Montage of a Dream

Montage of a Dream

The Art and Life of
Langston Hughes

Edited by

John Edgar Tidwell and Cheryl R. Ragar

with a foreword by Arnold Rampersad

University of Missouri Press   Columbia and London

Library of Congress Cataloging-in-Publication Data

Montage of a dream : the art and life of Langston Hughes / edited by John
Edgar Tidwell and Cheryl R. Ragar ; with a foreword by Arnold Rampersad.
    p. cm.
    Summary: "Contributors reexamine the continuing relevance of Langston
Hughes's work and life to American, African American, and diasporic liter-
atures and cultures. Includes fresh perspectives on the often overlooked
"Luani of the Jungles," Black Magic, and works for children, as well as
Hughes's more familiar fiction, poetry, essays, dramas, and other writings"
—Provided by publisher.
    Includes bibliographical references and index.
    ISBN 978-0-8262-1716-5 (hardcover : alk. paper)
    1. Hughes, Langston, 1902–1967.   2. Harlem (New York, N.Y.)—Intel-
lectual life—20th century.   3. Poets, American—20th century—Biography.
4. African American poets—Biography.   5. African Americans in literature.
6. Harlem Renaissance.   I. Tidwell, John Edgar.   II. Ragar, Cheryl R.
    PS3515.U274Z6845 2007
    818'.5209—dc22
    [B]
                                                            2006102013

Designer: Jennifer Cropp
Typesetter: The Composing Room of Michigan, Inc.
Printer and binder: Thomson-Shore, Inc.
Typefaces: Palatino, Georgia, and Flamme

For permissions, see p. 351

The University of Missouri Press offers its grateful acknowledgment for a
generous contribution from the Office of the Chancellor, University of
Kansas, in support of the publication of this volume.

Contents

II. *The Public and the Private*

III. *Revolutions Literary and Political*

IV. *Other Words and Other Worlds*

Foreword

Arnold Rampersad

This book, like a well-known speaker being welcomed to the stage before a large audience, needs no introduction—but it has one, expertly written by its editors, John Edgar Tidwell and Cheryl R. Ragar. What I offer here at the start of this book would be superfluous and also inferior were I to call it an introduction to the collection of essays they have so imaginatively put together. Instead, it is my honor to have been asked to provide a foreword. An honor it is indeed, since this volume is the smartest collection of work on Hughes to appear in many a year. It's a tribute to the editors and contributors but also, of course, a tribute to Langston Hughes as he continues to exert a power over us that seems at last to be embedded and destined perhaps to be permanent.

If we are to judge by reputation but also by the hard evidence of visits to the web sites of organizations such as the Academy of American Poets, Hughes's work may well be the main gateway through which many younger people and especially small children enter the world of formal poetry. It's hard to imagine a poet better suited to that almost sacred task. His verse, like his prose, is typically as clear as water, and just as essential to life. It is intensely musical, so it is no wonder that the composer Elie Siegmeister called Hughes the most musical poet of the twentieth century. It covers a range of emotions, from the nihilistic to the earthy, exuberant, and idealistic. Now that the children seem to have him (and with his love of children, for whom he wrote many books, he is surely where he wishes to be), his important place in our process of literacy and learning is assured for some time to come. Books such as this one build on that elementary and elemental connection. The appeal of Hughes's work to children is wonderfully complemented by the increasing attraction of his work to teachers, scholars, and other committed lovers of literature.

More than one hundred years after he was born in 1902, Langston Hughes lives! If he had died at the age of twenty-one, in 1922, he would have been remembered, perhaps, as the author of a single, transcendent poem, "The Negro Speaks of Rivers." This was the first poem he published in a national magazine (the *Crisis*), and it remained his signature poem for the rest of his life. If he had died when he was thirty, in 1932, he would doubtless be remembered as one of the brightest stars of the Harlem Renaissance, with his two important books of poems *The Weary Blues* (1926) and *Fine Clothes to the Jew* (1927), his novel *Not without Laughter* (1930), and his landmark essay of 1926 in the *Nation*, "The Negro Artist and the Racial Mountain." If Hughes had died when he was forty, in 1942, we might also remember him for having written and published some of the most radical poems ever by an American, and for having composed several plays that illustrate that he was more than simply a poet.

Instead, Hughes lived to be sixty-five. More important, he continued to write and publish to the very end, as if writing and publishing were as necessary to him as blood itself. He was working on the collection *The Panther and the Lash* when he died in 1967, in the often fiery heyday of the Black Arts and Black Power movements. Appearing later that year, that volume showed how relentlessly attuned Hughes was to the evolution of African American culture in his lifetime, and how deeply he cared about the status and the future of black America and for America as a whole.

By the time of his death, he had created over his forty-six-year career one of the most remarkable bodies of literary work in our language. He was not always highly prized. He was sometimes seen as mainly modish, as in the Harlem Renaissance; or as mainly dangerous, as in the politically charged 1930s and the Depression; or as largely irrelevant, as in the 1950s and the 1960s when, having survived the attacks of the anticommunist right and even Sen. Joseph McCarthy himself, he became in the eyes of our sterner judges, including writers as accomplished as Ralph Ellison, a hack. To many of these judges, he was really never much more than a hack. And yet Langston lives.

Some forty years after his death, most of us who are not blinded by needlessly elitist ideas about art see him as someone far greater than the sum of his parts—the sum of the often troubled and troubling parts that racism compelled him to play as a writer and as a black man seeking to live almost exclusively by his writings. He played those parts as best he could, even as he sought to fulfill the core desire of his life. That core wish was to write principally—though not entirely—about black America, and also to honor the dignity of the poor and politically oppressed people of all colors and nationalities around the world. At the same time, he aimed, as any truly inspired artist would, to rise above the local, the provincial, and the national to the level of the universal (which most certainly exists, despite those who cynically disparage its existence in art and culture). Thus Hughes sought to take his place, at a level that posterity would decide, in the grand tradition of writers around the world, from the ancients to the moderns, who had stirred in him his devotion to the word.

His sense of that grand tradition of writers was large. As a youth, for starters, he loved Whitman, Sandburg, De Maupassant, Millay, Dunbar, and Du Bois. He only widened his definition from that point on, so that it would eventually take in García Lorca, Yevtushenko, and Césaire, among many others. He believed in encouraging a love of art and in encouraging younger artists. He was famous for his generosity. He believed, as most of these men and women did, that few callings are more hallowed than that of the artist who, wrestling with the elusive angel of the word, seeks to express the heights and complexity of humanity despite our often urgent compulsion toward the vile.

Given up for dead as a writer at various times in the distant past, Hughes is now seen, in the words of a shrewd academic critic, as one of the major world writers of his century, even if his own nation, with its sad prejudices, so often found it hard to see him as an outstanding *American* writer. Now that colonialism (politically, mentally, and intellectually), is largely finished, a genuine cosmopolitanism is taking its place as the way we see the world, including the world of art. Supplanting definitions of success in literature that were often chained to imperial power, world writing in English is now recognized as a strange and yet familiar, beautiful, and brave new world. In this new world, the art of Langston Hughes positively glitters. To love his work is not to insist on the obsolescence of older, whiter versions of tradition. Nevertheless, we see now that he was an unconventionally marvelous artist, one who anticipated the world in which we live, the truly international, dark-skinned as well as white future of humanity, its revolutionary core, its dangers, and its glories.

This collection of essays is constantly alert to Hughes's multiple meanings. Even the essay I find the least convincing—I name no names, of course—is provocative and peppery. Here is no supine hero worship but a willingness and an eagerness to test the quality of Hughes's work against fresh ideas and attitudes. For example, his passion for the blues, not simply as entertainment but as the basic fabric of his art and of black life, is interrogated from a number of viewpoints. Critics here scrutinize the place of the blues both in the collage of his various poetical utterances and also close up, within the discrete boundaries of *Not without Laughter*, where Hughes not only creates a character who is a bluesman but also filters large parts of his narrative through the chiaroscuro of the blues. As it should do, in order to keep us honest, skepticism laces and braces the polite language of scholarship and criticism in order to bring our understanding of this topic or that work by Hughes to a new place.

This lively sense of poised conflict among ideas informs the other major areas of inquiry served by the collection. Was Langston Hughes gay? If one question above all others has added tangy spice to commentary on Hughes's life and work in recent years, this is surely it. Again we have here dynamic analyses that are also notably respectful of the integrity of contrary opinions. One essay poses the dramatic query: "Was Hughes a 'down low' brother"? Was he surreptitiously an active gay man? Answering the basic question leads, in another essay, to an invaluable study of Hughes's relationship to his mother as seen in a shrewd analysis of her letters to him over the last decade of her life.

The other principal topics addressed in this volume speak both to Hughes's intellectual and artistic range, on the one hand, and to the editors' understanding of that range, on the other. Subjects such as modernism, Africa, the African diaspora, Russia, Spain, Hollywood, children's literature, and Communism, treated with assurance by a variety of scholars, help to do justice to the legacy of Langston Hughes. As someone who has lived for almost thirty years with Langston Hughes as a primary focus of my teaching and scholarship, and who remembers clearly stepping into his world when very few scholars and critics could see his genius (ordinary black people always did!), I find this volume truly gratifying. My thanks to the editors and all of the contributors. Langston Hughes lives on!

Acknowledgments

The essays herein, with two exceptions, are all written expressly for this collection. In sum, they represent the first major reassessment of Langston Hughes's life and art since the emergence of Therman B. O'Daniel's important *Langston Hughes, Black Genius: A Critical Evaluation* in 1971. *Montage of a Dream* appears in the wake of the 2002 celebrations of the centenary of Hughes's birth. Among the most prominent programs, Hughes was feted at Missouri State Southern University, the University of Kansas, Yale University, and the Schomburg Center for Research in Black Culture. What made these commemorations special was that their foci were not simply honorific. At each event, scholars and nonacademics engaged in a major reconsideration of Hughes's place in the history of American and African American cultures. This collection complements and greatly extends the scholarly undertaking that emerged from each of these events.

In his lifetime and well after his death in 1967, Hughes's life and work were subjected to a variety of analyses and interpretations and even made to serve a number of different aesthetic and political uses. By gathering the voices represented in this volume, we self-consciously build onto previous scholarship and, using new critical methodologies and theoretical approaches, provide new and fresh ways of determining Hughes's importance. To that end, this collection would not be what it is without the many fine pieces of scholarship provided by the contributors to this volume. To each of you, we express our heartfelt gratitude. As we assembled this collection, we lost Lorenzo Thomas. While we mourn his passing, we commemorate his commitment to excellence in creative and scholarly writing by including his essay, "'It Is the Same for Me': Langston Hughes and the African Diaspora's Everyman."

We are also indebted to Professors Maryemma Graham, Leslie Sanders, and Carmaletta M. Williams for reading the manuscript in its entirety and making insightful comments. Our overall task was made much easier by Andrea Craig Gruenbaum, our very capable student assistant, who conscientiously read copyedited manuscripts and page proofs. If any errors have crept in, we, as editors, accept full responsibility for them. For their patience and expeditious work in preparing this manuscript, we would like to express our appreciation to Paula Courtney, Pam LeRow, Gwen Claassen, and the late Lynn Porter of the CLAS Word Processing Center at the University of Kansas. To Robert E. Hemenway, chancellor of the University of Kansas, and Victor Bailey, who directs Kansas's Hall Center for the Humanities, we cannot say thank you enough for the financial and collegial support you've shown for this project. Collegial aptly applies to the encouragement we received from the English Department at Kansas and especially from its Ad Hoc Committee on African American Literature. Finally, we wish to heartily thank Director Beverly Jarrett and the University of Missouri Press for their extraordinary vision in reconsidering Langston Hughes's significance and especially for including us in that vision.

Abbreviations

To assist the reader in locating quotations taken specifically from Hughes's works, the contributors have, in common, used *The Collected Works of Langston Hughes*, with citations listed parenthetically using volume and page citations, separated by a colon, as in *CW* 8:45. Those works by Hughes that are not included in the *Collected Works* are cited in the footnotes and bibliography.

CW 1   The Poems: 1921–1940
CW 2   The Poems: 1941–1950
CW 3   The Poems: 1951–1967
CW 4   The Novels: *Not without Laughter* and *Tambourines to Glory*
CW 5   The Plays to 1942: *Mulatto* to *The Sun Do Move*
CW 6   Gospel Plays, Operas, and Later Dramatic Works
CW 7   The Early Simple Stories
CW 8   The Later Simple Stories
CW 9   Essays on Art, Race, Politics, and World Affairs
CW 10   *Fight for Freedom* and Other Writings on Civil Rights
CW 11   Works for Children and Young Adults: Poetry, Fiction, and Other Writing
CW 12   Works for Children and Young Adults: Biographies
CW 13   Autobiography: *The Big Sea*
CW 14   Autobiography: *I Wonder As I Wander*
CW 15   The Short Stories
CW 16   The Translations: Federico García Lorca, Nicolás Guillén, and Jacques Roumain

Poème pour Langston

Cheikh Ahmadou Dieng

Volée de papillons blancs
   Sur le blanc de l'écume
   Sur le bleu de l'eau
Ils passent et papillonnent
   Au rythme des vagues lasses
   Qui languissent perdues
   Dans l'or du soleil couchant
Volée de papillons verts, couleur
   De la mer coquette
   Qui étale ses charmes parés
   De rayons pourpres
Les papillons blancs mais noirs mais jaunes
   Virevoltent et puis
   Se laissent happer entre soleil et mer
   Dans leur vol éperdu entre ciel et terre
Les papillons bivouaquent du côté de Goulaine
   A Gorée, Nouméa
   Ces marais de corail
Cagous cendrés qui dansent et dansent
   Le tam-tam
Papillons qui s'égarent mais reviennent toujours
   entre rivage et large
Papillonnent papillonnent du côté de Lawrence

Dakar, December 11, 2001

Poem for Langston

Translated by Mame Selbee Diouf

Flock of white butterflies
   On the white foam
   On the blue water
They pass and flutter
   To the rhythm of weary waves
   That hang around lost
   In the gold of the sunset
Flock of green butterflies, color
   Of the charming sea
   That spreads its adorned charms
   Of purple rays
White butterflies but black but yellow
   Twirl around and then
   Snapped between the sun and the sea
   In their frantic flight between the sky and the earth
The butterflies bivouac towards Goulaine
   At Gorée, Nouméa
   These coral tides
Ash-colored cagous* that dance and dance
   The tam-tam**
Butterflies that wander but always come back
   Between shore and open sea
   Flutter flutter toward Lawrence

* Ash-colored birds, similar to parrots.
** The music produced by a variety of drums

Montage of a Dream

Langston Hughes Revisited and Revised

An Introduction

John Edgar Tidwell and Cheryl R. Ragar

The month of February 2002 resounded with well-earned commemorations and reconsiderations for one of America's most influential poetic voices: James Mercer Langston Hughes (1902–1967). From Joplin, Missouri, Hughes's birthplace; to Lawrence, Kansas, the site of his formative years; to the Schomburg Research Center, located in his beloved Harlem, scholars and nonacademics alike celebrated the centenary birthday of a writer whose passion for black people enabled readers to see the extraordinary in ordinary black life. If these remembrances shared a vision or controlling theme, it was the idea that Hughes's value to the development of African American and American art and culture has been inestimable. More than delineating a cultural past, his life and work, as these symposia wonderfully demonstrate, continue to have an enduring significance. Since, as Arnold Rampersad once reminded us, no single book has the absolute last word on any subject and thus cannot lay claim to being "definitive," we must continually "redefine and reexamine and reevaluate" art and life.[1] This prescient insight describes the context in which literary historians, critics, and community people participating in these symposia saw Hughes's life and work: as narratives that are ever-evolving and, as

1. Rampersad, "Future Scholarly Projects on Langston Hughes," 314.

new information becomes available, constantly growing. They understood that the pursuit of a subject's life and art cannot be static or mired
in "received opinion." This book shares this vision. Conceptually, it de-
rives its shape and definition from the synergy of a *dynamic* context—one
that engages past literary study and offers fresh perspectives in considering a contemporary importance for Hughes's life and art.

A Life Distilled

The world into which Langston Hughes was born in 1902 was, for
African Americans, one of racial uncertainty and contradiction—the end
of what historian Rayford Logan called "the nadir" of African American
history. The promises of Reconstruction had been systematically broken,
leaving blacks virtually without legal protection. The Hughes family
found itself vulnerable. Hughes was born in Joplin and moved the next
year to Lawrence, Kansas. During his formative years there (1903–1915),
he discovered that he was not immune to the vagaries of interracial and
intraracial tensions. His father, James Nathaniel Hughes, exacerbated
these feelings when he abandoned his family shortly after Langston's
birth and sought refuge in Cuba and then Mexico because a series of
racially discriminatory events denied him the opportunity to sit for the
bar and practice law in Oklahoma. His mother, Carolina or "Carrie," as
she was known, also contributed to Hughes's sense of social dislocation
when she essentially deserted her son and became an itinerant, searching
for economic stability and romantic happiness. The task of rearing him fell
to his grandmother, Mary Leary Langston, whose life in Lawrence was
largely defined by maintaining the historic family pride as acute poverty
and deprivation constantly dogged her doorstep. Despite her best efforts,
her grandson became predisposed to loneliness and sought his own
refuge in a world of books provided by the public library. As painful as
many of these personal experiences were, he would return to them imaginatively time and again for the values that formed the moral and spiritual foundation of his early fiction and poetry.

Following his grandmother's death in 1915, Hughes lived for a short
time with family friends Aunty and Uncle Reed, before embarking on his
own pilgrimage in search of family and stability. In an effort to keep pace
with his mother's movements, he lived for a while in Lincoln, Illinois, before finishing high school in Cleveland, Ohio, in 1920. By then, wanderlust characterized his reason for being. All paths, though, led him to

Harlem, which became a spiritual touchstone for racial authenticity and his love for black people. For the remainder of his life, he made his living solely on the strength of his writing—becoming the only African American writer of his generation to do so. His commitment to the life of a writer usually did not equate with financial success, but it enabled him to experience life and to experiment with representing it in different genres, including poetry, fiction, drama, essay, translation, and libretto.

Apart from economics, the principal challenge Hughes faced was how to reinvent himself as a writer in order to find new modes of self-expression. For a while, many literary historians and critics thought of Hughes's work as simple, uncomplicated, and undifferentiated. More astute writers demonstrated the fallacy in this thinking. *Montage of a Dream* builds on the success of these historians and critics, using new theories, methodologies, and approaches now available.

Era of the New Negro

Quite naturally, a literary life as varied as Hughes's invites different interpretations, depending on the social, political, and aesthetic positions of his commentators. What has consistently earned Hughes the unconditional praise of critics was his unfailing commitment to represent common, everyday black people with reverence and respect, with simplicity and depth. He did not yield to the temptation of the "putting the best foot forward" theory of racial representation, because, as he writes poignantly in his "The Negro Artist and the Racial Mountain," the people farthest down were the repositories of racial authenticity. These "low-down folks" were unafraid to be themselves. As creators of blues, jazz, and spirituals, they did not suffer the "second-generation respectability" or racial embarrassment of their middle- and upper-class brethren. These folks were not enamored with Euro-American values. For such a preoccupation was merely an impossible wish to be like someone else and a silent admission of self-hate.

In today's critical parlance, Hughes's idea of racial and cultural authenticity would no doubt be dismissed as an essentialist argument. But in the 1920s, the representational wars demanded an approach that countered the proliferation of black racial stereotypes. In representing the folk as they actually were, with all their faults and foibles, the truth offset the lies engendered in stereotypes. The literary struggle for the humanity of African Americans necessitated, in the view of Hughes and others, authentic representation.

The debate waged among the New Negro writers and critics attempted to define the nature of authenticity. For those in agreement with Hughes, *The Weary Blues* (1926) and *Fine Clothes to the Jew* (1927) established a standard of excellence to which other poets should aspire. W. E. B. Du Bois, from his editor's chair at *The Crisis: A Record of the Darker Races*, temporarily abandoned his late Victorian sense of art and uncharacteristically lavished high praise on *The Weary Blues* and *Fine Clothes to the Jew.* According to David Levering Lewis, Du Bois, in an unattributed quote, saw *Weary Blues* as reflecting "the fine qualities of force, passion, directness, and sensitive perception." Lewis also reported that Du Bois ordered the race to buy the book because "Du Bois instantly recognized in the Hughes volume a breakthrough in the genre, an uncanny distilling of the soul of ordinary black men and women struggling to make their way in the cities."[2] Others were simply hyperbolic. They greeted Hughes's folk-based writing as innovative and conferred upon him the honorific title of "poet laureate of the people."

In the debate about who should wear the crown of archetypal New Negro poet, a consensus was never reached. The result was critical ambivalence. One who waffled on Hughes's importance was Alain Locke, the self-described midwife of the younger generation of Negro writers. Locke attempted to put in place a cultural movement and enlisted Hughes as one of the linchpins in this effort. His vision for this movement was nicely articulated in his review of Claude McKay's 1937 autobiography, *A Long Way from Home:* "The task confronting the present younger generation of Negro writers and artists is to approach the home scene and the folk with high seriousness, deep loyalty, racial reverence of the unspectacular, unmelodramatic sort and when necessary, sacrificial devotion." After a brief period of celebrating Hughes, Locke accused him of failing to build on his "revelation of the emotional color of Negro life and his brilliant discovery of the flow and rhythm of the modern and especially the city Negro." This failure, Locke said, resulted in "essentially a jazz version of Negro life . . . and though fascinating and true to an epoch this version was *surface quality after all.*"[3]

Still others, such as the renowned Countee Cullen, were simply detractors. To them, the idea of finding anything of poetic value in cabaret, blues, and jazz merely cast aspersions on the race. Cullen had studied versifica-

2. Lewis, *W. E. B. Du Bois: The Fight for Equality and the American Century, 1919–1963*, 605–6, 206.

3. Locke, "Spiritual Truancy," 84, and "Sterling Brown: The New Negro Folk-Poet," 92 (emphasis added).

tion at Harvard and represented a more traditional approach to writing poetry, one rooted in European forms. Because he embraced Western poetic ideals, he found little merit in Hughes's experiments with a folk-based aesthetic. It hardly surprises that he found Hughes's "jazz poems as interlopers in the company of the truly beautiful poems in the other sections of [*The Weary Blues*]." As if to drive the point home, Cullen, in a more damning comment, wrote:

> Taken as a group the selections in this book seem one-sided to me. They tend to hurl this poet into the gaping pit that lies before all Negro writers in the confines of which they become racial artists instead of artists pure and simple. There is too much emphasis here on strictly Negro themes; and this is probably an added reason for my coldness toward the jazz poems—they seem to set a too definite limit upon an already limited field.[4]

An unnamed reviewer, writing for the Chicago *Whip*, was downright scurrilous when he wrote that the poems in *Fine Clothes to the Jew* were "unsanitary, insipid, and repulsing"; he ended by bestowing on Hughes the unceremonious distinction of "poet low-rate" of Harlem.[5]

For most of his life, Hughes had to confront the few who held on to this class-bound aesthetic vision. His literary reception and legacy constantly shifted, leading to his falling in and out of critical favor, depending on the needs of the individuals writing about him. Hughes, of course, was not dissuaded about the efficacy of his art. Except for his proletarian period, arguably, he never strayed too far from the aesthetic principles he expressed in "The Negro Artist and the Racial Mountain," his most explicit statement about his love and need for black people. Despite his father's expressed hatred of them, which Hughes inferred was self-hate, Langston acknowledged his own emotional commitment to black people. His love was so deep that, in the next period, he changed the nature of his aesthetic expression to make his work even more accessible to them.

Social Art and Reform in the 1930s

After a period in the 1920s of immersion in black folk culture and expression, Hughes turned in the 1930s to a more directly political view of

---

4. Cullen, "Poet on Poet," 7.
5. *Chicago Whip*, February 26, 1927; see also Hughes's reference in *CW* 13:203.

art. In this aesthetic shift, Hughes committed himself to addressing the folk more polemically, by way of pageants and proletarian poetry. In 1932, he published *Scottsboro Limited: Four Poems and a Play in Verse* in support of the nine men falsely accused of raping two white women hoboing on a train in Alabama. In 1932–1933, he spent time in the Soviet Union, where he encountered socialism up close. From 1937 to 1938, he served for five months as a war correspondent for the *Baltimore Afro-American* covering the Spanish Civil War. As a result, his militancy increased, leading to his *A New Song* (1938), a pamphlet of radical verse published by the International Workers Order, a socialist organization.

Overall, critics in the United States were not impressed with the political turn Hughes took in his poetry. Most withheld public comment on the privately published books of verse. The more vocal ones agreed with Alain Locke, who, in an *Opportunity* column in January 1933, expressed his disdain for Hughes's new attitude by suggesting that "the poet of *Scottsboro Limited* is a militant and indignant proletarian reformer."[6] During this decade Hughes also came under fire from leaders of black churches for his perceived attack on religion in such poems as "Goodbye Christ" and "Christ in Alabama," which he later explained was "misinterpreted . . . as an anti-Christian poem. I intended it to be just the opposite" (*CW* 9:274).

The Ways of White Folks (1934), as Maryemma Graham has argued, "pulsates with the themes and sentiments of the radical movement." Even though Hughes never officially joined the party, she points out that his work reflected Marxist ideological concerns; as Graham says, Hughes "successfully fused the black folk heritage with what was considered a revolutionary consciousness." Locke once again revealed his ambivalence in a qualified endorsement of the stories: "Their sociological significance is as important as their literary value, perhaps more so, because . . . they reflect the growing resentment and desperation which is on the increase in the Negro world today." Locke recognized the significance of these stories for black Americans in reflecting their concerns in the midst of the bleak days of the Depression. The stories' polemical nature, however, led him to conclude, "This is an important book for the present times; greater artistry, deeper sympathy and less resentment would have made it a book for all times."[7]

On the basis of his Marxist approach, Hughes gained a strong interna-

6. Locke, "Black Truth and Black Beauty: A Retrospective Review of the Literature of the Negro for 1932," 15.
7. Graham, "The Practice of a Social Art," 213, 214; Locke, "Negro Angle," 565.

tional following. "It was critics from abroad," according to Edward J. Mullen, "who were most receptive to Hughes's leanings toward poetry of social commitment." By traveling to the Soviet Union, China, Cuba, Haiti, Mexico, and Spain during the late-1920s and 1930s, Hughes gained both new perspectives from which to write and new readers for his work. As Mullen points out, Hughes's celebration of blackness linked him to other African diaspora writers: "It was during this period that Hughes was discovered by the francophone writers of the black Diaspora, including Léopold Sédar Senghor, Paulette Nardal, and Etienne Léro, the founders of the Negritude school of ethnic consciousness."[8]

A New Song (1938) represents a coda for that period in Hughes's life and art. It would be his last poetry overtly shaped and defined by a socialist ideology. With the advent of World War II, Hughes would continue his social protest less directly.

A Poetics of Indirection in the 1940s

Beginning in the 1940s, Hughes responded to the pressure he incurred as a result of his political and social critiques of America. Reflecting on the fallout about his work from the previous decade in a 1947 essay called "My Adventures as a Social Poet," Hughes stated, "I have never been a Communist, but I soon learned that anyone visiting the Soviet Union and speaking with favor of it upon returning is liable to be so labeled" (*CW* 9:273). He also acknowledged the controversial effect of his earlier poetry: "But when poems stop talking about the moon and begin to mention poverty, trade unions, color lines, and colonies, somebody tells the police" (*CW* 9:270).

His first autobiography, *The Big Sea*, appeared in 1940. As if to forestall further criticism, he ended this life story in 1932, at a point when the Depression exerted its tightest grip on the nation. Hughes understood that to critique America and its failure to honor its commitment to African Americans might be ill advised, given the governmental scrutiny he attracted by virtue of his 1930s political activism. By the early 1940s, Hughes realized that he needed another way to express the problems he saw in society if he wanted to continue commenting through his writing. Thus he turned to satire. He created a character, Jesse B. Semple (also known as Simple), through whom he humorously expressed his criticism of Amer-

8. Mullen, "Introduction," in *Critical Essays on Langston Hughes*, 11.

ica. Simple first appeared in 1943 in what would become a weekly column for the *Chicago Defender*. Rampersad recounted how the character of Simple, the Black Everyman, came to life as Hughes looked for a new vehicle for expressing his views: "the idea came to him that he should turn to prose, instead of verse, and use the man in Patsy's Bar [Simple] as 'a foil for patriotic propaganda.'"[9] Although Simple was widely praised, the House Un-American Activities Committee found nothing funny in his critiques and, in 1953, called Hughes to account for his political and aesthetic vision.

Literary Sharecropping in the 1950s

The 1950s, the purportedly placid, homogeneous, almost bland era in American social history, barely concealed an undercurrent of international paranoia and interracial tension. In the United States, the cold war coerced citizens into an uncritical acceptance of patriotism and nationalism, forcing either allegiance to America or accusations of fealty to foreign powers. The Soviet Union, a metonym for all things communistic, became the political antagonist that caused the United States to purge this philosophy at home and march boldly, jingoistically into saber rattling abroad. In this climate of political paranoia, Hughes survived Sen. Joseph McCarthy's witch hunts, while Du Bois and artist-activist Paul Robeson fared less well. Despite the perceived threat of nuclear warfare with foreign powers, social change was imminent at home. The underlying current of black political protest carrying over from the 1940s became more pronounced in 1954 with *Brown v. Board of Education* of Topeka. In a decision that shook the very foundations of interracial relations in the United States, the Supreme Court dislodged the hegemonic cornerstone of "separate but equal" by declaring separate educational facilities to be inherently unequal. In the resulting white backlash, blacks suffered abuses that inspired the civil rights movement: the heinous lynching of fourteen-year-old Emmett Till in 1955, Rosa Parks's unwillingness to vacate her bus seat later in that same year, the federal government–enforced integration of Little Rock High School in 1957, and much more.

In response to these events, Hughes vacillated between indirect and direct confrontations with the sociopolitical realities facing black America and about how best to represent them. These events notwithstanding,

9. Rampersad, *The Life of Langston Hughes: Volume 2, 1941–1967, I Dream a World*, 62.

Hughes found himself somewhat at the mercy of an economic reality: that to continue making a living as a full-time writer he had to broaden and extend his modes of expression even further. He became, as he said in describing himself, a "literary sharecropper."[10] This meant committing himself to more children's books, translations, editorial work, and other forms that would help generate some income. At the same time, Hughes did not lose his subversive nature; it continued subtly in such works as *Montage of a Dream Deferred* (1951), *I Wonder As I Wander* (1956), four collections of the Simple stories, *The Selected Poems* (1959), and many others.

The critical reception accorded the writer that some still acknowledged as the "poet laureate of black American letters" was, at best, mixed in the early years of this decade. In considering the achievement of his *Montage,* reviewers and critics debated whether his poetic experiment with this new form of music called bebop advanced the writing of poetry or failed miserably, mired, as reviewer Babette Deutsch said, in the supposed "limitations of folk art." At the end of that decade, James Baldwin, writing in the *New York Times,* was considerably less tactful in his judgment about *The Selected Poems:* "This book contains a great deal which a more disciplined poet would have thrown into the wastebasket." Moreover, he accused Hughes of writing "in a fake simplicity in order to avoid the very difficult simplicity of the experience." Essentially repeating Cullen's earlier dismissive critique of Hughes, Baldwin concluded: "Hughes is an American Negro poet and has no choice but to be acutely aware of it. He is not the first American Negro to find the war between his social and artistic responsibilities all but irreconcilable."[11]

Constructing a Legacy

The volatile 1960s saw dramatic shifts in black political, social, and aesthetic expression. Because of the primary loci of its struggles, the civil rights movement seemed to be a southern experience, while the North appeared to define itself in terms of Black Power. These geographic locations loosely translated into a series of binary oppositions, including nonviolence versus self-defense, moral suasion versus self-determination, racial

10. Hughes to Bontemps, December 27, 1950, in Charles H. Nichols, ed., *Arna Bontemps–Langston Hughes: Letters, 1925–1967,* 277.
11. Deutsch, "Waste Land of Harlem: A Review of Montage of a Dream Deferred"; Baldwin, "Sermons and Blues," 6.

integration versus racial separation, and more. In the midst of these upheavals, Hughes found himself at a crossroads in his life and career: he had to confront changes in aesthetic practice occasioned by the politics of the times. His own political vision had certainly been broadened by his participation in a number of conferences held in West African nations. At the same time, he found himself outraged at the brutality and deaths experienced by his beloved people at home. In the years leading up to his death in 1967, he reaffirmed the commitment he had expressed earlier in poems such as "I, Too" and "Freedom Train": a decision to remain centered in the values articulated in such governing documents as the Bill of Rights, the Constitution, and the Declaration of Independence.

In declaring his allegiance to the fundamentals of American democracy, Hughes raised an important question: what should the writer's role be in "the struggle"? His manifesto "The Negro Artist and the Racial Mountain" (1926) suggested that "it is the duty of the younger Negro artist, if he accepts any duties at all from outsiders, to change through the force of his art that old whispering 'I want to be white,' hidden in the aspirations of his people, to 'Why should I want to be white? I am a Negro—and beautiful!'" (CW 9:35). This sounds remarkably similar to Maulana Karenga's 1968 prescription for writing: "Black art, like everything else in the black community, must respond positively to the reality of revolution."[12] The obvious difference, of course, is that while Karenga sought to dismantle "the master's house," Hughes fought vigorously to prove it belonged just as much to blacks. Hughes was guided by the very imperative Baldwin declared to be a weakness in Hughes's poetry. In effect, Baldwin accused Hughes of aesthetic timidity or a reluctance to ground his work more deeply in conceptions of art. Hughes, though, found common ground among personal need, social responsibility, and aesthetic expression. As Rampersad wrote: "While Langston psychologically needed the race in order to survive, [Baldwin's] deepest needs as [artist and human being were] evidently elsewhere." He further observed: "Langston was one of the few black writers of any consequence to champion racial consciousness as a source of inspiration for black artists" in the six years following the Brown decision.[13]

Hughes's differences with Baldwin did not deter him from offering assistance to younger writers and artists. Among many others, Alice Walker and Paule Marshall have been effusive in expressing their gratitude.

12. Maulana Ron Karenga, "Black Art: Mute Matter Given Force and Function," 477.
13. Rampersad, Life, 2:297.

Writing in his "Introduction" to *The Best Short Stories by Negro Writers* (1967), Hughes argued that writers, especially black writers, needed financial support so that they could have time to think about and create literature. In this spirit, he nominated his longtime friend and confidant Arna Bontemps; however, "if it must be a young talent as first choice for a subsidy, then why not the astounding Miss Alice Walker? Neither you nor I have ever read a story like 'To Hell with Dying' before. At least I do not think you have" (*CW* 9:528–29). Paule Marshall received a comparable boost when, in May 1965, she received a letter from the U.S. Information Service, a part of the State Department, inviting her to accompany Hughes on a European tour, where they would read their work, lecture, and conduct seminars on African American writing. Years later, both Walker and Marshall spoke with heartfelt gratitude for being chosen by arguably the preeminent black writer of the era, whom neither one had met before being honored by him.

At the same time Hughes was aiding the careers of Walker and Marshall, he continued to define what he considered the essence of great art. In his aesthetic vision, the Black Arts writers' use of scatological language was a poor substitute for well-written poetry. For instance, the poetry of LeRoi Jones (Amiri Baraka) contained a sense of urgency. His poem "SOS" served in a few short lines to scream out the need for all black people to come together because the perilous times demanded unified, concerted action. Baraka's "Black Art" continued that same theme by defining poetic expression in clearly pragmatic terms: "Poems are bullshit unless they are / teeth or trees or lemons piled / on a step."[14] It was volatile, incendiary poetry, intended to incinerate the perception of Western aesthetic hegemony, while proselytizing black readers about the necessity of taking political action.

Throughout his lifetime of writing committed work, Hughes was also driven by urgency. The clearest, most sustained statement of his radicalism in poetry is contained in *The Panther and the Lash: Poems of Our Times*, published posthumously in 1967. A remarkable feature of the collection is that it draws poems from his oeuvre as early as 1932. Even though many of the poems were topical—"The Backlash Blues" and "Black Panther" provide the title for the book—Hughes raised questions, not consciousness; he moved readers to change, rather than inflaming them into action. His approach no doubt placed him out of touch with many of the Black Aestheticians, who, in their early years, preached an antiwhite propa-

14. Baraka, *The LeRoi Jones/Amiri Baraka Reader*, 219.

ganda in their art. His death, in 1967, represented the end of one era and the beginning of a new one. In the younger generation, a new spirit of proclaiming the beauty of blackness emerged and replaced the anti-Euro-American rhetoric. Like rivers remembering their sources, these insurgents ultimately came to understand and applaud the social commitment of their predecessors. Their own writing revised the ahistorical premises of their earlier aesthetic and paid homage to their forebears for doing courageous cultural work. One of the principals so honored was Langston Hughes.

Revisioning Langston Hughes

Arnold Rampersad, in his 1987 essay "Future Scholarly Projects on Langston Hughes," documented the need for more scholarly attention on Hughes. He argued especially for the republication of more of Hughes's wide body of work. For instance, he suggested that the vast expanse of Hughes's poetry be published in a collection so that readers would have a chance to understand his work more fully within the broad contexts in which it was created. This, in turn, would lead to more opportunities to study neglected aspects of his career, such as his abiding role as a social activist or the thread of religious themes that runs throughout his work. Since the appearance of this directional essay, publishers and editors have taken heed and produced a number of new books that bring more of Hughes's work to contemporary audiences. The University of Missouri Press has been the leader in this huge undertaking, bringing out nearly all of Hughes's published works in reprint editions. The uncovering of this material, in concert with the use of new theoretical tools, set the stage for the innovative analyses presented in this volume.

This recuperative process revealed the extent to which many earlier critics were unable to discern how complicated Hughes the man was or how his aesthetic vision belied an apparent simplicity. They were not privy to such new developments as psychological, performance, gender, and postcolonial theories as well as approaches rooted in modernism and postmodernism. *Montage of a Dream* avails itself of these new methodologies and perspectives to conduct nuanced studies of Hughes's life and work. In its five parts, we have included conversations that reexamine and extend earlier interpretations of his creative output. Essays here not only offer fresh ways of looking at Hughes's best-known works but also provide new examinations of previously understudied or unstudied works.

Part I, "The Sacred and the Secular," provides an overview by foregrounding two contrasting impulses. For most of his early writing career, Hughes was well known for his blues and jazz-based literature. Thus these musical forms are foundational in any consideration of his writings. These secular forms are counterbalanced by the recurrence of religious themes in many of these same works. As Hughes affectionately wrote in "The Negro Artist and the Racial Mountain," both impulses were crucial to definitions of black racial and cultural specificity. The writers in this section interrogate, in their individual ways, Hughes's notion of the significance of the "low-down folk" and what it meant for his aesthetic vision.

"The Public and the Private," the collection's second part, is framed, on one end, by a reading of the personal and textual silences in Hughes's life and work. On the other, a look at significant letters exchanged by Hughes and his mother, Carrie, illuminates several recurring themes in his life. The call issued by this frame elicits the response of two provocative close readings of Hughes's autobiographies and his first novel, *Not without Laughter* (1931). As a result, Juda Bennett and Kimberly Banks use Hughes's life to open up broader, more theoretical discussions about identity formation and performance.

The subject of Part III is "Revolutions Literary and Political." Politics, of course, have always crucially shaped Hughes's writings. This leaves open the question of whether Hughes, at times, is merely polemical. The contributors to this section, in their individual ways, refute this notion. Their essays are connected, using the words of Robert Young, by their exploration of "form, structure, and textuality" in Hughes's work.

In Part IV, "Other Words and Other Worlds," more than in any other section, the contributors recontextualize Hughes and place him on a broader, global stage. We have always known about Hughes's internationalism, via his travels and adventures. Collectively, though, these writers enable us to rethink what have almost become pro forma interpretations of Hughes abroad. Under their studied analyses, we are given new and deeper insights into his political and aesthetic excursions into Spain, Russia, and the negritude movement in France, francophone Africa, and the Caribbean.

"Langston Hughes and the Boundaries of Art," the last part, is more than a reminder that Hughes created in diverse forms and avidly took up different subjects. The contributors here focus on four areas that have received little notice: his children's literature, dance, the essay, and movies. Certainly, each author provides some understanding about why Hughes's engagement with these areas has received so little attention. More important, they reveal a dynamic that illustrates Hughes's ability to work in multiple genres with equal facility and still locate the spiritual nature in peoples' lives.

Revising literary history, Cary Nelson reminds us, "is never an innocent process." He continues: "We recover what we are culturally and psychologically prepared to recover and what we 'recover' we necessarily rewrite, giving it meanings that are inescapably contemporary, giving it a new discursive life in the present, a life it cannot have had before."[15] An example of Nelson's theory can be seen in Sen. John Kerry's rearticulation of the phrase "Let America be America again" from Langston Hughes's 1938 poem. In commemorating the fiftieth anniversary of *Brown v. Board of Education*, Kerry broke from his usual presidential campaign rhetoric and made these words evoke a sense of patriotism, national unity, and civic duty. In true democratic fashion, his speech urged a return to the highest values of citizenship, such as those purportedly experienced in the 1990s.

This position, of course, is fraught with irony. While Kerry sought to *reinscribe* a belief in what he felt were generally accepted political ideals, Hughes actually had issued a call for *establishing* those ideals. From his privileged social station, Kerry assumed a humanity for all Americans, including African Americans. But from his origins in the imprimatur of Jim Crow, Hughes used his poem to argue for the inclusion of a people whose very humanity had been denied. Kerry, therefore, called for a return to noble ideals, while Hughes cried out for an experience that most African Americans never had. To his credit, Kerry's revisionist comments placed Hughes once again in the public sphere, making this people's poet part of a national discourse on art, race, and politics.

This is the achievement of *Montage of a Dream: The Art and Life of Langston Hughes.* By thoughtfully arguing his importance for the twenty-first century, it ushers in a new life for Hughes. Our era is dominated by such "-isms" as multiculturalism, nihilism, whiteness studies, and interracialism. Moreover, the interpretive categories of race and class engender fervent debates over the significance and place of the very people about

---

15. Nelson, *Repression and Recovery: Modern American Poetry and the Politics of Cultural Memory, 1910–1945, Repression and Recovery,* 11.

whom Hughes wrote so passionately. Updated, reframed, and refocused, a number of issues carry over from Hughes's lifetime. Has cultural ni-hilism, for example, become the defining spiritual mode of economically less fortunate African Americans? Or has hip-hop culture come to be both salvation and source of hope for those who are virtually disenfran-chised—the very people who provided Hughes with idea and inspira-tion? Who is an American? Indeed, what is America? Collectively, the es-says gathered here not only demonstrate Hughes's continuing relevance for those seeking answers to these and many other contemporary ques-tions; they also offer proof that he is truly a man for all times.

I

The Sacred and the Secular

Langston Hughes and Aunt Hager's Children's Blues Performance

"Six-Bits Blues"

Steven C. Tracy

The music of the blues . . . precedes the rise of the curtain

Langston Hughes stated in the stage directions to act 2, scene 1 of his play *Simply Heavenly* (CW 6:215) what I believe to be a directive with implications for Hughes's aesthetic and art, as well as for the critic who wishes to read, understand, and teach his work. A few years ago, when I was writing the dissertation that eventually became *Langston Hughes and the Blues,* one of my readers admonished that Hughes's mere statement of the a priori idea constituted no concrete proof that it was so—though I would argue that it is better proof than Hughes saying that the blues did not precede the rise of the curtain. Of course, he was right in part: the statement is merely a clue to Hughes's usage, an acknowledgment, an invitation: "hear the blues." It is not an insubstantial statement, but it is one that needs illumination: in what ways does this blues material effectively permeate Hughes's work?

Several questions occur: (1) What is blues literature (as opposed to literature with blues in it)? (2) What are its characteristics? (3) What does it try to accomplish? (4) Is blues literature an oxymoron, given that the blues is an oral genre? (5) Is this literature a blues literature because its characteristics are of the blues and the blues only, or are the characteristics ones found in African American expressive culture or the vernacular more generally? Would they be better labeled in that way?

Louis Armstrong's famous reply to the question "what is jazz"—"man, if you have to ask . . . "—bespeaks the sometimes visceral recognition that can be difficult to describe concretely. Which brings us to the question of how we can recognize the blues in a literary work. There are many possibilities. A work may be called a blues, or use the title of a blues song; make use of language associated with the blues in the language of the author or characters; attempt explicitly to define or portray the blues and its philosophy; attempt to use the ethos of the blues to portray its emotional, psychic, spiritual, community, and political implications; attempt to portray the historical and social background leading up to the time of the emergence of the blues as a major expressive African American form crucial to its times; use blues singers as characters; interpolate selections from songs or performances (lyrics, notations, descriptions of music or responsive reaction); name real blues singers in the text, as characters or touchstones or icons; employ or extend the traditional forms or subject matter of the blues; employ elements associated in literal or symbolic ways with the blues, such as call and response, stanzas, syncopation, melisma, glissandi, or voice masking; make references to common emotions portrayed in the blues, such as loneliness, isolation, frustration, or sexual desire; make references to the color blue itself as evocative of emotion and tradition; or refer to the position of the performer in relation to a community or a social class through its attitudes toward music.

A number of these elements do not stand by themselves as an indication of a "blues literature." After all, the language that we associate with blues songs, such as "easy rider," "let me be your sidetrack til your mainline comes along," or "laughin' to keep from cryin'," may have originated in the community speech itself, and not in blues songs. The philosophy of hope and perseverance in the face of overwhelming odds—"the sun's gonna shine in my back door some day"—describes an optimism present not only in the blues. Call and response is characteristic of a variety of not only African American musics. Loneliness and isolation are not solely the province of the blues, nor do the blues limit themselves to those feelings. There is also a question as to how crucial these elements are to the meaning of the text: do they permeate style and subject matter, or are they merely decorative?

It may be, then, that we want to speak more generally of an African American vernacular literature rather than of a blues literature. This can be particularly true in the case of Langston Hughes's work. That is, Hughes frequently pointed out how elements of religious music were related to elements of the blues and jazz traditions, even as he explored how some people in the community had difficulty negotiating what they saw as the oppositions between the two musics. So while Hughes used many elements of the blues tradition in his work, we need to understand that those elements were sometimes neither exclusive to the blues tradition nor, for Hughes, divorced from the spirit and wisdom of the spirituals, jubilees, and gospel songs that he celebrated as well. Indeed, at times Hughes made the connections explicit and sought to reconcile those elements of the culture that to some seemed irreconcilable, particularly what would be described by some as the dichotomy between sacred and secular.

Ultimately, if we wish to call something "blues literature," we must insist that the blues is demonstrably and necessarily part of the work both stylistically and substantively, and that the work bases its central meaning on the social, historical, political, musical, and / or aesthetic context of the blues. Of course, determining the presence of the blues can be a subjective exercise, but the more specifically we can connect manifestations of the blues to the work itself, the more confidently we can call it blues literature. We must also acknowledge that to call it blues literature is not to suggest that nonblues elements are absent; in fact, such elements can be used, as is the case with Hughes, to effect a unity Hughes hoped we would achieve in life itself.

All of which brings us to Hughes's novel *Not without Laughter,* a work that itself evidences a variety of the characteristics noted above. Admittedly, the idea of a novel seems somewhat alien to the blues tradition. The novel, which emerged in the form we know it today as an essentially eighteenth-century European middle-class long narrative in written form, seems grossly unlike the blues. The blues is essentially a twentieth-century form, with its Afro-European-inspired, generally pithy lyric and its dramatic moments expressed orally. (Actually, we have the novel's remote ancestors in XII Dynasty Middle Kingdom Egyptian prose fiction.) That is not to say that there have not been lengthy blues compositions, such as the eighty-stanza song labeled "The African Iliad" collected from Floyd Canada by W. Prescott Webb circa 1915, which Webb excerpted and rearranged in thirty-five stanzas according to his own notions of coherence. Interestingly, Webb identifies "wanderlust" as the central informing spirit of the performance and then proceeds to taxonomize the lyrics to produce not a lusty and gregarious narrative, but a logical and directed artifact.[1] Still, Webb's version of Canada's composition is unlike a novel, as was the original composition itself, in terms of style, subject matter, and intended audience. The point here is that Hughes has presented us with a hybrid, Afro-European form that must be understood in each context in order to communicate its full meaning.

Hughes's choice of a title, *Not without Laughter*, is significant in the context of his work and the blues tradition. One thinks of Hughes's tribute to his people, "loud laughers in the hands of Fate," as described in the poem "Laughers" (*CW* 1:107). Additionally, his frequent repetition of the word at the beginning of *The Big Sea* is associated with his rebirth aboard the SS *Malone* and his voyage to Africa in search of the ancestral significance of his "homeland." More important, Hughes knew and employed the proverbial phrase "laughing to keep from crying" as the title of his 1952 short story collection. For Hughes, the sentiment associated with this phrase as a response to the harshness of the lives of African Americans represented the indomitable spirit of the folk. Hughes defined the blues in a review of W. C. Handy's *Blues: An Anthology* as "hopeless weariness mixed with an absurdly incongruous laughter." Later, in the *Book of Negro Humor*, he emphasized that "there is always something in the blues that makes people laugh or at least smile."[2] The lyric that traditionally precedes "I'm laughing to keep from crying" indicates at least one of Hughes's aims in employing the phrase: "you don't know, you don't know my mind / when you see me laughing." Thus, Hughes is calling attention to the fact that there are things and times that people do not see—*when* you see me laughing. And what people sometimes see—and he applied this to slummers during the Harlem Renaissance pointedly in the poem "Cabaret" and in the "boogie" poems of *Montage of a Dream Deferred*—is not the reality, but a superficial preconception of it. Finally, we need to recognize that laughter is in fact an oral, nonverbal medium, one associated with sound rather than writing. As such, Hughes reinforced the importance of oral expression through his evocation of laughter in the title.

The title of the novel seems to be a play on the traditional lyric. Some editors might be tempted to say that this title could be changed to "With Laughter" and express virtually the same idea. But "With Laughter" is not

---

1. Webb, "Notes on Folk-Lore of Texas," 292.
2. Hughes, "Review of W. C. Handy's *Blues: An Anthology*"; Hughes, *The Book of Negro Humor*, 97.

the same as "Not without Laughter." The use of the double negative here gives a particularly appropriate sense of difficulty and denial; yet we arrive, as is consistent in English grammar, at a positive statement by the end of the phrase, taking all elements into account. "Not without Laughter" negates the negative, implying a difficult-to-imagine laughter to be delineated in the text. While the title does not mention the presence of hard times and sadness, it certainly implies them through the way that the laughter is almost backgrounded or withheld. And when the title phrase occurs in the text, it refers specifically to the hard lives of "poverty-stricken old Negroes" who "lived so long—because to them, no matter how hard life might be, it was not without laughter" (CW 4:175).

In addition to the title, Hughes employs a number of the other potential uses of the blues in the novel. On occasion, the characters, some of whom speak in the vernacular, use phraseology associated with the blues. Even Hughes's narrator, entering into the oral tradition of the characters, employs a traditional blues lyric in reporting the lack of communication from Jimboy: "But for Annjee, 'the mail-man passed and didn't leave no news,' because Jimboy hadn't written yet, nor had Harriett thanked her for the three dollars she had mailed to Memphis before Christmas" (CW 4:118). In line with the association of the blues with the seamy side of life, Hughes's narrator describes the blues as "speaking an earthly language" (CW 4:48), sounding "like a blare from hell" (CW 4:72), and being sexual "like the body of a ravished woman" (CW 4:75). However, just as Hughes attempts to portray sexuality as natural in the text, so he associates the music of the band at the dance hall, including its blues, with nature: "It was true that men and women were dancing together, but their feet had gone down through the floor into the earth, each dancer's alone—down into the center of things" (CW 4:77). And though Hughes describes the "profane frenzy" (CW 4:53) of Jimboy's music, he has Maudel assert that the dance hall music is "certainly righteous, chile" (CW: 4:72), whereupon Sandy reflects on how much he likes her, though his grandmother didn't. Clearly, Hughes means to define the blues in all its earthly and spiritual aspects. One of the high compliments that a blues performer can receive is that his performance is "righteous," that is, commensurate with the truth and force of God's will. Under these circumstances, it possesses and evokes an uplifting spiritual force comparable to that conjured in the realms of spirituals and gospel music.

Obviously, there are references in the text to blues songs, blues singers as characters, and actual blues figures. Sandy's and Annjee's loneliness, Sandy's isolation, Annjee's and Harriett's frustrations, frequent expressions of sexual desire, including Annjee's, Jimboy's, and Sandy's, are all present here, as they are common in the blues. And sometimes religious or class values are portrayed through the responses of characters to the blues. In all, Hughes employs a great many of the uses of the blues outlined above in the novel.

The novel attempts to go beyond preconceptions about the lives of African Americans to the more complete realities of the life of this young, bright, impressionable boy as he confronts the difficulties of childhood, classism, and racism in a complicated home environment. And it attempts to break down barriers between segments within the community as well, particularly what traditionally have been termed the sacred and secular elements of strict Christian adherents and the low-down folks of the blues, respectively. A bildungsroman in regard to the central plot involving Sandy, the novel is, in its subplot dealing with Aunt Harriett, a kuntslerroman. Her development and insights crucially impact the development of the central plot and connect the Baptist and middle-class-influenced Sandy to the values and wisdom of the community of "low-down folks" in the "bottoms." As R. Baxter Miller rightly pointed out, "Sandy synthesizes the diverse strains of his folk roots."[3] As Harriett emerges through her associations with and acceptance of Jimboy's blues artistry to become a blues performer, she nonetheless retains elements of the "Baptist" forgiveness, thoughtfulness, and compassion she saw in Aunt Hager. Harriett therefore represents how the religious and the secular may be brought together in peaceful and natural coexistence and provides crucial assistance that allows Sandy to flourish as the novel ends.

The blues are associated by Hughes with sexuality and sin in a number of places, from hips "speaking an earthly language" (CW 4:48) to the second encore of "Easy Rider" coming "like a blare from hell" (CW: 4:472). Yet Hughes presents Jimboy and Harriett as having "innocent fun" as they sing bawdy blues lyrics and dance with definite movements of the hips: if one thought about the lyrics, it might not seem so innocent, "but neither Harriett nor Jimboy soiled their minds by thinking" (CW 4:50). Such thinking Hughes associates in the text with white folks, for whom the natural and joyous expression of sexuality was foreign. Here, the so-called profane blues are really only a carefree celebration of sexuality, not a sinful call to debauchery as some would have it. A sort of "everybody singin' 'bout coitus ain't goin' there." As is frequently the case in Hughes's work, the hierarchy is explored and challenged, here to delineate the sub-

---

3. Miller, *Langston Hughes and Gwendolyn Brooks: A Reference Guide*, 369.

jectivity of values that privilege traditional middle-class Christian sexual mores over a more spontaneous and open sexual expression.

Certainly, in this novel, Sandy confronts a number of negative experiences—being young, black, poor, and class-embattled in a racist American society—that climax in a positive outcome as he negotiates his way in the worlds of his grandmother, mother and father, and Aunt Tempy, as well as that represented and supported by Harriett, his blues-singing aunt.

Although it is not literally true, Sandy is like the proverbial motherless child of the spirituals. His mother, Annjee, frequently disregards his needs in order to please or follow after Jimboy. His surrogate mother, Aunt Hager, cares deeply for him but dies as he enters puberty. Tempy, who takes Sandy into her house out of a sense of responsibility, is too busy trying to mold him into a middle-class automaton to treat him humanely, though she does regret his leaving when he joins his mother in Chicago. Even that reunion springs from Annjee's selfishness: she needs the income that Sandy can provide as an elevator operator. His experience with father figures is no better. From the absentee father Jimboy, who offers Sandy some guidance in terms of musicianship and honesty but ultimately goes his own way, to the henpecked and ineffectual Mr. Siles, to the pianist Billy Sanderlee, who encourages Sandy to play the numbers until Harriett intercedes, Sandy has little luck with parental figures. In fact, perhaps a blues lyric characterizes Sandy's situation better than the spiritual: "I am motherless, fatherless, sisterless, and brotherless, too / Reason I tried so hard to make the trip with you." This stanza from Blind Lemon Jefferson's "Broke and Hungry" reflects perfectly Sandy's sense of abandonment, isolation, and loneliness, as well as his desperation to find someone to accompany or guide him, from Earl, who goes around with him at the carnival, to Pansetta, the guys at the pool hall, and the men at the barbershop.

Sandy's relationship with Aunt Hager is the most tender and touching one in the text. The long-suffering Hager, born into slavery and demonstrating a remarkable capacity to forgive and empathize with her enslavers, provides economic, spiritual, and personal support for the young, abandoned child. Recognizing that "po' colored womens have it hard" (CW 4:103), she nonetheless refuses to capitulate to bitterness and hatred and thus pass on to Sandy the hatred he hears expressed by Harriett, Annjee, and others.

Significantly, the name *Hager* references both the biblical and the blues traditions. Genesis 16 and 21 provide the story of Hagar, the Egyptian servant of a seemingly sterile Sarah, who is presented to Abraham to provide him with the male heir that Sarah cannot produce. After the pregnant Hagar is expelled from the household, she meets with a messenger of God in the wilderness and gives birth to Abraham's son Ishmael, prophesied to be a wild and embattled outcast. When Sarah bears a child to Abraham fourteen years later, Hagar and Ishmael are cast out once more but once again encounter a divine messenger, who affirms Ishmael's legitimacy by prophesying that Ishmael, even from his humble beginnings, will become patriarch of a great nation.

The biblical Hagar is a vulnerable woman, a foreigner and a servant, who nevertheless demonstrates strength and a commitment to her son in the face of horrendous mistreatment. The suggestions of miscegenation, hints of ethnic tension in the narrative, and rather insulting sexual innuendo applied to the character of Hagar all have their counterparts in the experiences of African Americans. Indeed, Hughes's novel confronts the reality of miscegenation directly through the various colors in Sandy's family: black Hager and Harriett, dark Annjee, light yellow Jimboy, and brown Sandy. Additionally, the text includes the story of Buster, the "white man's child" (CW 4:31) who announces his intention to pass (CW 4:180), as well as a number of clashes between people of different hues, from black versus yellow (CW 4:74) to dark purple and yellow (CW 4:75) to mustard colored, black, and maple sugar (CW 4:95). An unidentified speaker admonishes at the dance to which Harriett takes Sandy, "High yallers, draw nigh! Brown skins, come near! . . . But black gals, stay where you are!" (CW 4:75). But as in the biblical story of Hagar's commitment to Ishmael, Aunt Hager's perseverance and love for all her children—however they disappoint her—and the issues of sexual exploitation, marginalization, and betrayal (associated, perhaps, with the era of Reconstruction) all resonate in the novel. Hager is an ex-slave woman symbolic of the treatment of African women in America, and her children are symbolic of a variety of paths—economic, social, and religious—open to African Americans in the post-Reconstruction world of the late nineteenth and early twentieth centuries. Of course, the great promise of the (grand)son Sandy at the end of the novel relates to the prophecy regarding the unfairly stereotyped Ishmael as well.

Significantly, the blues themselves began to emerge as a distinct musical genre as the first generation of African Americans born outside slavery reached their majority. One of the figures responsible for midwifing the blues into popular culture was W. C. Handy. Handy's name is mentioned in the text by Jimboy, who met Handy in Memphis when Jimboy was a child (*CW* 4:51), and Handy's famous composition "St. Louis Blues" is also named (*CW* 4:76). Hughes himself knew Handy and collaborated with him on a blues song, "Golden Brown Blues," that was dedicated to Madame Mamie Hightower and recorded by Maude Mills twice in 1927. Hughes also wrote in a variety of places about Handy's significance to American culture.

In 1921, Handy Brothers copyrighted a W. C. Handy–Tim Brymn collaboration, "Aunt Hagar's Children's Blues," that was recorded some two dozen times before 1942, including the debut vocal recording by Alice Leslie Carter in September 1921. The song presents us with an assertive Aunt Hagar, a member of Old Deacon Splivins's flock, who jumps up and shouts her objection to the deacon's prohibition against secular music and dance. Splivins acquiesces to Hagar's admonitions to listen to her children harmonize on the latest sweet melody. The song is "one mournful blues," but the performers are compared to a choir from on high as they perform it. This combination of supposed sacred and secular elements is significant: "If the devil brought it, the good Lord sent it right down to me," Hagar exclaims, and this heavenly blues provokes dance and rejoicing in the congregation. The music and performance, in effect, challenge and destroy the artificial Manichaean dichotomy of sacred versus secular music.

It is not difficult to see Hughes's Aunt Hager in the lyrics of the Handy blues song, though she is not an exact match. Hughes's Hager is unfailingly religious in her taste in music: Jimboy's religious performances made Hager forget he was the "enemy" (*CW* 4:38), but she was appalled by his, and Harriett's, blues. Her recognition of the stylistic value of Jimboy's technique when pressed into the service of the Lord underscores the closeness in technique of what she saw as the competing sacred and secular music traditions. Significantly, two of her "children," Harriett and Sandy, grow up to appreciate the blues, even as they demonstrate a humanity and compassion that draw on the spiritual backgrounds of the church services and songs that are referenced in the text. Aunt Hager's children bring the blues to the "congregation," supported by Hager herself. Back of it all, the author Hughes is, like Hager, preparing the way for his own literary progeny as well as, like Harriett, bridging the gap between the two genres and carrying the wisdom and spirituality of the blues to the community as a whole.

Nowhere is this more evident than in the final chapter of Hughes's novel, "Princess of the Blues." This chapter offers a portrait not only of Harrietta the vaudeville blues singer and her very secular act but also of Harriett the sister and protector of Sandy, who scolds Annjee for insisting Sandy sacrifice his education for a fourteen-dollar-a-week dead-end job. In fact, Harrietta offers Annjee the weekly money, earned from plying her blues singing trade, to enable Sandy to purchase his books and attend school. The symbolism is clear: the religious Aunt Hager's child uses a complementary secular African American tradition to provide Sandy with the opportunity to improve his standing and help the black race through education. Thus the oral blues tradition supports the gaining of literacy, especially in one like Sandy, who seems able to accept the power and beauty of the blues side by side with an appreciation of the spirituals.

Certainly the book's final scene, where Sandy affirms the great beauty of the spirituals sung in the little down-home church in Chicago, juxtaposes what Hughes sees as two complementary musical traditions that can both teach Sandy about humanity and compassion and support him in his quest for knowledge, understanding, and financial stability. In the penultimate chapter, Sandy tries to sort through his relation to the members of his family. He rejects Jimboy's lifestyle as being as aimless and tiresome as his elevator job, asserting,

> "I'm more like Harriett—not wanting to be a servant at the mercy of white people for ever. . . . I want to do something for myself, by myself. . . . Free. . . . I want a house to live in, too, when I'm older—like Tempy's and Mr. Siles's. . . . But I wouldn't want to be like Tempy's friends—or her husband, dull and colorless, putting all his money away in a white bank, ashamed of colored people." (CW 4:202)

Rather, he ends his reverie focused on Aunt Hager's admonition to be a success. It will be a success based on sorting through the attitudes and temperaments of his family and embracing the complementary sacred and secular elements that reinforce the lessons of love, humanity, responsibility, education, and frugality he culls from his family.

What is important here is that Hughes does not envision the oral blues tradition as being inimical to the written imperative of the educational tradition in which Sandy wishes to participate. He explores this in his contrasts of Hager, Annjee, Harriett, and Tempy. Significantly, Sandy's character learns and develops in a kind of call and response to what these women especially (though of course he observes and learns from men, too) say and do in their lives around him. From Hager, Sandy gets his sense that the best way to respond to hatred in the world is with love. In addition to his sensitivity, he also inherits from her his ethic of hard work, his love of spirituals, his pride in his African American heritage, and his commitment to becoming a great man "fo' de glory o' God an' de black race" (*CW* 4:139). Annjee, on the other hand, demonstrates what happens when Hager's values are reflected through a selfish prism. She is luke-warm religiously, and her hard work is put in service of her aim to save enough to join Jimboy. Annjee is, in fact, primarily a body in orbit of Jim-boy, being almost monomaniacally committed to a man whose own ad-vice to Sandy about women is, "Treat 'em like chickens": "Throw 'em a little corn and they'll run after you, but don't give 'em too much. If you do, they'll stop layin' and expect you to wait on 'em" (*CW* 4:56). Sandy's response is "will they?" He answers Jimboy's call as he does the calls of many characters in the novel—with thoughtful consideration of where the idea fits into his own experiences, core feelings, and maturing philos-ophy about life.

Harriett, on the surface, seems to be not as religious as Hager and Ann-jee, criticizing "Your old Jesus is white" (*CW* 4:44) and preferring the blues and jazz of the joints in the Bottoms and the traveling stage and road shows to Hager's Baptist services. And it is the youthful Harriett, bump-ing up against the ceiling of her limited possibilities, who allows her frus-tration to spill over into a hatred of white folks so vehemently expressed that "Sandy was afraid" (*CW* 4:68). Nonetheless, it is Harriett who laments at the end of the novel that she and Annjee did not follow Hager's lead, breaking her heart and leaving school. By the end of the novel, it is the "prodigal daughter" whose response to Annjee's selfish desire to keep Sandy out of school is in line with Hager's sense of pride, encouragement, commitment, and mission. And it is her money, earned with the fruits of her labors as a singer of blues songs—learned over nine years from Jim-boy, plied in joints and dances and on the tough performance circuit, and lived in all their harshness in her experience as a streetwalker—that al-lows Hager's dream for Sandy, now Harriett's too, to be actualized.

Sandy, significantly, embraces them both and recognizes the closeness of their spirits. He has learned to reconcile the different ideas and natures of those around him without being harshly judgmental or hateful, and without segregating segments of the community from each other. After all, he notices that the Bottoms is the place, the only place, where blacks and whites mingle freely and happily in their activities, and thus cannot force himself to reject it out of hand as a place of sin and ignominy. But he also cannot reject the loving spirit of Hager, who welcomed back all her children, no matter how far they strayed or how much they hurt her. Al-though Sandy may have agreed at times that, as Harriett thinks, "it was hard to have a Christian mother" (*CW* 4:70), he realized it was good to have a Christian (grand)mother as well.

Sandy even has something to gain from his Aunt Tempy. Her sense of order and propriety, learned from the white Mrs. Barr-Grant, is decidedly middle class and oppressive. On his first day at her house after Hager's death, Sandy learns that he "must get up on time" (*CW* 4:165), hence the appropriateness of her name (tempus), which associates her in a way with the father Hughes laments in *The Big Sea*, whose mantra "hurry up" so sickened the young Langston (*CW* 13:59–62). Still, though the proudly Episcopal Tempy rejects blues and spirituals as beneath her middle-class dignity and condescends to her mother and other members of that household, she does expose Sandy to *The Crisis* and a sense of the greatness of a "race leader" like W. E. B. Du Bois, whose lead she would like Sandy to follow. Tempy's admiration of Du Bois is a response to Hager's for Booker T. Washington, who is for her the great beacon of commitment to race. Sandy listens to both, and decides, "I guess they are both great men" (*CW* 4:171).

Although in a typically browbeating manner, Tempy encourages Sandy educationally as well. While Hager encouraged Sandy to read, the only books Sandy had around were schoolbooks. The one nice book that Tempy brought to Sandy for Christmas he rejected out of frustration, pride, and disappointment. However, later it is Tempy's money that provides access to the books Sandy is able to read with frequency and avidity while he lives with her. Significantly, her books are dusty from misuse—she has clearly bought them for show—but Sandy uses her resources advantageously. Although Tempy has a more conventional relationship with her man—he is her husband, though he is like Jimboy and Harriett's johns, frequently absent in his position in the railway postal service—their relationship does not provide Sandy with a satisfactory example of conjugal bliss. Neither do they provide him with healthy attitudes toward the opposite sex. Tempy and Mr. Siles label Pansetta, and perhaps all women in Sandy's sphere, dangerous, social-climbing gold diggers, imputing, of course, their own values to others.

In the climactic scene, when Sandy attempts to sort through his feelings about these different family members, he decides to leave his job as an elevator operator and return to school. Feeling guilty about leaving a paying position to continue his education, Sandy begins arguing with himself. Accusing himself of being like Jimboy in his irresponsibility, he counters by rejecting his father and embracing Harriett's independence, the creature comforts of the Sileses, and the loving vision of Aunt Hager.

He even connects the religious ecstasy of Hager with the joie de vivre of Harriett, and then reintegrates Jimboy into the circle of value for his artistic contributions to the community and to Sandy's life:

> Sandy remembered his grandmother whirling around in front of the altar at revival meetings in the midst of the other sisters, her face shining with light, arms outstretched as though all the cares of the world had been cast away; Harriett in the back yard, under the apple-tree, eagle-rocking in the summer evenings to the tunes of the guitar; Jimboy singing. (CW 4:202)

It is this vision that prepares the way for Harriett to become Sandy's deliverer in the final chapter of the novel and foreshadows the words of the spiritual "Bye and Bye" that bring the novel to its unified conclusion. On that cold northern urban street, a little bit of the southern rural past, represented by the church in which the singing of the old ones strikes Sandy as so beautiful, describes the reconciliation that Hughes has tried so hard to achieve in Sandy. "By an' by when de mawnin' comes," at the dawning of the new day signaled by the marshaling of various segments of the African American community in the service of the black race, "Saints an' sinners all are gathered home" (CW 4:209). This is home indeed for Sandy, whose growing comprehension of race, class, sexuality, society, and humanity finds him uniting the sacred and secular strands of the community in a unified and loving vision that could help bring about a unified and loving world.

Almost — But Not Quite — Bluesmen
in Langston Hughes's Poetry

Trudier Harris

If we were to paint a picture of the quintessential bluesman of literary tradition, he might take a couple of guises. He is Albert Murray's Luzana Cholly from *Train Whistle Guitar* (1974), with his guitar strapped over his shoulder as he contemplates hopping the next freight train, a quiet man surrounded by a mysterious aura that isolates him from others in his community and makes him heroic simply because his chosen life is so dramatically different from theirs, so strikingly free of communal and family obligations. In another guise, that literary bluesman is surrounded by beautiful women who adore his phallic guitar as much as they adore the bluesman himself. He ranges from Langston Hughes's and Sterling Brown's poetry in the 1920s and 1930s to Arthur Flowers's *Another Good Loving Blues* (1993). This bluesman emphasizes his attraction to women and his inability to live without female attention. Indeed, presumed sexual attractiveness is the essence of his understanding of himself as a man.

Hughes invents personae who attempt to fit this second guise of the bluesman as well as others who move the male blues persona toward drama that transcends sexuality or toward humor that is incompatible with sexuality. For a couple of the bluesmen who do define themselves in terms of sexuality, namely Sylvester in "Sylvester's Dying Bed" and the unnamed persona in "As Befits a Man," their declarations exist only in the realm of imagination, thus their abilities to be convincing as bluesmen are compromised severely. Consider Sylvester. He wakes up from some undisclosed ailment after three o'clock one morning with "All de womens in town" (*CW* 2:48) gathered around his bed lamenting his departure and begging him to stay. This scenario would suggest that his hammer has hung heavy in this territory, that he has cooled a lot of hot engines, or that he has been a particularly efficient coffee grinder. Resolving to live up to his reputation as a sexual bluesman and embrace the women as long "as life do last," he hollers "Com'ere babies, / Fo' to love yo' daddy right!" and "reaches up to hug 'em— / When de Lawd put out de light" (*CW* 2:48–49).

A couple of strange things happen in this poem in terms of the blues tradition. While we applaud Hughes for "getting it right," so to speak, in generally imitating the blues stanzaic form, he didn't quite get it right in portraying the male blues persona. The first problem is that Sylvester's reputation rests in his own imagination, not in some confirmed, exterior reality. I reach this conclusion by avowing that Sylvester is alone in this room and delirious. His reputation, therefore, exists only in that disease-induced delirium. There are no women present beyond the ones he conjures up. Second, no serious bluesman would ever take himself to the physical point of his own death (Hughes does get this right in other poems), not to mention Sylvester's inability to continue his narrative if he had indeed died. This almost bluesman, therefore, becomes a sacrifice to Hughes's love of the humorous. In order to wrap Sylvester in laughter, Hughes positions him where no bluesman can reside—that is, posthumously. Indeed, such a place is antithetical to the blues. Remember that, even in "The Weary Blues," the narrator only wishes for death; its reality is never a serious consideration.

By locating Sylvester's blues stature in the realm of the sexual and then undercutting that very potential for sexuality—lights out rather than sex—Hughes forces Sylvester to suffer an impotence that is not registered in any part of the African American blues tradition with which I am familiar. Ironically, then, in this reading Sylvester is only *almost* sexual, almost a bluesman. By substituting talk for action, delirium for reality, imagination for substance, Hughes allows Sylvester only to approach what a true bluesman might be. In contrast to the blues stanzaic that Hughes imitated, which allowed him form and substance in revealing the blues, the presentation of the persona in "Sylvester's Dying Bed" allows neither form nor impressive substance. It can be argued that Sylvester has the lingo of the blues culture, for he knows how to label the women as "pretty mamas" and "brown-skins" and to refer to himself as "Sweet Papa

'Vester" (*CW* 2:48), but naming operates on the same level as imagination; it exists without action. Sylvester is thus a humorous sham, a declarer of deeds for which there is little evidence in the poem. His almost blues life dissolves into him imaging God turning out the light, which could even be read as punishment for Sylvester's professed deeds and their implicit excess.

The persona in "As Befits a Man" is no less problematic as a male blues persona. He, like Sylvester, begins in a position near death or contemplating death: "I don't mind dying—/ But I'd hate to die all alone!" (*CW* 3:236). Like Sylvester, he wants pretty women hollering and moaning his departure. He imagines a funeral at which "A row of long tall mamas" will be "fainting, fanning, and crying" (*CW* 3:236), which again introduces sexuality as the realm in which he defines himself in the blues tradition. "When they let me down, / Down into the clay, / I want the women to holler: / *Please don't take him away! / Ow-ooo-oo-o! / Don't take daddy away!*" (*CW* 3:237). By lamenting his departure, making clear that his absence will mean great sexual denial for them, the women name his right to the blues tradition. At least that's the way the traditional script is written. With this persona, however, even more clearly than with Sylvester, the script is an imagined one. At some future moment, this speaker avows, when death comes, this is what he wants. His contemplation of his demise and what will happen then, no matter how dramatic, has no independent corroboration. He leaves us with the dream, not with his present reality.

Again like Sylvester, this persona knows the blues culture. He is aware of the women, the status cars, and the importance of "a whole truck load of flowers" (*CW* 3:236) for a fine funeral. He can mouth the lament of the women as they imaginatively refer to him as "*daddy*," but his reputation, too, depends on an after-death scenario. The gap between who he is now and who he plans to be at his funeral is the gap between reality and imagination. His imagined John Henry–like exploits with women leave him as static in the blues tradition as John Henry is in the ballad tradition, that is, locked into a moment of inactivity—the moment of death.

In two other blues poems in which relationships with women dominate, the personae fail as blues heroic figures because of inaction and because of domination by the object of affection. In "Wide River," the persona asserts, "Ma baby lives across de river / An' I ain't got no boat / . . . I ain't a good swimmer / An' I don't know how to float" (*CW* 1:176). Although the river is the only thing that stands between himself and his baby, he cannot figure out how to get to her. He's "got to cross that river" and get to his baby "somehow," but instead of acting he lingers in contemplation. Finally he claims, "Cause if I don't see ma baby / I'll lay down an' die right now" (CW 1:177). Given his inability to find a solution to his dilemma, he may well end up quitting, as these final lines suggest. Whatever sexual or emotional urgency his baby offers is not sufficient to move his complaint from the abstract to the concrete, from whining about lack of transportation to acquiring transportation. Given the rail-riding, guitar-over-the-shoulder bluesman of tradition who would as easily hop a freight train as walk, this lover merely seems pathetic. As Sonny Terry and Brownie McGee assert in "Walk On," when you ain't got no bus fare or train fare, you just put your feet in the road and walk. Obviously this bluesman cannot walk across water, but his lack of imagination in how to get across paints him as ineffectual and perhaps even cowardly in his relationship to his lover.

His plight, however, is precisely that because he is not in the presence of his "baby." The persona in "Only Woman Blues" suffers because he has been in the presence of a woman. This "meanest woman" that he has ever seen has mistreated him, but he maintains that she is the only woman who will have the opportunity to do so. What she has done, according to his testimony, is rather life-changing. "She could make me holler like a sissie, / Bark like a dog. / She could chase me up a tree / And then cut down de log—/ Cause she's de only / Woman that could mistreat me" (CW 2:41). These metaphoric representations of mistreatment place the speaker in a "go long" situation comparable to that in which Tea Cake asserts that Janie places him in Zora Neale Hurston's *Their Eyes Were Watching God* (1937). The woman in the poem seems to have total sexual and emotional control without an accompanying generosity of spirit. The speaker tries to redirect attention from his own submissive, "sissie" status by claiming that the woman had "long black hair" and "big black eyes," features that might have made her sexually attractive enough for him to endure domination, but then he demands "forgive them lies!" and we know that he has merely been weak. For the male to lack control within a blues situation without immediately extricating himself from it marks the failure of this potential bluesman. The woman apparently stays as long as she wants. When she leaves voluntarily, his response is: "I said, Go, hot damn!" Circumstances, which could possibly include the woman's boredom with her lover, rescue this burdened speaker, not any severing action of his own. In fact, he carries the woman from Mississippi to Alabama, where she finally leaves him, which means that he enables her livelihood and her departure. Such a scenario of lack of control shows yet again a persona who knows the blues lingo and the blues life, but who is ultimately victimized by it or cannot live it because of some lack in himself. At least we can assume in this instance that sex is a part of the relationship, which is a contrast to the scenes with Sylvester and the persona in "As Befits a Man."

The almost bluesmen who imagine sexuality but fall short of its execution are matched in Hughes's poetry by the potential bluesmen who are too spastic to settle comfortably into a blues lament or a blues lifestyle. In "Life Is Fine," for example, one of Hughes's most humorously engaging and memorable poems, the persona, presumably stereotypically male, is driven to contemplate ending his life by drowning or by jumping from a sixteen-story building. When he jumps into the water and discovers how cold it is, he pauses, but the poem leaps to his next episode. He takes the elevator sixteen stories up and pauses again when he realizes that it is too high for him to commit suicide. He then leaps to avowing that life is fine and to giving up on his attempts to do himself in. The spaces in which physicality overcomes mental resolve—that is, when his body experiences cold and vertigo—are the spaces in which Hughes makes his persona too spastic to be considered a true bluesman. Unlike the previous personae, who imagine blues scenes, the persona in "Life Is Fine" not only acts but ends up in a traditional blues posture, that is, focusing on women, wine, and song.

What makes the difference here is that Hughes so overlays the poem with humor that it slants the potentially serious actions. This enables me to label this persona a "feinting man." He does not whine and cry about his lover leaving him, as many of the blues women in Hughes's poetry do; he simply leaps to another condition. He leads the reader to expect drama, then "feints" into humor. In other words, this persona is only *almost* a bluesman because he does not pause to contemplate his situations into seriousness; he passes over them in slapstick mode. His "baby" has obviously driven him to think of suicide, and that love motive certainly fits into traditional blues culture. However, his humorous responses to his attempts to resolve his love troubles by committing suicide inadvertently negate the seriousness of those troubles. When the persona ends up declaring, "You may hear me holler / You may see me cry—/ But I'll be dogged, sweet baby, / If you gonna see me die. / *Life is fine! / Fine as wine! / Life is fine!*" (CW 2:180), the journey to that perspective has prevented readers from having taken it seriously. Certainly bluesmen and -women sing themselves into reconciliation to their situations, but listeners to their music seldom conclude that the situations the singers have portrayed so graphically are ones that could be dismissed by the ends of the songs. Transcended, yes. Overcome, yes. Dismissed, no. It is that nuance of distinction in arriving at the point of claiming life that makes the difference between Hughes's personae and traditional bluesmen.

In "The Weary Blues," perhaps the most classic of all of Hughes's poems centering on the blues ethos, the persona shares with his predecessors an *almost* status. While the blues stanzaic form and the function of the blues are effectively presented for the blues musician whom the speaker observes, the persona himself is merely an imaginative voyeur to the blues life. He can observe a musician singing about not having anybody but himself and declaring that he will "quit" his "frownin" and put his "troubles on the shelf" (*CW* 1:23), but the speaker himself is beyond that experience. His purpose in the poem is to observe, record, and imagine an ending; the life of the bluesman is not his to live. Even when he imagines an ending that is commensurate with the blues tradition, he is himself still beyond that tradition. Claiming that the musician "slept like a rock or a man that's dead" (*CW* 1:24), the persona easily fits him into blues culture, for he recognizes the exorcising function of the blues—one sings about one's troubles and, as a result of that singing, is able to carry on until another set of troubles supplants the current one. However, not having followed the musician home or witnessed for himself the result of his singing, the speaker is left to imagine the blues result just as he must stand back from and merely observe the blues life.

Like his counterparts, this persona is drawn to the blues life. While there are no explicit overtones of sexuality in the poem, there is implicit blues-based sexuality in the way the musician plays his piano as well as in his noting that he does not have anyone in this world but himself. It might easily be concluded that there has been a recent female departure from his life. That possibility, however, is far removed from the narrator. He remains one of those to whom the blues life is not available.

Seldom in reading these poems do we pause to contemplate the gaps between what the personae describe, claim, or avow and their concrete relationships to those claims. Closer examination, however, reveals that Hughes frequently stops short of allowing his male personae the blues existence to which he seems so robustly drawn. While several women blues personae are portrayed as being in the throes of the blues situations that undo them, many of the men are somewhat removed; they are allowed an active or imaginative escape that is not usually available to the women. These gaps in representation, then, raise issues about Hughes's conceptualization of the accessibility of the blues life to men as opposed to women. Or, perhaps more troubling, they posit that the blues life was more appropriately realized fully in the traditional form of a woman lamenting the departure of her lover. In this reading, sexism in the blues thus moves from song to poetry and provides another lens through which to view Langston Hughes as a blues poet.

Natural and Unnatural Circumstances in *Not without Laughter*

Elizabeth Schultz

The Harlem Renaissance was a big-city phenomenon. It was generated and supported by African Americans living, working, and creating in New York City's streets, tenements, brownstones, cabarets, clubs, offices, and publishing houses. Yet the imagery in literary texts produced by the Harlem Renaissance's major writers—Countee Cullen, Jean Toomer, Zora Neale Hurston, Eric Walrond, Langston Hughes, among others—is not all urban. Rather, it reflects these writers' intimate familiarity with nature—in places as distant from New York as Jamaica, Florida, and Kansas.[1]

Hughes's *Not without Laughter* (1930), based on his boyhood years in Lawrence, Kansas, was written fifteen years after his departure from Kansas; during those intervening years Hughes traveled the world, becoming a consummate urbanite and cosmopolitan. Yet, as *Not without Laughter* reveals, Hughes forgot neither the individuals and experiences he encountered during his Kansas years nor the features of that land. Among the aspects of Kansas that he recalls throughout the novel are those explicitly related to nature—plants, seasons, weather, earth, and sky.

Hughes perceives nature in his novel as the source of neither transcendental reverie nor Darwinian determinism as European American writers

1. This essay appeared previously in *Callaloo* 25.4 (2002): 1177–87.

were doing in the 1920s and 1930s. It can be argued that in drawing on natural imagery, Hughes, like other Harlem Renaissance writers, was referring explicitly to his personal experiences prior to moving to New York as well as to the rural experiences of thousands of other African Americans who participated in the Great Migration. Unlike the narratives of his contemporary and collaborator, Zora Neale Hurston, Hughes does not engage in extensive reenvisionings of African American animal tales in *Not without Laughter*.[2] Nor does he romanticize or exoticize nature in his novel, as Countee Cullen does African nature in his poetry. Instead Hughes, recognizing the conventionality and neutrality of nature as imagery and subject matter for middle- and upper-class readers, exploits its rhetorical possibilities for representing complex social concerns.

From the time he wrote "The Negro Speaks of Rivers" in 1921 at the precocious age of nineteen, Hughes appears to have recognized the rhetorical possibilities for linking African American experience and nature. The impetus for "The Negro Speaks of Rivers" might have been the Kaw River, which flows through Lawrence and which Hughes would have seen as a boy. His early description of the Mississippi in "The Negro Speaks of Rivers," with "its muddy bosom turn[ing] all golden in the sunset," anticipates his later description of the river in *Not without Laughter* where Sandy and his father go fishing: "The warm afternoon sun made [it] a languid sheet of muddy gold" (*CW* 4:56). However, more significant than the description of the Mississippi is the symbiosis Hughes generates in the poem by seeing several rivers as embodying African history, the African diaspora, and himself, the representative "Negro" of the poem's title, whose "soul has grown deep like the rivers" (*CW* 1:36).

Hughes's descriptions of Kansas's natural features in *Not without Laughter* establish not only the authenticity of place as a vividly textured backdrop for human affairs but also the boundaries of class. In addition, they provide him with the rhetorical means for generating what Mikhail Bakhtin calls "a double-directed discourse."[3] Thus Hughes constructs a

---

2. Although Hager tells Sandy, "Slavery-time stories, myths, folk-tales like the Rabbit and the Tar Baby" (*CW* 4:129), Hughes's only folktale in *Not without Laughter* is told by Uncle Dan Givens about two black slaves who borrow their master's horse to go to a dance and, when the horse dies, manage to fool him into thinking it died of natural causes. The tale, coming late in the novel, not only balances Hager's genteel view of slavery but also indicates the significance of his title, explicitly demonstrating the means by which "poverty-stricken old Negroes like Uncle Dan Givens lived so long— because to them, no matter how hard life might be, it was not without laughter" (*CW* 4:175).

3. Bakhtin, *The Dialogic Imagination*, 324.

dominant narrative in *Not without Laughter* that relies on natural imagery to appeal to mainstream readers, including his wealthy and aged white patron, Charlotte Mason, even as he slips a significant subversive subtext into the narrative under this conventional and noncontroversial guise. Thus in Hughes's "double-directed discourse," a "natural" story of a boy's coming of age reveals the "unnatural" circumstances of racism and poverty. This subtext explicitly introduces middle- and upper-class readers to the ubiquity and injustices of racism in American society as well as to the richness of African American culture.

In small midwestern towns in the early twentieth century, as is the case with Stanton, Kansas—Hughes's pseudonym for Lawrence in *Not without Laughter*—lower-class African Americans lived in close proximity to nature. In Stanton, nature intersects with the lives of Hughes's characters on a daily and nightly basis. As the novel develops, a class difference as well as a difference in the quality of life itself is revealed through descriptions of nature. Hager's house, the setting for twenty-two of the novel's thirty-three chapters, is open to the elements. Throughout the summer, its windows are open, with lights "lurin' all sorts o' night-bugs an' creepers into de house" (*CW* 4:39). Both the porch and the backyard are extensions of the house into the outdoors. Members of the family are often on the porch, talking, telling stories, catching fireflies, or watching the world go by, while the backyard with its gardens and apple tree is a playground for Sandy, the novel's protagonist, and his friends as well as an open-air pavilion where the family members dance, sing, and make music. For the middle and upper classes, whose lawns are well trimmed and who stay inside for the most part, Hughes implies life is pretentious and sterile.

However, during the winter, Hager's house is permeated with cold and damp. An elderly woman comments on the difficulties for poor blacks during those months, "'folks is out o' work ever' where, an', wid all dis sleet an' rain, it's a terror fo' de po' peoples'" (*CW* 4:102). In Hughes's representation of lower-class African American life in Stanton, work also necessitates intimate interaction with nature. Hager and her neighbors are frequently shown engaged in the laborious task of hanging the laundry out in the open. Sis Whitehead gardens and sells her produce from the back of a wagon. Black men work the railroad, lay brick, or dig sewers. Sandy's chores all involve nature:

> In the mornings he helped Aunt Hager by feeding the chickens, bringing in the water for her wash-tubs and filling the buckets from which

they drank. He chopped wood, too, and piled it behind the kitchen-stove; then he would take the broom and sweep dust-clean the space around the pump and under the apple-tree where he played. (*CW* 4:90–91)

Cultivated, nature in *Not without Laughter* can be bountiful even as it can be brutal. Both flower and vegetable gardens are represented as lush. Food, constantly evident in the novel's scenes, comes most often from the garden—peas, corn, eggplant, yams, apples, peaches, watermelon—with an occasional fish from the river or possum from the woods.

Frank Baum's *The Wizard of Oz* (1900), in opening with a Kansas tornado, gave the state a signature meteorological event. Hughes picked up on this event for the opening of *Not without Laughter*, as Gordon Parks would do later for the opening of his Kansas novel *The Learning Tree* (1963). Hughes's gradual evocation of the tornado in his first chapter, presented from Sandy's perspective, is realistic and terrifying: trees sway in the wind; a pail tips over; finally there appears "a black cloud twisting like a ribbon in the western sky . . . [with] sooty grey-green light that was rapidly turning to blackness" (*CW* 4:22). However, the tornado that devastates the Stanton community does more than designate Kansas as the specific geographical setting for the novel; rather than whisking its protagonist off to a fantasy land, it locates him in a specific social setting, one that initially functions to captivate readers of all classes and races in a sympathetic response. As Sandy is separated in the aftermath of the tornado from his beloved grandmother, Hager, and his mother, Annjee, Hughes presents him as any isolated and terrified young boy. In his distress and disorientation, Sandy's reality turns into a surreal nightmare: "a piano [lay] flat on its back in the grass. Its ivory keys gleamed in the moonlight like grinning teeth, and the strange sight made his little body shiver" (*CW* 4:24). Desperate for his mother, he imagines that she "had been carried off by the great black wind" (*CW* 4:25). The color imagery in these passages describing the tornado's power is non-race-specific, with white and black equally appalling to the small boy. Similarly, Hughes's tornado is non-judgmental, discriminating among neither races nor classes in Stanton—a kindly, elderly white couple is killed by this natural force, while Hager loses her porch, and her neighbor loses her trees. Thus, nature, in Hughes's opening chapter, while threatening, appears to create an open playing field with all human beings equally vulnerable.

The tornado, however, also introduces *Not without Laughter*'s readers to the African American way of responding to calamity "not without laughter": Hager laughs at her missing porch—"Cyclone sho did a good job. . . . Looks like I ain't never had no porch," while her neighbor exclaims, "But praise God for sparing our lives! It might've been worse . . . ! It might've been more calamitouser! As it is, I lost nothin' more'n a chimney and two wash-tubs which was settin' in the back yard. A few trees broke down don't 'mount to nothin'. We's livin', ain't we? And we's more importanter than trees is any day!" (*CW* 4:23). As the novel evolves, however, racism becomes the tornado that threatens African American lives on a daily basis, even when the weather is benign and the season is spring; its effects prove "calamitouser."

In subsequent chapters, Hughes represents nature seasonally, thereby underscoring the generic structure of *Not without Laughter* as a bildungsroman. Natural changes occurring with summer, fall, winter, and spring, with specific seasonal references to the family's apple tree and corn patch, provide a descriptive correlative for Sandy's growth. The "natural" process of Sandy's coming of age consequently becomes generalized, so that readers can relate his experiences to those of any youth, regardless of race, class, or gender. Thus in the course of Sandy's growing up, Hughes repeatedly aligns the changing seasons with his protagonist's developing consciousness of an existential and sexual identity as well as with his developing consciousness of social and racial inequities and of his own racial identity.

Hughes's description of early summer in the second chapter evokes pastoral innocence with an array of plants as colorful as the people in his community and only a hint of sexual fecundity:

> The air was warm with sunlight, and hundreds of purple and white morning-glories laughed on the back fence. Earth and sky were fresh and clean after the heavy night-rain, and the young corn-shoots stood straight in the garden, and green pea-vines wound themselves around their crooked sticks. There was the mingled scent of wet soil and golden pollen on the breeze that blew carelessly through the clear air. (*CW* 4:28)

In the course of the summer, Sandy gradually awakens from sexual innocence. At night he listens to the sounds of his parents making love, sounds "he already knew accompanied the grown-up embraces of bodily love." As he listens, he associates these sounds with ripening corn: "sometimes through the window he could see the moonlight glinting on the tall, tassel-crowned stalks of corn in the garden" (*CW* 4:90).

Marking Sandy's fall from innocence as well as the season of fall, Hughes describes "sunny August mornings" giving way to September mornings with the apple tree "loaded with ripe fruit" and "pans of apple juice boiled to jelly" (*CW* 4:96). Here Hughes's conventional description of nature emphatically reveals an unnatural subtext. In late fall, summer's Edenic pastoral is clearly replaced by a fallen world:

> September passed and the corn-stalks in the garden were cut. There were no more apples left on the trees, and chilly rains came to beat down the falling leaves from the maples and the elms. Cold and drearily wet October passed, too, with no hint of Indian summer or golden forests. (*CW* 4:100)

In September, Sandy enters a new school, and both he and the reader are introduced to Kansas's institutionalized racism when the young boy confronts the racial cruelties of his new classroom teacher and the shame of his family's poverty. This painful knowledge intensifies in chapters 12 and 13, "Hard Winter" and "Christmas," which mark the midpoint in the novel. In Hughes's complex description of winter, which operates symbolically, psychologically, and realistically, it is apparent that nature cannot be neutral in a society permeated by the unnatural circumstances of racism and poverty.

In these pivotal chapters, Sandy's home life is miserable: his father is absent; his mother, grieving, becomes ill herself; his beloved Aunt Harriet has departed; his strong grandmother is overworked. With freezing temperatures outside, the only warmth in Sandy's home is in the kitchen, where Hager hangs out the wash; yet as Sandy eats "under dripping lines of white folks' garments while he listened to his mother coughing in the next room," Hughes's imagery evokes the oppression and humiliation of an omnipresent racism and poverty. A neighbor observes, "so many colored men's out o' work here, wid Christmas comin', it sho' is too bad!" Hager laments, "we ain't gwine have no money a-tall. Ain't no mo'n got through payin' ma taxes good, an' de interest on ma mortgage, when Annjee get sick here! Lawd, I tells you, po' colored womens have it hard!" (*CW* 4:102–3).

In depicting the coming of snow, Hughes implies a symbolic connection, as Richard Wright was later to do so effectively in *Native Son* (1941), with the prevalence of white power: "The great heavy flakes fell with languid gentility over the town and silently the whiteness covered everything. The next morning the snow froze to a hard sparkling crust on roofs and ground" (*CW* 4:110). Like the snow, whites, in this winter season, are indifferent to the sufferings of others, frozen-hearted and absorbed in the "languid gentility" of their respectable holidays. The contrast between the economic situations of whites and blacks as well as the connection between the indifference of whites and the snow is further suggested by Hughes's description of Sandy's misery on Christmas Eve:

> Sandy passed the windows of many white folks' houses where the curtains were up and warm floods of electric light made bright the cozy rooms. In Negro shacks, too, there was the dim warmth of oil-lamps and Christmas candles glowing. But at home there wasn't even a holly wreath. And the snow was whiter and harder than ever on the ground. (*CW* 4:111)

In describing the following winter, Hughes retains the symbolic association between snow and white racism and, in addition, associates Sandy with blackness and darkness, indicating that he has matured enough not only to assume his own racial identity but also to protest against both racism and the snow. Working as a shoeshine boy and facing the degrading demands of a drunken white southerner, Sandy throws his "bootblack box" at the "group of laughing white men" and races out through "the falling snow." Although voices pursue him, Hughes explains that they blow away in "the darkness" (*CW* 4:153).

Spring melts the snow; it brings a softening to the earth and the return of sensuality to Sandy's life. "You could smell the spring," but "the odor of cheap and poignant drugstore violets dripped across the house" from Aunt Harriet's broken perfume bottle, anticipating and accentuating spring's unnatural potential for pain (*CW* 4:122, 121). In his subtext, Hughes implies that for Sandy spring is the cruelest season. Its sensuality intensifies his sexual questions, while its frequent bleakness and grayness intensify his questions of racial identity and racial justice. By the latter part of *Not without Laughter*, nature thus becomes a vivid correlative both for the unnatural anxieties generated by America's endemic racism as well as for Sandy's natural anxieties regarding both his sexual and his racial identity. Following his description of the March wind rattling windowpanes, "humming through the leafless branches of the trees, [and blowing] terrifically" (*CW* 4:126), Hughes generates three pages of questions, indicating Sandy's commitment to questing for selfhood. Spring's burgeoning fecundity is set in antithesis to his lonely search for answers. "[B]efore the first buds opened on the apple-tree in the back yard,"

Sandy's mother leaves him. "And when the apple-blossoms came in full bloom, there was no one living in the little house but a grey-headed old woman and her grandchild" (*CW* 4:128).

In his description of later springs, Hughes intensifies Sandy's growing pains. Racial prejudice becomes personal at Easter, when, although the days are depicted as clear and balmy, Sandy and his friends are rejected from the citywide children's party. Recognizing the insidious spread of racism, Sandy realizes, "Kansas is getting like the South. . . . They don't like us here either" (*CW* 4:144). During the spring his lonely suffering and confusion are suggested by the prevalence of rain and fog, a conventional literary correlative for disorientation, occurring during the days of Sandy's grandmother's death and funeral.

In *Not without Laughter*'s first twenty-two chapters, Hughes's seasonal references thus generate a "double-directed discourse" that initiates both his readers and Sandy into the racial and class inequities impacting African American life. Throughout the novel, however, Hughes also integrates images and metaphors of nature into his narrative in order to celebrate his people, their color, and their culture. His imagistic and metaphorical association of African Americans with nature might be interpreted as promoting the exotic expectations of white readers at the risk of primitivizing the very people and culture he praises. However, the effect of this bold rhetorical move is to energize, even to flaunt, African American diversity, beauty, and accomplishment in creating a vibrant culture in the face of the persistent degradations of racism and poverty.

This is especially evident in Hughes's treatment of color. His appreciation for nature's diverse colors is unmistakable in his description of a summer garden:

> The sunflowers in Willie-Mae's back yard were taller than Tom Johnson's head, and the holly-hocks in the fence corners were almost as high. The nasturtiums, blood-orange and gold, tumbled over themselves all around Madam de Carter's house. Aunt Hager's sweet-william, her pinks, and her tiger-lilies were abloom and the apples on her single tree would soon be ripe. The adjoining yards of the three neighbors were gay with flowers. . . . Bees were heavy with honey, great green flies hummed through the air, [and] yellow-black butterflies suckled at the rambling roses. (*CW* 4:55)

Hughes's pleasure in nature's mosaic is no less, however, than his pleasure in the colors of African American people as he glories in the diversity of skin tones throughout *Not without Laughter*. During the summer months that dominate the novel's early chapters, Hughes presents Sandy, who is "the shade of a nicely browned piece of toast with dark, brown-black eyes," in relation to his friends, "coal-colored" Willie-Mae and "ivory-white" Buster. Hager, Harriet, and Annjee are dark-skinned, but Sandy's father, Jimboy, is a "good-looking yellow fellow" (CW 4:29). In chapter 8, "Dance," Hughes's description of African American skin tones rivals nature's colors:

> Sandy looked down drowsily on the men and women, the boys and girls, circling and turning beneath him. Dresses and suits of all shades and colors, and . . . [f]aces gleaming . . . lemon-yellow, coal-black, powder-grey, ebony-black, blue-black faces; chocolate, brown, orange, tan, creamy-gold faces. (CW 4:76)

Elsewhere in the novel, Hughes also relates skin colors to nature, associating people with clay, roaches, blackberries, sealskins, maple sugar, or autumn leaves.[4] In thus using aspects of the natural world to emphasize racial coloration, Hughes not only openly delights in the diversity within the African American community but also undermines the possibility of categorizing blacks monolithically.

Despite whites' enthusiasm for African American music and dance in Harlem in the 1920s, Hughes was conscious that in small-town U.S.A. these vibrant and innovative manifestations of African American culture were antithetical to dominant social concepts of respectability and propriety. Yet from the opening of chapter 5, "Guitar," Hughes foregrounds his sense of the cultural significance of the blues by inserting them unadulterated into his narrative, a procedure he continues throughout the novel, assuring that the energy and the poetry of these African American lyrics are recognized and experienced directly by his readers. In *Not without Laughter*, Hughes seduces a sexually puritanical readership—both white and black—by assuring them that his young protagonist's sexual awakening occurs gradually, vicariously, and as naturally as corn and apples ripen and as bees pollinate flowers. Similarly, natural metaphors become the means for both conveying and mitigating the powerful sexual subtext of the blues and dance.[5]

---

4. Hughes continued to delight in the multiple colors of African Americans, as is apparent in "Harlem Sweeties," which appeared in *Shakespeare in Harlem* (1942) (CW 2:30).

5. Through his characterization of Hager, Hughes deflects anxious responses to the

He specifically chooses blues lines that rely on natural metaphors, thus introducing his readers to the vitality of the lyrics:

> Baby, throw yo' arms around me
> Like de circle round de sun!
> An' tell yo' pretty papa
> How you want yo' lovin' done!

and

> Did you ever see peaches
> Growin' on a watermelon vine?
> Says did you ever see peaches
> On a watermelon vine?
> Did you ever see a woman
> That I couldn't get for mine? (CW 4:47)

Hughes conveys the sexuality of Jimboy's singing by describing his fingers, running softly, "light as a breeze, over his guitar strings, imitating the wind rustling through the long leaves of the corn" (CW 4:50), as he glances toward the sexually attuned Annjee. Sandy is fascinated by the pulsating life in the blues from his childhood in Stanton, where he hears his father and his Aunt Harriet singing and playing, until the end of the novel, when he attends Harriet's concert in Chicago. In her blues songs, nature resonates with the loss of sexual love:

> Red sun, red sun, why don't you rise today?
> Red sun, O sun, Why don't you rise today?
> Ma heart is breakin'—my baby's gone away.

and

---

overt sexuality of the blues. Hager not only is associated with the spirituals, but she also repeatedly expresses her moral indignation at the blues as they are sung by Jimboy and Harriet. In addition, she expresses her concern that the ostensible immorality of the blues would present a dangerous view of her community to whites, "I don't want too much o' them a 'larmin' de white neighbors." Hughes implies, however, that the blues are irrepressible: "the sun had scarcely fallen below the horizon before the music had begun to float down the alley, over back fences and into kitchen-windows where nice white ladies sedately washed their supper dishes" (CW 4:47).

Little birds, little birds, ain't you gonna sing this morn?
Says, little chirpin' birds, ain't you gonna sing this morn?
I cannot sleep—ma lovin' man is gone. (*CW* 4:205)

Chapter 8, "Dance," the longest chapter in *Not without Laughter*, focuses on an extended description of music and dance. Here Hughes also constructs natural metaphors to evoke his conviction that African American music and dance, irresistible in their urgency and energy, cross racial, class, and geographic boundaries:

> [T]he music was like a lazy river flowing between mountains, carving a canyon coolly, calmly, and without insistence. . . . the piano was the water flowing, and the high, thin chords of the banjo were the mountains floating in the clouds. But in sultry tones, alone and always, the brass cornet spoke harshly about the earth. (*CW* 4:72)

> [T]he drum-beats had become sharp with surly sound, like heavy waves that beat angrily on a granite rock. . . . Cruel, desolate, unadorned was the music now, like the body of a ravished woman on the sun-baked earth. . . .
> The earth rolls relentlessly, and the sun blazes for ever on the earth, breeding, breeding. But why do you insist like the earth, music? Rolling and breeding, earth and sun for ever relentlessly. But why do you insist like the sun? Like the lips of women? Like the bodies of men, relentlessly? . . .
> Who understands the earth? . . . Who understands the sun? (*CW* 4:75)

Exalting these passages of elevated poetic rhetoric, Hughes depends on generic natural references to relate the music and the dance of his people to all peoples, in all times and places.

Balancing the sun and the earth, metaphors he repeatedly relates to African American music and dance in *Not without Laughter*, Hughes poses another cosmic sign: stars.[6] Stars shine throughout the novel, in relation to multiple episodes. They shine after the tornado, above the blues-singing Jimboy; a star drops over the porch following Sis Johnson's account of a race riot; and they fade "to points of dying fire" when Sandy returns from the dance with Harriet (*CW* 4:23, 50, 65, 80). Although stars initially appear as an erratic and indifferent sign, as his narrative evolves

---

6. In "Stars," a short poem published in 1926 in *Lincoln University News*, Hughes reveals that he had long considered the possibility of interpreting stars as secular signs of hope.

Hughes associates them increasingly with Hager and Sandy and with transcendent possibilities for a better life on earth. "[W]hile the lightning-bugs glowed and glimmered and the katydids chirruped, and the stars sparkled in the far-off heavens," Sandy listens on the porch to Aunt Hager's stories of "years of faith and labor, love and struggle" (*CW* 4:129). When he is sorrowfully disillusioned by the whites' refusal to allow black children to participate in "Children's Day," he and Hager watch the evening star. In the spiritual she sings, Hughes transforms the star into a beacon of hope:

> From this world o' trouble free,
> Stars beyond!
> Stars beyond! . . .
> There's a star fo' you an' me
> Stars beyond! (*CW* 4:144)

During Hager's illness, on the morning of her funeral, and after her death, Sandy focuses on the stars (*CW* 4:144, 159, 187). Through connecting the imagery of stars to the spirituals, Hughes reinforces Hager's particular legacy to her grandson—the legacy of her dream that through hard work and hope he will prevail. Like the earthy legacy of music and dance that Sandy receives from his father and his Aunt Harriet, Hager's heavenly legacy is one that Sandy knows has been passed down historically from "generations of toil-worn Negroes" (*CW* 4:144).

In the final eight chapters—five focusing on Sandy's life under his Aunt Tempy's tutelage and three on his life in Chicago—nature almost entirely disappears from the narrative. The dominant imagery of these concluding chapters concerns architecture, books, streets, trains, and elevators. This erasure begins with the death of Sandy's beloved grandmother and his adoption by his Aunt Tempy, whom Hughes associates with the black bourgeoisie. By alienating her from nature, Hughes underscores her desire not only to identify with the color and the material prosperity of Stanton's upper-class whites but also to distance herself from the rich African American culture embraced by the other members of her family.

Although Sandy submits to his Aunt Tempy's demands that he develop intellectually, he resists her insistence that he reject his African American cultural identity. In a single natural image in the chapters describing Sandy's life with Tempy, Hughes indicates his resistance to her unnatural commitment to white superiority and capitalism. One evening prior to his departure from her constricting house, Sandy becomes conscious of a "cool earth-smelling breeze [which] lifted the white curtains" in his up-stairs bedroom, allowing him to appreciate the "stars and the tops of the budding maple-trees . . . under the night sky" (*CW* 4:187). Hughes thus suggests that Sandy here lifts the unnatural white curtains of racism and emphatically claims his natural African American heritage of both earth and heaven.

Later in Chicago he discovers yearningly that there are "No trees, no yards, no grass such as he had known at home" (*CW* 4:194). Yet, at the end of *Not without Laughter*, Hughes makes it apparent that the now mature Sandy has the capacity to remember the significant legacies from his rur-al home and to integrate them into his new urban life. After all, it was from his own boyhood memories of diverse natural and unnatural circum-stances that Hughes himself—a small-town, midwestern boy transplant-ed to a major metropolis—created many of his major poems as well as *Not without Laughter* itself.

II

The Public and the Private

The Sounds of Silence

Langston Hughes as a "Down Low" Brother?

John Edgar Tidwell

Do nothing till you hear from me
    Pay no attention to what's been said
    Why people should tear the seam of anyone's dream
    Is over my head.

   —Duke Ellington and Bob Russell

And the rest is silence.

   —*Hamlet* 5.2.5

Arguably, the gay and lesbian movement can be credited with opening up a discourse once considered taboo, invasive, unsettling, or even unseemly. Formerly, life writers were reluctant to inquire into the nature of their black subjects' intimate relationships. Instead, they were often protective of their subjects, as if their privacy was sacrosanct. An honor-bound commitment to preserve the image and reputation of their subjects at all costs dominated the approach and thinking of these writers. Today, writers express a different attitude. It has become increasingly more common for biographers, literary historians, and critics to reject the rather circumspect models of "decorum" in favor of deeper, more probing analyses of the private lives of African American subjects, a practice that extends to explorations of sexual orientation. This change in interpretative strategy effectively represents a significant paradigm shift in studies about black life. The notion of the personal being political has emboldened scholars to probe formerly protected areas for any new light that might be shed on the lives of their subjects.

The private life of Langston Hughes is a case in point. Faith Berry opened an inquiry into the formerly quiet whisperings about Hughes's sexual identity and set off a full-scale, cacophonous debate among scholars in her *Langston Hughes: Before and beyond Harlem* (1983).[1] In her wake, Arnold Rampersad deftly set forth the available documented evidence in *The Life of Langston Hughes* (1988),[2] which was followed by the most undisguised artistic claim laid on Hughes's iconic stature—Isaac Julien's tour-de-force film *Looking for Langston* (1989). Although Berry and Rampersad offer undocumented comments on Hughes's alleged relationship with a sailor, the Julien film, as Henry Louis Gates Jr. helps us to understand, frames one of the most interesting means of investigation. Gates commented that there are two reductive ways of viewing the film: as "fixing the historical question about Hughes's sex life" and as establishing the claim that "the film is an imaginative meditation, and 'real' history is completely immaterial to it." The solution Gates proffers is, like the figure of "sankofa," a "partnership of past and present."[3] It calls for unity between the real and the imaginative, thus broadening and extending discussions of Hughes's private life.

This strategy enables an examination of Hughes's past as he constructed it and the relevance it holds for our present thinking; it also permits us to analyze his private and public selves, within historical contexts. In other words, this heuristic provides a thoughtful interrogation of Hughes's private life, one that emanates from a reconsideration of the silences, both textual and personal, in his art and life. Biographers, literary historians, and even his closest friends have commented on the most crucial paradox defining Hughes's life: how an outgoing, gregarious, fun-loving man nevertheless carefully guarded the innermost sanctum of his personal being from those closest to him. "His reticence about certain aspects of his personal life," as Berry wrote, "was legendary."[4]

1. Berry, *Langston Hughes: Before and beyond Harlem*, 38.
2. Arnold Rampersad, *The Life of Langston Hughes: Volume 1, 1902–1941, I, Too, Sing America*, 45–46.
3. Gates, "The Black Man's Burden," 235.
4. Berry, *Langston Hughes*, 187.

Clearly, exploring his autobiographies for instances of a confessional or introspective mode will result in disappointment, for the most part. Instead of a deliberately creative and imaginative engagement with his past, Hughes more comfortably represented his past as history and fact. Especially in *The Big Sea*, readers find little that qualifies as a sense of discovery, a new stage in self-knowledge, or the like that would reveal an interrogation of his past for what it reveals about his present. The results are unanswered questions, speculation about the unaddressed spaces in his life, or simply "silences."

In self-conscious efforts to fill those spaces, biographers and literary historians, using new theoretical and critical models, have ingeniously assigned meaning to Hughes's silences, from reclaiming him for political purposes to subjecting him to psychological explanation. These efforts have resulted in several provocative readings of Hughes's sexual identity, conducted by such excellent scholars as Rampersad and Berry and more recently Juda Bennett and Lindon Barrett, among many others, grounding their theories in concepts such as "closet," "passing," and "desire." Each of these concepts, relying on ideas about masquerading, invites another heuristic device for probing Hughes's interior: the concept of the "down low," or "DL."

As an analytical construct, "down low" has yet to emerge in the discourse of literary theory or criticism. In popular or vernacular culture, though, it describes a phenomenon lately proposed by J. L. King in which "straight" men, either married or in committed relationships with women, secretly engage in sexual relations with other men.[5] At best, this definition is sensational because it is not rooted in studied science or social science.[6] Suggested in this formulation is something secretive, deceitful, duplicitous, or even untoward or manipulative. These themes persist in the efforts of many scholars to account for the spaces in Hughes's personal life and art.

In this essay, I use the term *down low* as a heuristic through which to explore how Hughes inscribes his own choice to keep his most intimate experiences shielded from friends and fans alike. The term conveys the idea of being secret without signifying salaciousness. The silences in Hughes's life and art are self-constructed, inspired by social pressure, on one hand, and personal need, on the other. But his art of concealment has less to do

---

5. King, *On the Down Low: A Journey into the Lives of "Straight" Black Men Who Sleep with Men*, 9–11.

6. See Keith Boykin, *Beyond the Down Low: Sex, Lies and Denial in Black America*, 19–20.

with masking or obscuring a clandestine sexual relationship than with engaging in a form of self-protection against those who would invade his privacy. As will be seen, Hughes participated in a number of heterosexual relationships—all of which proved disastrous. The common reason critics assign for these failed romances is a supposed predisposition for same-sex involvements. Either Hughes secretly practiced homosexual behavior, critics argue, or his writing quietly revealed a homosexual identity, thus a distaste for heterosexual love. This binary represents a conflict between sexual preference and sexual identity, both of which view a veiled homosexuality for Hughes as a given. A focus on the self-construction of his private life reveals how Hughes guides and directs us to what was important to him. A glimpse into the known courtships Hughes had with women not only tempers the idea he only desired same-sex relationships but also lays the foundation for understanding his decision to be self-protective.

Romance, Love, and Sex

Both Berry and Rampersad have provided full and informed accounts of Hughes's heterosexual love interests and the significance they hold for understanding Hughes's public and private personas. In the rush to shift attention to Hughes's sexual orientation, many scholars have neglected the fact that Hughes had meaningful relationships with Anne Coussey, Zora Neale Hurston, Si-Lan Chen, Natasha, and Elsie Roxborough—who bear brief mention, if for no other reason than to remind us that Hughes did have documented relationships with women.

Berry's chronicle of Hughes and Anne Coussey's relationship leans heavily on Hughes's own rendition in *The Big Sea*. In *Big Sea*, where Anne is renamed Mary, Hughes offers what seems to be an honest, heartfelt retelling of their affair, which occurred in the spring of 1924 in Paris. The attractive Anglo-African became enamored with Hughes and even entertained thoughts of marriage. It is arguable whether the relationship would have lasted more than the month it supposedly did. Her father cut off her source of income and demanded she return to London. Hughes certainly was incapable of supporting them financially. In a brief summary, Berry noted: "She had indeed proposed to Hughes, and though he was perhaps as deeply infatuated with Anne as he would ever be with anyone, the seriousness of her devotion frightened him. At age twenty-two, he was hardly ready to cope with it. Nor did he seem to trust the feeling as more than fleeting. The experience, brief though it was, probably influenced his subsequent relations with women."[7] Berry's conclusions here, as elsewhere, derive from her own reading of Hughes's life. She provides little evidence to support her claims. It is never clear how this reading of Hughes's feelings informs subsequent interpretations of his life.

Rampersad, in a more detailed analysis, was nearly in agreement with Berry about the gist of the relationship. Teddy and Nan, as Rampersad reports Hughes's and Coussey's pet names for each other, ultimately seemed destined not to enjoy the longevity promised by marriage. Nan was "very fond" of Teddy, according to Rampersad, and "[b]y May, Teddy was in love." Despite his amorous feelings, Hughes was not entirely forthcoming, since he did not divulge a great deal about his family. Ultimately, Hughes's "love" clashed with his feeling of being a "rover, troubadour, [and] poet."[8] Given this dilemma, the intervention by Coussey's father was probably not as necessary as it seemed at the time because Anne's wishes for a baby and a more conventional life were enough to convince Hughes that he was unprepared for that kind of commitment.

The complex relationship between Hughes and Zora Neale Hurston has led to considerable speculation about the role romance might have played in their friendship. Even though there is little evidence to confirm a romantic involvement between them, historians have interpreted or divined motives from the antagonistic cooperation they shared in their failed collaboration on the play *Mule Bone: A Comedy of Negro Life*. Biographers generally read romance into Hughes and Hurston's accidental meeting in Mobile, Alabama, in July 1927, because the usual three-day trip back to New York evolved into a thirty-day excursion. However, the cordiality they shared during that idyllic moment deteriorated rapidly between March and June 1930, after they began work on the play.

Sequestered in Westfield, New Jersey, away from the distractions of New York City, Hughes and Hurston set out to make theater history by innovatively incorporating vernacular practices and language in a play. The drama that resulted, though, was the outgrowth of Louise Thompson joining the artistic team as a stenographer and typist. Hughes proposed that Thompson be accorded equal billing as a writer. Hurston responded by hitting the roof! Was she angry because she failed to see how a secretary-typist had earned such consideration? Was she angry because Thompson's joining the team was aesthetically intrusive? Or did Hurston see

---

7. Berry, *Langston Hughes*, 50.
8. Rampersad, *Life*, 1:86.

what Hughes and Thompson denied—a romantic relationship? Many writers have concluded that Hurston's reactions were those of a woman scorned. To them, unreciprocated love and subsequent jealousy accounted for her irrational behavior.[9]

By early 1933, according to Berry's account, Hughes's once ambivalent feelings about being in love had given way to greater certitude about wanting to be with a woman. Si-Lan or Sylvia Chen, a gorgeous Afro-Asian ballerina, elicited dramatic overtures of love from Hughes. But even in making these expressions, Hughes proved to be very complicated. As Berry learned in a 1977 interview, Chen discovered him to be "a serious person who found his outlet in his work, not in committed, physical emotion."[10] Whether Chen meant passion, sex, or physical intimacy is a question Berry does not take up. Nevertheless, the oxymoronic phrase *physical emotion* wonderfully contains Chen's desire for greater intimacy and Hughes's reluctance or inability to provide it for her. According to Rampersad, the problem preceded Chen; it went back to the embittered experience of breaking away from the dominance of his patron, Mrs. Charlotte Osgood Mason, in December 1930.

The anxiety of this separation, according to Rampersad, "consolidated in Langston his tendency towards withdrawal from emotional involvement."[11] For Rampersad, the break from Mrs. Mason resulted in Hughes's near decline into what some of his contemporaries thought to be almost childlike behavior. As the relationship became more intense with Chen, Hughes became more reserved. Eventually, Chen's thoughts of marriage and motherhood caused Hughes to rethink the nature of a committed relationship, and he once again slipped into a pattern of procrastination and self-doubt.

It seems almost certain that during the same time he was sorting out his feelings about Chen, Hughes had an intense physical relationship with a Russian actress named Natasha. When she left her husband for him, Hughes felt trapped in a wholly unsatisfactory arrangement. That he was able to convince her not to accompany him as he continued his travels in Russia was an enormous relief. This scenario represented to Berry a confused romanticism and further indicated Hughes's inability to communicate deep feeling. Berry concludes, "At age thirty-one, he had lost his battle against homosexuality, but it was not easy for him to accept defeat. He

9. Henry Louis Gates Jr., "A Tragedy of Negro Life," 8–10.
10. Berry, *Langston Hughes*, 184.
11. Rampersad, *Life*, 1:260.

knew that his most intense emotional attachment had been not to a woman but to a man, whom he identified as 'F.S.' in a dedicatory poem in *The Weary Blues*."[12] Berry's conclusion is hastily reached. Perhaps she inferred this lost battle from her interview with Chen, who felt Hughes always thought he was expressing deep emotional commitment, when he actually betrayed a confused sense of his own emotions.

Not to be completely defeated, Hughes, in 1936, again constituted his pattern of expressiveness and reticence, this time with the extremely bright and beautiful Elsie Roxborough. Hughes, at age thirty-four, seemed unconcerned that she was twelve years younger. A senior at the University of Michigan, Roxborough had demonstrated a maturity and sophistication far beyond her years; however, she was not without flaw. Being so fair-skinned that she could pass for white invested her with the same dilemmas literary historians have attributed to the "tragic mulatto." Notwithstanding his own opposition to the classism and the discriminatory color consciousness important to Roxborough, Hughes found himself trying to project a romantic future with her, which, as Berry notes, was at best problematic: "Whether Hughes was really capable of any deeper emotional or more lasting commitment to Elsie than he had felt for Si-Lan is doubtful. But he wanted to believe he was in love, and he wanted the world to think he was."[13]

Rampersad probes the relationship with Roxborough more deeply. Roxborough, he wrote, "tumbled into love." Like Coussey and Natasha before her, she went so far as to propose marriage, even a marriage of convenience in which Hughes would have the widest latitude. When Hughes proved to be less than enthusiastic about this arrangement, Roxborough found herself in the uncomfortable position of feeling very strongly for a man who seemed wholly incapable of adequately reciprocating her love. Just as in his previous relationships with women, Hughes vacillated between interest and disinterest; conveyed what he thought was love but, what in reality, was a feeling only he could understand; and tried without success to resolve the dilemma of being a free-spirited artist with the demands of a more conventional, committed marriage. This led Rampersad to conclude: "The romance, or such as it was, ended for him less than six months after their first meeting, when the black papers began to report, to Hughes's amazement and anger, that they were about to marry. . . . Towards Roxborough herself, Hughes was outwardly friendly, but glacial at

---

12. Berry, *Langston Hughes*, 185.
13. Ibid., 249.

any hint of intimacy. Their affair was definitely over."[14] She wound up passing for white in New York and, like many of her fictional sisters, ended her life tragically by committing suicide—an act that caused Hughes remorse but no feeling of responsibility.

Hughes on the Down Low?

Without a doubt, Langston Hughes was a brother on the "down low." But characterizing the precise nature of that term requires a revisionist reading, one that radically departs from its conventional meaning. In describing the distinctive qualities of Hughes's DL, it is prudent to keep in mind the issue Essex Hemphill raises in his polemical essay "Undressing Icons": "The controversy surrounding Looking for Langston has posed far more urgent questions than whether Langston Hughes, black America's best-known poet and writer, practiced an asexual, bisexual, homosexual, or heterosexual lifestyle." Hemphill rightly focuses on a reticence by many black historians to probe such issues about black subjects because the image of the subjects might be tarnished. Seeking to quiet such discussions, in his view, is little more than erecting electric fences around these subjects: "fences of silence, confoundment, and denial. This is done in an attempt to prevent black icons from being undressed to discover whether they were really kings, queens, or ordinary tramps."[15] Unlike Hemphill, I am interested in what happens when the *subject* constructs that fence, as Hughes did. Hughes had specific reasons that impelled him toward self-protection, but these motives have little to do with the commonly received notions of DL.

King's assertion about the DL, in the long run, does not neatly apply to a characterization of Hughes's DL. Certainly, the heterosexual relations Hughes had with Coussey, Hurston, Chen, Natasha, and Roxborough satisfy one critical part of King's prescription—men engaged in relationships with women. But the formulation is incomplete because there appears to be no incontrovertible evidence of Hughes persistently engaging in sexual relations with men. It bears repeating that, as Thomas Wirth notes, of the New Negro Renaissance writers, Hughes "was perhaps the most circumspect of all" about divulging personal secrets. Paule Marshall confirmed this idea when she recalled that Hughes, in 1965, selected her and

14. Rampersad, *Life*, 1:332, 333–34.
15. Hemphill, "Undressing Icons," 181.

William Melvin Kelley to accompany him on a U.S. Information Service tour of Europe, where they would read their own work and conduct seminars about contemporary African American writing. Hughes, she said, would escort her back to her hotel and then disappear into the Parisian night, not to return until the reading the next day. Where he disappeared to, she maintained, was not her place to inquire.[16] His disappearing acts offer no direct testimony or admission; we are left with these troublesome absences, personal and textual "silences."

These silences have been interpreted by many writers as unconditional admissions by Hughes of his sexual orientation—that is, of his supposed homosexuality. As a consequence, a number of aspersions have been cast on those writers who elected not to climb on the bandwagon to celebrate an admission that Hughes himself chose not to articulate. In particular, Rampersad has been unfairly singled out for not reading those silences as tacit proof of a same-sex identity for Hughes. This argument assumes that the reason Hughes retreated from the society of his friends and fellow writers was to disappear into a private, mysterious world of homosexuality. Alden Reimonenq has been especially critical, calling Rampersad's failure to accept Hughes's supposed homosexuality as fact "a political agenda." He further accuses him of viewing Hughes as having "a perceived abnormality." In the face of what we know about Hughes, Reimonenq's accusations betray his own political agenda. His footing seems surer and certainly less acerbic when he argues: "finding physical traces of overt homosexuality is rare indeed. The closet, by the turn of the [twentieth] century, had been so firmly erected by heterosexism that the fear of coming out could last a lifetime, especially for public figures."[17] The metaphor of the closet is appropriate for describing Hughes's self-constructed silences. It is an image that supersedes questions of "was he or wasn't he" and allows a telling discussion of what it meant for Hughes to circle the wagons around his inner self for protection.

Hughes's time in Harlem during the Renaissance certainly permitted him to become aware of and participate in its gay and lesbian culture. Eric Garber, in a general discussion of this era, reminds us of the proliferation of the public spectacles of drag balls and rent parties and the privacy of buffet flats ("often offering a variety of sexual pleasures cafeteria style") and the speakeasies catering specifically to "pansy" trade.[18] Hughes him-

16. Wirth, "Introduction," 55; Marshall, untitled luncheon speech, February 9, 2002.
17. Reimonenq, "Hughes, Langston."
18. Garber, "A Spectacle in Color: The Lesbian and Gay Subculture of Jazz Age Harlem," 323–25.

self references these in *The Big Sea* (*CW* 13:208–9). Also, Hughes undoubtedly agreed with one historian who remarked that the crucial cultural work done in the Renaissance was by homosexuals. Within the group, there seems to have been an unqualified acceptance; however, outside the circle lay a less tolerant world. Richard Bruce Nugent, Ma Rainey, and Harold Jackman were just a few gay people for whom public attention was no problem. An artist like Hughes, who customarily closed himself off from scrutiny by even his closest friends, certainly felt the need to exercise caution in publicly announcing affairs related to sexual habits, especially when his personal predilection might clash with public mores and beliefs.

Such reticence by Hughes, as previously noted, was made necessary because of his deeply felt need for the approval and creative stimulation provided by the common, everyday black people he affectionately called "the low-down folks." Despite what probably was a quiet acceptance of homosexuality among black intellectuals and the elite, the broader audience he spoke to was largely unforgiving about homosexuality in their heroes. Often rooted in traditional Christian belief, they considered homosexuality an abomination. Hughes could not risk alienating them because they furnished him the love and inspiration so crucial to his sense of self and his art. Because Hughes was predisposed to loneliness and a protracted sense of abandonment, the significance of this transaction between artist and audience becomes an even greater indication of his need for black people in his life. Clearly, these mitigating circumstances denied him an opportunity for full disclosure, making him fundamentally repressed and therefore unable to express himself fully, openly, and unreservedly. What remained pent-up or unspoken because of his self-constructed fence no doubt affected him deleteriously. This means Hughes himself played a large role in this map of (mis)reading his moments of personal and textual silences. He did not and theoretically could not have made such a confession. To express the dilemma of his entrapment, he turned to metaphor. In the words of his favorite song, "Do Nothing Til You Hear from Me," he expressed an entreaty and possibly a warning to those who would define those silences for him: "pay no attention to what's been said."

This plea obviously did not stop critical speculation. In an otherwise carefully considered review of Rampersad's two-volume biography, the eminent cultural historian Daniel Aaron asks: "Does it really matter whether Hughes was asexual, heterosexual, homosexual? To the biographer, it must matter."[19] An unfortunate consequence of the question—

19. Aaron, "Reds, Whites, and Blues," 111.

and perhaps this is placing an undue burden on a book review—is that Aaron fails to explain why it should matter. Many writers, in effect, have proffered answers to Aaron's question. The effort to unravel Hughes's life has resulted in a variety of interpretive strategies, speculations, and conclusions—all of which raise a fundamental question: what is to be gained from such an inquiry?

For members of the gay and lesbian movement, Hughes represents an iconic figure, whose "example" they selected for guidance for their political interests. It matters little whether Hughes was a brother on the DL, aptly described by the figure of the closet. His name makes him invaluable as a figurehead and as an individual who was "one of the children," to use the title of William Hawkeswood's book. Certainly, Hemphill's metaphor of "undressing icons" appropriately describes the position of those who would deny discussion of a celebrated figure's sexual orientation. Even so, placing a claim on a celebrity who has chosen not to "out" himself is little more than appropriation, a political gesture with the potential to place claims on another's spirit or soul. Assigning a gay identity to Hughes, in effect, imposes on him a way of life he did not openly confess, acknowledge, or commit to.

This problem is clearly generational. The gay culture Hughes knew in the 1920s and 1930s differed immeasurably from its more recent emergence in the 1960s and 1970s, riding the coattails of the modern civil rights movement. Hughes came of age during a more circumspect era, when gay cultural expression was necessarily less visible, except for the aforementioned public spectacles. Rarely does the literature in the Renaissance reveal a discussion such as the one Charles Henry Rowell conducts in his afterword to *Shade.* After asking rhetorically what it means to be "black and male" and then "black and male and *gay*," he responds: "If we interrogate these issues with the thoroughness they require, we will discover that to be black and male and gay in the United States is to live in a state of *perpetual siege:* either to endure, in silence, the debilitating circumstances which threaten to destroy the very core of your humanity, your selfhood; or, as the result of living publicly as a gay black male, to risk physical and psychological violence from black and white heterosexist communities."[20] Rowell's cogent analysis reveals the agency currently expressed in the black gay male voice. His bold observations are obvious indications of the extent to which the gay and lesbian movement has become self-reflexive and simply political about problems Hughes's generation discussed less publicly.

20. Rowell, "Signing Yourself: An Afterword," 342.

When the question "what is to be gained" is raised with more equanimity, as in *Looking for Langston*, the issue of foregrounding Hughes as gay still rests on shifting ground. One of the achievements of this stunning experimental film is the manner in which Hughes's subjectivity is invoked. Isaac Julien subtitled his film *A Meditation on the Harlem Renaissance*. As others have observed, the film's intention is not that of a documentary. Its experimental structure enables Julien to "meditate" on important questions, especially the "role of the black artist in relationship to the black community, and specifically the role of the black gay artist both within the black community and in the context of the larger society as well."[21] Perhaps more here than in the politically motivated use of Hughes, we find the need for a greater definition of terms, such as the idea of a gay aesthetic and how it can be applied to Hughes.

In place of a full-blown theory of gay art, Hughes has been assigned a gay identity most often on a reading of several of his poems. The poems generally acknowledged as containing the evidence of his sexual orientation include "Poem (To F.S.)," "Desire," "Star Seeker," "Shadows," and "To Beauty." As powerful as these poems are, none has the aesthetic force or expressive directness of Bruce Nugent's novel excerpt "Smoke, Lillies, and Jade" or Ma Rainey's "Prove It on Me Blues." In the absence of a codified aesthetic—one better defined than the Black Aesthetic in the 1960s—the case for reading Hughes's poems through a "gay lens" is fraught with contradiction and conflict. What is often left is the use of expressions such as "a potential link to make same-sex desire" or "Hughes could well have known,"[22] where possibility substitutes for certainty.

So What?

The number of people claiming Hughes for their own political, aesthetic, or personal causes is legion. This fact alone serves as a poignant reminder of how, nearly four decades after his death, he has a continuing importance. Rampersad makes a valuable point when he suggests: "We investigate and recreate the past, ultimately, in order to understand better our own lives and society."[23] In our zeal to make relevant the lives of our cultural heroes, we should not throw caution to the wind. As we re-

---

21. Essex Hemphill, "Looking for Langston: An Interview with Isaac Julien," 174.
22. A. B. Christa Schwarz, *Gay Voices of the Harlem Renaissance*, 75.
23. Rampersad, "Biography and Afro-American Culture," 202.

cover and rewrite the lives and works of our cultural forebears, new trends in scholarship will make possible new examinations of their public and private lives. But therein lies the rub. We have an obligation to proceed cautiously, respectfully, and intelligently. Speculation in the name of scholarship will undoubtedly remove the protective covering Hughes so carefully crafted as he represented himself to the people he loved and needed. Guessing and surmising will not reveal the truth. They will only serve to alter the way we engage the work by forcing us to read through private lives possibly to reveal private lies.

Having bequeathed a long legacy of art and an example of personal sacrifice, Hughes no doubt shared the belief with Hamlet that, after he was gone, "the rest is silence." However, despite his best efforts, Hughes's silences are deafening. I am sure he would be mortified to find his name at the vortex of speculation about his sexual identity and sexual practice. He would probably ask: "Why tear the seam of anyone's dream?" Whatever can be gleaned from this life, a self-constructed "down low" existence, it has to make our lives better. His life cannot be used narrowly for self-serving or political gain. Hughes himself was larger than that. Whatever the use to which he is put, it has to enrich our lives so that we can feel Hughes's sense of racial pride, a renewed relationship to our cultural past, and, above all, a deeper appreciation for his love of humanity. These are the gifts he left us. These are the treasures he would want us to enjoy.

Langston Hughes on the Open Road

Compulsory Heterosexuality
and the Question of Presence

Juda Bennett

Langston Hughes, as Richard Bruce Nugent would tell Arnold Rampersad, was "like the legendary Virgin who walks through mud without soiling even the hem of her robe."[1] This desexualized, yet curiously crossgendered, characterization of Hughes is not entirely out of keeping with other versions, which have seen him as "asexual, without noticeable erotic feeling for either women or men" and "an outsider." He has been described as having a certain "sexual reticence," as having an "ageless, sexless, inspired innocence, Peter Pan-like," as having a "desire to remain a child," and as having a "childlike innocence."[2] His writing has been called dispassionate (read asexual), distant (read sexually reticent), and simple (read childlike).[3] How is this distant, dispassionate, and simple writing a

1. Arnold Rampersad, *The Life of Langston Hughes: Volume 1, 1902–1941, I, Too, Sing America*, 46, 402.
2. Ibid, 1:20, 22, 35, 46, 66, 69. It is a testament to the thoroughness of Rampersad's two-volume biography that it not only promotes a consistent version of Hughes as asexual (and perhaps this is the artistry of bringing a historical figure to life) but also includes a wide range of materials, many of which allow for alternate, complicated, and even contradictory versions of Hughes.
3. See Harold Bloom's introduction to *Langston Hughes* and James Baldwin's "Ser-

reflection of his life, his personality, his closet? I will argue that an epistemology of the closet is crucial to an understanding and appreciation of
Langston Hughes, and perhaps nothing more aptly reflects Langston
Hughes's closet than the trilogy of texts that was written to explore the
maturation of an African American male.

Between the publication of *Not without Laughter* (1930) and that of *The
Big Sea* (1940), Langston Hughes considered writing a second novel, one
that might "form a continuation of *Not Without Laughter.*" In a proposal to
the Guggenheim Foundation, Hughes indicated his plan for this project
to "develop into a trilogy of Negro life covering the childhood, youth, and
manhood of a black boy in this country."[4] Hughes's second novel, *Tambourines to Glory* (1958), does not build upon this vision of a trilogy, and
so it would seem that there was no fulfillment of the promise. However,
the poet's two autobiographies may be productively read as a continuation of the work begun in the novel.

As a trilogy, *Not without Laughter*, *The Big Sea*, and *I Wonder As I Wander*
(1956) follow the maturation of an African American male from childhood
to adulthood. These works, furthermore, envision maturation as a process
built upon various dislocations—most notably geographical and sexual
ones. These two types of dislocations are, in fact, linked. In the novel and
the two autobiographies, sexual knowledge is associated with—and even
dependent upon—a geographical displacement. The newly found awareness of sex, however, produces yet another dislocation, and it is this psychic
dislocation that most dramatically resembles the dynamics of the closet.[5]

When a dynamics of the closet is used to inform a reading of Hughes,
strategies that once seemed to create distance begin to seem less like
weaknesses and more like necessary strategies or clever solutions to the
burden of representation.[6] This burden, which is arguably most present

---

mons and Blues," his 1959 review of Hughes's *Selected Poems* for the *New York Times*,
which argues that "one sometimes has the impression . . . that Hughes has had to hold
the experience outside him in order to be able to write at all." For more positive as-
sessments, see the introduction to *Langston Hughes: Critical Perspectives Past and Present*, ed. Henry Louis Gates Jr. and K. A. Appiah, and Gregory Woods, *A History of Gay
Literature: The Male Tradition*.

4. Rampersad, *Life*, 1:297.

5. In arguing "that many of the major modes of thought and knowledge in twentieth-
century Western culture as a whole are structured—indeed fractured—by a chronic,
now endemic crisis of homo/heterosexual definition, indicatively male, dating from
the end of the nineteenth century" (1), Eve Kosofsky Sedgwick's *Epistemology of the
Closet* is crucial to my reading of Hughes's work.

6. Henry Louis Gates Jr. discusses the politics of representation in "The Black Man's

in Hughes's autobiographies, becomes manifest in the doubling of dislocations—geographical and sexual—and may appear as a failure of craft to readers who feel that Hughes keeps them at a distance, outside the experience and unable to identify.[7] The closet, moreover, seems antithetical to the tradition of autobiography, and Rampersad reminds us, "In a genre defined in its modern mode by confession, Hughes appears to give virtually nothing away of a personal nature."[8] The resistance to confessing, of course, is one of the unforgivable sins of autobiography, and so it should not surprise us that Hughes has been criticized for his silences and distances.

In its exploration of masculinity and the maturation process, the trilogy does indirectly address systems of oppression, such as homophobia, compulsory heterosexuality, and gender conformity. With a goal of highlighting Hughes's exploration of those systems of oppression, I will focus on those scenes that most effectively represent the nonnormative male within them. It is this figure, sometimes clearly defined as homosexual and sometimes defined as sexually ambiguous or uninterested, that most powerfully speaks to heterosexist systems of oppression. It provides, moreover, a provocative entrance into the vexed question of the poet's conceptions of sexual identity and self.

Eve Sedgwick argues persuasively for the "endemic crisis of homo/heterosexual definition" as informing twentieth-century culture and experience.[9] Certainly, the scholarly debate over Hughes's sexuality, which is arguably more contentious than other debates about the author or his work, supports Sedgwick's privileging of this crisis. In searching to expose Hughes's closet, I do not, however, strive to impose an essential identity on Hughes as much as hope to reveal a structure of thinking that informs his work. Hughes scholars, moreover, will never fully appreciate

---

Burden," celebrating Isaac Julien's solution to the problem of representing Langston Hughes by presenting the problem itself, giving special notice to the "articulation of interests" (237).

7. In "Sermons and Blues," Baldwin faults Hughes for holding "experience outside." Other critics have recognized a similar quality to Hughes's work, accounting for it in different ways. In "The Gaze of Langston Hughes: Subjectivity, Homoeroticism, and the Feminine in *The Big Sea*," Lindon Barrett presents a fascinating reading of the tensions between public and private spheres in Hughes's *The Big Sea*. His reading, however, focuses more on text and author and less on how this public/private divide affects the reader. I will return to Barrett's essay to support my own reading of *The Big Sea*.

8. Rampersad, Introduction to *The Big Sea* by Langston Hughes, xvii.

9. Sedgwick, *Epistemology*, 1.

the rhetorical complexity of the fiction, nonfiction, and poetry unless they understand the specific place—constrained but also enriched—from which the author writes about identity and, more specifically, sexual identity.

Hughes scholarship has already powerfully addressed the politics of race and location in essays and books devoted to understanding the poet's work through the legacy of the African diaspora, the Great Migration, and Jim Crow. It is, in fact, impossible to fully appreciate such works as "The Negro Speaks of Rivers" or "Slave on a Block" without understanding how place and dislocation affected Hughes's politics and aesthetics. The closet, however, provides a different challenge, one that Hughes scholars have only recently addressed.[10]

The Great Migration toward Sexual Knowledge

Not without Laughter presents a scene that, perhaps more directly than any other passage or phrase in Hughes's oeuvre, shows him wrestling with the politics of sexuality. In a novel that is marked by several physical dislocations created by storms, death, and war, it is the migration of blacks to urban centers that anticipates not only a new racial map but also a remapping of sexual experiences and opportunities.[11] Sandy, the protagonist, participates in the great wave of African Americans to the cities and witnesses the sexual liberation associated with modernity.

Although he has worked in several male-dominated environments, including a barbershop and a hotel, Sandy avoids sex and conversations about sex. His grandmother Hager, representative of the female-centered world, warns him about women and the city, and Sandy proves himself virtuous. In the course of the novel, Sandy hears the men at the barbershop talk about sex and women—and even in sexual terms about his aunt

10. Despite the pathbreaking work of Isaac Julien, *Looking for Langston;* Charles I. Nero, "Re/Membering Langston: Homophobic Textuality and Arnold Rampersad's *Life of Langston Hughes*"; and Barrett, "Gaze of Langston Hughes," the queering of Hughes remains relatively controversial.

11. See George Chauncey, *Gay New York: Gender, Urban Culture, and the Making of the Gay Male World, 1890–1940:* "Whatever the numbers, gay men's migration was clearly part of the much larger migration of single men and women to the city from Europe and rural America alike. A disproportionate number of the people who moved to the cities were young and unmarried, and while for many of them migration was part of a carefully considered strategy designed to address the broader economic needs of their families, for many it also provided a welcome relief from family control" (135).

Harriet. Sandy learns that his aunt has been arrested for prostitution; he is told that Pansetta, his best friend and schoolmate, is having sex with Jimmy Lane; and he witnesses the promiscuity that takes place in the local hotel. In each of these scenes, the protagonist is depicted as innocent despite his years. But when Sandy moves to Chicago to be with his mother, it seems as if he may finally cross the threshold to manhood. It is at this point in the narrative, in the closing chapters, that Hughes introduces homosexuality as a threat.

The chapter "Chicago" follows "Beware the Women," and so the scene of homosexual panic is preceded by a chapter emphasizing the conflict between religious abstinence and the heterosexual imperative. While "Beware the Women" shows Sandy—as influenced by his family and the church—resisting a young girl who is his age, "Chicago" shows Sandy resisting the advances of an adult homosexual. This is a defining moment in the novel because Sandy is new to the city and venturing out on his own for the first time. The scene between Sandy and the homosexual helps to prove that Sandy can handle himself without the help of family, friends, and community.

The homosexual predator represents all that is unknown and threatening. He is first marked by his size, color, and voice.

> "Nice evening?" said a small yellow man with a womanish kind of voice, smiling at Sandy. (CW 4:196)

He is further defined as inappropriately gendered with details about his scent and appearance.

> He smelled of perfume, and his face looked as though it had been powdered with white talcum as he lit a tiny pocket-lighter. (CW 4:196)

Although Sandy tries to move away from the man, he finally smokes a cigarette with him and reluctantly responds to the man's questions and assumptions. Hughes shows Sandy's discomfort with this predator but also marks the yellow man's unclassifiable quality with a gender-neutral pronoun, perhaps to designate this man's intermediate status between male and female.

> "Say, kid" it whispered smoothly, touching the boy's arm, "listen, I got some swell French pictures up in my room—naked women and everything! Want to come up and see them?" (CW 4:197)

After this exchange, one of the longest in the novel, Hughes provides the following description of Sandy's slow awakening.

> But Sandy was beginning to understand. A warm sweat broke out on his neck and forehead. Sometimes, at the pool hall in Stanton, he had heard the men talk about queer fellows who stopped boys in the streets and tried to coax them to their rooms. (*CW* 4:197)

This scene, built upon stereotypes of the homosexual predator, is less interesting for its depiction of the stranger than for its depiction of Sandy and his growing awareness of sex. In placing this scene at the end of the novel, Hughes seems to suggest that Sandy has finally moved from innocence to knowledge. But Hughes suggests not only that Sandy is now capable of recognizing perversity but also that he is curious to learn more.

> "He thinks I'm dumb," thought Sandy, "but I'm wise to him!" Yet he wondered what such men did with the boys who accompanied them. Curious, he'd like to find out—but he was afraid; so at the next corner he turned and started rapidly towards State Street, but the queer fellow kept close beside him, begging. (*CW* 4:197)

The begging continues, becoming menacing in its insistence, and Hughes ends this interaction with Sandy fleeing as "panic seized him." Sandy, furthermore, is no longer aware of what he is doing; there is a sort of dislocation of mind and body as, "almost without knowing it, his legs began swerving swiftly between the crowds along the curb" (*CW* 4:197).

In this protracted scene, Hughes safely represents the homosexual as diseased and predatory. The protagonist, however, is situated between disgust and curiosity, a conflict that does not appear in the following two scenes of heterosexual solicitations. As if the scene of homosexual panic needed to be placed within a larger frame of threats, Hughes adds—in rapid succession—two more scenes of solicitation. But these two scenes of predatory heterosexuality are brief when compared to the previous scene. The women elicit no curiosity from Sandy, and Hughes himself, in keeping the scenes brief, seems to display little interest in developing the women and their relationship with Sandy.

In a few paragraphs, Sandy meets first a "very ugly, skinny girl" and then "a painted woman" (*CW* 4:198), both of whom prey upon the youth. Although these women are not as insistent and the interactions are not as developed, they repeat the drama of solicitation and rejection. Sandy survives each experience, just as he has survived countless similar sexual threats throughout the novel. His maturation, therefore, is defined not through the sexual act but through the experience of knowing how to retain his virginity.

In contrast to the narrative of Sandy's slow and even stunted sexual maturation, Hughes creates the subplot of Aunt Harriett's escape into a life clearly marked as sexual. Hughes, in fact, weaves the stories together, allowing the two plotlines to merge at the end. In moving to Chicago to help his mother, Sandy must quit school and begin work, but then Aunt Harriett appears to save the day. It is only through her that Sandy will be able to return to school and continue his path toward knowledge. Harriett herself has pursued an opposite path to success, a path defined by sexual improprieties. The novel begins with Harriett in her teens, lured into an independence that is associated with sex and sexuality, and then the novel ends with Sandy in his teens and on the verge of his own independence. His independence, however, is possible only because of Harriett's good fortune, and so their stories are interdependent and structured as mirror images of one another.[12]

Harriett's excess of sexuality might be read as a displacement of Sandy's unarticulated sexuality. She takes risks, defies tradition, and ventures into a taboo sexuality (prostitution), while Sandy remains silent in the face of an array of temptations.[13] In her evolution, Harriett in fact resembles the protagonist of a bildungsroman far more than does Sandy, and her importance to the novel has been noted by early reviewers and recent critics. Sandy, on the other hand, resembles the autobiographical Hughes who "give[s] virtually nothing away of a personal nature." Alain

12. Early reviewers and later critics have argued for the importance of Harriett to this novel. The interweaving of Harriett's and Sandy's stories, however, invites further psychoanalytical readings. See Sterling A. Brown's review and Cheryl Wall, "'Whose Sweet Angel Child?' Blueswomen, Langston Hughes, and Writing during the Harlem Renaissance."

13. In considering Harriett as a sort of wish-fulfillment to compensate for all that Sandy is denied, it is interesting to consider what Hughes has said about the creation of the characters. Although Hughes admits mining his own experience as a "typical Negro boy" in order to write the novel, he describes himself as being much more excited about developing those characters distant from his own experience (see CW 13:228–30). After writing about Harriett running away to join a carnival, he felt, for example, that it was "almost more than [he] could stand" (CW 13:229). Harriett, of course, represents the freedom from sexual inhibition that Sandy never moves toward. How, then, does Harriet represent the autobiographical impulse as much as Sandy does?

Locke's desire to see more of the protagonist's "inner emotional conflict" could easily be applied to the autobiographical Hughes. James Baldwin's argument that Hughes always kept himself outside experience can also be applied to both the fiction and the nonfiction.[14]

What happens if we read Harriett and Sandy as addressing the tensions of a sex system built upon compulsory heterosexuality and homophobia? How does the novel move from a rather simple account of a boy's entrance into a world of heterosexuality to exploring a boy's entrance into a heterosexist world of compulsory heterosexuality and homophobia? This latter reading does not require that we know the sexual orientation of the author or the protagonist; however, it is my contention that the prevailing notions of Hughes as either asexual or as implicitly heterosexual have helped produce readings that do not fully consider the complexity of the sexual tension in the novel.

It is important, for example, to recognize the effort the novel makes to close the narrative of sexual maturation with a final acceptance of Harriett's peccadillos. The novel comments upon the two characters and their very different paths by quoting from a spiritual.

> By an' by when de mawnin' comes,
> Saints an' sinners all are gathered home. . . . (CW 4:209)

Sandy and Harriett are linked, therefore, by the spiritual, by their shared destinies, and by their experiences as desired objects. Ironically, Sandy gets propositioned more than Harriett, though most readers will probably lose sight of this insistent role for the protagonist. Because he is an innocent youth and because we do not often think of males as objects of desire, Sandy's role as a siren remains inchoate and essentially invisible. It would, perhaps, seem risible if we were to allow ourselves to think of him in those terms. When he is propositioned three times in the final moments of the novel, the narrative—perhaps recognizing the dangerous shift in character—quickly infantilizes Sandy upon his return home. He returns from the scene of sexual panic to his mother, who says, significantly, "You're still little enough to sleep with your mother, ain't you?" (CW 4:195). In this way, the narrative struggles to retract itself from its venture into the unknown, seeking to forget the geographical and sexual dislocations introduced in the context of Chicago's sexual landscape. It is this

---

14. Rampersad, Introduction to The Big Sea, xvii; Rampersad, Life, 1:175; Baldwin, "Sermons and Blues."

turning away from the sexual that links the autobiographical novel to the two autobiographies.

The Big Sea of Other Men and Other Sexualities

The first chapter of *The Big Sea* is entitled "Beyond Sandy Hook," as if the chapter will move beyond the fictional Sandy. This connection is perhaps serendipitous, but there are more compelling links between the novel and the autobiography. Both focus on the maturation of an African American male, significantly emphasizing his entrance into manhood. *The Big Sea*, in fact, conveys its concern with maturation in its tripartite structure, with sections entitled "Twenty-One," "Big Sea," and "Black Renaissance." These sections essentially cover the three stages mentioned in Hughes's letter to the Guggenheim foundation, essentially fulfilling the promise of a trilogy in a single book. But *The Big Sea* plays with chronology.

While *Not without Laughter* brings the reader to the very edge of Sandy's manhood, *The Big Sea* begins with the arrival into manhood. Although "Twenty-One" does address Hughes's early background in Kansas, it begins—out of sequence—with Hughes's twenty-first year and his voyage to Africa. "Beyond Sandy Hook," in other words, belongs temporally to the second section, "Big Sea," but proleptically begins this first section because of its significance to the overall text. Thus, Hughes temporarily disrupts the tripart chronological structure in order to highlight his dominant theme: the transition into manhood.

"Beyond Sandy Hook" begins with two intensely symbolic scenes that invite explication. The first, which describes Hughes throwing his books into the water as if he were "throwing a million bricks out of [his] heart," has generated various interpretations, while the second has received less attention. This second scene, however, answers the call to action of the first by moving Hughes away from the past, represented by his books, and into the future, represented by two sailors, George and Ramon, who provide a new fraternity for the poet. Hughes characterizes these men as opposites, and, although he remains essentially outside looking in, he reveals much about his conceptions of masculinity and sexuality.

Lindon Barrett provides a compelling reading of this second scene's use of public and private sexualities: "Readers are prompted to speculate about the sexuality of an autobiographer doggedly close-mouthed about his sexual encounters but who, on the second page of his narrative, gratuitously directs the gaze of his reader, through his own gaze, to the animated penis of another man and, furthermore, in this spectatorial act, to the discursive subordination of a female agent."[15] Barrett contrasts the silence of Hughes to the loquacious and rather public performance of George. I would like to extend this concern with the public and private to the other figure found in this scene: Ramon.

Hughes distinguishes one of the men as loquacious and the other as taciturn, noting that "George had a thousand tales to tell," while "Ramon of the upper bunk didn't talk much" (CW 13:33). But Hughes was not the only one who recognized these differences: "Everybody knew all about George long before we reached the coast of Africa. But nobody ever knew much about Ramon" (CW 13:32). George and Ramon, therefore, become representative of the spectrum of men aboard ship and of men in general.

George and Ramon, furthermore, become texts to be read, not unlike the books in the first scene and—more pointedly—not unlike the gesture of throwing the books overboard. But as subjects to be read, these men prove to be unreliable narrators of their lives. George, for example, offers two contradictory versions of his past.

> George had a thousand tales to tell about every town he'd ever been in. And several versions of each tale. No doubt, some of the stories were true—and some of them not true at all, but they sounded true. Sometimes George said he had relatives down South. Then, again, he said he didn't have anybody in the whole world. Both versions concerning his relatives were probably correct. (CW 13:33)

Unconcerned with George's contradictions, Hughes celebrates his new cabin mate for his stories and playfulness. Although the poet has less to say about Ramon, one salient fact again invites him to consider the issue of reliability: "Ramon told us once that his mother was a seamstress in Ponce." With this simple fact related, the author quickly adds that, according to another Puerto Rican sailor, "'seamstress' was just another name for something else" (CW 13:33). Not unlike his handling of George's biography, Hughes undercuts Ramon's story, effectively raising the question of reliability once again. He does not explicitly state that Ramon's mother was a prostitute; instead he emphasizes that she was not really a seamstress and that Ramon was circumspect.

Although Hughes underlines the impossibility of fully knowing these men, emphasizing George's contradictions and Ramon's opaqueness, he also celebrates the immediacy of their presence. The scene begins, after

---

15. Barrett, "Gaze of Langston Hughes," 384.

all, with George "stark naked," "talking about women" and waving "one of his appendages" (the one he could fit in his hand) for emphasis. This is, arguably, one of the most graphic scenes in the Hughes canon, unique in its display (albeit euphemistically) of the penis. Hughes also describes George as "good-natured and comical," heading off any readings that might impose a more aggressive or sexual tone to the passage.[16] The passage, nevertheless, associates George, the representative heterosexual, with talk of women and displays of manhood. Ramon, on the other hand, is associated with lingerie, silence, and a disinterest in women.

> He seldom drew any money, and when he did he spent it on sweets— seldom on a woman. The only thing that came out of his mouth in six months that I remember is that he said he didn't care much for women, anyway. He preferred silk stockings—so halfway down the African coast, he bought a pair of silk stockings and slept with them under his pillow. (CW 13:33)

Hughes recognizes, as will most readers, that Ramon's behavior and pronouncements are considered unmanly, but he neither comments nor criticizes. Although he does call Ramon "decent enough as a cabin mate," these words precede the startling information about Ramon's preferences. Hughes, as in much of his writing, rarely judges or offers commentary, and it is left to the reader to make sense of Hughes's beliefs and values.

What, then, can this account of men, placed at the beginning of Hughes's first autobiography, tell us about the author's conceptions of masculinity and sexuality? Can it help us better understand the author's identity? We learn that Hughes is the same age as the other men and that he has formed a bond with them, but if George and Ramon mark the two ends of a masculine continuum, we never learn where along it Hughes is situated. If George is represented as a masculine presence, waving his manhood about and speaking of women, and Ramon is described as the opposite, confined to his bed and hiding silk stockings beneath his pillow, then the continuum is structured upon hierarchies not only of presence versus absence but also of performance versus inhibition. George displays his manhood, waving his appendage around, but he also performs his

16. See Phillip Brian Harper, *Are We Not Men? Masculine Anxiety and the Problem of African-American Identity* (esp. 3–38) for a fascinating exploration of black sexuality and representation. Harper notes, "Indeed, some segments of the black population have colluded in this defusing of black sexuality, attempting to explode whites' stereotypes of blacks as oversexed by stifling discussion of black sexuality generally" (10).

heterosexuality each time he mentions his experience with women. Ramon, on the other hand, represents absence in his reluctance to speak and in his choice to confine himself, as much as possible, to bed. Preferring sweets to women, he rarely performs as a heterosexual, and his preference for silk stockings, furthermore, associates him with the feminine.

The counterpointing of a hyper-masculine male against a nonnormative male certainly does more than establish character in *The Big Sea*. Thematically, the counterpointing establishes the importance of masculinity to the autobiographical project. More important, the scene establishes the significance of male bonding free from the divisiveness of homophobia or compulsory heterosexuality. Instead of representing Ramon as a problem, Hughes uses him to argue for a utopian celebration of differences. In contrast to the scene of homosexual panic that appears at the end of the autobiographical novel, *The Big Sea* celebrates acceptance and tolerance. Both scenes, moreover, make use of a geographical dislocation as a necessary condition for new epistemologies of sex and sexuality.

Hughes professes to bond with George, but he presents himself as not that different from Ramon. He is reluctant to speak about himself, and he even indicates a weak interest in women. Although many scholars have focused on the homosocial bond created through the discussion of women, this scene might also be inspected for its tepid, if not resistant, performance of heterosexuality. Hughes tells us that the sailors can be defined as having two different "temperaments": there are those who prefer, upon docking, to head for women, and there are those who prefer to go straight for the wine. In choosing wine, Hughes does not necessarily uncover a nonnormative sexuality, but he does—especially in using the term *temperaments*—suggest that there are different orientations. He furthermore disrupts the stereotypical scene of a homosocial bond built upon discussing and trafficking in women, replacing it with alternatives to compulsory heterosexuality. Even when Hughes states, "We kept thinking about the girls," he quickly undercuts this claim with a very different and more compelling interest in something else: "But all those days I was waiting anxiously to see Africa" (*CW* 13:36).

These scenes—with their resistance to a performative and constricted heterosexuality—are important documents of one writer's resistance to compulsory heterosexuality and homophobia, and it is important to recognize that this subversion of the heterosexist hegemony could come from either a heterosexual or an asexual author. Hughes, however, both performs his heterosexuality and submerges that performance, effectively constructing a sexual identity upon the trope of turning away from women. It is this consistent positioning of the autobiographer as turning away from the performance of heterosexuality that invites our attention.

The Autobiographer as a Gay Wanderer

While *Not without Laughter* explores the inchoate sexuality of a young boy as he develops into an adolescent, and *The Big Sea* continues this story past the threshold of adulthood, *I Wonder As I Wander* documents the life of a mature man. In the latter text, Hughes places less emphasis on sex and sexuality as a defining feature of identity. The theme of sexuality, for example, is not introduced in the opening, and it does not grow to be a crucial concern of the ending. Sexuality, however, does appear in various scenes almost as a necessary subject to be raised and then dispensed with.

Hughes, in fact, repeatedly represents his sexuality in a way that is strangely reminiscent of Sandy from *Not without Laughter*—both are presented as objects of desire, and both resist and turn away from the sexual act. But in *I Wonder As I Wander*, Hughes turns away from sex in a way that also suggests that he wishes to perform or announce his heterosexuality. It is this tension between the performance of heterosexuality and the turning away from that performance that makes the second autobiography such a fascinating exploration into the system of compulsory heterosexuality.

I Wonder As I Wander, which covers the poet's time traveling the world as a successful and somewhat famous author, provides several scenes suggestive of the poet's heterosexual life. Each of these scenes, however, depicts the author as turning away from sex—still an innocent and/or reluctant performer of heterosexuality. Amid many scenes of being the foreigner, which may be read as a metaphor for the virgin, Hughes describes arriving in Berlin and locating what he "thought was a candy-bar machine." After inserting a coin, "a package of prophylactics came out instead." Hughes does little more than describe this scene and the street, which was teeming "with prostitutes, pimps, panderers and vendors of dirty pictures" (*CW* 14:96). But the scene characterizes him as an innocent child, expecting candy and getting something very different. This characterization of Hughes as an innocent, which is strangely reminiscent of Sandy, is repeated in another more fully developed chapter called "Tartar Rendezvous."

As in many other scenes in the trilogy, a hyper-masculine male (not

Hughes) is introduced, while women, although not incidental, are the excuse for a certain exchange between men. This exchange between men is probably nowhere more clearly articulated than in the passages devoted to Nichan, Hughes's roommate in Uzbekistan. Hughes describes him as a "muscularly handsome youth with skin as brown as my own and very black hair, crew-cut, heavy and shiny as silk. His eyes were jolly, his smile broad and bright, and his disposition sunny" (*CW* 14:160). Hughes represents Nichan as having boundless energy: "When Nichan burst into the room, a dynamo of life always came with him. He was one of the most energetic of young men, happily occupied most of the time with sports, dancing, girls, or talking to his scores of friends" (*CW* 14:170). It is not sports or conversation, however, that Hughes highlights but rather Nichan's interest in and experience with women.

Hughes describes overhearing his friend making love to a woman, and the passage contributes to the image of Hughes as an innocent virgin in the shadow of yet another hyper-masculine man. Although Hughes suggests that he is, in this case, innocent because he is foreign to the ways of the Uzbeks, he makes strategic use of geographical displacement as a way of addressing a displaced sexuality: "when I first overheard such sounds, I thought [they] must be indicative of rape. Later I heard that it was just the way Uzbeks make love" (*CW* 14:171).

Hughes's interest in documenting the way Russian men interact with women extends to a second man, Hajir, who takes Nichan's place: "My personal experience with the details of such love-making came about through the good offices of a dashing young Red Army man from Tajikistan." This "dashing young Red Army man" offers to take Hughes "to meet one of the local girls." Although Hughes is at first reluctant, the "tall fair-skinned Asiatic soldier" arouses Hughes's "curiosity" by presenting "a graphic pantomimed description of the evening before" (*CW* 14:172).

Hughes wrote this scene as a humorous one, describing his need for a drink and his fear that the girls might be in their sixties. The girls, of course, turn out to be quite unattractive, but Hughes decides to fulfill his role as a heterosexual male. He faces, however, some problems. When he sees Hajir give his girl "a bearlike squeeze that caused her to scream, 'Ow!'" Hughes is unable to replicate the act.

[Hajir] motioned for me to attack mine in the same manner, but the other woman was busy putting a knot of desert wood on the fire. With this warming procedure I did not wish to interfere as my feet were wet with snow and I was chilled to the bone. (*CW* 14:174)

Hughes's humor is fully alive in this passage. As the two couples separate, Hughes describes his continued inability to communicate either verbally or physically with this woman. As Hughes tries to undress the "Tartar girl," he finds that she fights him off violently only to later encourage him to proceed. As he proceeds, however, she again resists and even "sat bolt upright, vaulted over me, and jumped out of bed" (*CW* 14:176).

Casting himself again as the innocent virgin—even as he introduces a competing notion of himself as a reluctant predator—Hughes relates a conversation he has with an American. Hughes, of course, is once again the naive student who is to be schooled, in this case by a knowledgeable road engineer.

> In Tashkent even a prostitute doesn't take off her own clothes for a client. The man has to do it. It's a ritual, that's all. Next time you'll know.
> I understood then why so much commotion went on with Nichan and his girls in the middle of the night. Nichan wasn't raping them. He was just trying to unbutton their sweaters or untie a sash. (*CW* 14:177)

Hughes ends the account not with this piece of cultural awareness, but with Hajir's offer to take Hughes back to the Tartar women. Hughes does not inform the reader if he ever returned. Instead, he ends the chapter marveling at Hajir, who is "[s]till fresh as a daisy after an amorous night of no sleep and a long day in school . . . , raring to wrestle a Tartar again" (*CW* 14:178).

Hughes leaves the reader—as he so often does—with an image of the poet in flight from women and finally turning away from the performance of heterosexuality. Even when Hughes works hardest to represent himself as a heterosexual, he continues to fall into this pattern of turning away. In the passages devoted to Natasha, which are the poet's most sustained attempt at depicting his heterosexuality, Hughes again resists and even expresses annoyance with his inamorata. As a way of emphasizing his role as a desired object, Hughes begins two chapters with a recounting of Natasha's outrageous display of desire.

> Without advance warning, Natasha simply came to my room in the New Moscow Hotel one night when I was out—and was in bed when I got back. (*CW* 14:210)

> The first evening that I came back to my room in the hotel and found Natasha in bed, I said, "But, listen, Natasha, you've got a husband." (*CW* 14:219)

As the object of desire, Hughes can resist and even turn away from the desiring subject, and, of course, he does. He expresses frustration and annoyance with Natasha, constructing the scene as a display not only of her outrageous sexuality but also of his resistance to her free and insistent sexuality. This scene, however, offers more than a representation of one relationship gone bad when we read it alongside the many other scenes found in the trilogy. It is this structure of displacement and evasion that finally invites a consideration of the closet as a structuring element of the work.

Because Hughes provides the literary critic with few expressions of desire for either the male or the female body, older models of gay and lesbian scholarship—models built upon the exploration of homoerotic elements—seem insufficient when applied to his work.[17] Certainly, a case might be made for the displacement of desire, a suppressed or occluded homoerotics or perhaps an examination of significant triangulations, but queer studies should not rely solely on an examination of desire in any of its many forms. Because Hughes studiously avoids a language of erotics and instead builds his representations of sexuality upon omissions and evasions, other models of reading must be employed.[18]

The complicated impulse to confront and avoid the subject of sexuality is, finally, what Hughes offers us. I have argued that a physical and sexual displacement takes place in the three autobiographical works. The effort to assert a sexual persona while also maintaining a persona of innocence and virginity makes Hughes's trilogy a fascinating document of an African American male's maturation. The closet also offers a compelling metaphor for understanding the extreme pressures placed upon the poet. It provides an explanation for the various omissions, occlusions, and circumnavigations found in the trilogy. The trilogy itself, which exists more as an imaginary construct, may testify to the difficulty Hughes had with documenting Sandy's life beyond his sexual awakening and to the problem of writing in a genre, autobiography, founded on the confession. More important, this difficulty makes most sense as a negotiation of the demands of the closet with the demands of writing.

To those who would argue that "asexuality" is also an identity that might make use of the closet, I would hasten to add that the pressures of compulsory heterosexuality, indeed, affect many. But Hughes does not

17. See Gregory Woods, "Gay Re-readings of the Harlem Renaissance."
18. Eve Sedgwick's first book, *Between Men: English Literature and Male Homosocial Desire*, examines triangulations, displacements, and homosocial desire, but her second, *Epistemology of the Closet*, suggests an even wider range of strategies of reading.

simply present an image of himself turning away from women; he also provides significant glimpses into his reactions to homosexuality. In *Not without Laughter,* curiosity for the homosexual male contrasts with the protagonist's easy dismissal of women. And in *The Big Sea,* it is George's heterosexual manhood and Ramon's very different and nonnormative sexual secrets that provide a frame for the autobiography. Finally, in *I Wonder As I Wander,* Hughes studiously turns away from women, allowing us only once or twice a glimpse into his fascination for the sexuality and the prowess of men like Hajir. In this final autobiography, Hughes also addresses a certain sensibility that is announced in the title and throughout the text as that of a wanderer. It makes sense, therefore, that he quotes from Whitman's "Song of the Open Road," but Hughes highlights a passage that speaks to notions of presence and absence and, more indirectly, epistemological questions about identity.

When referring to his friend Noel Sullivan, Hughes considers a line from Walt Whitman.[19] "As Noël Sullivan sat there listening to my recent adventures, saying little, but radiating kindness, good will and sympathy, I thought of a phrase in one of Walt Whitman's poems as applying to him, 'I and mine . . . convince by our presence'" (*CW* 14:278). With this line, Hughes invites us to consider "presence" as an assuring thing, as a spiritual connection between two men. The connective speaks to us from across the ages, encouraging us to consider Whitman's notion of "adhesive love" and asking us to consider the shared closet that these men— Whitman, Sullivan, and Hughes—inhabit. The quote, taken from "Song of the Open Road," brings together Hughes's theme of wandering with notions of presence/absence or, as I am reading it, the closet.

The closet cannot help but allude to its opposite: presence. That is the one thing that can save it from oblivion. It should not surprise us, therefore, that Hughes enlists Whitman to speak to the contradictory gestures of celebrating and also silencing the self. The quote, furthermore, addresses presence with two noticeable signs of absence: an ellipsis, which announces that words are missing, and the allusion to Whitman, which encourages us to consider the absent poet and all that he represents. Both absences effectively allow us to consider Hughes and his closet.

---

19. Rampersad indicates that there was much speculation about Sullivan and even some speculation about Hughes and Sullivan. I am not entering that level of speculation, but rather inviting a consideration of the homosocial bond between the two men. "Although homosexuality was largely an unspoken word in public, Noel Sullivan's status as an inveterate bachelor, and his relationship then and over the coming years with the equally resolute Hughes, may have caused some speculation" (*Life,* 1:289).

The missing words of the quote can be easily restored: "I and mine *do not convince by arguments, similes, rhymes, / We* convince by our presence."[20] These words celebrate a transcendent and romantic sense of debate resolved by presence, and so it would seem at first glance that this message—so out of keeping with our age—would do little to solve epistemological questions about Hughes and his sexuality. But Hughes, in celebrating presence and in dismissing verbal strategies as ineffectual, argues—yet again—from a place structured upon the silence of the closet.

This quote, moreover, imagines a homosocial and transhistorical community that includes Whitman, Sullivan, and Hughes. The quote, after all, applies not simply—as Hughes suggests—to Sullivan but also to Hughes himself. "I and mine," Hughes begins the quote, allowing the dead poet to express what Hughes so rarely permitted himself: an affectionate moment. "I and mine," the poet announces, perhaps describing a platonic friendship but also getting at something more, something celebrated in the possessive pronoun *mine*. Hughes celebrates his connection to a small but fragmented community of like-minded men. Through Whitman, Hughes announces that he belongs to this community, not separate from Whitman and Sullivan, but as a convincing presence despite the dark shadows of his closet.

20. Walt Whitman, *Walt Whitman: Complete Poetry and Prose*, 303 (emphasis added to the restored words).

Gender Performance and Sexual Subjectivity in *Not without Laughter*

Sandy's Emergent Masculinity

Kimberly J. Banks

In *Not without Laughter* Langston Hughes explores sexual subjectivity in terms of relative restraint or license on desire as well as legitimate or illegitimate objects of sexual desire. The private sphere, in terms of familial authority, conditions the development of sexual subjectivity, while the public sphere offers the scripts that regulate the enactment of gender. Such scripts, whether ultimately rejected or reinforced, must be continually processed and negotiated. Gender is not a static given; it is a social process that must be repeatedly enacted to create the appearance of permanence and timelessness. In his characterization of Harriett, Hughes refuses to present one enactment of gender; her enactments explicitly and publicly shift. Hughes chooses a different strategy in his characterization of Sandy, who reinforces a "wholesome masculinity," the assurance of which is undercut by curiosity about other versions of gender performance.

Sandy's emergent masculinity in *Not without Laughter* is not predicated on that of his father, Jimboy. The novel is not about fathers teaching sons how to be men. The novel shows how boys learn masculine scripts outside the home and how these scripts shape their visions of masculinity. Although home is depicted as a feminine space of Sandy's mother Annjee, his grandmother Hager, and his aunt Harriett, the feminine script is not as straightforward as it might at first appear. Harriett, as the youngest girl-child, does not want to be a domestic and works to become a blues artist. Therefore her feminine script is learned outside the home as well. Her rebellion serves as a model, to be confirmed, denied, or negotiated, for the development of Sandy's sexual subjectivity.

One way in which Hughes explores cross-gender subjectivity is by using the blueswoman as a nexus for Sandy's emerging masculinity. It is fairly commonplace to think of the blueswoman as a model for sexual subjectivity, starting with the pioneering work of Hazel Carby.[1] In her argument, such a model appeals equally to northern and southern, rural and urban black women. The blueswoman is a mediating figure for numerous cultural contradictions. *Not without Laughter* suggests that the blueswoman performs such a role, not only for women, but also at the very least for boys.

In contrast to the blueswoman, who is a public figure, the maternal Hager is a private one. Both Harriett and Sandy develop their sexual subjectivity against the authority of Hager, who attempts to police that subjectivity despite the external pressures involved. In the context of working at a hotel and accompanying their peers, Harriett and Sandy have the potential to define their sexual development. Hager denies such potential to Harriett, equating her work environment, a hotel, to her soul, evil. When Harriett defies Hager to go out at night with boys and girls of her age, Hughes consigns Harriett to anonymous sexual encounters. In contrast, when Sandy wants to work at a hotel, Hager still considers his soul good and innocent. After Hager's death, when Sandy walks his girlfriend Pansetta home, her identity is very specific and Hughes rehearses Sandy's anxieties around sexual knowledge and performance. At the level of nar-

---

1. On blueswomen and their importance as models of black feminist sexuality, see Michele Russell, "Slave Codes and Liner Notes"; Deborah E. McDowell, "'That name-less . . . shameful impulse': Sexuality in Nella Larsen's *Quicksand* and *Passing*"; and Carol Batker, "'Love Me Like I like to Be': The Sexual Politics of Hurston's *Their Eyes Were Watching God*, the Classic Blues, and the Black Women's Club Movement." Ann duCille has raised important questions about the commercial context in which black blueswomen performed in *The Coupling Convention: Sex, Text, and Tradition in Black Women's Fiction*. Linkages between black women and prostitution are explored in Sander L. Gilman, "Black Bodies, White Bodies: Toward an Iconography of Female Sexuality in Late Nineteenth-Century Art, Medicine, and Literature"; Hazel Carby, "Policing the Black Woman's Body in an Urban Context"; and Kimberley Roberts, "The Clothes Make the Woman: The Symbolics of Prostitution in Nella Larsen's *Quicksand* and Claude McKay's *Home to Harlem*."

rative, the blueswoman is not only denied sexual subjectivity, her objectified condition becomes the mediating point for Sandy's sexual subjectivity. The extent to which Harriett resists such objectification is the extent to which Sandy can exercise choice about his own gender performativity.

Hortense Spillers focuses on the consumption of blues music as an active process in the constitution of subjectivity. She frames the problem posed by blueswomen: "the black woman must translate the female vocalist's gestures into an apposite structure of terms that will articulate both her kinship to other women and the particular nuances of her own experience."[2] The listener is searching both for identification with other women in a community of women and for a structure within which to differentiate her experience from those of other women. In the case of Sandy, *Not without Laughter* positions the listener as a young boy and creates a community of men through a shared reaction to the blueswoman. It is in the pool hall that Sandy learns to differentiate his experience from that of the blueswoman, but the moment of gender performativity leaves open the possibility that Sandy could choose to identify with the blueswoman. If blueswomen are a nexus, a "locus of contradictions,"[3] they are just as much a problem of interpretation as of (re)presentation. Hughes provides a way to examine a young boy's negotiation of this locus of contradictions.

In achieving sexual subjectivity, characters have to negotiate culturally prescribed channels for recognizing and expressing desire. In *Gender Trouble*, Judith Butler makes an important distinction between gender expressivity and performativity. She explains that "there is no gender identity behind the expressions of gender; that identity is performatively constituted by the very 'expressions' that are said to be its results." What appears to be "an abiding substance or gendered self" is "produced by the regulation of attributes along culturally established lines of coherence."[4] While we generally acknowledge the public nature of gender performance, expressions of sexuality are expected to be private. However, Hughes explores the public constitution of sexual subjectivity. There is no sexual self waiting to be expressed in spite of a repressive social milieu; the sexual self is constituted by the social system that in fact attempts to regulate it in a multiplicity of ways. The men at the pool hall define the parameters of legitimate and illegitimate desire. They dismiss both Harriett and homosexual men as degenerates. While Hughes denies Harriett

2. Spillers, "Interstices: A Small Drama of Words," 167.
3. Hazel Carby, *Reconstructing Womanhood: The Emergence of the Afro-American Woman Novelist*, 15.
4. Butler, *Gender Trouble: Feminism and the Subversion of Identity*, 32–33.

gender subjectivity as a result of her lack of interiority, she illuminates a very sophisticated sense of gender performativity. Hughes tends to take Sandy's gender subjectivity for granted. His interiority is produced through self-reflection and dreams. Ironically, through his persistent "innocence," Sandy achieves sexual subjectivity. As he decides how to act on the information provided in the pool hall narratives, he achieves awareness of gender performativity. Ostensibly Harriett's and Sandy's sexual subjectivities develop with the same influences in the private sphere while their options for gender performativity have very different influences in the public sphere.

Hughes offers an interesting exploration of sexuality that is tied to reconstructions of masculinity. Such reconstructions follow the kind of masculine consolidation that Robyn Wiegman explores in *American Anatomies*. Wiegman explains, "Black Power's rhetorical inversion—to assert the black phallus in the context of metaphorical and literal castration—elides black liberation struggle with a universal masculine position, thereby displacing both the specificity and legitimacy of black female articulations of political disempowerment, as well as a variety of claims from African-American sexual minorities."[5] Functioning similarly to Black Power rhetoric, the rhetoric of black male leadership is central to *Not without Laughter* because of how it consolidates masculinity. Sandy and Harriett negotiate their gendered scripts within very different public spheres; such differentiation within the public sphere heightens rather than replaces sexual differentiation within the private sphere. Both kinds of differentiation work to reproduce gendered and sexualized hierarchies while consolidating racial identification.

This level of complexity in Hughes's exploration of race, gender, and sexuality has not been acknowledged by scholars. In "Natural and Unnatural Circumstances in *Not without Laughter*," for example, Elizabeth Schultz provides a classic argument about the double-voiced discourse of the novel in African American literature. She explains, "Thus in Hughes's 'double-directed discourse,' a 'natural' story of a boy's coming of age reveals the 'unnatural' circumstances of racism and poverty. This subtext explicitly introduces middle- and upper-class readers to the ubiquity and injustices of racism in American society as well as to the richness of African-American culture."[6] In an era when it is critical to not only acknowledge but also delineate the consequences of not all black people

---

5. Wiegman, *American Anatomies: Theorizing Race and Gender*, 86.
6. See above, p. 41.

being men and not all women being white, the counterpoint between mainstream and African American cultures and natural and unnatural development has consequences for how we understand gender and sexuality in *Not without Laughter*. Schultz assumes that Sandy's sexual identity is a "natural" heterosexual one, and therefore an "unnatural" homosexual identity works in conjunction with racial and economic oppression. In a different context, Timothy S. Chin points out that the "valorization of 'indigenous' [here substitute African American] culture also entails the affirmation of a 'native' sexuality, specifically coded as 'natural' and therefore necessarily counterposed to the possibility of an 'unnatural' or 'aberrant' sexuality."[7] Chin forces a careful consideration of the consequences of sexual representation within African American and Caribbean culture. Schultz falls back on an early argument in the recuperation of African American literature, one that counterposes the "exotic expectations of white readers" to an author's ability "to energize, even to flaunt, African American diversity, beauty, and accomplishment in creating a vibrant culture." Such an opposition does not leave room for an analysis of how African American culture reproduces gender and sexual hierarchies while furthering an agenda of racial consolidation. By carefully examining how racial consolidation reproduces sexual and gender hierarchies, I will deconstruct simplistic dichotomies between mainstream and African American or natural and unnatural as well as the long-contested but difficult to dislodge idea that all oppressions are equally oppressive or oppressive through similar strategies.

Parallel Sexualities

Hughes offers two sets of parallel moments in *Not without Laughter* for exploring the relationship between Harriett's sexual subjectivity and Sandy's. These moments illuminate the ways in which women and men are positioned within gender hierarchies and also how such hierarchies are reinforced. They also offer ways to think about the regulation of sexuality and how certain constructions are valorized and thereby reinforced while other constructions are denigrated and thereby made illicit or illegitimate.

The first parallel revolves around the employment of Harriett and then

7. Chin, "'Bullers' and 'Battymen': Contesting Homophobia in Black Popular Culture and Contemporary Caribbean Literature," 131.

Sandy at a hotel. For both, Hager is the regulator of sexual boundaries. Anne Borden employs the term *genderracial* to account for the relationship between race and gender in Hughes's work. However, Borden does not acknowledge the hierarchical nature of the family relationships. She says, "The perspectives of the four women coexist in Sandy's consciousness. There is no clear-cut right or wrong; their realities survive in the flashes of joy and conflict that make up family. Despite varying views and lifestyles, a spirit of collectivity is maintained; a polyrhythmic quality . . . suffuses the novel."[8] Borden's approach does not acknowledge the disciplinary and regulatory roles that certain family members perform for other family members. Focusing on the harmonious interplay of difference, Borden ignores the fundamental differences over the nature of reality between the characters. "Genderracial" fails to account for the multiple subject positions held among black women. Hager plays a regulatory role and tells Harriett, "You ain't gonna work in no hotel. You hear me! They's dives o' sin, that's what they is, an' a child o' mine ain't goin' in one. If you was a boy, I wouldn't let you go, much less a girl! They ain't nothin' but strumpets works in hotels" (*CW* 4:42). Hager offers gender equivalence in suggesting that she would not let a boy or a girl work in a hotel at the same time that she offers differentiation in also suggesting that boys have greater freedom than girls and she would not let *even* a boy work in a hotel. The space of a hotel produces a kind of sexual license to which Hager does not want her daughter or grandson to have access. Hager effectively forecloses Harriet's access to this particular space, while she is less successful at foreclosing her access to other spaces such as the dance hall and the carnival.

The fact that Hughes valorizes Hager's role as the unifying force within the family means that he does not overtly critique her role as a sexual regulator. However, a critique does emerge in his complicated representation of sexual "essences" and the gender assumptions that accompany such essences. While Hager claims equal treatment in the potential for her descendants to gain sexual subjectivity, she grants Sandy more negotiating power. In contrast to Hager's success at steering Harriett clear of hotels, she allows Sandy to work at one. As the only male in the household, Sandy makes the decision to work at a hotel and makes a case to his grandmother later: "I want to send mama a Christmas present. And just look at my shoes, all worn out! I don't make much money any more since that

8. Borden, "Heroic 'Hussies' and 'Brilliant Queers': Genderracial Resistance in the Works of Langston Hughes," 335.

new colored barber-shop opened up . . . and I have to start working regular some time, don't I?" While Hager still believes that hotels are "evil, full o' nastiness, an' you don't learn nothin' good in 'em," she relents with, "But don't forget, honey, no matter where you works—you be good an' do right . . . I reckon you'll get along" (*CW* 4:146).

The differentiation that Hager makes in her attitude toward boys and girls becomes a reality when Sandy decides to work in a hotel and his grandmother acquiesces. Sandy's working options are structured very differently from Harriett's. Sandy works at the barbershop, the hotel, and later at a print shop. His greater degree of latitude and Hager's willingness to let him work in a hotel show that she regulates sexual boundaries differently based on gender. Hager's sexual practice illustrates the hierarchical nature of subjectivity.

In Hager's conversation with Harriett, sin is located both within the space of the hotel and within the workers of the hotel, that is, "dives o' sin" equal "strumpets." With Sandy, the exterior space of the hotel can be disconnected from the interiority of the person, that is, "evil" hotel does not equal "good" boy. Women's sexual subjectivity is denied because such subjectivity is made equivalent to social situations. Not only does Hager not make any assumptions about Sandy's subjectivity in relation to working in a hotel, she does not assume that Sandy is initiated into sexual experience through such work. As a girl, Harriett has to be careful of her exterior environment and appearance because they are equated to interior attitudes; the same is not true for Sandy. Although Harriett is not a "strumpet" at the moment of Hager's assertion, her essence as a strumpet is confirmed through such a gesture. Hughes suggests that whether or not Harriett recognizes her nature as a strumpet is immaterial to her condition as such.

Two early reviews of *Not without Laughter* emphasize the purity of Sandy and therefore the value of the novel. In one dated July 26, 1930, Wilson Jefferson articulated the relationship between the characterizations of Sandy and Harriett: "Sandy is perhaps the finest fictional type of a Negro boy that literary America has yet produced. He sees and experiences things that would warp a nature less resolute, or embitter a nature less poised. He feels the touch of poverty from his tenderest years, is thrown around barber shops and second-rate hotels in his efforts to earn a few dollars and help his grandmother—and yet, unlike his Aunt Harriett, keeps clean and wholesome." Similarly in a August 29, 1930, review, Mary White Ovington substituted the word *decent* for Jefferson's "clean and wholesome." Sandy "works at the barber's shop and in the hotel and sees the seamy side of white and colored life, but keeps decent through it all."[9]

The focus on Sandy's purity is also important in the context of Hughes's patron, Charlotte Osgood Mason, who approved of the portrayal of Sandy as incorruptibly innocent. She wrote to Hughes: "Thank you, Child, for sending it to me with this dedication, remembering how precious the true spirit of Sandy is to Godmother. Oh Alamari, as the sun sets on the Western slope of Godmother's life her spirit holds in its eternal relief the morning star that Sandy was destined to carry into the hearts of his people."[10] Mason clearly saw Sandy as having redemptive value to African American people. Both H. Nigel Thomas and John P. Shields have written about the influence of Mason on the writing of *Not without Laughter*. While Thomas argues that Mason's injunction to steer clear of propaganda saved the novel, Shields argues that her suggestions tempered Hughes's left-wing politics. Both critics understand race as the only significant politics of the novel. Because Hughes's treatment of sexuality and gender was less subject to Mason's interest, these aspects of the novel are more likely to be a result of Hughes's own editorial choices.

The hotel functions in the novel as a contrast to the notion of purity. If the hotel is a site of sexual license, more inclined to produce a loose attitude toward sex, it is also a nexus for negotiating a wider range of options for sexual subjectivity. A number of examples reinforce the presentation of hotels as "dives o' sin." In her conversation with Sandy, Hager explains that the populations of hotels are "all them low-down Bottoms niggers, and bad womens" (*CW* 4:146). The omniscient narrator is more specific about the people who frequent Drummer's Hotel: "the poorest of travelling salesmen, transient railroad workers, occasionally a few show-people, and the ladies of the streets with their clients" (*CW* 4:149). Charlie Nutter, who arranges for Sandy to get the job at the hotel, "had taken only a dollar" (*CW* 4:151) and promised to teach Sandy the hotel trade. Despite such a guide, Sandy remains "a dumb little joker" (*CW* 4:150, 151). His dumbness equals an "essential," incorruptible innocence. Such essentialization of Sandy's character raises questions about the essentialization of Harriet's. Is Harriet evil to the same extent that Sandy is good? Is this general-

9. Jefferson, "Life Comes 'Not without Laughter' to Kansas Negroes," 139; Ovington, "Praises Hughes an Unusual Colored Writer," 158.

10. Charlotte Mason to Langston Hughes, July 10, 1930, Langston Hughes Papers, JWJ Collection, Beinecke Rare Book and Manuscript Library, Yale University, New Haven, Conn.

ization applicable to all men and women in the novel? Unlike other women in the novel who appear unsexed, Harriett's expressed interest in sexuality makes her evil. When Sandy sees a naked white woman, there is no expression of sexual desire. The narrator explains, "The child was scared because he had often heard of colored boys' being lynched for looking at white women, even with their clothes on—but the bell-boy only laughed" (CW 4:151). While Sandy understands the political terror of lynching, he does not understand the desire for a naked woman. Hughes fails to delineate desire as a part of Sandy's characterization, and the lack of such desire makes him good. The charged racial-political context of the hotel is further reinforced by a drunken white southerner who gets Sandy to shine his shoes and asks him to dance. Sandy insists that he does not dance and ultimately throws his shoeshine materials at the man and runs away from his job and the hotel. By juxtaposing Sandy's expectation of lynching and his refusal to perform a particular racial role, Hughes highlights Sandy's transgression of racial boundaries in two very different ways, both of which are crucial to Sandy's emergent masculinity. To the same extent that Sandy transgresses racial boundaries in the public sphere, Harriett is firmly inscribed and sexualized within such boundaries.

The second parallel between Harriett and Sandy revolves around their relationships to peers of the opposite sex and how their ability to negotiate such social factors influences their production of a sexual subjectivity. In the parallel of the hotel, Harriett becomes a reflection of her environment while Sandy is defined against his environment through his ability to resist its demands. In this second parallel, Hughes casts Harriett's environment as one of numerous, anonymous men while Sandy's environment is the negative influence or danger of a specific individual, Pansetta Young. Harriett's encounters with the opposite sex are cast in shadow. She comes to town on Monday night "with the cook and some of the boys" (CW 4:41) from the Stanton County Country Club. Thursday, Harriett goes to Willow Grove with "Maudel's brother and some fellows" (CW 4:44). When "a big red car" pulls up to the house that night, it is full of "coatless, slick-headed black boys in green and yellow silk shirts" (CW 4:45). The boys are always mentioned in aggregate, and the implication is that Harriett has fairly anonymous sexual encounters. In such encounters, red is a predominant color. She wears red silk stockings; she gets into a red car; Hager and Sandy watch a red taillight fade into the night. Again Harriett's sexuality is implied through exterior signs, and such signs are no more indicative of her subjectivity in going to Willow Grove than they would have been had she worked at a hotel. In *Not without Laughter*, the regulation of sexual boundaries is more clearly represented than is the creation or performance of sexual desire. Desire itself is an element of interiority that is always presumed. The lack of specificity about Harriett's companions and her desire further inscribes her within stereotypes about black women's hypersexuality.

For Sandy, although his sexual desire awakens in relationship to Pansetta Young, such desire does not foreclose the possibility of sexual innocence. Hughes reveals this desire through waking fantasy and nighttime dreams. Ironically, Sandy's sexual awakening must be represented in a way that is consistent with his "essential" innocence, and one way Hughes does this is through Sandy's approach to Pansetta. It is love at first sight: "he would sit looking at her for hours in every class that they had together—for she was a little baby-doll kind of girl, with big black eyes and a smooth pinkish-brown skin, and her hair was curly on top of her head" (*CW* 4:172). Sandy spends a year walking Pansetta halfway home and is known as her boyfriend, but he never enters the Young house. When he is alone at night in bed thinking of her, it is a scene ripe for masturbation. Even the ellipses of the narration suggest masturbation: "Black youth . . . Dark hands knocking, knocking! Pansetta's little brown hands knocking on the doors of life! Baby-doll hands, tiny autumn-leaf girl-hands! . . . Gee, Pansetta! . . . The Doors of Life . . . the great big doors . . . Sandy was asleep . . . of life" (*CW* 4:183). The phrase "Sandy was asleep" could easily be more suggestive than it at first appears. He could fall asleep dreaming of Pansetta or he could use the image of Pansetta to fuel an erotic fantasy. The dual interpretation indicates the degree to which Sandy's desire is just as much real as ideal.

Sandy's innocence is further reinforced when his aunt Tempy delineates the inevitable outcome for his relationship with Pansetta: "First thing you know you'll be getting in trouble with her and she'll be having a baby—I see I have to be plain—and whether it's yours or not, she'll say it is" (*CW* 4:185). Sandy is still confused about the relationship between sexual intercourse and pregnancy despite his constant association with peers Buster, Jimmy Lane, and Jap Logan, all of whom are clearly more sexually experienced. As a result of Tempy's lecture, Sandy stops walking Pansetta home. After some days of regret, he goes to Pansetta's home to resume their prior relationship and finds that Jimmy Lane is already Pansetta's new boyfriend. He calls Sandy a "God-damn fool!" (*CW* 4:190) for not capitalizing on Pansetta's sexual availability. Sandy recognizes his desire for Pansetta but does not understand how to express it and is unwilling to be initiated into the forms of expression that his friends have already learned. The need for such explicit initiation into forms of sexual expression reinforces Butler's assertion about gender identity as something produced along "culturally established lines of coherence."

During his childhood Sandy seems to maneuver through the obstacles presented by what Hazel Carby has called, in the context of Claude McKay's *Home to Harlem*, "the degenerate female element" to achieve "wholesome masculinity."[11] While Hughes does not provide space for women's sexual subjectivity, unlike McKay he raises questions about "degeneracy" and its construction for both men and women. Concomitantly he raises questions about "wholesomeness" and the forms of masculinity that would be desirable. In Chicago, Harriett loses the association with prostitution, which in the context of Sandy's characterization is a kind of corruption and capitulation to sin. She then becomes, instead of a degenerate female element, Sandy's guide, charting a course for him through other degenerate female elements so that he can achieve "wholesome masculinity" as defined through the achievement of a high school diploma. R. Baxter Miller explains that "in the last three chapters, Sandy moves to an understanding of his racial heritage. He rejects Tempy's material success less than the condescension with which she and her circle look down on folk blacks; he chooses Harriett as a model because of Harriett's independence and self-content."[12] In Miller's reading, Harriett provides a model of racial consolidation. He does not explore the cost of such consolidation in terms of sex and gender, however, and Harriet does not serve the same function throughout the novel. In fact, she serves oppositional functions. Harriett moves from a symbol of degeneracy to one of regeneracy. The first role is subject to social opprobrium, while the second represents a social model.

The regulation of sexual and gender boundaries shifts from the level of characterization, the attitudes of Hager and Tempy, to the level of narrative. While Pansetta's status as a degenerate female is introduced through the perspective of Tempy (and her perspective is subject to tremendous ridicule), that status is reinforced by the end of the novel by the narrative itself. The importance of a high school diploma is arguable given the job and career opportunities available to black people. But such a critique is undermined when the diploma symbolizes the evasion of becoming a

11. Carby, "'It Jus Be's Dat Way Sometime': The Sexual Politics of Women's Blues," 12.

12. Miller, "'Done Made Us Leave Our Home': Langston Hughes's *Not without Laughter*—Unifying Image and Three Dimensions," 368.

"degenerate female" or becoming ensnared by one. Hager tells a friend that Harriett sees "no use in learnin' books fo' nothin' but to work in white · folks' kitchens when she's graduated" (*CW* 4:32). With Sandy, Harriett fails to point out that black men with an education become Pullman porters and elevator operators, a job Sandy already holds. Sandy's promise of becoming a great male leader like Frederick Douglass, Booker T. Washington, and W. E. B. Du Bois is unrealistic given the jobs awaiting the majority of black people with or without high school diplomas. The differential gender expectations in the context of education operate in the same way as do those in the context of work.

The two sets of parallels, work at the hotel and relationship to peers, are the clearest indication in *Not without Laughter* of how adolescents learn to perform sexual subjectivity. In terms of the hotel work, Hughes devotes a considerable amount of space to Hager's regulation of sexuality. Such regulation succeeds when Harriett refuses work at the hotel and does not succeed when Harriett goes to Willow Grove. Harriett makes a conscious decision not to work at a hotel when she leaves the country club and goes to Willow Grove. However, in the novel Harriett's choices are not represented in a rational way. In addition, her desire is not represented from an interior perspective. These narrative choices reinforce the equivalence between exterior and interior perspectives. In contrast, Sandy's rationalizations for working at the hotel and for walking Pansetta home are presented in very specific terms. The narrative maintains Sandy's "essential" innocence and fashions his performance of sexuality. Illicit sexual knowledge, whether at Drummer's Hotel, through Pansetta, or through Jimmy Lane, cannot penetrate Sandy's interior innocence. When applied to the male character Sandy, such sexual knowledge is only surface knowledge.

Gendered Publics

Hughes is quite self-consciously invested in the production of masculinity through masculine public spaces. The implications for sexual subjectivity through such masculine public spaces are fraught with ambiguity. Since both Harriett and Sandy are initiated into gender identity through gendered public spheres, exploring such spheres should provide a better understanding of gender performance as predicated on sexual subjectivity. Harriett's options for participating in a gendered public sphere, based on the choices of the women around her, are the Baptist church (Hager), colored women's clubs (Tempy), and the lodge (Annjee).

Sandy's options are the barbershop, hotel, and pool hall. Harriett's options are more formal than Sandy's, and the kind of information available to each character is therefore very different. The clearest representation of Harriett's options is with Hager and the church. When Harriett wants to go to Willow Grove, Hager tells her, "Harriett, honey, I wants you to be good . . . I just wants you to grow up decent, chile. I don't want you runnin' to Willer Grove with them boys. It ain't no place fo' you in the nighttime—an' you knows it. You's mammy's baby girl. She wants you to be good, honey, and follow Jesus, that's all" (CW 4:46). For Hager, goodness is a Christian goodness that means acceptance of Jesus into one's life and heart. The exterior of the church exemplifies the interior spirituality. Otherwise, environments such as those associated with being a washerwoman are relatively meaningless.

Hager's powerlessness to communicate this perspective to her descendants foreshadows the helplessness of Nanny in *Their Eyes Were Watching God* in protecting her daughter Leafy. Nanny explains to her granddaughter Janie that she would "take a broom and a cook-pot and throw up a highway through de wilderness for [Leafy]. . . . But somehow she got lost offa de highway." Just as important as the sense of available tools, represented by the broom and the pot, is the sense of having a text to preach but no pulpit from which to preach it. Whereas Hager eclipses one environment over the other, Nanny justifies the need for materialism because the environment does not provide a forum in which to express women's spiritual knowledge. Whereas for Hager spirituality does offer protection, for Nanny spiritual protection is connected to material resources. Nanny offers a very gendered initiation into the world, but Hager attempts to transcend gender through reference to spirituality. Both Janie and Harriett are sixteen when the significance of gender emerges. At sixteen, Harriett has such a strong will that she rejects her mother's idea of salvation, whereas Janie thinks love will come with marriage because "Nanny and the old folks had said it, so it must be so."[13]

Harriett's rejection of Christianity is related to the inability of Christianity to acknowledge questions of racial discrimination. She sees the streets and Maudel's friendship as capable of addressing these questions. In contrast, Barbara Burkhardt reads *Not without Laughter* as offering the spirituals and the blues as equivalent releases: "While belonging to separate spheres in the black community, both seek to address and assuage the contrast between the promise of the American dream and the disap-

13. Zora Neale Hurston, *Their Eyes Were Watching God*, 15, 20.

pointing realities of post-slavery, African-American life."[14] Early in the novel the blues and spirituals are not equivalent, but by the end of the novel they become so because Harriett assumes Hager's regulatory role. Harriett refuses to privilege the demands of the spiritual over the material. Before walking out the door, Harriett calls her mother an "old Christian fool" (*CW* 4:46). Harriett offers a reading of Christianity that makes it complicit with racism and thereby marks her mother as a fool for failing to see it. She tells Hager that "the church has made a lot of you old Negroes act like Salvation Army people. . . . Afraid to even laugh on Sundays, afraid for a girl and boy to look at one another, or for people to go to dances. Your old Jesus is white, I guess, that's why! He's white and stiff and don't like niggers!" (*CW* 4:44). Although there are cases to be made for how Christian institutions regulate sexual subjectivity and / or provide possibilities for gender performativity, Hughes avoids such representations in his novel, and such choices have consequences for how we understand feminine public spaces.

Hughes creates only one viable public space for Harriett's feminine performance, and that is vaudeville, a space complicated by the perpetuation of a variety of stereotypes and their commercialization. Harriett creates a public space for herself through performance, but she also recognizes that women's options for gender performativity are inadequate. Harriett does not assimilate her mother's Christian values, nor does she have other models through which she can assimilate a feminine script. In contrast to her mother and others who would like to define her "essence" as negative, bad, or evil, Harriett asserts a performative self without an essence. All roles, then, are performed, whether perceived as good or evil. When Harriett appears on stage, she is "stepping out from among the blue curtains . . . in a dress of glowing orange, flame-like against the ebony of her skin, barbaric, yet beautiful as a jungle princess" (*CW* 4:205). Such an outfit reinforces black women as the feminine Other, not feminine at all but containing everything excluded from conventional feminine roles. In "Rejuvenation through Joy," David Chinitz sees Harriett's clothing for her first act as an affirmation of Hughes's inability to escape primitivism.[15] The outfit indicates less about Hughes the author than it does about the options of self-presentation available to Harriett the character. Appearances are only appearances here. Precisely because this outfit is singular

14. Burkhardt, "The Blues in Langston Hughes's *Not without Laughter*," 122.
15. Chinitz, "Rejuvenation through Joy: Langston Hughes, Primitivism, and Jazz," 69.

as a representation of Harriett, its nature as performance is highlighted rather than Hughes's fall into primitivism.[16]

In her next two changes of clothing, Harriett plays to other vaudeville images. In her second act, she wears "an apron of blue calico, with a bandanna handkerchief knotted about her head" (CW 4:205). Her voice is described as moaning throughout her performance. Observers can interpret this image as a plantation stereotype. Whereas the exotic primitive is a stereotypical representation of Africa and hence all blacks, the bandanna image is associated more specifically with the domestic and service status of most black women. Harriett makes yet another move in her final change of clothing. She wears "a sparkling dress of white sequins" and ends by dancing "a mad collection of steps and a swift sudden whirl across the whole stage" (CW 4:206). The sparkling dress of white sequins attests both to Harriett's success and to fantasies of that success. The dress represents the north as promised land; it is the lure of the good life, the lure of dreams fulfilled. The reality of women on vaudeville circuits is much less attractive than the images of glitter and glory suggested by the dress. In addition, the northward migrations of women in the 1920s did not fulfill promises of increased opportunities for achieving the good life. Cheryl Wall sees the final change in clothing as critical: "Its placement at the end of her performance suggests that this is the persona which embodies Harriett's greatest achievement as an artist. The triumph inheres as well in Harriett's successful invention of a life which she can lead without denying her self."[17] "Invention" is important here as Harriett continues to self-consciously construct and deconstruct images of herself for consumption by others. Her recognition of the need for such manipulation calls attention to her self-possession as the denial of any role in particular. On stage, Harriett continues to adapt her image to a series of audience expectations. As readers and voyeurs, we cannot assume the authenticity of any of the images. The images trace continued negotiation over the meaning of sex and sensuality in black women's lives.

Continuing negotiation over the meaning of sex and sensuality in black

16. Wall also locates this initial image of Harriett as one of exotic primitivism, but "the description of the song she sings ... helps the reader deconstruct the image as commercial and counterfeit" ("'Whose Sweet Angel Child,'" 44–45). Deconstruction of the image is key for active reader participation in the production of subjectivity. However, this image is not significantly different from other kinds of mediated social relations. The commercial context of the image extends the analysis of other kinds of social relations rather than contrasts with them.

17. Ibid., 45.

men's lives is traced in very different contexts. Nonetheless, this idea that self-possession, whether sexual or gendered, is the denial of any particular role has consequences for Sandy's sexual possibilities. When Sandy starts to work at the barbershop, its importance as a space to reinforce male gendered norms is clearly highlighted against the fact that Sandy had spent the entire summer close to his grandmother, "tied to [her] apron-strings." This chapter is equally explicit about the contrast between the world of the barbershop and the world of women at home: "But the barber-shop then was a man's world, and, on Saturdays, while a dozen or more big laborers awaited their turns, the place was filled with loud man-talk and smoke and laughter" (*CW* 4:135). One of Sandy's initiations into manhood at the barbershop involves the ritual of playing the dozens. When Sandy first starts to work there, he does not have a comeback for customers who tease him about his sandy hair. Eventually he learns to return the insult with "So's your pa's." Within this clearly masculine space, the men talk about various women, including Sandy's aunt Harriett. Her name regularly comes up "in less proper connections" (*CW* 4:136) than chambermaid. The barbershop owner tries to protect Sandy from such knowledge of his aunt. While the owner is out one day, a young teamster discusses Harriett's beauty combined with her darkness. Uncle Dan Givens says, "I admits Harrietta's all right . . . all right to look at but— sput-t-tsss!" The suggestion of "but" indicates there should be something more to women at the very moment that they are in the process of dissecting women by exterior standards. The teamster's response is "O, I know that! . . . But I ain't talkin' 'bout what she is! I'm talkin' 'bout how she looks. An' a songster out o' this world don't care if she is a——!" (*CW* 4:137).

The novel repeatedly returns to the question of the relationship between exteriors and interiors, between beauty and goodness. These comments at the barbershop shift Harriett's work environment from the hotel and street to the stage. The first environment is ugly and evil, while the second is beautiful but not good. This contradiction emerges in the transition between Harriett's roles. Although Sandy is silent during this exchange about his aunt, he is initiated into the barbershop's rituals surrounding women. When a woman comes in asking where she can buy a Chicago *Defender*, Sandy asserts, "She wouldn't have to pay me" (*CW* 4:138) to shine her shoes. Sandy has successfully assimilated the male repartee of the barbershop and pool hall and can employ its rhetoric when the proper time presents itself. His silence about his aunt suggests agreement with the judgments of men at the pool hall. Having learned the dozens and how to rap about if not to women, Sandy could choose to defend his aunt in the same terms with which he chooses to defend himself against taunts about his hair.

In another context where Harriett becomes the men's topic, Sandy completely ignores the sexual text and attends solely to the racial one. At the pool hall, after Hager's death, the gambler tells Sandy, "Yo' Aunt Harrie's a whang, son!" (*CW* 4:178). This comment about Harriett is less clear-cut than the comments in the barbershop. Sandy is just as silent here as he was in the earlier example, and no one else contests the gambler's judgment either. The only commentary occurs through juxtaposition. In this chapter, Uncle Dan tells a story, bragging, about being a stud while in slavery and having forty-nine children. Sandy is initiated into a world where boys could sit on the "benches outside, talking and looking at the girls as they passed" (*CW* 4:174). In a context where men and boys pass the time watching women and Uncle Dan brags about his reproductive capacity when women had no choice about reproduction, aspersions on Harriett's character are undercut by the credibility of those casting the aspersions. The other boys, Buster, Jap Logan, and Jimmy Lane, all question Uncle Dan's credibility. However, Sandy finds him to be a credible storyteller and asks, "Weren't you scared?" (*CW* 4:177). Such a naive response indicates that Sandy fails to grasp the import of the stories heard in the pool hall. Uncle Dan's tale of his own prowess as a young man arises in response to young men asserting their own sexual prowess. Regardless of whether the story is true, Sandy's response highlights the racial dimensions of slavery (being scared of bondage), rather than the sexual politics in which the story clearly participates, both within Uncle Dan's narrative and within the pool-hall context in which it is shared.

The successful completion of Sandy's masculine initiations is very clear when he moves to Chicago. While in Stanton, the lessons of the barbershop and the pool hall and the examples of his friends could not penetrate his innocence. Once Sandy is in Chicago, Hughes shifts the representation of Sandy's innocence without any explanation or development. Sandy's innocence is shattered, and Sandy becomes wise and knowing. When Sandy arrives in Chicago, he decides to explore the neighborhood. Almost immediately after Sandy exits his residence building alone, an effeminate man approaches him. The narrative description is of "a small yellow man with a womanish kind of voice" (*CW* 4:196). Other narrative indicators are the "murmur[ing of] the soft voice," "the powdered voice . . . softly persistent," and the insistent voice. Taken on its own, the voice is a synecdoche for femininity. Hughes upsets such a synecdoche and thereby upsets all of the equivalencies between interiors and exteriors, parts and wholes, both those questioned and those reinforced in the novel. Juda Bennett approaches this question of sexual curiosity in *Not without Laughter* in relationship to other instances in Hughes's work: "'Curious' ends with a question not unlike the question at the end of 'Café: 3 a.m.' Both poems begin with the promise of knowing—'spotting fairies' and 'I can see your house'—but both poems end with not knowing. The curiosity is not unlike the curiosity that the protagonist of *Not without Laughter* has for 'such men [who do things] with the boys who accompanied them' [*CW* 4:197]. It is perhaps even the same curiosity that John has as he watches his son 'turning out to be a queer.' It is the curiosity of the outsider, the homophobe and the innocent. But then Hughes, we must remember, always collapses outside with inside."[18] Rather than always collapsing interiors and exteriors, Hughes can simultaneously or successively collapse interiors with exteriors, disavow the relationship between interiors and exteriors, or do both at the same time.

Upon hearing the effeminate voice, Sandy recalls the cautionary narrative of the men in the pool hall: "But Sandy was beginning to understand. A warm sweat broke out on his neck and forehead. Sometimes, at the pool hall in Stanton, he had heard the men talk about queer fellows who stopped boys in the streets and tried to coax them to their rooms." For the first time in the novel, Sandy has a body of experience to draw on in order to make decisions about his sexuality. While pool hall narratives are designed to foreclose entrapment, Sandy's reaction works against the expected outcomes of such narratives. Instead of immediate revulsion, he feels curiosity: "Yet he wondered what such men did with the boys who accompanied them. Curious, he'd like to find out—but he was afraid." This fear of sexuality, through its parallel to Sandy's question to Uncle Dan about fear of slavery, is implicitly naive. In his question to Uncle Dan, Sandy sidestepped the issue of sexuality to focus on race. The issue of sexuality in that case was one of violently enforced heterosexuality. In the explicit confrontation with homosexuality, the issue of violence is constructed through narrative rather than physical practice. The pool hall narratives seem to ensure Sandy's revulsion, even if delayed, because his expression of curiosity is almost immediately disavowed: "The whining voice made him sick inside—and, almost without knowing it, his legs began swerving swiftly between the crowds along the curb" (*CW* 4:197). This is the first time in the novel that Sandy demonstrates the degree to

18. Bennett, "Multiple Passings and the Double Death of Langston Hughes," 687.

which he has assimilated the pool hall narratives. Immediately before his departure to Chicago, he still seems immune to such narratives in his experience with Pansetta. In Chicago, Sandy both recalls the narratives and uses them as the basis of action.

The fact that Hughes uses various forms of initiation in his works to explore masculine and feminine scripts as they relate to race is clear in two essays, "The Fascination of Cities" and "The Streets of Chicago," about his own initiation experiences in Chicago. In both he focuses on a very different kind of masculine initiation, physical violence. In "The Fascination of Cities," Hughes explains that he explored the streets of Chicago upon his arrival. When he wandered into an immigrant neighborhood, the boys informed him, "We don't 'low no niggers in this street." A fight ensued and, Hughes relates, "the lanky boy stuns me with a blow to the jaw. A shrill whistle brings the gang. Blows and counter-blows, oaths and kicks. We butt and fight and scratch" (*CW* 9:28). Over twenty years later, in "The Streets of Chicago," Hughes explained, "From the first week that I arrived in Chicago, I learned that it was a tough town. . . . Being a youngster who always liked to explore on my own, my first Sunday in town I went out walking. Not knowing any better I continued across State Street, past Wentworth, and on into what was then a Polish neighborhood. I had gone only a few blocks when I was set upon by a group of white boys who tripped me up, knocked me down, and beat me thoroughly. Then they chased me all the way back to the Negro area" (*CW* 9:327–28). This autobiographical account of a masculine initiation is clearly racially coded, while the fictional account is sexually coded, but they serve similar purposes despite their overt differences.

In contrast to Sandy's propositioning by a man, his next encounter with a young woman is more typical of what we have been taught to expect in sexual cautionary tales of the city. A young woman approaches Sandy outside the Monogram Theatre to buy her entrance ticket. The parallel to the man is clear, but in this instance there is no desire: "This time it was a girl—a very ugly, skinny girl, whose smile revealed a row of dirty teeth. She sidled up to the startled boy whom she had accosted and took his hand." After Sandy rejects the woman's dubious advance, "some men standing on the edge of the sidewalk laughed as Sandy went up the street" (*CW* 4:198). Such laughter seems to reinforce a specific kind of initiation into manhood, a successful initiation indeed. This initiation is a rejection of dependent women. Unlike with Sandy's encounter with the queer man, his revulsion is not qualified or culturally coerced. The laughter is approbation of a choice already made.

At the end of the novel, Sandy has achieved masculinity because he has assimilated the cautions and scripts of those around him. At the same time, there is room to doubt the efficacy of such narratives because they do not preclude curiosity. Such narratives instill awareness of the norms governing sexual behavior, for both men and women, and the consequences of transgressing such sexual boundaries. Sandy's two encounters in Chicago demonstrate the extent to which gender is performative. He learns stories about sexuality in the barbershop. For such stories to be effective, he has to assimilate them into his consciousness and rely on their parameters for action. Were Sandy to unquestioningly rely on such narratives, he would simply reproduce cultural norms. However, Hughes raises the possibility that such narratives could be assimilated without becoming scripts for action. If only momentarily, curiosity wins out over fear. With the woman at the Monogram, a group of men on the street reinforces appropriate masculine behavior through laughter. The laughter of the title is not only racially encoded. Its gender and sexual dimensions are equally if not explicitly key to understanding the importance of the novel. Laughter is not only a coping strategy for racial violence, it is also a regulatory instrument for enforcing sexual and gendered scripts.

What is at stake is the question of whether gender and sexuality are always hierarchical. In order to achieve masculine subjectivity, does a boy have to develop personal narratives about women as "degenerate female elements"? If heterosexual subjectivity is predicated on such an understanding of degeneracy, then any kind of heterosexual subjectivity forecloses the possibility of homosexual (or feminine) subjectivity. However, Harriett's characterization in *Not without Laughter* leaves the question of sexual subjectivity more open-ended. Gender performance is predicated on sexual subjectivity. To what extent is it possible for young boys to learn masculine scripts without assimilating them? Under what circumstances do young boys refuse to enact such scripts? When Sandy does not buy the woman's ticket, he asserts his wiseness to the scripts governing masculine behavior on the street. By the end of the novel, Sandy's masculinity is fully achieved.

Mother to Son

The Letters from Carrie Hughes Clark to Langston Hughes, 1928–1938

Regennia N. Williams and Carmaletta M. Williams

The advice and admonition given by the anonymous mother in Langston Hughes's well-known poem "Mother to Son" (1922) could easily have been recited by millions of African American women in predepression America encouraging their sons to strive for success. It is the story of hard times. Life becomes analogous to a house with tacks, splinters, and bare floors. There is none of the beauty and elegance of castles, none of the luxurious opulence that would include crystal stairs. But the narrator doesn't collapse under the sparseness and hardness of her life. Instead, she keeps "a-climbin' on," making progress through harsh and dark conditions. To conclude that Hughes wrote this poem about his relation with his mother, Carolina "Carrie" Langston Hughes,[1] would be too pat and largely inaccurate. It more closely represents the relationship between Hughes and his proud but very poor grandmother, Mary Leary Langston. Carrie's life was

---

1. Langston Hughes's mother was born Carolina Mercer Langston. In her adult life, she was alternately referred to as "Carolyn Hughes" (after her marriage to James Nathaniel Hughes, Langston's father), "Carolyn Hughes Clark" (after her divorce from Langston's father and marriage to Homer Clark), and "Carrie Clark." We will use "Carrie" throughout this essay.

no crystal stair, but most of the lessons Langston learned early in his life about striving for survival were taught by his grandmother.

Critical commentary on Carrie is mixed. She was a complex woman who lived a complicated life, and her relationship with her son reflected those complexities. Admittedly, Carrie had more than her share of trials and tribulations, and what is usually perceived as selfishness on her part can also be interpreted as exercising her survival instinct. Born Carolina Mercer Langston in Reconstruction-era Kansas, this theatrical, fun-loving, and usually cash-strapped mother spent most of her adult years in search of a better life away from her son.

It is Carrie's role as a mother to Langston that brings her character into question. Carrie gave birth to Langston in Joplin, Missouri, in 1902. Shortly afterward her husband, James N. Hughes, abandoned Carrie and the baby to seek a life free from the rigid, racial conditions in America that had not allowed him the opportunity to practice law or to make a successful living. He moved first to Cuba but found the freedom and economic opportunities he was searching for in Mexico. There, James Hughes practiced law, was a successful farmer, and made the money that he used in an attempt to control Langston's life. There was no money for Carrie that would allow her to control even her own life, let alone her son's. Life for Carrie had taken a much different road. When the stress of taking care of an infant with no money became too much for her, Carrie deposited the child with her mother. After her mother, Mary Leary Langston, died in 1915, Carrie did not rush to Lawrence, Kansas, to retrieve her then teenage son. Instead she kept traveling around the country searching for her errant new husband, Homer Clark, a better job, or another place to live, "where the rent was cheaper or there was at least a bathroom or a backyard to hang out clothes" (CW 13:53). Carrie's journeys carried her to Kansas, Missouri, Illinois, Ohio, New York, and Washington, D.C., among other places. She eventually spent many years of her adult life in depression-era Cleveland and Oberlin, Ohio.

In biographical and autobiographical essays, articles, and books about Langston, Carrie is presented all too often as the vagabond traveling mother who put her own interests ahead of her son's in her effort to "find herself" and a better life. Fortunately for him, there were other people in Langston's family who were important to his formation. What troubles our insights into Carrie's relationship with her son is the depth of influence of those people. Carrie's father and uncle were famous abolitionists. Her father, Charles Langston, rode with the God-provoked abolitionist John Brown, and, indeed, Langston recounted his pride in attending a program where his grandmother was recognized by President Teddy Roosevelt as one of the last surviving widows of the raid on Harpers Ferry. Carrie's uncle, John Mercer Langston, was the first African American elected to office. Later, she would live with his children, her first cousins, in Washington, D.C. Carrie's mother, Mary Leary Langston, part indigenous American and part African American, was the proud but poor matriarch with whom she left her infant son as she attempted to make her way through life. Carrie and Langston's family also included his underemployed stepfather, Homer Clark; his mischievous stepbrother, Gwyn "Kit" Clark; and his money-loving, self-hating father, James Nathaniel Hughes.

Langston's self-examination and documentation of his life in relation to the other family members, and his willingness to contribute his voluminous correspondence to the James Weldon Johnson Manuscript Collection at Yale University, have made it possible for others to reappraise his life and work since his death in 1967. One popular theme in these reappraisals is the impact of the frequent absences of his mother and the differing views critics have reached on the mother/son relationship when Carrie and Langston were together.

In reflecting on his youth, Langston confesses that his feelings about his divorced and still bitter parents were problematic. He came to understand that his father hated Negroes, and by extension himself as well as Langston and Carrie. On his fateful trip to pick up Langston in Chicago and carry him to Mexico, James disparagingly referred to neighborhood folk as "niggers." As a consequence Langston came to know that he did not love his father; in fact, he admitted hating him. His relationship with his mother was not that clear. The letters reveal Carrie's very obvious manipulation of Langston for money, and a son who fell prey to that manipulation out of love for his mother. Hughes did, however, attempt to carve a place for himself in Carrie's life by pointing out the similarities between them. He went to great lengths to make note of his mother's love for the arts and entertainment and the fact that she always tried to have a "good time" after working hours. In this regard, mother and son were very much alike. There is evidence that Langston's hatred for his father was enough to make him physically ill; in *The Big Sea*, for example, he described faking an illness to keep from going to Mexico City with his father and later remaining in a hospital needlessly because it was costing his father twenty dollars a day. Life with his father was so unhappy for the young Langston that he even considered suicide but changed his mind out of fear of missing something. The hate and indifference so deeply affected Langston that even in the hour of the father's death he remained distant. There is also abundant evidence in Carrie's personal letters to Langston to support biographer Arnold Rampersad's contention that, even as a child and throughout their infamously combative adult years, "Langston was his mother's son in his passion for the theater and the road."[2] But their relationship ran much deeper than that. The letters also reveal that Carrie was her son's mother in her determination to survive, even when survival meant relying on the support of family and friends.

While the nearly one hundred and thirty pages of written correspondence from Carrie to Langston are but a tiny part of his manuscript collection, they are important as primary sources for researchers interested in the social history of twentieth-century African American women. Carrie's letters provide a better understanding of Langston's relationships with the women in his life as well as a firsthand account of life throughout the Midwest, but particularly in two Ohio communities, from the vantage point of a working-class woman.[3]

What is significant about these letters is the manner in which Carrie establishes and reveals the relationship between herself and Langston. In *The Big Sea*, Langston wrote of the personal sacrifices he made, like going hungry, to help his mother. In reading the letters, it becomes clear that Carrie either didn't know of his sacrifices or ignored them for her personal gain. The tone of the letters is also interesting. In an almost begging posture, Carrie manipulates Langston with guilt and love into helping her. In a letter dated October 29, 1928, Carrie announces her desire to attend the "39th meeting of the Interstate Literary Society of Kansas and the West." Langston recalled in his autobiography his mother's attachment to this organization, which was founded by her father, Charles Langston, in 1891. The conference was scheduled for December 28–30, 1928, in Lawrence, Kansas—the place she described as "home." Carrie makes several confessions in this letter. She follows her earlier pattern by informing Langston that she can't take him with her. Her compromise is that she can

2. Rampersad, *The Life of Langston Hughes, Volume 1: 1902–1941, I, Too, Sing America,* 12.

3. In recent years, the debate about Langston's relationships with women has frequently focused on his sexual orientation, with some writers insisting that he was gay or bisexual, since there is evidence to suggest that he had both heterosexual and homosexual experiences. Others suggest that he was asexual, desiring intimacy with neither men nor women. For a brief discussion of some of these issues, see Rampersad, *Life,* vol. 1, and Devon W. Carbado et al., eds., *Black Like Us: A Century of Lesbian, Gay, and Bisexual African American Fiction,* 56–57. See, in this volume, the essays by Juda Bennett, John Edgar Tidwell, and Kimberly Banks.

take his books and sell them and possibly "do well with them." What she doesn't say is whether she will use the money for her own needs or send it on to Langston. Carrie lets us into the depths of their relationship by revealing that they "never agree." She begs:

> Instead of giving me an xmas present could you give me $15.00 between now and then on a coat? Oh! Langston you don't know how bad I want to go to the meeting. I'd love to take you, but I can take your books, and sell them there and I know I'd do well with them. Dear Heart we never agree on anything, but please be interested in this. . . .
>
> Dear, why don't you love me, why aren't we more loving and chummy, why don't you ever confide in me. I know I have no sense to help you in your work but I'd enjoy your confiding. Now Langston, I have no one else to talk to. You will agree with me and help me if you can?[4]

Her emotional manipulations are obvious. She begins by pleading her case: how much she wants to go and how little she needs to get there, only fifteen dollars for a new coat. In the second paragraph she switches to emotional guilt by blaming Langston for the problems in their relationship, accusing him of not loving her and charging him with responsibility for the distance in their relationship, for their not being "loving and chummy." Then Carrie becomes the victim. She portrays herself as lonely and isolated with no one other than Langston to even talk with. Her voice softens at the end as she asks him to agree to help her. This almost shameless manipulation ends when she promises never to bother him again with requests for money if he helps her out this time. Carrie closes this letter by reminding Langston that he would also benefit from a trip to Kansas for this purpose, since the "learned men of the U.S." that his grandfather had organized would have a chance to see his work. "I'd be so proud of you," she insists. Then she expands her market and possibly her income: "Could I sell copies of your songs out there too? Write. Yours, Mother."

This letter, sent from a New York address to Langston, who was then a student at Lincoln University in Pennsylvania, illustrates Carrie's flair for the dramatic, her desire to live a full life, her need to interact with "the better class of colored people," and the requests for money that would

4. Letters from Carrie to Langston, along with other Hughes correspondence, are in the James Weldon Johnson Collection, which is part of the Yale Collection of American Literature, Beinecke Rare Book and Manuscript Library, Yale University. When the city and / or state is given in the original letters, that information is also included here.

come to characterize most of her correspondence with Langston until her death in 1938. What it does not reveal is that Langston was living off a modest allowance sent to him by Charlotte Osgood Mason. If he sent Carrie the money she requested, he would not have any for himself. Also noteworthy is Carrie's compromise. She was always willing to support her son's writing career. This is, perhaps, the most important revelation to emerge from her letters. Carrie demanded a lot from her son, but she was also quite capable of sharing what she had with him, as Langston would discover when he moved into her tiny basement apartment in Cleveland in 1930. According to Langston, "My mother then lived in three rooms in a basement on Carnegie Avenue, with my step-father and my brother. Very kindly my mother gave me the only bed and they slept on the davenport. My brother stayed with some cousins, because we had only two sleeping rooms and a kitchen" (CW 13:247).

In a 1929 letter, Carrie used the matter of her "generosity" to draw an important distinction between herself and Langston's father:

Well, so you again heard from Mexico. Of course your father has also seen of your success. I am glad. You will answer those old souls of course. . . . I am of the opinion that God has been very, very good to you and I, even though we have been wicked, he has blessed us wonderfully. Just to think, although I have had to work hard, glad I could, I lived to be very, very, exceedingly happy to see you graduate.

The reference to hard work is significant, because it is so appropriate in any considerations of Carrie. Based on evidence provided by mother, son, and others, the adult Carrie worked as a waitress, a nanny, and an actress, among other things, and she expected other family members to work just as hard and to help take care of her when she was not working.[5] This is one of several dominant and recurring themes in Carrie's letters to her son: (1) family ties and the importance of friends and functional kin; (2) African American institutions and organizations, including literary societies and churches; (3) education for both her son and her stepson; (4) success and employment; (5) cultural and other amenities in small towns and big cities; (6) Carrie's emotional and physical health; and (7) money, or the lack thereof. Carrie repeatedly voices all these concerns and, in the process, ensures that they are always on Langston's mind and in his budget.

Money was, it appears, a constant concern for both mother and son.

5. See CW 13:35, 39; Rampersad, Life, 1:9; Carrie to Langston, February 15, [1933], and [March, 1935].

When Carrie lived in or near Cleveland in the 1930s, the city where Langston spent his high school years was in the depths of an economic depression. Residential segregation became more rigid, as racism, unemployment, and poverty combined to create an African American ghetto on the city's eastside.[6] Writing to her son, who was away in Russia with a troupe of would-be movie stars,[7] on September 19, 1932, Carrie said:

> This is the worse [sic] depression U.S. ever had, people are just committing suicide for fun . . . the charities are overcrowded, plenty foreigners who can't even speak English, crowding to get food. The law cannot make anyone pay rent and all teachers have not been paid part still owed for last year.

And, on a more personal note:

> No, after Homer lost his job we did not take $15.00 to send Gwyn to summer school, because that was all we had until someone got work, as yet, none of us have made nothing.

Constant unemployment seemed the bane of Carrie's life. Both she and her second husband, Homer Clark, were constantly out of work. Because he continually needed to search for employment, Homer repeatedly abandoned Carrie. It appears that each time he left she fell into direr straits, which precipitated her leaning financially more on Langston. Carrie, however, refused to let it keep her down. Although no one in the household had a job, Carrie wrote that she was grateful for the family car. "[I]t is good for driving to the Employment Offices. . . . If I don't get work I will have to drive to Russia." Carrie's threat to go to Russia in search of employment contained as much truth as exaggeration, since job searches for Carrie and Homer Clark had taken the family to many places in Illinois, Kansas, Ohio, and other states. If it had been possible for her to drive to Russia to join Langston for a better life, Carrie would likely have tried.

Yet, even in the midst of great suffering, Carrie's letters reveal her zeal for life and an interesting, if unusual, sense of humor, both on and off stage, mixed with her appeal for money. On the road as a cast member in a play, Carrie wrote Langston from the Garrick Theatre in Philadelphia in 1932:

---

6. See Kenneth L. Kusmer, *A Ghetto Takes Shape: Black Cleveland, 1870–1930,* esp. chaps. 10 and 11.

7. On the ill-fated Soviet film project, see Rampersad, *Life,* 1:242–51.

My dearest I am sending you a Philly clipping. We opened last night with a wonderful house. I hope that you will get to see the show while I am with it. I want you to send the money to Gwyn next time, and I think you need not send but $12.00 this time as I will take care of the rest. After I get a start I can get along o.k., I think, but this month I had lots to do and I was bare for clothes and must finish my debts. Just help me out awhile. I don't like to ask you to do so much, I must try to send $10 to get Homer to Oberlin, so he can cook for Gwyn.

The show was *Run Little Chillun,* a musical written by the celebrated African American composer and choral conductor Hall Johnson. It appears that this show was one of the few truly bright moments in the last years of Carrie's life. In February 1933, one letter proclaimed, "Yes, your mother is an actress at last. The dream I dreamed as a little child is very near realized. I am one of the principals in Hall Johnson's show *Run Little Chillun.*"[8]

By March, her enthusiasm was diminished somewhat, but not completely, by the depression. The country's dire financial condition was affecting the show, but Carrie sounds a bit relieved to reveal that she is still making money. However, she does not allow that fact to free Langston from any financial obligation to her, informing him that her pay is not enough to assure her financial security. She wrote from New York: "As the show opened, the banks closed. Everything seemed against us, but we are fighting on with a cast of 175, and the cast was cut today to 125 plenty." On November 14, 1933, she wrote from the Shubert Theatre in Newark, New Jersey, that she was still on the job, but not quite ready to declare her financial independence: "I hope we can do some good so I can make a little money. It has been so tight with me these last two years." Carrie found little comfort in the fact that millions of Americans shared her depression-era misery. President Franklin D. Roosevelt's promise of a "New Deal" for the American people was just coming into being, and the first round of programs designed to bring about "relief, reform and recovery" was only then being implemented.[9]

Carrie returned to Oberlin, a community reeling from three solid years

8. For a brief discussion of *Run Little Chillun* in the history of American musical theater, see Langston Hughes and Milton Meltzer, *Black Magic: A Pictorial History of the Negro in American Entertainment.*

9. On the particular experiences of African Americans during the Great Depression, see Harvard Sitkoff, *A New Deal for Blacks: The Emergence of Civil Rights as a National Issue, Volume I: The Depression Decade.*

of depression by the fall of 1933, but neither promises from the president nor the bright lights and several months of work with *Run Little Chillun* had lifted her financial burdens. She still had high hopes, however, for the education of her stepson, Gwyn, and for jobs for the adults in the family. The car that earlier she was so grateful to have for visits to the unemployment office had apparently disappeared, as had Homer.

> Dear Son, We have moved and as yet have no gas, but will get along o.k. until we can get it. . . . Langston, I walked everywhere yesterday trying to find a job, but as yet have none. . . . Gwyn worked today, will get most of his books . . . . Have not heard a word from Dad. . . . I went up to the library and read your story in Scribner. It sure was good. Oh! I want work so bad, but don't know what to do.

Here, Carrie introduces the possibility of marital problems and abandonment by Homer (Dad). In another instance she wrote on February 15, 1933, "Dad is crazy. I do not know what he will do. He just stays out there & does not send us a thing nor write. I am just sick of everything so I don't bother." After 1933, Carrie's letters rarely present Homer in a positive light.

Although Carrie consistently began her letters to the adult Langston by asserting her authority over him as his mother and reducing him to child status with "My Dearest Boy," "My Own Boy," "My Dear Boy," "My Baby Boy," and similar salutations, her pleas for support suggest that she saw her son increasingly after 1933 as a replacement for Homer. The support she asks from him places him in the roles of a surrogate father for Gwyn and a financial and emotional substitute for her missing husband.[10] Even when she wrote on April 12, 1934, that she had recently received word from Homer, her letter contained a thinly veiled request for bus fare to get Homer to a place where he might find employment. She suggested that her son "do as you think best and can" for his stepfather.

In considering Carrie's ties to other family members, it is important to note that while she frequently called upon Langston for financial assistance, like other African Americans of the time she also came to rely on the kindness and generosity of members of her extended family for basic creature comforts. Before the end of 1933, Carrie wrote:

> Cousin Lucy has given us an oil stove that does fine now. Every one of the relatives are lovely to us and are all wanting you for dinner Thanks-

---

10. See, for example, the following letters from Carrie to Langston: [Oct. 18, 1934]; November 1, [1934]; March 29, [1935]; and [May 14, 1935].

giving. Oberlin people are very proud of you. Oh, I cannot tell you how I thank you, and if I can get work, you won't have to do so much. I am praying every day for a job.

Langston and Carrie were also the beneficiaries of the hospitality of non-relatives, including "Aunt Toy," Ethel Dudley Brown Harper—described by Rampersad as "a friend from Carrie's Kansas days"—and her husband, Emerson, when the Hugheses resided in New York.[11]

New York, especially Harlem, was the cultural capital of black America. Carrie was very much aware of shifting cultural conditions for black Americans. As a reminder of the ever-present threat of violence and court-sanctioned injustice facing African Americans, Carrie wrote in an undated letter of the plight of the "Scottsboro Boys," who had been accused of raping two white women at knifepoint in 1931. With the exception of the youngest, all had been sentenced to death by an all-white jury.[12] "It is all a graft," Carrie wrote. "Now everyone is trying to get money, Scottsboro boys! And most all of it the poor boys don't even get a 'smell.' But I don't believe anything will get them out but God, and he will have to destroy every jail in Alabama."

The Scottsboro case was one of the most infamous in the early twentieth-century South, attracting attention and support from such disparate groups as the National Association for the Advancement of Colored People (NAACP) and the Communist Party.[13] As the objects of international consciousness-raising and fund-raising campaigns for their legal defense, the Scottsboro Boys became celebrities in their own right. Langston visited Alabama during his 1931–1932 southern book tour, read poetry to the imprisoned "Boys," and wrote about their plight, even though Carrie begged her son to stay away from Alabama and the Scottsboro case and reminded him that her entire church congregation was praying that he would.[14]

By early 1934, Carrie had turned her attention from southern racism to other major problems facing African Americans: a shortage of affordable

11. Rampersad, *Life*, 1:124, 312.

12. See Sitkoff, *A New Deal for Blacks*, 145–46.

13. On the NAACP's reaction to Scottsboro, see David Levering Lewis, *W. E. B. Du Bois: The Fight for Equality and the American Century, 1919–1963*, 256–65.

14. On Langston's activities in Alabama and writings on Scottsboro, see Rampersad, *Life*, 1:218–19, 224, 229–31, 235, 238, 246, 283–85, 344; and Emily Bernard, ed., *Remember Me to Harlem: The Letters of Langston Hughes and Carl Van Vechten, 1925–1964*, 91–104.

community health care services and the pathological behavior that many young people were engaging in:

> I have had a throat trouble for about three weeks. I do not know what it is but when I get paid [I] can go to Cleveland, I will go to the Clinic, there is none here, and find out. It is $2 round trip on bus to Cleveland and with my food and rent, gas & eats and Gwyn I can't get nothing yet to spare but hope to soon. Oh! if I was just at work somewhere. These times are terrible. Just making bums, desperadoes, and gangsters out of the young people. . . . But Langston, neighbors, relatives and all have been so kind to me.[15]

That Cleveland offered services that were not readily available to Oberlin residents became a major concern for Carrie after she was diagnosed with breast cancer and had to move back to Cleveland to receive treatment. Cleveland was, according to the 1930 census, the nation's sixth largest city. During the depression, it was home to some of the highest unemployment and some of the best publicly and privately financed relief efforts. In time, Carrie would benefit from both types of relief.[16]

That the economic downturn was driving many people to desperation was something of which Carrie and Langston were painfully aware. While his mother reacted with a sense of hopelessness, Langston's writing began to reflect his growing radicalism and concern that capitalism had failed miserably to provide a safety net for unemployed American workers and their families.[17]

Reading Carrie's letters from the late fall of 1934, one has to wonder whether her priorities were in need of the same kind of radical reordering that Langston envisioned for the American government relief programs. In the beginning of a letter dated October 1, 1934, she wrote from Oberlin requesting "a few dollars to catch up" on payments for groceries and gas. Later in the same letter, she asks for money to travel to Cleveland to see *Green Pastures*, one of the few all–African American musicals still making money and, to Langston's dismay, playing before segregated audiences. "I want to go," she pleaded. "[C]ould you send me enough to go on? If you have it, if not o.k., but I do want to see it so bad. Write me at

15. Carrie to Langston, April 12, 1934.

16. Carol Poh Miller and Robert A. Wheeler, *Cleveland: A Concise History, 1796–1996*, 2d ed., 131–38.

17. For more on an especially radical period in Langston's life, see Rampersad's discussion of his activities in 1934 in *Life*, 1:284–95.

once." Carrie seems to be letting Langston off the financial hook when she says that it's all right if he doesn't have the money, then she pulls him right back on to it with her plea of how badly she wants to see the play. Her voice shifts again as she demands that he respond "at once."

Yet letters from the following month indicate that Carrie was able to differentiate between wants and needs—and to consider someone's feelings besides her own. It was a thoughtful and forgiving Carrie who wrote to Langston in November following the death of her first husband and Langston's father, James Nathaniel Hughes, even as she continued to insist that Langston "belonged" to her:

> I am so sorry to hear of James' death. All of the misunderstandings are now wiped away, and I sorrow much at his passing. Can't help it, as he, after all, counting everything was your father, the father of the only being in the world, that really belongs to me.

Her last statement in claiming Langston as "the only being in the world, that really belongs to [her]" is a bit problematic. After all, there was "Kit" to consider. Arguably, Carrie saw Langston as solely hers because Kit came with Homer. Langston tells us in the *Big Sea* of his joy in being reunited with Carrie after his grandmother's death and his time living with people who functioned as his relatives, the Reeds. He says that his mother "had married a chef cook named Homer Clark" who couldn't stand the heat of the kitchen, so he worked at a series of odd jobs and "by now [Langston] had a little brother" (*CW* 13:44). When Carrie traipsed around the country following Homer, Kit was always in tow. This was quite different from her relationship with Langston, who as a young child was left with relatives. But after Langston's reunion with Carrie, Homer, and Kit, Carrie often left the teenage Langston alone. Carrie talks about needing money to send to Homer so that he can come cook for Kit, yet Langston reveals his self-cooked meals of hotdogs and rice. Carrie's relationships with her sons were obviously different, arguably because Kit had Homer.

The holidays immediately following James's death were especially trying for the family. Financially the death had no effect as James had cut off Langston emotionally and financially after Langston informed him that he was quitting Columbia University. After that, James not only did not send any more money, he also never again wrote Langston. James's death, in which he left Langston nothing in his will, worked an emotional hardship on an already emotionally strained family. Carrie admits the stress in a letter in which she acknowledges that Langston is having a tough emotional time, too. She also voices her feelings about Oberlin. When she applied for public assistance, the fact that Carrie had established only semi-transient residence there came back to haunt her. She was told at the end of November that "no relief is available to non-residents of Oberlin." Out of frustration she wrote on January 14, 1935:

> Langston, I think the strain is too much for you and it is becoming too much for me. . . . I never want to read anything ever about Oberlin. If I ever get away from it, I'll wash my hands of it forever. It [is] the narrowest, "confound it," talking, lying, meanest, contemptible hole in God's whole country. Oberlin, Eh! I hate the whole name—I've had more trouble, more worry, more everything here. No more for me.

She then shifts from a self-focus back to considering the feelings of her son. She adds, "Sad about Wallace Thurman and Rudolph Fisher's death. Poor Boys," demonstrating that she is not so obsessed with her own problems that she fails to notice the passing of two of Langston's Harlem Renaissance literary associates.

Many Roosevelt New Dealers held out the hope that 1935 would be the year of the American worker. In fact, millions would receive important assistance with the creation of the Works Projects Administration (WPA) and the passage of the Social Security Act. While Carrie did not benefit immediately from the make-work programs of the WPA or the retirement benefits authorized by the Social Security Act, some economic relief had come her way by the time that she wrote the following on January 15, 1935:

> Well, I am now to my humiliation and embarrassment on government relief. . . . Now I can get eats and coal—no rent or gas or light—The poor is supposed to live without either. Ha! Ha! . . . I get salt pork and bacon, which I can't eat, as I have no teeth. . . . I am old, I can get the old age pension soon, a few years, but I am willing to try to make it or go to the poor house one.

Even in the family's impoverished state, Carrie lamented that Gwyn was still "wild." "He wants wine, women, and song," she wrote. What he got, however, was a job in Cleveland, which allowed him to rent living quarters in the city's Collinwood community. According to Carrie in a letter dated March 29, 1935, Gwyn and his friend were determined to live on their own and refused to allow her to live with them, even after her offers to act as housekeeper. Two weeks later, on April 15, a dejected Carrie considered the other options available to her, while trying to shame Langston into giving her more money, including the subtle emotional ploy of replacing him with another child:

> Maybe later I could get a welfare child, and I would not be alone all the time. They pay $4 per week, and I could live on $12 per month with relief food. . . . I must have somewhere, or go to the county farm. I'd hate to do that, for I am your mother and everyone knows it and I don't want to hurt you.

It is surprising that Carrie resorted to this kind of manipulation so late in life, given that Langston had readily contributed to the household finances since he was a teenager, often with funds from an allowance sent from Mexico by his father. Carrie, whose work record clearly shows that she was not lazy, never seemed to understand that Langston's fame was not always accompanied by fortune.

In May 1935, Carrie received alarming news when she was diagnosed with breast cancer. Although the deathblow from the disease would not be delivered for three years, almost immediately Carrie's letters began to speak of illness, mortality, and loneliness as much as they spoke of jobs and money. This is especially true of the letter in which she broke the news to Langston: "I have a very bad blood tumor on my breast. . . . I'd love to have you just a little while once in my life."

The 1930s were trying for both Carrie and Langston. In addition to the personal and financial problems detailed in Carrie's letters, Langston's public career suffered because of his growing radicalism; these problems resulted from, in part, his publication of the poem "Goodbye Christ," which sparked protests in several communities and would come back to haunt him in later years. Carrie's correspondence suggested, however, that she still knew her son better than did many of his critics. In June 1935, she wrote that a local preacher said, "[A] certain Negro writer, a poet says there is no Christ. It was real funny, he was talking of you." But the family, it seemed, was still in Langston's corner and still interested in what he had to say for himself: "We have cousins in Detroit, who want to know where you'll speak," Carrie wrote in the same letter, reminding Hughes that family still mattered.

Carrie's need to keep in touch with family and to know that someone cared became more urgent as her health declined. On one occasion, she described being held up by two "confidence men" while coming from a doctor's appointment in Cleveland. Carrie wrote Langston to say that although the men "scared her out of six weeks' growth," they didn't get any money, because she didn't have any. Carrie becomes self-depreciating, and her tone softens toward Langston and seems to be more considerate of him as a person instead of just an easily manipulated money machine. Emotionally, their relationship seems to have come full circle to the time of just the grown-up Carrie and her baby, Langston. There is no mention of Homer or Kit in a letter written on the day after Christmas 1935, which illustrates how desperately the downhearted Carrie needed reassurance and money from Langston, even though she had worked on Christmas Eve and Christmas day:

> It was great to get the telegram [and the money] after all you have done. I am not worthy of half your sweetness, I am just an old cranky, worrying soul. No good to anyone much—But I am so proud of you and so fond of you. You are my very life. I know no interest scarcely outside of you and how you are and how you get on and all. I know you are so very lovely to me, but Langston it hurts to take for I don't want to deprive you of what you need.

> The year is only a few days from closing and I am just thinking that one year ago, I was well and working. Now I am hurt, not much good, no work or money—no good.

With her sense of security severely shaken and her medical bills mounting, Carrie found temporary shelter at the Phillis Wheatley Home for two dollars and fifty cents per week.[18] This residential facility for women had been founded earlier in the century by Jane Edna Hunter, a leading African American clubwoman and renowned community activist. One letter to Langston from 1936 describes in great detail the dire financial situation in which the ailing Carrie found herself. She claims a coownership of Langston's money, referring to his savings as theirs. Carrie also indicates that she still believes she can be of service to Langston, even if the service is secretarial:

> I will get a room at the Phillys Wheatly [sic] for $2.50 per week. Then I will go out every day for a treatment. A pass will cost me $1.25 per week and the treatments will be $15.00—12 x-ray. I may not need the 12 but must pay the $15.00. . . . Now send the money at once by Thursday any way. I have to start treatments at once. . . .

18. Carrie to Langston, January 1936. For additional information on the Phillis Wheatley Association, see Jane Edna Hunter, *A Nickel and a Prayer.*

Now Langston you wanted this done. Dr. said out of the clinic it would cost me $100.00. So you see what we saved . . .

P.S.
I arranged about your mail. No more has come for you.

Although the letters, with their emphasis on the relationship between Langston and Carrie, make no mention of the rest of her family, in later correspondence it is clear that both Carrie and Gwyn continued to reap benefits from having a famous writer for a son and brother.

Carrie was proud of Langston's artistic successes but doesn't seem to have given his work a very close read. Hughes confessed that *Not without Laughter* is a semi-autobiographical novel, and Stanton is clearly a fictionalized version of Lawrence, Kansas. Although they are both traveling men and frequently abandon their families, Homer Clark has none of the romantic attributes of Jimboy, whose life is defined by music; however, Mary Langston cared for her grandson Langston as deeply as Aunt Hager cares for Sandy. The three sisters, Tempy, Harriett, and Anjee, definitely represent different aspects of Carrie. Tempy is the Carrie who could write her son and beg for money to go to a literary society meeting, where she had recited her poetry and hoped to do so again. She's the Carrie who carried her little son to the vine-covered libraries in Topeka where he fell in love with libraries and librarians; and she's the Carrie who was still impressed with the "important" people her father knew. Harriett is the Carrie who loved performing on the stage, was serious about her acting, and loved to be in front of an audience. She was also the Carrie who spent some of her hard-earned money partying on paydays. Annjee is the Carrie who followed her man from town to town without hesitating to leave her young son at home with her mother. She is the Carrie who was incensed when Langston wanted to go away to college when she was "there working like a dog" (*CW* 13:64). If she had seen the similarities, Carrie would not have written in February 1936 to request two autographed copies of *Not without Laughter*. She wanted to share those copies with "important" people in her life: "I want to give them to my doctor and nurse . . . both know you."

Carrie also maintained connections with important people in the arts. She sent another letter the following month to announce that "Gwyn got a job today also through Mr. Jelliffe," the cofounder of Cleveland's Karamu House Theatre. Russell Jelliffe and his wife, Rowena, were among the earliest and most consistent supporters of Langston's career, and he spent a significant amount of time in Cleveland—at Karamu and with Carrie—in 1936.

In 1937, as her health continued to deteriorate, Carrie still tried her hand at mothering her then thirty-five-year-old son. In a letter filled with grammatical errors, most likely as a result of her cancer treatments, she warned him to stay out of wartorn Madrid, Spain, where he was serving as a correspondent for several African American newspapers, and then made a subtle plea for money.

> I can't bear for you to be over in that war zone. I am so worried. Won't you leave there? Just think what it means to hear every day that Madrid is bomed [*sic*] and surrounded with troops ect. . . . When I pay next rent (Sept) I'll have about $10.00—But Langston please come out of Madrid. Please do this for me, for I am just worried sick.

Another letter, dated August 22, expressed relief that she now knew (thanks to a wire from Noel Sullivan) that Langston was not "prison barred in Spain" and warned him never to worry her that way again: "Langston don't go to foreign countries like things are now and not write," she pleaded.[19]

The depression continued to take its toll on Carrie, but it also created somewhat regular employment for Gwyn. According to her 1937 letters, "Kit" was often away at "camp" working for the Civilian Conservation Corps.[20] Thus, there were fewer requests for money from Langston to buy Kit's books and clothes.

One of the last letters from Carrie to Langston speaks volumes about how the lives of mother and son had become intertwined. References to the fact that she had given his address to a reporter from the *Plain Dealer*—a major daily newspaper in Cleveland—who apparently needed to get in touch with Langston right away indicate that she saw herself caring for him, at least in a business sense. There were also statements regarding checks received and deposited by Carrie into his bank account, including payments from the *Afro-American* for $50.00 and the American Society of Composers for $27.50. The letter also states that she was forwarding some of Langston's mail. She continued to track and support his career and included her comments on the Shanghai edition of *Not without Laughter*: "It is the most comical looking book with your picture on the back and front." Surprisingly, however, she did not ask for money. While

19. Noel Sullivan was Langston's trusted friend and patron from the early 1930s on. See Rampersad, *Life*, esp. 1:276–305.
20. Carrie to Langston, [November 3, 1937].

the letter is dated simply "January 20th," it was certainly written during the depression, since *Not without Laughter* was not completed until 1930. This omission of the year, though, is noteworthy in that it is uncharacteristic of Carrie's long history of writing for support of various kinds.

On February 3, 1938, two days after Langston's thirty-sixth birthday, Carrie wrote to wish her son "all the happiness in the world," since she "was not well enough to go out for a card." Again, she did not ask for additional money, but she did acknowledge that she had already received some by simply mentioning that she would "make the money go far as it will." It is also important to note that Carrie disavowed having ever used the money purely for selfish reasons: "It's not for me it's been or being used—I never have none for myself. It's for bills, bills,—Rent, etc. It will last I think. If not it will be ok." After informing Langston that she had "6 months," that the St. James African Methodist Episcopal Church had burned down, and that her arm was "almost so I can't use it at all anymore," she closed this letter with "Yours truly—lovingly Mother." Exactly four months later, on Friday, June 3, 1938, Carrie died at Deaconess Hospital in Manhattan.

Carrie's letters document clear changes in her mood and her actions from 1928 to 1938. In 1928, she had finally accepted the reality of her son's career as a writer, and in 1938 she remained convinced that Langston had a responsibility to care for her, even as he enjoyed his publicly successful although not particularly lucrative writing career. The letters also clearly document the fact that Carrie followed her son's career and supported him by receiving and forwarding his mail; passing along information on inquiries about interviews and speaking engagements; packing and shipping to him clothing, stories, and other documents left in her care in Ohio; and on occasion handling his banking. These letters also demonstrate a strong yet troubled relationship between mother and son, a relationship that neither of them was able or willing to change.

By the last year of her life, the woman who had worked at any number of odd jobs—and even cooked and cleaned for friends and relatives when she couldn't afford to pay rent to live in their homes—was no longer willing or able to continue a lonely struggle against overwhelming social and economic conditions. After Carrie succumbed to cancer, her loving, dutiful, and famous but not wealthy son made sure that she had a nice funeral, although he had to borrow money to pay for it.[21]

21. Bernard, ed., *Remember Me to Harlem*, 42; Rampersad, *Life*, 1:360–61.

Carrie's letters assure her place in American social history, as surely as Langston's work assures him a place in literary history. In *A Shining Thread of Hope*, historian Darlene Clark Hine suggests that thousands of wartime migrants like Carrie, who came to Ohio just as Langston started high school in 1916, "carried their freedom bags" to northern urban areas like Cleveland. They searched for a better life for themselves and their families. Frequently "better" meant a life that was more financially rewarding. Unfortunately for Carrie and thousands of others, "they faced almost two decades of digging in and hanging on, of basic survival and sheer endurance." Fortunately, Carrie had a son who was willing to sacrifice so that he could help with her day-to-day expenses during the closing years of her life.[22]

Carrie often comes across as greedy, selfish, and manipulative in her correspondence with Langston and in accounts provided by others.[23] However, we must read more closely and listen to the voices. The letters also reveal her as proud and hardworking. Theirs was no idyllic relationship. It had no chance to become so. From the time James Hughes abandoned them in Joplin, their relationship was one of struggling to remain connected in an emotional sense. Sometimes this connection seemed to be rooted in a mother's manipulation and a son's acquiescence to her demands. But the manipulations served a real purpose for both of them. Carrie was able to reclaim and hold on to the role of Langston's mother, the role she had transferred to her mother when her son was an infant. And Langston was able to reclaim the mother that he so desperately needed, the mother who had come to represent the instability in his life. In the final analysis, neither of their lives was a crystal stair. Carrie's life appears to have had more tacks and bare spots than Langston's, but neither gave up. Neither sat down and accepted failure. Langston Hughes has earned a piece of immortality as the "people's poet." Carrie's life, in both its positive and its negative aspects, stands as an example to all women. Her life and work in the early decades of the twentieth century, as revealed in her letters, help to explain, if not excuse, her actions in those financially difficult days of the 1930s.

22. Hine with Kathleen Thompson, *A Shining Thread of Hope: The History of Black Women in America*, 239.

23. According to Langston's longtime friend Arna Bontemps, "She kept him terribly broke, you see, so that sometimes I had to lend him money. . . . She imagined that he was rich" (quote from a 1972 oral history interview in Rampersad, *Life*, 1:319).

III

Revolutions Literary and Political

"Luani of the Jungles"

Reimagining the Africa of *Heart of Darkness*

Jeffrey A. Schwarz

First published by Wallace Thurman in his new magazine *Harlem* in 1928, Langston Hughes's "Luani of the Jungles" tells the story of a European man who falls in love with an African woman and subsequently moves to West Africa to live with her in her African community. Hughes wrote this story after his experiences as a sailor on the American freighter SS *Malone*,[1] which sailed to the west coast of Africa in the summer of 1923. While Hughes's African voyage clearly influenced the writing of "Luani," he was preparing for both his journey and his story before his enlistment on the Africa-bound freighter.

In October 1922, prior to his African voyage, Hughes signed onboard the freighter SS *West Hassayampa* as a mess boy, only to discover that the freighter would merely be traveling up the Hudson River. Although initially dismayed at the prospect of remaining on the Hudson, Hughes took the opportunity to absorb ship culture and to read. In his autobiography *The Big Sea,* he noted that during the winter of 1922, while serving on this ship, he read Joseph Conrad's *Heart of Darkness,* which was in the ship's

1. In his autobiography *The Big Sea,* Hughes refers to the Africa-bound freighter on which he served as the SS *Malone,* and most Hughes biographers use that name for the ship. However, in his biography Arnold Rampersad refers to the ship as the SS *West Hesseltine* (*The Life of Langston Hughes: Volume I, 1902–1941: I, Too, Sing America,* 71–81).

library (*CW* 13:92). While Hughes's reading of *Heart of Darkness* may have influenced his decision to travel to Africa, it certainly affected "Luani of the Jungles."[2] In *The Life of Langston Hughes*, Arnold Rampersad notes the effects that *Heart of Darkness* and the African American political scene had on Hughes's conceptions of Africa before his voyage there in 1923:

> As a child Hughes had dreamed of exploring its forbidding jungles and mighty kingdoms. Over the winter he had struggled with the Africa of Conrad's *Heart of Darkness*, consoling himself with Jessie Fauset's confirmation that Conrad was very difficult reading indeed. He knew of Dr. Du Bois's gallant if futile efforts, through the meetings of his Pan African Congress in 1919 and 1921, and scheduled again for that year, 1923, to alter the destructive patterns of European imperialism which had despoiled Africa; certainly Hughes also knew about Marcus Garvey's hope to return blacks from America to Africa.[3]

With all of these things in mind, Hughes traveled to Africa to see for himself the continent to which he felt so connected. Upon arriving on the west coast of Africa, Hughes observed, "The white man dominates Africa. He takes produce, and lives, very much as he chooses. The yield of the earth for Europe and America. The yield of men for Europe's colonial armies" (*CW* 13:95). Finally, after seeing Africa and its political climate for himself, Hughes wrote "Luani of the Jungles."

Through this story, Hughes rewrote and revised *Heart of Darkness*, critiquing Conrad's racist novel and rethinking images of Africa and African peoples. Like many of his contemporary Harlem Renaissance writers, Hughes sought to revise negative stereotypes of African peoples and to create a new understanding and appreciation of African beauty. To borrow a term from Henry Louis Gates Jr., "Luani of the Jungles" is an African American text that "signifies" upon *Heart of Darkness* as it revises the racism against Africans so prevalent in Conrad's novel. As Gates wrote in *The Signifying Monkey*, "Just as the ex-slaves wrote to end slavery, so too did free black authors write to redress the myriad forms that the fluid mask of racism assumed between the end of the Civil War and the end of the Jazz Age."[4]

In fact, through his writing of "Luani," Hughes anticipated later Con-

---

2. In *When Harlem Was in Vogue*, David Levering Lewis also notes that "Luani of the Jungles" "bear[s] the clear imprint of Joseph Conrad" (84).

3. Rampersad, *Life*, 1:71.

4. Gates, *The Signifying Monkey: A Theory of Afro-American Literary Criticism*, 171.

rad criticism by almost fifty years. In his famous lecture "An Image of Africa," given on February 18, 1975, Chinua Achebe discussed the racism inherent in *Heart of Darkness,* calling Conrad a "bloody racist." Achebe argued that "it is the desire—one might indeed say the need—in Western psychology to set up Africa as a foil to Europe, a place of negations at once remote and vaguely familiar in comparison with which Europe's own state of spiritual grace will be manifest."[5] While Achebe's presentation has influenced many scholars' readings of *Heart of Darkness,* Hughes's "Luani of the Jungles" can just as clearly (though more subtly) reshape one's reading of Conrad's novel. By examining the parallels between "Luani of the Jungles" and *Heart of Darkness,* one can easily see how Hughes inverted Conrad's story in order to actualize his racial ideology as a Harlem Renaissance writer. Through the narrative framework, plot, language, imagery, and characters of "Luani," Hughes signified upon, as he repeated elements of, Conrad's white colonial text, but he simultaneously revised it in order to create an African American text through which Africa becomes a place of beauty rather than a "heart of darkness."

The narrative frameworks of *Heart of Darkness* and "Luani of the Jungles" parallel one another and are both double-layered narratives in which orality and aurality become privileged. Both works begin from the point of view of a secondary narrator and quickly move into the stories of the primary narrator. The stories of the primary narrator, aside from a few brief interruptions, dominate both texts, but both texts end with a return to the points of view of the secondary narrator. In *Heart of Darkness,* Marlow narrates his tale to the group of sailors aboard the *Nellie,* though it is just one of these sailors who communicates the story to us as readers. Likewise, in "Luani," the European narrator who has moved to Africa with his African bride narrates his tale to Hughes's narrator aboard the *West Illana,* though it is Hughes's narrator, also presumably a sailor, who communicates the story to us. These double-layered narratives are what Gates would call "speakerly texts," for "the narrative strategy signals attention to its own importance, an importance which would seem to be the privileging of oral speech and its inherent linguistic features."[6]

While Marlow, the sailor on the *Nellie,* and the European narrator in "Luani" are all most certainly white Europeans, the race of the sailor aboard the *West Illana* is unknown.[7] This uncertainty is important, for it

5. Achebe, "An Image of Africa," 319, 314.
6. Gates, *Signifying Monkey,* 181.
7. While some critics may argue that the sailor aboard the *West Illana* is raced be-

"opens up" the audience for the European narrator's tale. While Marlow's tale to the group of sailors aboard the *Nellie* about the mysteries, evils, and darkness of Africa is clearly a tale for European "white" men, and almost becomes a collusion to propagate negative African stereotypes, the European narrator's tale in "Luani" is told to only one man of unknown race. Thus, the message in "Luani" is not solely for "white" Europeans or African Americans but for all groups; yet it is a tale to be listened to individually.

The fact that the storytelling in both of the texts takes place on ships is also significant. As Paul Gilroy explains in *The Black Atlantic*, "Ships immediately focus attention on the middle passage, on the various projects for redemptive return to an African homeland, on the circulation of ideas and activists as well as the movement of key cultural and political artefacts." Gilroy goes on to explain that "the ship provides a chance to explore the articulations between the discontinuous histories of England's ports, its interfaces with the wider world."[8]

While in *Heart of Darkness* the storytelling takes place on a ship anchored in the Thames River in England, in "Luani" the storytelling takes place on a ship anchored in one of the tributaries of the Niger in Africa. The setting of the Thames positions the story within a European framework, while the setting of the Niger in "Luani" antithetically positions the story within an African framework. Nevertheless, the fact that the two narrators in "Luani" are a sailor of unknown race and a white European man, coupled with the fact that the story is told on the African Niger, prevents the story from being fixed within any one national or racial construct. The names of the two ships, the *Nellie* in *Heart of Darkness* and the *West Illana* in "Luani," likewise position the stories within two very different spheres, for the name *Nellie* connotes European origins, while the name *West Illana* connotes more African or African American origins.[9] In "Luani," unlike *Heart of Darkness*, ships take on all of the meanings that Gilroy describes and, like the storytelling in "Luani," become a means of bringing together individuals from diverse national and racial backgrounds.

---

cause the character is actually Hughes himself, "Luani" is fiction, and there is no autobiographical evidence to support the argument that Hughes is the secondary narrator in his story.

8. Gilroy, *The Black Atlantic: Modernity and Double Consciousness*, 4, 17.

9. Ships also appear within the tales themselves. Within the primary narratives, both Marlow and the European narrator leave for Africa in French ships, but Marlow returns to England, while the European narrator remains in Africa.

In addition to the oral narrative framework of Hughes's story, its plot, language, and imagery also clearly revise Conrad's *Heart of Darkness,* thereby transforming the tale into an inverse imperialist story that embraces Africa and African beauty rather than vilifying it. Both Marlow and the European narrator in "Luani" are Europeans who journey to Africa, but their motivations are quite different. Marlow travels to Africa for the adventure of the exploration and with the desire to conquer the wild continent. In truth, Marlow is the quintessential colonialist, for the means he has to explore what he calls the "darkness" of Africa is through a trading company, whose goal is "to run an overseas empire, and make no end of coin by trade."[10] In contrast, the European narrator in "Luani" travels to Africa because of love; while in France, he marries Luani, an African woman, and then he returns to Africa with her.

Marlow's and the European narrator's contrasting motivations for journeying to Africa consequently affect their impressions of the continent when they arrive there. When describing his boat trip into the center of Africa, Marlow narrates, "We penetrated deeper and deeper into the heart of darkness."[11] Africa again represents a place of darkness for Marlow, but the use of *penetrated* also connotes his aggressive and forceful movement into this land. Compare Marlow's description of his boat trip into the center of Africa to the secondary narrator's description in "Luani": "we seemed to be floating through the heart of a dense, sullen jungle" (*CW* 15:420). The structure and word choice of this sentence mirror those of Marlow's sentence in *Heart of Darkness* but completely revise Marlow's negative impression of Africa and his adversarial advancement into this land. In "Luani," the narrator passively "floats" on the river, rather than aggressively "penetrating" into the continent. Likewise, the narrator in "Luani" describes what he sees as "the heart of a dense sullen jungle," rather than a "heart of darkness."

The subsequent descriptions of the Africans that Marlow and the European narrator in "Luani" encounter within the "heart" of the continent also contrast sharply. Marlow views the Africans he meets as subhuman and therefore condescends to them in his descriptions of them and his interactions with them. He notes that cannibals are "[f]ine fellows . . . in their place." Along with his frequent use of the word *nigger* when describing the Africans, Marlow also describes them as "prehistoric": "We were wanderers on a prehistoric earth, on a earth that wore the aspect of

10. Joseph Conrad, *Heart of Darkness,* 24.
11. Ibid., 51.

an unknown planet. . . . The prehistoric man was cursing us, praying to us, welcoming us—who could tell?"[12]

The Eurocentrism so prevalent in Conrad's novel progresses as Marlow continues further into Africa, particularly as he describes the peoples he encounters: "They howled and leaped, and spun, and made horrid faces; but what thrilled you was just the thought of their humanity—like yours—the thought of your remote kinship with this wild and passionate uproar. Ugly. Yes, it was ugly enough."[13] Marlow is singularly disturbed that he, and the rest of European society, could in some way be related to these "prehistoric" and bestial people.

In contrast, the European narrator in "Luani" describes the Africans of his wife's tribe as beautiful, and he is ashamed and disturbed by the fact that he does not fit in with them. Upon first arriving at his wife's African village, he narrates, "There a hundred or more members of the tribe were waiting to receive her—beautiful brown-black people whose perfect bodies glistened in the sunlight, bodies that shamed me and the weakness under my European clothing." He points out the flaccid weakness of his own body, thereby unconsciously positioning himself as the antithesis of the powerful colonial conqueror. Unlike the violent "savages" Marlow describes in *Heart of Darkness*, the Africans presented in "Luani" are peaceful. The narrator accounts, "No one molested me. I was seemingly respected or at least ignored" (*CW* 15:423). Unlike Marlow, the European narrator understands that he will be neither attacked nor worshipped by the Africans.

While Kurtz and Marlow believe the Africans should worship them, in "Luani" it is the European narrator who worships Luani, the African woman. He recalls that upon first meeting her, "She seemed to me the most beautiful thing I had ever seen—dark and wild, exotic and strange—accustomed as I had been to only pale white women" (*CW* 15:421). He even refers to Luani as a goddess: "You'll be the ebony goddess of my heart, the dark princess who saved me from the corrupt tangle of white civilization, who took me away from my books into life, who discovered for me the soul of your dark countries" (*CW* 15:422). According to the European narrator, Luani is a goddess, a princess, and a savior. And Africa, though "dark," is not a place of evil, but a place of beauty and passion. It is white civilization that he sees as "corrupt."

Though a representation of Africa, Luani takes on the roles of both the

12. Ibid., 50, 51.
13. Ibid., 51.

African woman on the riverbank and the Intended in *Heart of Darkness* and is thus able to bridge the hemispheres of Europe and Africa. Like Luani, the African woman on the riverbank in *Heart of Darkness* is beautiful, but unlike Luani her darkness is considered dangerous, for in her warrior's garb she becomes for Marlow "the heart of darkness" itself; she is the antithesis of Europe, and therefore a threat to Marlow and his European way of life. Conversely, Marlow constructs Kurtz's Intended as distinctly separate from Africa and as a foil to the African woman on the riverbank. Marlow's repeated descriptions of the Intended as "white" clearly differ from his descriptions of the dark African woman on the riverbank. For Marlow, the Intended becomes the feminine embodiment of Europe: "This fair hair, this pale visage, this pure brow, seemed surrounded by an ashy halo." As Johanna M. Smith argues in "'Too Beautiful Altogether,'" "Marlow's construction of these women dramatizes the point of his story, its manful effort to shore up an ideology of imperialism with an ideology of separate spheres."[14]

The character of Luani, however, succeeds in dissolving the separate spheres of "man" and "woman" and of "Europe" and "Africa." Interestingly, while Marlow does not give either the African woman or the Intended proper names in his narration, the European narrator in "Luani" does refer to Luani by her proper name; conversely, while Marlow and Kurtz do have proper names, the European narrator in "Luani" does not. Luani not only becomes more central to the story, but she displaces the names of the European men. In addition, as Smith points out, Marlow silences the African woman on the riverbank by not giving her a voice in his narrative.[15] This lack of voice stands in sharp contrast to Luani's very potent voice in the European narrator's story. In fact, Luani tells her European husband: "You are coming with me back to my people. . . . You with your whiteness coming to me and my dark land. Maybe I won't love you then. Maybe you won't love me—but the jungle'll take you and you'll stay there forever" (*CW* 15:422).

Educated in England, though living in Africa, Luani is fully able to exist in both European and African society. She is intellectual, and yet physical, and adjusts to the culture of her surroundings as easily as she dons different clothing. She tells her European husband, "A woman can have two lovers and love them both" (*CW* 15:424). As the wife of the European

14. Ibid., 91; Smith, "'Too Beautiful Altogether': Ideologies of Gender and Empire in *Heart of Darkness*," 177.
15. Smith, "'Too Beautiful Altogether,'" 174.

narrator and the lover of Awa Unabo, the African chief's son, Luani is able to embrace the cultures of both Europe and Africa. And, though she loves both cultures, she is controlled by neither. The character of Luani thus serves to critique both the colonialization of Africa and the colonialization of women.

As is exemplified in "Luani of the Jungles," when Langston Hughes voyaged to the west coast of Africa in 1923 he saw the inherent beauty of Africa, rather than its darkness; perhaps the only "horror" he saw while in Africa was the prevalent European colonialization that was taking place there. When Hughes finally met Africans on his journey, he was disappointed that they called him a "white man," for he was hoping for a brotherly connection with the African people and did not want to be associated with the Europeans who were conquering their land. Hughes recalls, "They looked at my copper-brown skin and straight black hair—like my grandmother's Indian hair, except a little curly—and they said: 'You—white man'" (CW 13:96). Perhaps Hughes's desire both to connect with Africa and its people and to elevate the conceptions and preconceptions Americans had about the "dark continent" explain his somewhat Garveyist idealism of Africa in "Luani of the Jungles."

More important, however, through "Luani," Hughes succeeded in revising Conrad's racist novel and imagining a more beautiful and pure Africa. Hughes inverted Conrad's imperialist story by presenting Luani as a strong and beautiful African woman who can successfully exist in both Africa and Europe. In a sense, the European narrator is "conquered," though not violently or corruptly, by Luani and Africa, and the Eurocentrism of *Heart of Darkness* is thus displaced. Hughes's revision of the double-layered narrative framework of *Heart of Darkness* likewise inverts Eurocentrism by "opening up" the story to a more racially and culturally diverse group of listeners. Hughes saw within Conrad's novel a representation of Africa that undermined the goals of the Harlem Renaissance, and he subsequently endeavored to revise this racism through his literary work, just as so many of his contemporary Harlem Renaissance writers were doing through theirs.

Langston Hughes's Red Poetics
and the Practice of "Disalienation"

Robert Young

In celebrating Langston Hughes's centennial birthday, I hope to recover the other Langston Hughes—the "red" Hughes—by engaging his proletarian poetry and discerning his theoretical contributions to Marxist aesthetics. During the 1930s, Hughes published poems such as "Open Letter to the South" (1932), "Good Morning Revolution" (1932), "Black Workers" (1933), "Revolution" (1934), and "Ballads of Lenin" (1935) that clearly foreground his revolutionary political commitment. I am interested in how such a political commitment shaped the form, structure, and textuality of Hughes's poetics and, more specifically, in the ideological effects generated by Hughes's poetics.

As Hughes called for a transracial/transnational worker-based political collectivity, for example in "Open Letter to the South," how did such a political/ideological commitment encode itself, not just in the content, but also in the formal structure of his poetics? I argue that Hughes encoded revolutionary political commitment through a poetic practice I call "disalienation," a practice whereby Hughes intersected vernacular culture with materialist theory. To illustrate this practice, I symptomatically engage Hughes's revolutionary poem "White Man" (1936).

In addressing this question, I situate Hughes within the larger debate during the 1930s between Georg Lukács, a proponent of realism, and Bertolt Brecht, a proponent of modernism. In "Realism in the Balance,"

Lukács critiques modernist forms of literature, such as expressionism and surrealism, because they deny any reference to objective reality. For Lukács, a Marxist theory of literature "is a particular form by means of which objective reality is reflected." Consequently, "it becomes of crucial importance for it to grasp that reality as it truly is, and not merely confine itself to reproducing whatever manifests itself immediately and on the surface." Hence, Lukács privileges the issue of totality, and, on this analytic and political premise, he articulates the goal of the realist writer: "to penetrate the laws governing objective reality and to uncover the deeper, hidden, mediated, not immediately perceptible network of relationships that go to make up society." Thus, for Lukács, "a campaign against realism, whether conscious or not, and a resultant impoverishment and isolation of literature and art is one of the crucial manifestations of decadence in the realm of art."[1]

As materialists, Lukács and Brecht shared a commitment to realism; however, Brecht believed that Lukacs articulated a formalistic notion of realism. For Brecht, Lukács's formalism "is demonstrated by the fact that not only is it exclusively based on the form of a few bourgeois novels of the previous century . . . but also exclusively on the particular genre of the novel." While Lukács proposes a dialectical understanding of the social totality, Brecht offers a dialectical understanding of history because "[r]eality changes; in order to represent it, modes of representation must also change." For Brecht, the "truth can be suppressed in many ways and must be expressed in many ways." He continues: "One can arouse a sense of outrage at inhuman conditions by many methods—by direct description (emotional or objective), by narrative and parable, by jokes, by over- and under-emphasis."[2] Brecht argued that realism is not a question of form since the issue of form is itself historical and not metaphysical.

In short, Lukács critiqued modernists, like Brecht, for decadent formalism; in turn, Brecht critiqued Lukács for a formalistic notion of realism. Hughes resolved this tension, not in an abstract academic way, but in his poetic practice, which, in turn, generated a new theoretical practice—a red poetics that I am calling "disalienation." By disalienation, I mean a project that interpellates and then alienates the reader to produce new subjectivities. In part, I delineate this new theoretical practice because—surprisingly—there has been little work dealing with the theoretical contributions of Hughes to radical aesthetics and the theoretical effects of his

1. Georg Lukács, "Realism in the Balance," 33, 38, 58.
2. Brecht, "Against Georg Lukács," 70, 82, 83.

discourse.[3] In reclaiming Hughes as a theorist, I argue that the concepts of race and jazz, in particular, and folk culture, in general, along with a materialist philosophic substructure, provided Hughes with the basis for his theoretical innovation.

More specifically, Hughes used examples of racial oppression to historicize his diverse intellectual practices, specifically his poetic practice. Consequently, Hughes would avoid the (Brechtian) charge of an ahistorical and formalist notion of realism. Along with the historicization of race, Hughes appropriated vernacular forms, like jazz, which gave him an analytic basis from which to theorize new poetic forms—forms that are historical, modernist, and aligned to a politically progressive project. Hughes's poetics points to the objective reality of African American racial oppression and economic exploitation. Hence, Hughes would escape the Lukácsian charge of "decadent formalism." For Hughes, the forms are derived from the proletariat, reflect the experiences of the proletariat, and position the proletariat as agents of change. The poetic forms reproduce cultural aesthetics and, in doing so, render the form accessible, thereby providing the presupposition for understanding the social and inaugurating new subjectivities. In the project of rendering reality in a form men and women can master, as Brecht once put it, Hughes's red poetics provides a compelling example.

Hughes's poem "White Man" exemplifies disalienation: it interpellates and alienates in the interest of developing class consciousness. The first part of the poem constructs the familiar by drawing upon commonsense notions of racial experience; this, in turn, makes interpellation possible. Thus, the title of the poem—"White Man"—signals the historicity of Jim Crow racial oppression, and as such it generates (self-)identification. The title provides a poetic space for the ideological (mis)recognition (and reification) of the racialized subject position, a positionality reinforced by the declarative opening line of the poem: "Sure, I know you!" (CW 1:247). Upon this structure of identification, the poem proceeds to (re)produce familiar racially encoded binary oppositions: "You're a White Man / I'm a Negro." Then, it traces the social implications: "You take all the best jobs / And leave us the garbage cans to empty / and / The halls to clean" (CW

3. Hughes is readily seen as a poet, short story writer, and novelist but rarely as a theorist, that is, someone who produces concepts. For example, the volume edited by Henry Louis Gates Jr. and K. A. Appiah, *Langston Hughes: Critical Perspectives Past and Present*, contains historical and contemporary essays on Hughes but little on Hughes as theorist. Moreover, his theoretical relationship to Marxist aesthetics is a relatively underdeveloped field.

1:247–48). Hughes invokes commonsense understandings of racial experience and renders them in a common language to effectuate a poetic interpellation. In this regard, he articulates what Maryemma Graham calls a social art, "an art that uses a popular literary style, derived from vernacular language and other forms of oral folk (national) expression, for conveying social content."[4] At this point in the poem, Hughes conveys racial content to recruit the reader; upon this base, he will produce an estrangement and introduce revolutionary content.

Hughes continues with a discussion of jazz and the exploitation of black musicians, such as Louis Armstrong, by the White Man. Unlike the 1920s poem "Weary Blues," in which Hughes deploys the vernacular/blues form, here he encodes the vernacular music in the content. However, there is a thematic continuity, and, whether Hughes discusses jazz through questions of form or through content, the political aim remains the same: to interpellate the subject. Again, for this purpose, Hughes draws upon common sense: "White Man! White Man! / Let Louis Armstrong play it— / And you copyright it / And make the money." Of course, within the logic of common sense, the exploitation of black musicians would readily register, and, because of such recognition, it would seem as if the White Man symbolizes hegemonic authority: "You're the smart guy, White Man! / You got everything!" Until this point, Hughes has been interpellating (self-same) racial subjects through the deployment of common sense, but later, in the same stanza—which suggests a dialectic unity of common sense and theory or, better yet, the concrete and the abstract—he shifts toward a poetic practice of estrangement: "But now, / I hear your name ain't really White / Man" (CW 1:248).

Hughes offers an ideological critique of racial common sense and its underlying empiricism and puts in place something unfamiliar: red theory, the other to common sense. Similar to Lukács's and Brecht's notion of realism, Hughes's poetic realism also moves beyond appearance, which reifies whiteness, and foregrounds underlying socioeconomic relationships. Indeed, at the moment the shift occurs, the poem seems to structurally replicate the Marxist base-superstructure model. Marx articulates the classic formulation of the base-superstructure model in his preface to *A Contribution to the Critique of Political Economy*: "The sum total of these relations of production constitutes the economic structure of society, the real foundation, on which rises a legal and political superstructure and to which correspond definite forms of social consciousness." Hence for

4. Graham, "The Practice of Social Art," 214.

Marx, "It is not the consciousness of men that determines their being, but, on the contrary, their social being that determines their consciousness."[5] Hughes extends Marx's materialist framework into the domain of race and thus, in a very concrete fashion, poetically demonstrates that whiteness is not constitutive of the social but rather an effect of capitalist social conditions.

Hughes, then, replicates a base-superstructure model in poetic form:

> I hear your name ain't really White
>   Man.
> I hear it's something
> Marx wrote down
> Fifty years ago—
> That rich people don't like to read. (CW 1:248)

Lines 21–22 ("I hear your name ain't really White / Man") rest on top of lines 23–26, ("I hear it's something / Marx wrote down / Fifty years ago / That rich people don't like to read"), which form a poetic base. Hughes locates "White Man," or whiteness, as an ideological and political discourse—a superstructure articulation—dialectically structured by an underlying economic base, poetically signified by "rich people." The specific formal structure of lines 21–26 parallels the larger dialectical movement of the poem, from the White Man to its negation, the Capitalist. This double dialectical structure provides the philosophical coordinates for Hughes's practice of disalienation. The poem moves the reader from (mis)recognition to estrangement, and this opens the possibility for a radical intervention.

Hughes's red theory deconstructs the metaphysics of whiteness and opens a space for conceptual and revolutionary literacy. In other words, Hughes's critique of racial ideology generates a crisis, and, in this crisis, Hughes introduces radical content: Marx. Hughes produces a (poetic) crisis but then provides a modality for reading the crisis. The crisis in not immanent to the poetic space, and therefore Hughes moves beyond a formalist concern with the crisis of representation. He links the poetic space to history, inviting the reader to implicate the poetic text in history by foregrounding the historicity of exploitative social relationships, by raising unfamiliar (red) questions: "Is your name in a book / Called the *Communist Manifesto*? / Is your name spelled / C-A-P-I-T-A-L-I-S-T?" (CW

---

5. Marx, preface to *A Contribution to the Critique of Political Economy*, 4.

1:248). The syntactic structure of the signifier, capitalist, deliberately draws attention to a new object, and its capitalization signals the (economic) location of social power—the capitalist class—and the geopolitical location of this class—the capital cities of Western imperialist nations (and their colonies).

Hughes's red poetics puts the focus on a new object of critique: capitalism. In conjunction with this new object, Hughes also articulates a new political vision: internationalism. Hughes's internationalism structures poems such as "Good Morning Revolution," which concludes with a greeting of proletarian solidarity: "And we'll sign it: *Germany* / Sign it: *China* / Sign it: *Africa* / Sign it: *Poland* / Sign it: *Italy* / Sign it: *America* / Sign it with my one name: *Worker*" (CW 1:226). Similarly, "Always the Same" (1932) contains a call for international solidarity to resist exploitation: "Until the Red Armies of the International Proletariat / Their faces, black, white, olive, yellow, brown, / Unite to raise the blood-red flag that / Never will come down!" (CW 1:228).

Hughes identifies a new (poetic) object, capitalism, and a political formation, the international proletariat, intended to carry out social change. For some, Hughes's internationalism represents a rupture from his 1920s poetry, which drew upon African American expressive forms and is considered a poetics of cultural nationalism. For example, Anthony Dawahare surmises that Hughes "no longer believed that they [vernacular forms] were appropriate vehicles for the content of his ideas." Dawahare asserts that Hughes, during the 1930s, rejected vernacular forms because the "'national' aesthetic forms could not adequately express the subjectivity of the white worker," and the black cultural forms, like the blues and spirituals, "did not express (at least explicitly) militant politics against oppression."[6]

Dawahare's reasoning is problematic for at least two reasons. First, under capitalism white workers also experience alienation, and there is no intrinsic reason the blues, a form that deals with issues of social alienation, could not be made to speak to the alienation of white workers and highlight the common experience of alienation among black and white workers under capitalism. Second, even if the vernacular musical forms did not directly protest oppression, the forms certainly foreground the effects of racism and poverty. As Graham puts it, "Hughes . . . realized the political implications of the cultural manifestations of the national oppression of the black masses." Thus for Hughes, as Graham insightfully points out,

---

6. Dawahare, "Langston Hughes's Radical Poetry and the 'End of Race,'" 34, 35.

cultural nationalism is not divergent from class issues but is "the base upon which any consciousness of economic exploitation within the class structure of the American capitalist society would have to depend."[7] Hughes builds upon this African American cultural base and, ultimately, needs a different poetic form not to displace his concerns with the blues but rather to situate that form at a broader level of abstraction.

Therefore, Hughes's red poetics is not so much a displacement of his blues poetics as a deepening of his materialist inquiry. As Onwuchekwa Jemie reminds us, Hughes's class critique is evident in poems from the 1920s such as "God to Hungry Child" (1925) and "Johannesburg Mines" (1928). Furthermore, as Arnold Rampersad points out, Hughes acquired an introduction to socialism as a high school student between 1916 and 1920.[8] Thus, he had a long-standing awareness of class politics, and the 1930s poetry can be seen as a more sustained critique of class politics in poetic form. In other words, while Hughes's 1920s poetry deals with the effects of racial oppression, the 1930s poetry focuses more specifically on the cause of that oppression—an exploitative economic structure. Hence, the 1930s poetry produces a new object of critique—capitalism. To register this new perception, Hughes generates not just the poetics of recognition that characterizes his work of the 1920s but also an estrangement from the racially familiar in order to resituate the question of race within the capitalist social totality. This poetics of recognition and estrangement is what I have called "disalienation."

The shift from a poetics of recognition, which addresses the effects of oppression, to a poetics of estrangement, which foregrounds the cause of oppression, characterizes "White Man." The first part of the poem deals with the effects of racial oppression:

> Sure I know you!
> You're a White Man.
> I'm a Negro.
> You take all the best jobs
> And leave us the garbage cans to empty
> > and
> The halls to clean.
> You have a good time in a big house at

---

7. Graham, "Practice of Social Art," 229.
8. Jemie, "Or Does It Explode?" 154; Rampersad, "Langston Hughes and His Critics on the Left," 34.

> Palm Beach
> And rent us the back alleys
> And the dirty slums.
> You enjoy Rome—
> And *take* Ethiopia
> White Man! White Man!
> Let Louis Armstrong play it—
> And you copyright it
> And make the money.
> You're the smart guy, White Man!
> You got everything! (CW 1:247–48)

It is not difficult to imagine these lines being written during the 1920s. Consider "A Song to a Negro Wash-woman," a poem from that period paradigmatic of what I have been calling a poetics of recognition. It describes the racial experiences of discrimination and oppression: "Was it four o'clock or six o'clock on a winter afternoon, I saw you wringing out the last shirt in Miss White Lady's kitchen? Was it four o'clock or six o' clock? I don't remember" (CW 1:159). The poem provides a ready identification with such racial experiences. However, because the poem works descriptively rather than through explanation, it is not surprising that Hughes cannot find the words to express his songs: "For you I have many songs to make / Could I but find the words" (CW 1:160).

By the 1930s, Hughes had shifted to a poetic practice of estrangement, and with "White Man" this shift is inscribed in the poem itself:

> But now,
> I hear your name ain't really White
>   Man.
> I hear it's something
> Marx wrote down
> Fifty years ago—
> That rich people don't like to read.
> Is that true, White Man?
> Is your name in a book
> Called the *Communist Manifesto*?
>   Is your name spelled
>   C-A-P-I-T-A-L-I-S-T?
>   Are you always a White Man?
>   Huh? (CW 1:248)

The shift is not a displacement of racial concerns and the blues poetic form, which could readily address (multiracial) political issues. Rather, it suggests a more dialectically based, realist understanding of these issues, and here Hughes's notion of realism is similar to that found in the works of Lukács and Brecht. All three theorists aim to demystify the social and point up underlying social relations. Hughes situates questions of race and the blues within a larger socioeconomic context, and thus he moves from a poetics of description to one of explanation, providing the analytical ground for a radical, class-based political project.

In the 1920s, Hughes was still seeking a voice, as exemplified in the closing lines of "A Song to a Negro Wash-woman." By the 1930s, he had found political voice in such poems as "Chant for May Day," which poetically inscribes and celebrates the collective voice of workers, and "Sister Johnson Marches," which affirms the power of the working class: *"Who are all them people / Marching in a mass? / Lawd! Don't you know? / That's de working class! / It's de first of May!"* (CW 1:146). Hughes "sings" now because he is able not only to explain the cause of social misery but also to identify an agent to carry out social change.

The 1920s poetry and the blues poetic form, by and large, address the effects of racism. Inasmuch as these forms highlight the effects of racism and not the causation, they would have been seen by the "red" Hughes as offering a limited perspective, ultimately redirecting social struggle from changing the relations of production toward a cultural resolution that glosses over class inequities. As Dawahare puts it, in an effective critique of nationalism, "nationalist ideologies and movements during the interwar period . . . functioned for a time to divert the legitimate political desires of many black writers for a world without racism along channels that did not throw into question the capitalist foundation of modern racism."[9] Hughes's sense of political urgency led him to address the underlying structural causation of oppression rather than its mediating cultural forms, such as the blues.

Hughes poetically invoked racial common sense to interpellate the reader; at the same time, he also introduced a poetics of estrangement to combat racial common sense. Both of these strategies contribute toward Hughes's theoretical innovation—his practice of disalienation. On one hand, the element of estrangement distinguishes Hughes's work from his earlier race-based poetics; on the other, the element of interpellation dis-

9. Dawahare, *Nationalism, Marxism, and African-American Literature between the Wars: A New Pandora's Box*, xii.

tinguishes his work from the Brechtian notion of estrangement. For Brechtian theater, the starting point is to denaturalize the social. As Brecht puts it:

> What is involved here is, briefly, a technique of taking the human social incidents to be portrayed and labeling them as something striking, something that calls for explanation, not just to be taken for granted, not just natural. The object of this "effect" is to allow the spectator to criticize constructively from a social point of view.[10]

Brecht's project advances a critique of ideology because he assumes the hegemony of dominant ideology; hence, his theoretical-political priority is to demystify that dominant ideology.

Hughes's project, on the other hand, does not initially estrange; rather, it incorporates existing (working-class) black subjectivity via black vernacular forms, such as folk language and music, which encode their experiences and therefore enable recognition. This is the difference of race: African Americans, who occupy a subordinated social position, are already detached from the dominant (Eurocentric) ideology; hence, there is no need to estrange blacks from the dominant ideology. Indeed, the dominant ideology is premised on constructing and legitimating the African American as Other. Thus, Hughes uses vernacular culture to recruit agents for change; then he introduces an estrangement to produce a critical detachment from and a critique of existing social identities and the larger political and economic arrangements. As Graham puts it, Hughes uses the "particular facts of the experience of black people to reach a broader understanding of the general nature of society."[11]

Race, then, becomes a point of departure for Hughes's poetics. Yet he deploys race to deessentialize it; this, in turn, enables him to illuminate the underlying social relations of capitalist society. Hughes defetishizes the concrete in a fashion similar to Marx. He poetically inscribes a materialist understanding of the social—the poetic replication of the base-superstructure. In addition, Hughes's understanding of the concrete directly links to Marx's notion of the concrete. This theoretical relationship is worth elaborating, for it is this materialist understanding of the concrete that grounds Hughes's poetic practice.

In the *Grundrisse*, Marx theorizes his understanding of the concrete in

10. Brecht, *Brecht on Theater*, 125.
11. Graham, "Practice of Social Art," 229.

relation to his method of political economy. He critiques traditional political economists who typically begin with an analysis of the population when studying a country. Marx argues that it "seems to be correct to begin with the real and the concrete" but on "closer examination this proves false," because the population is an abstraction, if one leaves out the class structure, which in turn rests on such elements as wage labor and capital, which in turn presuppose exchange, division of labor, and prices. Thus, as Marx puts it:

> [I]f I were to begin with the population, this would be a chaotic conception of the whole, and I would then, by means of further determination, move analytically towards ever more simple concepts, from the imagined concrete towards ever thinner abstractions until I had arrived at the simplest determinations. From there the journey would have to be retraced until I had finally arrived at the population again, but this time not as the chaotic conception of a whole, but as a rich totality of many determinations and relations.

Hence, for Marx, the "concrete is concrete because it is the concentration of many determinations, hence unity of the diverse." Consequently, it "appears in the process of thinking, therefore, as a process of concentration, as a result, not as a point of departure, even though it is the point of departure in reality and hence also the point of departure for observation and conception."[12]

Marx's theorizing of the concrete provides the analytical substructure for Hughes's conception of the White Man. To shift from Marx's discussion of the methodology of political economy to the discourse of race, Hughes also suggests that it seems to be correct to begin with the concrete, and of course here the concrete is signaled by the White Man. However, Hughes poetically demonstrates that this is a false premise because the white man is an abstraction, if one leaves out the class divisions that structure white (and black) society, which in turn presuppose exchange and division of labor within a historically specific mode of production. To begin with, the White Man would produce "a chaotic conception of the whole" and consequently obscure the logic of exploitation—which occurs through the extraction of surplus value—that structures capitalist society. Therefore, Hughes poetically moves from the "imagined concrete" to "ever thinner abstractions" to arrive at the simplest determinations: class.

12. Karl Marx, *The Grundisse*, 237.

From such a broad conceptual scheme, Hughes now returns to the White Man, but this time the White Man is seen not in idealist terms but rather as a "rich totality of many determinations and relations."

Hughes understands that, in a racist society, the White Man would be seen as the point of departure, and he does not initially reject this idea. Instead, he uses it to produce a poetics of identification. Again, this is the interpellative aspect of Hughes's poetics. Then he moves to reveal how the White Man is not the point of departure, but rather an ideological and political effect of exploitative social relations, which in turn operate to mask the exploitative machinery. Hughes's poetics of estrangement aims to mark the historicity of class domination and demystify the concrete in the interests of change. As Marx once put it, the philosophers have only interpreted the world; the point is to change it. To this end, Hughes deploys a poetic practice of disalienation to recruit agents on behalf of social change.

Hughes's theoretical practice thus operates on two levels, interpellation and estrangement, and this process constitutes his disalienation. This practice represents a dialectical resolution of Hughes's earlier African American cultural poetics, which privileges the poetics of (cultural) recognition, and radical aesthetics, which privileges the poetics of estrangement. Hughes's poetic practice points toward the possibility for social change and the necessity for constructing revolutionary subjectivities to carry out such a historic task. Hence, the urgency, I believe, to reclaim the revolutionary Hughes.

Scholars have offered various reasons for the suppression of Hughes's red poetics. Some, such as Faith Berry, highlight the impact of McCarthyism, while others point to the rise in the U.S. academy of New Criticism, which privileged issues of form and thus ensured the suppression of overtly political poetry.[13] However, these reasons do not address the continuing suppression of Hughes's red poetry, a suppression I believe points to the ongoing ideological project to silence, if not erase, materialist knowledge—like Hughes's "red" poetry—that calls into question the exploitative mechanism inherent within capitalism as it actually exists.

By reclaiming the long suppressed "red" Hughes, we might better position contemporary African American literary and cultural practices to engage the economics of freedom and break the silence on class. On the other hand, for Marxist aesthetic theory, Hughes's intervention opens a space to more effectively historicize the relations between cultural articulations and capital.

13. Dawahare, *Nationalism, Marxism, and African-American Literature*, 92–93.

The Paradox of Modernism
in *The Ways of White Folks*

Sandra Y. Govan

Dear Blanche, I am delighted to report at once that I find myself tremendously excited about Langston's book from its splendid title straight through to the end. All of it is good and some of it, I should think, is great. . . . Something has happened to the lad; he has grown up, I guess. Anyway, this collection of stories is a step ahead of *Not Without Laughter*, his best work up to date. They are also written from a new formula, the complications that ensue between black and white lives, from the colored point of view. I am glad to feel this way.

—Carl Van Vechten to Blanche Knopf, December 14, 1932

Those of us in college classrooms who regularly teach the requisite twentieth-century American literature survey course generally pay some attention to what various literary histories designate as modernism, the modern period, or the modernist revolution. While the dates of this period may vary according to the texts consulted, they typically commence with 1910, 1913, or 1914 and conclude with 1945. Dependent on whether the social or literary historians date the period with the start of the so-called Aspirin Age in 1919, or the 1913 New York Armory art exhibit that featured the work of the new European cubist and abstract painters, or the start of World War I in 1914, they usually conclude that World War II effectively ended the modern period. What followed thereafter was deemed the postmodern.

As a parenthesis between two world wars, especially following the disruptive effects of World War I, American and European artists and intellectuals of the modern era began to characterize the postwar period as rife with alienated, disillusioned, rootless people suddenly freed from the cultural constraints of an alleged genteel past but suffering from acute anxiety and pessimism regarding the future of humanity. Given the recently demonstrated human capacity to wage war on a massive scale (one so grand that hundreds of thousands of human lives were weighed then discarded), given a war that thoroughly uprooted traditional notions of value and order, this pessimistic strain affecting the artistic community was understandable. Images of death and decay, decadence, sex, glitter, and glamour often appeared in the literature of this period juxtaposed against a certain sense of hollowness, against images of an emotional poverty manifesting itself both economically and spiritually. A sense of spiritual malaise became a strong undercurrent in the literature. The disillusionment that followed the aftermath of World War I led Gertrude Stein to describe the wandering souls she saw in Paris as a "Lost Generation"; in *This Side of Paradise,* F. Scott Fitzgerald declared that the alienation was such that a "new generation" had arrived that was "dedicated more than the last to the fear of poverty and the worship of success"; Fitzgerald's "new generation" grew up "to find all Gods dead; all wars fought, all faiths in man shaken."[1] Ironically, we also know one decade of the modern period popularly as "the roaring twenties" or "the jazz age." We know the 1920s as the era of the first sexual revolution; as a boom period for American business hustle and enterprise (or "Babbitry," as Sinclair Lewis was to say); and as a time of rapid social change thanks to the automobile, the radio, rural migration from the farm to the cities, Prohibition, illicit liquor, crime, and the factory assembly line.

When broaching the subject of modernist literature or modernist writing, the discussion usually centers around those writers initially identified as shapers of the modernist aesthetic. Ezra Pound, T. S. Eliot, Amy Lowell, E. E. Cummings, Edna St. Vincent Millay, and Robert Frost (though Frost's ties to "modernism" are perceived as deriving from an entirely different locus than do those of Pound, Eliot, or Lowell) are among

1. Fitzgerald, *This Side of Paradise,* 255.

the poets immediately associated with the new aesthetic. When the conversation turns to fiction, the writers whose names typically arise first are Sherwood Anderson, Ernest Hemingway, F. Scott Fitzgerald, Katherine Anne Porter, and William Faulkner. Seldom is Langston Hughes included in the discussion of American modernists as either a poet or a fiction writer. He may well be listed in an anthology's table of contents, but typically he is grouped together with other African American writers as a member of the Harlem Renaissance, the Negro Renaissance, or the New Negro movement; rarely is he discussed critically as a participant in the modernist movement.[2] Although Hughes and Jean Toomer show the influence of modernist ideas, or more specifically show how their works signify on, or "riff" off, those ideas (despite ostensibly standing on the racialized "margins" of American culture), they both borrowed from modernist precepts and tenets and adapted them to fit their own needs and work.

Anyone with a clear-eyed perspective on American literary history should be able to see in Toomer's rich, imagistic, multilayered, elegant, and evocative *Cane* (1923) a text that most certainly belongs in the modernist camp. It may, however, require more of a perceptual stretch, more critical acumen, to see that in the short fiction of Langston Hughes there are also subtle, more nuanced adaptations or applications of modernist tenets. The African American cultural contexts that so suffuse Hughes's stories sometimes have the unintended consequence of cloaking their other attributes. Yet I would argue that, in several tales, Langston Hughes deploys modernist techniques while simultaneously satirizing "the hype" surrounding modernism as a codified aesthetic. In his *The Ways of White Folks* (1934), with its assorted stories highlighting the dynamic racial tensions between blacks and whites in the modern age, Hughes deftly constructs three distinctive stories that paradoxically, or playfully, utilize, sabotage, and camouflage his adaptation of modernist precepts, themes, and techniques. Through these three tales, "Home," "Rejuvenation through Joy," and "The Blues I'm Playing," Hughes attacks and snipes at both lowbrow middle American culture and the pretentiousness of "modern age" patrician, highbrow, white American culture.

The major tensions persistently woven through the postwar modernist period recurred as writers confronted or dramatized such themes as disillusionment, alienation, rootlessness, pessimism, ennui, futility, anxiety, the place of beauty, and allusions to the world of art and the role of the

---

2. The exceptions to this caveat seem to be Steven C. Tracy, ed., *A Historical Guide to Langston Hughes,* and James E. Miller, *The Heritage of American Literature.*

"sensitive artist." Eliot's "The Love Song of J. Alfred Prufrock" demonstrates these themes perfectly. In addition, like several other tough-minded modernist masterpieces, "Prufrock" throughout prefigures images of death, decay, and decadence. The timid, fearful Prufrock alludes repeatedly to the rarefied world of classical art from which he is excluded. "In the room the women come and go / Talking of Michelangelo" (ll. 13–14, 35–36); he also speaks to his own temerity or lack thereof: "Do I dare / Disturb the Universe? / In a minute there is time / For decisions and revisions which a minute will reverse" (ll. 45–48).

While these themes echoed through the literary texts, those individuals consciously formulating an artistic credo in response to the age challenged their fellow artists to shape their art in a manner different from the forms and conventions of the past, to structure it in an entirely new way. "Make it new!" became the call postulated by Ezra Pound. Pound's dictum led to an amalgam of "new" literary techniques or conventions. Among those most associated with formal modernism were calls for the literary works to be spontaneous, full of emotional intensity, built upon an aggregation of images, and stylistically or technically innovative. Writers should be willing to employ disruptive or improvisational techniques with regard to syntax or narrative mode; writers should be willing to challenge an audience's perceptions regarding past or conventional notions of order and value; writers should be willing to attack conformity or conventionality. Writers could use irony, irreverence, experimentation, or fragmentary narrative devices to shape their art. Writers were artists and, as such, had a privileged place as self-conscious commentators on culture or as observers of society. According to the new dictum, it was the writer's role to investigate the culture—past or present—and to bring to an audience a new understanding of (or insight into) that culture whether the audience understood or appreciated the artistic rendering or not. Hence, some modernist work proved profoundly challenging to less informed readers as it was densely packed with direct and indirect allusions and fraught with fractured attenuated references and symbols, or images so sharply honed that readers were forced to struggle for apprehension. Again "Prufrock" makes the ideal exemplar: "And I have known the arms already, known them all—/ Arms that are braceleted and white and bare / (But in the lamplight, downed with light brown hair!)" (ll. 62–64). Or, take the poem's concluding lines, which speak cryptically of futility and death: "We have lingered in the chambers of the sea / By sea-girls wreathed with seaweed red and brown / Till human voices wake us, and we drown."

The work of Pound and Eliot came to signify the kind of inaccessible "high modernism" most associated with the period. The other side of modernism, that which James Miller described as a "revolt against realism but not against reality,"[3] was far more accessible to the average reader while still managing to be disruptive, discomforting, irreverent, or ironic; to be emotionally intense and yet spontaneous; to be improvisational while yet building upon an aggregation of images. It managed to be "new" while drawing upon old quest motifs and confronting the past or attacking convention. This form of modernism, the form that I contend Hughes adopted, still pointed to alienation or profound changes in the culture through the presentation of feelings in exquisite vivid images. Yet the art remained accessible, if uncomfortably biting, in its depiction of modern American life. Hughes's short stories embracing modernist tenets remain accessible to readers despite a tendency by scholars to overlook them entirely or to see them largely from a simple racialized cultural context, thus stripping them of their broader complexity.

In "Home," written in 1933 and published in *Esquire* in 1934 only after some difficulty and following active pursuit by his agent,[4] Hughes gives us the tragic, deeply disturbing story of Roy Williams, an African American musician who has lived and played abroad for years but who has instinctively returned to his small southern Missouri hometown to die. Easily the most uncompromising, unsettling, and emotionally intense tale in *The Ways of White Folks*, the archetypal "Home" early on presents readers with easily discernable presentiments of death. From the opening page we learn that Roy

> had come home from abroad to visit his folks, his mother and sister and brothers who remained in the old home town. Roy had been away [from Hopkinsville, Missouri] for seven or eight years, wandering the world. He came back very well dressed, but awfully thin. He wasn't well.

3. Miller, *Heritage of American Literature*, 2:765.
4. Arnold Rampersad, *The Life of Langston Hughes, Vol. 1: 1902–1941, I, Too, Sing America*, 282, cites a letter from Maxim Leiber, Hughes's new literary agent, that warned of difficulty placing powerful, deliberately shocking stories such as "Home" with magazine or book editors because of their content. "Nothing I can say or do will stop you," wrote Leiber, "but you may as well know that editors are frightfully squeamish and will not welcome such pieces." Leiber sent "Home" to several journals before *Esquire* accepted it in 1934. After rejecting the story, an exasperated editor for the *Atlantic Monthly* wrote, "Why is it that authors think it is their function to lay the flesh bare and rub salt in the wound?" "Most people," the editor argued, "read for pleasure and there certainly is no pleasure here."

It was this illness that made Roy come home, really. He had a feeling that he was going to die, and he wanted to see his mother again. (*CW* 15:37)

This passage immediately suggests several elements that contextualize the archetypal framework of the story. Hughes first posits the journey and the quest motif. Roy has been an expatriate; through travel in Europe, he has changed and broadened his worldview and his perceptions of a common humanity; he has been successful ("He came back very well dressed, but awfully thin"), but he has suffered and has seen suffering. He has forgotten neither his family nor his roots, but so long an absence has allowed him to forget his *place*. Preoccupied by his music and his illness, he has forgotten the codes of conduct, the deferential manner, and the appearance of lesser status demanded of a black man in the main streets of small-town America. With his different manner, his finely tailored European suits, his spats, his cane and yellow gloves, his luggage covered with bright customs stickers indicating the different countries he's been to and virtually shouting his success, Roy is immediately targeted as "an uppty nigger" by the white village loafers who chance to see him alight from a comfortable and expensive Pullman car. "He heard some one mutter, 'Nigger.' His skin burned. For the first time in half a dozen years he felt his color. He was home" (*CW* 15:39).

Roy returns from his long sojourn abroad in search of a place to ease his weariness, a place to die. Eventually, as the story takes us through six vividly drawn disjunctive segments, he finds death, though not from the lingering effects of the tuberculosis from which he appears to suffer. Rather, through his death Roy embodies the inverse of the sensitive respected black artist; he becomes instead the archetypal black victim, the black male "criminal," scapegoated and lynched as a common rapist solely because of his uncommon courtesy, his intellectual discourse (perhaps his intellectual intercourse) with a white woman and fellow lover of European classical music. Respecting his stature as an artist, the woman has simply spoken politely to him on the street. Acknowledging both her greeting and her appreciation of his music, Roy bows and speaks to her in return. Then he commits the unpardonable sin for a black American male in the south.

"Good evening, Miss Reese," [he said] and was glad to see her. Forgetting he wasn't in Europe, he took off his hat and his gloves, and held out his hand to this lady who understood music. . . . The movies had just let out and the crowd, passing by and seeing, objected to a Negro talking to a white woman—insulting a White Woman—attacking a WHITE woman—RAPING A WHITE WOMAN. (*CW* 15:44–45)

The highly dramatic progression of this passage, from its emphatic stylized emphasis on "white" and "woman" to the increasingly violent compilation of charged verbs cast in discrete images—from "talking," to "insulting," then "attacking," finally "RAPING"—is assuredly technically innovative. The disruptions to, or heightening of, the narrative strategy that Hughes uses here are thoroughly in keeping with the demand to take an old (in this case old American) story, the ritualized lynching of a black man, and "make it new" in a modernist mode.

Moreover, we have in Roy Williams the figure of the quintessential, if atypical, sensitive artist. Roy is a black artist who has mastered two discrete traditions—black American jazz and European classical music—brilliantly expressed through, not a drum, guitar, horn, or piano, but his violin. Interestingly, while jazz became the era's symbol for spontaneity, sensuality, and sexuality, traditional European classical music continued to symbolize cultured refinement and restraint. Roy has mastered both traditions; he now plays Brahms, Bach, Massenet, and Beethoven; he plays sonatas and concertos, all high art forms far removed from the musical grounding he received before going to Europe from church hymns, minstrel coon-shows, and night-club jazz bands. In Europe he learned how to hone his artistry on the violin and he learned to love "Music." As Roy reveals in a meditative stream-of-consciousness moment wherein he merges music, religion, and intimations of interracial sexuality (one of several modernist narrative techniques Hughes employs to tell Roy's story): "This, the dream and the dreamer, wandering in the desert from Hopkinsville to Vienna in love with a street-walker named Music. . . . Listen, you bitch, I want you to be beautiful as the moon in the night on the edge of the Missouri hills. I'll make you beautiful. . . . The *Meditation from Thaïs*" (*CW* 15:41).

"Home" shows Hughes displaying his socialist sympathies while reflecting a postwar arc from prosperity to poverty. It should also be noted that the poverty he dramatizes is both economic and spiritual. Here we can clearly see Hughes working through the modernist themes of world weariness, disillusionment, and despair at the living conditions for thousands surviving in Europe following the war. He contrasts the world of glitter and glamour still available to the privileged against the world of struggle and deprivation inhabited by the dispossessed. The narrative voice Hughes uses at this point in the tale explains that Roy developed his "feeling about death" over the several years he toured. Confiding information in melancholy tones, the omniscient voice reveals that the feeling "must have started in Vienna," and goes on to describe Vienna as "that gay but dying city in Central Europe where so many people were hungry, and yet some still had the money to buy champagne and caviar and women in the night-clubs where Roy's orchestra played" (CW 15:37). As the sensitive artist-observer, Roy must witness or endure scenes that directly affect his physical and emotional health. In one brief yet vivid paragraph, Hughes describes the suffering affecting Roy and the once proud Austrian people:

> But the glittering curtains of Roy's jazz were lined with death. It made
> him sick to see people fainting in the streets of Vienna from hunger,
> while others stuffed themselves with wine and food. And it made him
> sad to refuse the young white women trailing behind him when he came
> home from work late at night, offering their bodies for a little money to
> buy something to eat. (CW 15:37)

Hughes effectively wields irony, the largest shell in the modernist arsenal, to make the several tensions in "Home" that much more biting. As a student studying in Vienna with one of the most highly regarded violin teachers, Roy occupies a privileged position. He has the luxury of "a room to himself . . . to study and keep up his music," but he is also very well aware of the willingness of desperate "beautiful and hungry women" to prostitute themselves in an effort to feed their families. Compassionate as well as observant, Roy thinks, "Folks catch hell in Europe. . . . I never saw people as hungry as this, not even Negroes at home" (CW 15:37). Roy's allusion to the status of African Americans, contrasting it to that of poverty-stricken white Europeans, would at first suggest that despite their struggles with economic hardship, the Europeans emerge as the more honorable people. Yet Hughes explicitly reveals that the European police brutally beat protesters, thieves, or beggars. And in the cabarets where Roy played nightly, in a scene that rivals Fitzgerald's "Babylon Revisited" for dispelling illusions about this period, the rich "still spent good gold. They laughed and danced every night and didn't give a damn about the children sleeping in doorways outside, or the men who built houses of packing boxes, or the women who walked the streets to pick up trade," selling their bodies for survival (CW 15:38).
But neither his artistic sensibilities, nor his European training, nor his

sympathies for suffering humanity are enough to spare Roy the vagaries of his de facto "place" in American culture as a Negro. Roy Williams is a black man whose mother sacrificed for him to have violin lessons during his childhood, a black man whose uneducated but proud, hardworking, and deeply religious mother ("Honey, when you plays that violin o' your'n it makes me right weak, it's so purty. . . . Play yo' violin, boy! God's done give you a gift!" [CW 15:39]) saw her son run away to play for the coon-shows and nightclubs before he was able to return home as a maestro of white classical music. While his performances are recognized as "true art" by Miss Reese, the unappreciative white high school students of Hopkinsville are disdainful, reducing his accomplishments into their local vernacular as nothing more than "a dressed-up nigger" coming into their "school with a violin" to play "a lot of funny pieces that nobody but [their teacher] Miss Reese liked" (CW 15:43).

Several ironies conclude Roy's tragic tale. Home is not a safe haven for Roy; as an alienated expatriate, he remains an outsider in his hometown. In fact, since his journey abroad, Roy has become more distanced from the realities of his "home" community. Neither art nor discussions of art are enough to bridge that distance, no matter how superb his artistry. Despite his international accomplishments and grand dreams of the world's possibilities ("I had a dream, too, Mr. Brahms, a big dream that can't come true, now. Dream of a great stage in a huge hall, like Carnegie Hall or the Salle Gaveau"), Roy gives his first "concert in America for [his] mother and the Deacons of Shiloh Church and the quarters and fifty cent pieces they've collected from Brahms and me for the Glory of God. This ain't Carnegie Hall. I've only just come home" (CW 15:40–41). But this performance before his home audience becomes Roy's first and last American concert. The vaunted country hospitality of small-town rural America proves not only hollow but viciously brutal when mere common courtesy is extended by a white woman to a black man. Thus Hughes's ultimate irony, while still parodying art as an extremely vital force in the larger cultural realm, turns unsentimentally to dramatize all too traditional American racial constructs as its strongest punch. Roy's soul, into which he had poured his music, fuses with his body in a resonate crystalline image that Hughes paints following the attack of the mob:

> And the roar of their voices and the scuff of their feet were split by the moonlight into a thousand notes like a Beethoven sonata. And when the white folks left his brown body, stark naked, strung from a tree at the edge of town, it hung there all night, like a violin for the wind to play. (CW 15:45)

In contrast to the tragic, understated ironic tale of Roy Williams's homecoming, Hughes uses hilarious parody, farcical humor, and broad irony to satirize modernist conventions in "Rejuvenation through Joy." With tongue firmly planted in cheek, Hughes wrote "Joy," probably the most critically neglected tale in *The Ways of White Folks,* as a pointed critique that mocks and pillories those advocates of modernism who valorized and elevated a "cult of primitivism," particularly as this socially constructed "primitivism" presented distorted views of African American life and culture. In "The Diversity of American Fiction," Wendy Steiner called this preoccupation with the "primitive" an "aesthetic anthropology." Steiner goes on to declare, "Black and white writers alike were fascinated with the image of Africa and the values of authenticity and freedom from inhibition that it came to signify."[5] Other "aesthetic anthropological" premises connected to primitivism were promulgated in Sherwood Anderson's *Dark Laughter* (1925) and made prime targets for Hughes's rich wit.

According to Howard Mumford Jones, Anderson in 1924 wrote to photographer Alfred Stieglitz that he found New Orleans "marvelous" because of the "niggers, laughter, easy-swinging bodies, ships." Anderson thought the city illustrated "a rich and primitive value system combining indulgence, compassion, and acceptance of the truth that nature is both easy and cruel." He apparently also believed that "the Negro possesses a quality of emotion, an attitude toward existence that the white man has lost to an industrial and business order." Finally, Anderson thought his novel's title effectively contrasted "the relaxed culture of semi-tropical fecundity [read "sexuality"] and the tension-ridden sterility of post-war industrial society." In Anderson's view, there is an implied connection "between healthy art and healthy sexuality."[6] Such psychoanalytical posturing makes an excellent bull's-eye for Hughes in "Joy." He does not miss the mark.

Transfer the aforementioned ideologies regarding Africa, or New Orleans, to Harlem. Establish as conflicts the triad of art, beauty, and the primitive. Fold liquor, sex, jazz, and blues into the mix. Blend in the requisite themes of spiritual disillusionment, alienation, and ennui. Add to the mix a shaker of sterile, jaded white folks searching for a way to save their souls. Then, develop two intelligent hucksters, con men intent on capitalizing on the latest modern fad or cult. Stir, let sit, then allow to rise.

5. Steiner, "The Diversity of American Fiction," 854.
6. Jones, introduction to *Dark Laughter,* 1–4.

With such a recipe comes a story that is uproariously funny and highly satirical, one that provides an O. Henry–like surprise ending with a hook that takes the tale back to its black cultural roots.

Hughes's protagonists, the beautiful, "handsome beyond words" (*CW* 15:56) Eugene Lesche and his partner, Sol, decide to make their fortune on the primitivism hustle.[7] If George I. Gurdjieff and other Europeans could establish expensive, exclusive salons, institutes, or colonies to service the bored, disillusioned, and alienated rich, enterprising Americans Lesche and Sol foresaw no problem with capitalizing on the trend, establishing their colony in Harlem rather than Europe.[8] The impetus for their idea came from a wealthy white woman they met while vacationing in France. The two had first met Mrs. Oscar Willis, whose husband owned a railroad, in California when Lesche taught her to swim and later modeled for her; she had formerly been involved in an art expression colony there because "she was very unhappy. She was lonely in her soul—and her pictures expressed that loneliness" (*CW* 15:60). When Lesche and Sol meet Mrs. Willis again, this time in Paris, she announces, while listening to a frenetic jazz band playing at Bricktop's, that she plans to retire from life and give up art. She intends to "look for happiness" in Mogador Bonatz's colony, apparently one designed to repair the aches of the soul, for "Art does nothing," she says (*CW* 15:61). Struck by the daring simplicity of such a marketing idea, over drinks at Josephine Baker's club Lesche and Sol hatch their own design for a colony where the rich can come to relax and be relieved of their riches. "'Looks like to me,' said Lesche, 'a sure way to make money would be, combine a jazz band and a soul colony, and let it roll from there—black rhythm and happy souls'" (*CW* 15:61). The two lease an old Westchester mansion and some cottages and hire a decorator

7. The preoccupation with the notion of primitivism in regard to music was such that black Harold Jackman wrote Claude McKay, "Tell me frankly . . . do you think colored people feel as primitive as so many critics describe them as feeling when they hear jazz? [There is] so much hokum and myth about the Negro these days (since the Negro Renaissance, as it is called) that if a thinking person doesn't watch himself, he is liable to believe it" (David Levering Lewis, *When Harlem Was in Vogue*, 224).

8. Jean Toomer studied with Gurdjieff, the Armenian spiritualist who combined "mysticism, yoga, Freudian psycho-analysis and elements of dance" into a belief system he called Unitism, in 1924 at the Institute for Harmonious Development of Man and subsequently brought Gurdjieff's ideas home to Harlem in an attempt to establish a similar institute. While the Colony of Joy may be, in fact, laughing at both Gurdjieff and Toomer, the story itself has a much broader reach; its satirical commentary on the modernist aesthetic cannot be denied. See "Introduction to Jean Toomer" in Henry Louis Gates Jr. and Nellie McKay, eds., *The Norton Anthology of African American Literature*, 1088.

to, as Sol says, "do it over primitive—modernistic—on a percentage of the profits, if there are any" (*CW* 15:59).

In describing Lesche's Colony of Joy, Hughes hits every possible note to signify on the pretensions of modernism. His heroes recruit the services of a "man from Yale" to prepare their lecture series on "Joy in Relation to the Mind, Body, and Soul." These daily twenty-minute lectures are intended to be an integral part of their overall "program of action for a high brow cult of joy—featuring the primitive" (*CW* 15:62). For his sources the Yale man takes snippets from quick perusals of primitive art, German eurythmics, Indian mysticism, spiritualism, Eastern philosophy, "all of Krishnamurti, half of Havelock Ellis, and most of Freud" (*CW* 15:63). Lesche and Sol also hire their own jazz band and a dancer/blues singer. To this group Sol gives very explicit directions regarding expectations and decorum:

> [L]isten! Now I want to tell you all about this place. This will not be no night club. Nor will it be a dance hall. This place is more like a church. It's for the rebuilding of souls—and bodies. It's for helping people. People who are wore out and tired, sick and bored, *ennui-ed* in other words, will come here for treatments, the kind of treatments, that Mr. Lesche and I have devised, which includes music, the best music, jazz, real primitive jazz out of Africa (you know, Harlem) to help 'em learn to move, to walk, to live in harmony with their times and themselves (*CW* 15:64).

Lesche's first lecture, "*Joy, springing from the dark rhythm of the primitive*," is to be punctuated or underscored by the band's playing of Duke Ellington's "Mood Indigo." Carefully choreographing the nuanced, barely veiled sexuality of his presentations, Lesche demands that his dancer "glide in" when cued, using plenty of "hip movement" so that his perspective clientele will "learn to use their life-center." Blacks at the colony are to serve as living representatives of the primitive. "*See how the Negroes live, dark as the earth, the primitive earth, swaying like trees, rooted in the deepest source of life.*" At that point in his practice session, Lesche announces he will have his titillated audience "all rise and sway, like Miss Lucas here," suggesting that such action "ought to keep 'em from being bored until lunch time" (*CW* 15:65).

As Hughes depicts it, the Colony of Joy is an inordinate success. Although some accuse it of decadence and others of "neo-paganism," the colony attracts top names from the nation's social register. All goes well until two events, both rooted in primal emotion, coincide. The blues singer gets angry with the band's drummer for two-timing her; and, against Sol's advice, Lesche chooses to institute a "Private Hour" for certain female clients "to receive alone in confidence their troubles for contemplation." Regardless of a colony lecture that teaches "newness, eternal renewal" as the "source of all growth . . . , we shall be ever new, ever joyous and new," age-old basic, primitive jealousy effectively sabotaged the New Men, New Women, New One, and Lesche, the New Leader of the Colony of Joy (*CW* 15:68). One can feel viscerally the fun Hughes has at the expense of Ezra Pound ("Make it new!") in this passage and with Sherwood Anderson's vaunted primitivism in the passage cited above. But Hughes then takes the story to yet another level—slapstick comedy and ribald black folk humor. Gunshots ring out (though no one is hit); rich white women deprived of their cherished Private Hour go berserk; a madhouse fight scene ensues where love-crazed women attack their lovers while other women attack them. Word of the pandemonium leaks to the press; the police, plus scandalmongers, descend upon the colony. In a final hilarious ironic stroke, Hughes returns his pseudo-modernist fable to a black reality that touches on one of his own favorite motifs—surreptitious crossings of the color line. The beautiful, "handsome beyond words" Eugene Lesche is reputed by one of the tabloids to have committed a daring act, one implicitly laced with racially charged sexual innuendo. Supposedly, Lesche is uncovered as "a Negro—passing for white!" (*CW* 15:71).

If "Home" stands at the tragic end of the emotional spectrum, and "Rejuvenation through Joy" stands at the comedic end, then "The Blues I'm Playing" provides the balance in *The Ways of White Folk*. Intriguingly, the main characters in "The Blues" are both women. One is white, the other black; one is elderly, the other young. Further, there is no great human tragedy embedded here nor any sense of overwhelming loss; rather than farcical comedy, here Hughes turns to elegantly understated bittersweet humor. With "The Blues" Hughes effectively turns his dissection of modernism to a serious aesthetic debate on the role of art and the correct stance for the sensitive artist who happens to be black in the newly minted modernist world.

Actually, "The Blues" does revisit "Home" by the way in which it, too, dichotomizes art or, more specifically, by the way in which it valorizes music. Once again the high-art European tradition of classical music (European soul) is set against the period's "new music" that derived from a black cultural context or, more specifically, that sprang from the souls of

black folk—blues and jazz. In this tale, however, jazz is not used as merely the handmaiden of primitive impulses to tap into the psyche of world-
weary whites. Black music stands on its own as a vital force. When the story opens, readers learn that Mrs. Dora Ellsworth has become the patron
of the gifted, poor, young, black pianist Oceola Jones. Hughes's omniscient narrative voice immediately captures the rather generous but
sometimes shallow and muddled impulses of the genteel, refined Mrs.
Ellsworth, patron of the arts and of young artistic geniuses:

> Poor dear lady, she had no children of her own. Her husband was
> dead. And she had no interest in life now save art, and the young peo-
> ple who created art. She was very rich, and it gave her pleasure to share
> her richness with beauty. Except that she was sometimes confused as to
> where beauty lay—in the youngsters or in what they made, in the cre-
> ators or the creation. Mrs. Ellsworth had been known to help charming
> young people who wrote terrible poems, blue-eyed young men who
> painted awful pictures. And she once turned down a garlic-smelling so-
> prano-singing girl who, a few years later, had all the critics in New York
> at her feet. The girl was so sallow. (CW 15:72)

Mrs. Ellsworth, very likely modeled after Hughes's (and Zora Neale
Hurston's) own patron, Mrs. Charlotte Osgood Mason, has very decided
ideas about art.[9] As a consequence of her resolve to shape both the life and
the career of her new protégée, she has removed Oceola from Harlem and
placed her in a small Parisian apartment so that Oceola, without the disruptions of earning a living, may learn to refine her technique, to polish
her artistry as an interpreter of the classics. Having heard Oceola play
Rachmaninoff, List, and Ravel, along with W. C. Handy's "St. Louis
Blues," Mrs. Ellsworth falls in love with Oceola's talented rendering of the
classics ("I am quite overcome my dear. You play so beautifully" [CW
15:73]) and determines to give her, unasked, greater exposure to the world
of high art by conferring upon her both time and money so that Oceola can
study music in Paris—and not "waste" her time or talent teaching black
youngsters how to play, or rehearsing with church choirs, or playing for
benefit dances and Harlem parties, all familiar venues Oceola enjoys.

9. A note to "The Blues I'm Playing" in ibid., 1271, also makes this connection, suggesting that Mrs. Dora Ellsworth is "probably based on Charlotte Mason (1854–1946),
patron of Hughes and other leading figures of the Harlem Renaissance." For a fuller
look at Mrs. Mason's determination to assert her authority over Hughes, see Rampersad's Life, 1:185–188, 200.

The tension between Oceola as protégée and Mrs. Ellsworth as patron frames the essential conflict in the story, for Mrs. Ellsworth believes in supporting young artists so that they may live for their art alone and develop their genius. Hers is the elitist "art for art's sake" doctrine. She suspects that Oceola "mistrust[s] her generosity" and, indeed, Oceola does, "for she had never met anybody interested in pure art before. Just to be given things for *art's sake*" caused Oceola to wonder about Mrs. Ellsworth's motives (CW 15:74). Without engaging in philosophical debate, Oceola intuitively understands that the source of her music is grounded in her history, her life, and her experiences of the world. Pressed to reveal something about her past to her prospective patron, Oceola shares this personal background with Mrs. Ellsworth.

Both Oceola's stepfather and her mother had been musicians from Mobile, Alabama. Although prodded by the overly inquisitive Mrs. Ellsworth who wants to know all, Oceola never says a word about her "real" father, continuing to speak only of her stepfather, who had been in a band that played lodge meetings, community picnics, club dances, minstrel shows, and backyard barbecues. Her mother played both the church organ and the church piano; as a small child Oceola learned to play piano by ear "until her mother taught her notes" (CW 15:74). Multitalented, Oceola also learned to play the organ and cornet. Her parents left Mobile to go to Houston with Billy Kersands' Minstrels and settled there. In Houston, Oceola went to school; her mother also paid for her to have piano lessons from a German woman who gave her a foundation in classical music. There were times when her parents could not find work and the small family suffered hunger pangs, but Oceola's teacher continued her lessons and Oceola's aptitude grew. After Oceola's stepfather died, her mother moved them to St. Louis, where she took a job playing at movie theaters and Oceola played for a church choir. Oceola saved her money and was able to put herself through Wilberforce, where she studied piano, played for college dances, and eventually graduated. Then, like thousands of other African Americans who migrated out of the South, Oceola moved to New York, to Harlem. Following the death of her mother, she rented out a room to a student, a young man studying for medical school while working as a Pullman porter.

It is at this point in the recitation of Oceola's personal history that Mrs. Ellsworth flinches. For Oceola to have the distraction of a roomer is bad enough. But a male roomer! She is disturbed. Her fears, from her perspective, are well grounded, for rumor has it that Oceola does not charge her boarder rent; moreover, she even helps support him as he studies for entry into Meharry Medical School. The two, in fact, have a personal relationship. For Mrs. Ellsworth, Oceola, the fully grown, capable, independent, and self-supporting black woman, becomes a "poor child being preyed upon" who needs to be rescued. Immediately upon hearing Oceola's story, she decides to pay all of Oceola's expenses so that the girl can focus on her music lessons; in the interest of the art that she places such faith in, Mrs. Ellsworth also decides that Oceola should study music further first in the Village and then in France. Her theory is that Oceola, once removed from Harlem, won't need her roomer any more, or a relationship with any man, for "she will have her art" (CW 15:76).

The cultural rift between Mrs. Ellsworth's and Oceola's views on the power or nature of art fuels the rest of the story. Mrs. Ellsworth wants Oceola to have an unencumbered space high on some majestic mountain where she can gaze at the stars, "fill her soul with the vastness of the eternal, and forget about jazz. Mrs. Ellsworth really began to hate jazz—especially on a grand piano" (CW 15:78). Mrs. Ellsworth would also like to cut Oceola off from her connection with Pete, her roomer, her connection to a normal, healthy love life, and, in Mrs. Ellsworth's view, her distraction from art. Following a concert where the critics are merely mild in their assessment, Mrs. Ellsworth blames the absent Pete. "His spirit was here" she declaims. "All the time you were playing on that stage, he was here, the monster! Taking you out of yourself, taking you away from the piano" (CW 15:81). Her first black protégée, the strongest talent and the most interesting of the small group she supports, was supposed to set out upon "the wonderful road of art . . . until she became a great interpreter of the piano" with the ability to "sublimate her soul" to it (CW 15:78). However grateful she is for the opportunities Mrs. Ellsworth has provided—the chance to study music in Paris for two years; the apartment on the Left Bank; the opportunity to learn about Debussy; the opportunity to meet other black students from Algeria or the French West Indies who were also studying abroad—Oceola never loses her cultural and intellectual grounding; she never succumbs to intellectual elitism or pretentiousness, never loses sight of her own artistic identity. For her, the abstract "interminable arguments" the other students rehash over Marcus Garvey or Jean Cocteau, Spengler or Picasso are little more than frustrating exercises. "Why," Oceola wonders, would anyone "argue so much about life or art? Oceola merely lived—and loved it." Only the arguments of the Marxist students hold some relevance for her, "for they, at least, wanted people to have enough to eat" (CW 15:79).

Intriguingly, in the next segment Hughes clearly makes the blues-singing, jazz-playing Oceola his defiant aesthetic spokesperson. Oceola delivers in no uncertain terms a version of Hughes's own artistic credo. Showing impatience with lazy artistic pretentiousness, and again parodying the modernist emphasis on elevating art, the narrator tells us that "Oceola hated most artists, too, and the word *art* in French or English. If you wanted to play the piano or paint pictures or write books, go ahead! But why talk so much about it"? Hughes then forcefully attacks the position of Negro cultural critics of the 1920s such as Alain Locke and other idealists who once naively believed that art had the power to positively influence race relations—that it could break through the color barrier, save the race from prejudice, reduce race hatred, or stop lynchings. Refusing to break with reality, Oceola says "Bunk!" to these lofty notions and then describes the petty but brutish irrational realities her family endured. "My ma and pa were both artists when it came to making music, and the white folks ran them out of town for being dressed up in Alabama. And look at the Jews! Every other artist in the world's a Jew, and still folks hate them" (CW 15:79).

Even though Mrs. Ellsworth continues to attempt to place her cultural stamp on Oceola (until the moment Oceola announces that Pete the Pullman porter, who does become a doctor, has proposed marriage), she is unsuccessful with this independent protégée. This young black woman is too firmly rooted in Mobile and Houston and St. Louis, too anchored to "the Sanctified churches where religion was a joy, to stare mystically over the top of a grand piano like white folks and imagine that Beethoven had nothing to do with life, or that Schubert's love songs were only sublimations" (CW 15:80). Oceola chooses to marry Pete and eventually bear his children; she has no intention of trying to live off "nothing but art." Love of a man trumps art, to the total dismay of Mrs. Ellsworth. She then cuts most of her ties to Oceola, hurt and angry that her star protégée has not been willing to place art above life. Art, as she sees it, should be larger than love. As the narrator explains, when Mrs. Ellsworth "saw how love had triumphed over art, she decided she could no longer influence Oceola's life. The period of Oceola was over" (CW 15:83). At their final meeting, Oceola sings and plays a blues song that symbolizes the unbridgeable cultural chasm separating the two women, one elderly and white, the other young, vital, and black. Hughes notes their entirely different artistic visions, the distinctive personal value system each maintains. This final poignant and revelatory scene is carefully sketched as intensely dramatic and yet bittersweet.

Mrs. Ellsworth sits in her luxurious drawing room, gazing at fresh-picked lilies artistically arranged in her "priceless Persian vases," while Oceola first plays for her the technically masterful Beethoven sonatas and Chopin nocturnes she loves before moving on to play both jazz and blues on Mrs. Ellsworth's grand piano—because that music belongs to her. She makes the "bass notes throb like tomtoms deep in the earth," a sound that never came from that piano before.

> O, if I could holler
> sang the blues,
>> Like a mountain jack,
>> I'd go up on de mountain
> sang the blues,
>> And call my baby back.

Presented with new and different mountain imagery, Mrs. Ellsworth will not accept Oceola's playing of these blues because they concede the power of love. Rejecting both the singer and the song's premise, and confirming her own alienation from the possibilities of change with regard to art or culture, Mrs. Ellsworth, standing up from the chair where she has listened to Oceola play, frostily declares, "And I . . . would stand looking at the stars" (CW 15:84).

In The Ways of White Folks Langston Hughes subtly forces the question of whether he is a modernist writer. Is he part of the modernist revolution or not? How are we to see him, to read him? Herein lies the paradox. Anyone can read and enjoy Hughes's stories without knowledge of modernism as a distinct period or movement in American literature. The stories are engaging, powerful, and provocative. They speak elegantly as disturbing stories of race relations from a perspective that, at the time they appeared, was seldom heard. Yet they are, as are Hughes's poetry and his later Simple tales, deceptively simple, deceptively accessible. Because we know that Langston Hughes was a well-versed, well-read, and politically astute writer, we must acknowledge that he was most certainly alert to current literary trends and highly cognizant about the nature of his craft. Without question, he was familiar with and knew and used, when he chose, the tenets and innovative techniques of modernism. Through the use of irony, of parody, he questioned the notion of art as a bridge to help African Americans move from the margins of culture to the center. He examined the roles of art as an arbiter for cultural standards and the idea of the sensitive artist as the individual capable of orchestrating great cultural shifts. He also poked fun and satirized some of the dominant themes of modernism.

So can we read and understand or appreciate Hughes without knowing a thing about modernism? Without placing him in a modernist box? Yes. But when we bring to the table, or to the text, an awareness of the social and artistic dictates shaping the period, an awareness of the distinctive aesthetic debates and literary nuances filtering through the cultural conversations of that age, that knowledge enriches our reading. If knowledge is power, then a recognition of the traits of modernism definitely broadens and deepens our understanding, our perception, appreciation, and celebration of Langston Hughes's versatility as a multilayered, multitalented writer, an artist. Ultimately, Hughes is much like the strong-willed and independent Oceola Jones who can play both Ravel and W. C. Handy. Hughes, too, can "play" with or "ply" any style, any genre, any tradition. But while Hughes borrows at will from the modernist camp, using particular tenets of modernist prose in one story, satirizing other tenets in another, like Oceola his loyalties remain firmly rooted in an African American cultural tradition, in those jazzy blues changes he plays. Hence the paradox of modernism in his short stories.

IV

Other Words and Other Worlds

The Empowerment of Displacement

Isabel Soto

"Just like niggers," he spat out. "Always moving!"

—Langston Hughes, *The Big Sea*

Caren Kaplan's *Questions of Travel* offers a nuanced discussion of the critical practice surrounding modern Western experiences of dislocation, and she challenges readings that have traditionally provided aestheticized and ahistorical accounts of Euro-American displacement. Kaplan acknowledges the Euro-American modernist celebration and construction of "vanguard movements that rebel against traditional authorities in the humanities," a challenge that on the other hand has been normalized by "gatekeepers of modernist culture . . . circumscrib[ing] and contain[ing] these visions in the realm of aesthetics." This normalization seeks to suppress political and historical referents such as the colonial or imperial enterprise, thus preserving the binary opposition between the world and text, politics and aesthetics, a project that can be deconstructed, according to Kaplan, by applying the mediating element of travel: "The question of travel signifies the possibilities of multiple figures and tropes of displacement that might lead us to a more complex and accurate map of cultural production."[1]

1. Kaplan, *Questions of Travel: Postmodern Discourses of Displacement*, 9, 41.

Even while she persuasively critiques Euro-American discourses of displacement, Kaplan avoids prolonged discussion of transatlantic displacement on the part of Americans who are not of direct European lineage during the period that provides the historical springboard for her discussion, modernism. By focusing on a theoretical practice that promotes the (Euro-American) myth of the dehistoricized "modernist construction of authorship through displacement," she in fact also acquiesces in the well-established critical position that recognizes "two important literary traditions—the Harlem Renaissance and modernism" and which, as Laura Doyle concedes, "we have come to treat separately."[2] Indeed, until recent years, the treatment of transatlantic crossings by African Americans to the Old World during the period of literary modernism was more a purview of critics residing in Europe, or specialists in languages and literatures other than English. Michel Fabre's extensive work on black writers in France is emblematic of this, and for a time Hispanist Edward Mullen's *Langston Hughes in the Hispanic World and Haiti* (1977) was a lone work on Hughes's relationship with the Spanish-speaking world and part of the francophone Caribbean.[3]

The British Caribbean critic Paul Gilroy established a vocabulary that enables us to explicate a non-Euro-American cultural expressiveness marked, indeed enabled, by movement. *Black Atlantic, transatlantic, Atlanticist,* and *circumatlantic,* among others, are now essential terms at the service of a theoretical practice that seeks to represent western modernity as diasporic, *mestiza,* and always in the making. Not coincidentally, Kaplan invokes Gilroy's Black Atlantic as an alternative, historicized, theoretical model of explication of the modern. Kaplan notes the "vibrant set of diasporic experiences" recorded by Gilroy "that draw upon [the] . . . cross-cultural effects of moving back and forth and around the Atlantic Ocean."[4]

The Black Atlantic proposes a radical rethinking of the "history of blacks in the west," advancing "that the history of the African diaspora and a re-

2. Ibid., 41; Doyle, *Bordering on the Body*, 3.

3. There have been more recent path-breaking interventions by African American critics, in line with Kaplan's critique of the perception of modernism as an all-white, Euro-American phenomenon, or simply noting the ineluctable impurity of language. Houston A. Baker's *Modernism and the Harlem Renaissance* (1987), Toni Morrison's *Playing in the Dark: Whiteness and the Literary Imagination* (1992), and Brent Hayes Edwards's *The Practice of Diaspora: Literature, Translation, and the Rise of Black Internationalism* (2003) are a small sample of a growing critical field.

4. Kaplan, *Questions of Travel*, 134.

assessment of the relationship between modernity and slavery may require a . . . complete revision of the terms in which the modernity debates have been constructed. . . . [My] own concern [lies] with the variations and discontinuities in modern experience and with the decentred and inescapably plural nature of modern subjectivity and identity." Gilroy's goal, in short, is to contest universalist and utopian accounts of modernity that suppress the historical role of forcibly displaced Africans to the New World. For Gilroy, the victims of the slave trade must be recast as coparticipants in the ongoing reconstruction of modernity. This requires a critical repositioning, eschewing a Eurocentric (or Euro-American centered) focus in favor of "a more difficult option: the theorization of creolization, métissage, mestizaje, and hybridity," a theoretical refocusing that privileges an "explicitly transnational and intercultural perspective."[5]

My readings of Langston Hughes's prose and poetry draw on modes of inquiry that promote displacement, literal and figurative, as central to an understanding of cultural practice. I draw substantially on Paul Gilroy's Black Atlantic model and formulations of the diaspora—not least because, unaccountably, his influential study barely mentions Hughes, for whom the concept *Black Atlantic* might well have been coined. My central thesis is that travel (again, literal and figurative) was an aesthetically enabling experience for Hughes, articulating and enhancing what elsewhere I have termed his poetics of reciprocity or mutuality.[6] As illustration, I will draw on Hughes's autobiography, poetry, and translations of Federico García Lorca.

Ultimately, I propose the need to redraw Gilroy's foundational Black Atlantic map, which, while it usefully "encourages us to think of the diaspora as . . . a[n] . . . ocean that touches many shores—Africa, Europe, the Caribbean, the Americas—criss-crossed in all directions by people, goods and ideas,"[7] also promotes an Anglo-diasporic triangle. Excluded are major Old World slaving nations such as Portugal and Spain, the latter holding the dubious distinction of having played an inductive role in the transatlantic slave trade and ensuing African diaspora. A fresh mapping of the Black Atlantic to include the Iberian Peninsula would be justified in the first instance by this historical reality and ultimately by the wide range of responses prompted in twentieth-century African Ameri-

---

5. Gilroy, *The Black Atlantic: Modernity and Double Consciousness*, 44, 46.
6. Isabel Soto, "Langston Hughes: The Poetics of Reciprocity."
7. Alasdair Pettinger, ed., *Always Elsewhere: Travels of the Black Atlantic*, ix.

cans by pre- and post–Civil War Spain. As a result of his robust lifelong relationship with the country and things Spanish, Langston Hughes provides us with arguably the richest and most nuanced body of work to consider. Most of my examples, then, will come from Hughes's Spain-instantiated writings.

That travel was a major constituent of Hughes's life and work is evident from the titles of his two autobiographies, *The Big Sea* and *I Wonder As I Wander*. The second, whose title comes from the traditional Christmas carol, wonderfully conjoins aesthetics and life-in-the-making; the former outdoes Gilroy himself in its self-conscious appropriation of the oceanic metaphor. In both texts, as befits the genre, the itinerant shapes the narrative; not only are we presented with the purported facts and movements of the narrating subject's life, but the narrative itself performs a very deliberate trajectory, looping back and forth, ending recursively not with the first chapter but with the epigraph and title itself: "Literature is a big sea full of many fish. I let down my nets and pulled. I'm still pulling" (*CW* 13:250).

Hughes's first published poem celebrates the itinerant. This is what we know about the circumstances surrounding the writing of "The Negro Speaks of Rivers" (1921): that Hughes was traveling south toward the U.S.-Mexican border on his way to a prolonged stay in Toluca, where his father owned a ranch. Of the considerable literature spawned by Hughes's foundational poem, little, if anything, has been written in acknowledgment of the displacement that prompted the poet to write it. The estrangement between Hughes's parents provided part of the emotional backdrop: his father wanted him to visit, his mother did not. The poem was written "on the train during this trip to Mexico when I was feeling very bad" (*CW* 13:65). The mature, narrating Hughes recalls the precise moment of inspiration thus:

> Now it was just sunset, and we crossed the Mississippi, slowly, over a long bridge. I looked out the window of the Pullman at the great muddy river flowing down toward the heart of the South, and I began to think what that river, the old Mississippi, had meant to Negroes in the past—how to be sold down the river was the worst fate that could overtake a slave in times of bondage. Then I remembered reading how Abraham Lincoln had made a trip down the Mississippi on a raft to New Orleans, and how he had seen slavery at its worst, and had decided within himself that it should be removed from American life. Then I began to think about other rivers in our past—the Congo, and the Niger, and the

Nile in Africa—and the thought came to me: "I've known rivers." (*CW* 13:65–66)

This long quote performs the organizing principle at the heart of *The Big Sea* itself and indeed of the "The Negro Speaks of Rivers." Movement inheres both to the poem and to the factors that shaped its realization. In the above passage, movement takes us toward the end of the day—"it was just sunset"—and southwest across the Mississippi. The itinerary enacts further, less literal crossings to the relatively near and also a much more distant past, to a bygone America and Africa. The central image / metaphor—the river—does multiple duty, engaging the present and the not-present: it provides a literal topographical feature the poet is in the process of crossing while it simultaneously invokes other rivers. Each river, the here and the not-here, is historically and mythically freighted. The extract also traces a psychological passage, enabled by the preceding defiance of his mother's disapproval and parental control, this facilitating in turn the creative process. The ensuing poem marks the poet's coming of age, and the autobiographical explication provides the coming-of-age narrative; together they perform a double narrative act. The above passage inscribes Hughes within a tradition of "crossing the water" literatures; the topography invoked by both the autobiographical extract and the poem provides further a *mise-en-abyme* of the itinerary of *The Big Sea*, simultaneously touching American and African shores and traversing the imaginary of the Black Atlantic itself.

I have argued that the Mississippi crossing that accompanied the composition of "The Negro Speaks of Rivers" was not as simple as, well, crossing the Mississippi. The literal engaged the figurative across aesthetic, personal, and historical lines. This rich associational network sustains Hughes's writing motivated by his experiences at the Spanish Civil War front—indeed, I believe it sustains even his most racially specific works, including his 1926 manifesto "The Negro Artist and the Racial Mountain." For Hughes, the general or collective is not disbarred by the particular: it is the particular that facilitates the general, inscribing him within a Black Atlantic or diasporic sensibility that mediates between "the local and the global," here and there, self and other, paraphrased by Gilroy as one "involved in trying to face (at least) two ways at once."[8]

A fact implicitly lodged in the passage from *The Big Sea* is that Hughes

---

8. Gilroy, *Black Atlantic*, 6, 3.

is traveling not just geographically southwest, across the Mississippi, across time, but is also traveling across cultures. The teleological shape of his journey obliges him to alight at the other end in another country, another language. Discovery of another language, French, as Hughes declares in an earlier passage from *The Big Sea,* awoke him to the exigencies of his own language and his own internal need to write (*CW* 13:51). However, in later life it was Spanish that became Hughes's main "other language," and during the journey on which he wrote "The Negro Speaks of Rivers" he was traveling toward a decisive encounter with the language around which would cohere some of his most significant personal experiences as well as some of his most suggestive writing.

This, the summer of 1920, was Hughes's third trip to Mexico. His previous visit to his father's ranch in Toluca when he was seventeen ended with him leaving after a psychosomatic illness induced by "hatred" of his father, returning to the maternal home in Cleveland "without having seen Xochimilco, or a bullfight" (*CW* 13:62). His prolonged third stay in Toluca from 1920 to the following year proved somewhat more positive: relations with his father improved to the point that the latter agreed to bankroll Hughes's college education, and Hughes experienced his first major encounter with the Spanish language and culture. The latter took the form of reading Valencian realist writer Vicente Blasco Ibáñez's *Cuentos Valencianos* and *Cañas y Barro* and attending bullfights, where he saw *torero* Ignacio Sánchez Mejías in action, as well as the theater, where he watched performances by the actress Margarita Xirgu. Both Mejías and Xirgu were leading exponents of their respective crafts and, more suggestively, closely linked to Spanish writer Federico García Lorca and his coterie.

I want to examine the passage on bullfighting that occurs close to the end of the sequence on Hughes's third visit to Toluca. It provides an interesting counterpoint to Hemingway's canonical and coeval accounts of the Spanish *fiesta nacional* as well as substantiating my thesis that Hughes's aesthetics was expressive of a diasporic, restless sensibility. The entire short chapter is given over to witnessing and responding to the corrida. Hughes tells us, "Almost every week-end that winter [of 1920–1921], . . . I went to the bullfights in Mexico City." He is on his way to becoming a serious aficionado and feels confident enough to use the jargon and make value judgments: "Sanchez Mejias made the hair stand on your head and cold chills run down your back with the daring and beauty of his *veronicas* [*sic*]" (*CW* 13:75). Caught up in the excitement generated by the fight, Hughes joins the spectators in "leaping the *barrera*" and tearing "my only good trousers from knee to ankle—but I got my banderillas"

(*CW* 13:76). The chapter closes with a detailed description of the sensory aspects of the *corrida*—the sights, sounds, and smells generated by the ritual.

At several points in the chapter the narrator destabilizes his outsider gringo status. The trouser-tearing incident bespeaks an otherness that, not coincidentally, makes the passage spring to life. This is the narrator-as-bullfighter, "leaping the *barrera.*" Like the torero attired in his fabulously ornate and costly *traje de luces*, Hughes does not just crease or otherwise soil his "good trousers" but, as if the result of actual physical contact with the bull, tears his trousers "from knee to ankle." That he also claims his barbed "banderillas" intensifies the sense of the narrator's engagement, and the elliptical and bilingual "leaping the *barrera*" echoes syntactically the Spanish language, in which the expression is "saltar la barrera."

The bullfight continues to goad the young narrator's creative sensibility and to establish correspondences with otherwise unfamiliar cultural scenarios. Hughes recognizes the blood "gushing forth" from the side of a crucified Christ inside a Mexican church as "thick and red as the blood of the bulls I had seen killed in the afternoon." Significantly, the corrida experience prompts him "ambitiously, . . . to write prose" (*CW* 13:76). The actual representation of the bullfight eludes him, he confesses, though in the next breath he proceeds to produce a highly charged, sensory account. "I could not put the bullfights down [on paper]," he continues to fret at the start of the next chapter, yet write he does, albeit about other things— "an article about Toluca, and another about the Virgin of Guadalupe" (*CW* 13:77). Expressive of alterity, the corrida provides, much as the French language did for Hughes when still at high school, a matrix of self-recognition as a writer and the prompt to actually be one.

The ability to engage alterity as represented by the corrida, the gift of being able to "face (at least) two ways at once," drives Hughes aesthetically. This is vividly confirmed when, arriving in Harlem for the first time as a Columbia-registered freshman, Hughes morphs his first subway ride into a bullfight: "Like the bullfights, I can never put down on paper the thrill of that underground ride to Harlem" (*CW* 13:83). This is the writer-in-the-making, giving shape to experience by describing one thing in terms of another, offering us the metaphor made manifest. It hardly needs stressing that the movement that inheres to metaphor coheres with the movement of the subway ride as well as with the movement recently undergone by Hughes from the (deeper than the deep) South to the North. This is indeed dislocation as empowerment and confirms the itinerant as narrative.

Hughes did not stop traveling when he arrived at Columbia. Overwhelmingly at odds with the career his father wanted him to pursue, that of a mining engineer, he dropped out a year later, eventually finding work as a ship's cabin boy. This modest employment launched him on a several-month-long (1923–1924) nomadic lifestyle, during which he continued to produce some of his finest early poems, even as it transported him to major European capitals and ports of the Mediterranean—including Tenerife, Alicante, and Valencia, all in Spain—and Africa. He did not revisit Spain until 1937, posted by the *Baltimore Afro-American* to cover the 1936–1939 civil conflict from the Republican ranks. The five months or so (from late summer 1937 to January 1938) he spent there yielded a rich store of writing, from chapters in his autobiography to important antifascist poems, and a crucial literary encounter with the work of the recently assassinated Federico García Lorca. It was while Hughes was living in Madrid that he commenced his translation of Lorca's 1928 *Romancero Gitano*, eventually published in 1951 as *Gypsy Ballads*.[9]

I will not dwell on the Lorca-Hughes connection here, since this is ground I have covered elsewhere.[10] I do wish to reaffirm my view that the displacement inherent to translation provided fitting accommodation for Hughes's diasporic aesthetics. His translations of Lorca, as well as his appropriation and rewriting of such seminal Lorca texts as *Llanto por Ignacio Sánchez Mejías* (*Lament for Ignacio Sánchez Mejías*, the bullfighter Hughes saw perform in Toluca) in the politically charged "August 19th . . . ," offer eloquent testimony to a restless sensibility that enabled Hughes to cross over to another text, culture, and poetics. Travel, literary output, and, I would add, translation were mutually reinforcing enterprises for Hughes, all three never far from his ideological concerns and at a radical peak at the time he was posted to Spain and commenced his work on Lorca.

Close study of Hughes's translations of Lorca suggests that his practice leaned markedly toward the foreignizing paradigm advocated by Lawrence Venuti and based on "mov[ing] the reader towards the author," a strategy described by German theologian and philosopher Friedrich Schleiermacher as one of two translation methods.[11] "Wish I had written them myself, not

---

9. Other Lorca works Hughes was simultaneously translating were *Blood Wedding*, eventually staged by Melia Bensussen at the Joseph Papp Theater in downtown Manhattan in 1992, and *Poet in New York*, an extended surrealist meditation on the city inspired by Lorca's stay from October 1929 to March 1930.

10. Isabel Soto, "Crossing Over: Langston Hughes and Lorca."

11. Lawrence Venuti, *The Translator's Invisibility*, 18–19. Venuti quotes Schleiermacher: "There are only two [methods]. Either the translator leaves the author in peace,

just translated them" wrote Langston Hughes to Arna Bontemps in 1951 while revising the translation of fifteen of Lorca's eighteen ballads from the 1928 *Romancero Gitan*.[12] The remark reflects a desire to occupy the site of the foreign writer and "move the reader towards the author." The itinerant can shape translation as well as narrative, as briefly illustrated in the examples below of Hughes's foreignizing translation strategy.

In what is probably the most insightful reading of the Hughes's *Blood Wedding*, a translation of Lorca's play *Bodas de Sangre*, Paul Julian Smith commends Hughes's shadowing of the Lorca source, noting how his translation echoes the original's physicality and homoeroticism.[13] Close examination of the draft and published versions that preceded the 1951 published version of such gypsy ballads as "La Casada Infiel" ("The Faithless Wife"), "San Gabriel" (title unchanged), and "Romance del Emplazado" ("Ballad of One Doomed to Die") also reveals that in the revision process Hughes performed a restorative poetics that transported his translated text considerably closer to the Lorca source.[14] The third ballad, "Reyerta" ("Brawl"), shows this method at work. The first translated title, for instance, as revealed by the two draft versions, probably both from 1937, was "Quarrel." The greater accuracy of "Brawl" with respect to the Lorca title denotes a decision to privilege source-text faithfulness over poetic license. There are numerous further examples of this creative and / or editorial strategy:

A light hard as playing cards
in the *green roughness*
cuts away furious horses
and the profiles of riders.
In the nook of an olive tree
two old women cry.[15]

---

as much as possible, and moves the reader towards him; or he leaves the reader in peace, as much as possible, and moves the author towards him." Here is Venuti: "Foreignizing translations . . . are not transparent, . . . [they] eschew fluency for a . . . heterogeneous mix of discourses, [and] are . . . partial in their interpretation of the foreign text, but they tend to flaunt their partiality instead of concealing it."

12. Arnold Rampersad, *The Life of Langston Hughes: Volume 1, 1902–1941, I, Too, Sing America*, 193.

13. Smith, "Black Wedding: García Lorca, Langston Hughes, and the Translation of Introjection."

14. Soto, "Crossing Over," 126–28. The translations discussed in this essay are not included in my previous study.

15. Hughes, "Gypsy Ballads," 1937, unpublished draft translation of Lorca's *Ro-*

A light hard as playing cards
in the *green roughness*
silhouettes furious horses
and the profiles of riders.
In the nook of an olive tree
two old women cry.[16]

A light hard as playing cards
in the *acid greenness*
silhouettes furious horses
and the profiles of riders.
On the crest of an olive tree
two old women cry.[17]

Una dura luz de naipe
Recorta en el *agrio verde*,
caballos enfurecidos
y perfiles de jinetes.
En la copa de un olivo
lloran dos viejas mujeres.[18]

The italicized words point to a process of fine-tuning the translation. A further emendation of lines that were identical in both draft versions restored accuracy and the male agent as it moved Hughes's Anglo-American version closer to Lorca's:

Now a cross of fire
Flames on the road of death.

Now he rides a cross of fire
on the road to death.

Ahora monta cruz de fuego,
Carretera de la muerte.

---

mancero Gitano in the James Weldon Johnson Collection, Beinecke Rare Book and Manuscript Library, Yale University.

16. Hughes, "Gypsy Ballads," 1937, unpublished draft translation of Lorca's *Romancero Gitano* in the Langston Hughes Collection, Schomburg Center for Black Research and Culture, New York Public Library.

17. Hughes, "Gypsy Ballads," *Beloit Poetry Journal* 2:1 (Fall 1951): 9.

18. Federico García Lorca, *Obras Completas*, 1:398.

One might argue that Lorca's radical defamiliarization of language makes it relatively easy to adopt a semantic translation practice over a communicative one. One can simply treat words as building blocks, replacing the foreign lexicon with its target equivalent, and disregard other considerations such as syntax, word order, and, ultimately, intelligibility. This is hardly what Hughes did, however. To begin with, his renderings of Lorca's ballads are in intelligible English and, overall, evince a humility toward the source text and an absence of rhetorical self-indulgence that are markedly less in evidence in, for example, David K. Loughran's 1994 bilingual edition of Lorca's *Romancero*, which includes the 1922 *Primeras Canciones*. Loughran's version, while competent, reads as if there were no source text, as if, in short, the source text had been written in American English. So far does his domesticating practice go (Venti's term denoting the strategy whereby the source text is disguised to the point of virtual invisibility) that the target discourse not only obfuscates the foreign language source, and hence the entire translation process, but also normalizes the strangeness of Lorca's text. Here is the Loughram version of the lines quoted above:

A harsh light of gaming cards
etches the bitter green
with the profiles of riders
and infuriated steeds.
In the branches of an olive,
Two old women weep . . . [19]

The choice of "branches" for "copa" yields a relatively tame image of two old women sitting in a tree, unlike the more startling Lorca image of two old women sitting on the top branches of a tree. Hughes maintains the shock value of the source image by use of the word "crest." Similarly, Loughram's use of "harsh" diminishes the sensory charge of "dura," upheld in Hughes's choice of the literalist "hard," an adjective that resonates closely with the source connotations: tangibility, even physicality and homoeroticism.

In this necessarily cursory overview of Langston Hughes's poetics I have argued that dislocation or displacement both informed and empowered a creative output that spanned poetry, autobiographical narrative, and translation. The broad transoceanic paradigm Hughes seizes on

19. Loughram, trans. and ed., *Gypsy Ballads and Songs*, by Federico García Lorca, 10.

in his autobiography, I suggest, coheres with other, more specific, even local paradigms. I, for one, would welcome a retheorizing of modernist discourses of displacement to take account of a coeval cultural expressiveness traditionally inscribed within the terms *New Negro* or *Harlem Renaissance*. The Renaissance was, if anything, more implicated than its Euro-American counterpart in transatlantic explorations and renegotiations of territoriality, ethnicity, identity, and cultural practice. Although beyond the limited scope of this essay, such a retheorizing might commence with the massive intranational displacement of the first decades of the twentieth century that carried an urbanizing black America from southern to northern states. Farah Jasmine Griffin's important work on the vast range of creative, political, and social practices "set flowin'" in the works, say, of Dunbar, Toomer, Wright, and West, as well as contemporary artists such as Morrison and black rappers, provides overwhelming evidence of migration as a source of creativity.[20] The African American migration narrative—indeed, African American migration art as a whole, starting with slave narrative—provides us with one of the richest sources of representations of displacement in modernity.

20. Griffin, *"Who set you flowin'?": The African-American Migration Narrative.*

"It Is the Same Everywhere for Me"

Langston Hughes and the African Diaspora's Everyman

Lorenzo Thomas

Because of his breathtakingly accurate evocation of the daily lives and bittersweet yearnings of ordinary working-class black folk, his bold call for revolutionary political action, and his innovative blend of African American folk songs and the New Poetry movement's avant-garde interest in replacing stodgy nineteenth-century poetic diction with vernacular rhythms, Langston Hughes was widely acknowledged to be an important American writer in the 1930s. It is even more interesting to consider that, in the same period, Hughes also became a poet with an international influence that is astonishing in its reach.

Quite early on, the poets of what we call the Harlem Renaissance were known and appreciated by readers in French- and Spanish-speaking countries. Claude McKay's outspokenness and Countee Cullen's introspective lyrical beauty, coupled with their mastery of the traditions of English-language poetry and the apparent novelty that Cullen mentions in his sonnet "Yet Do I Marvel," brought them international attention. It was Langston Hughes, however, who—in person and in his poems—most effectively modeled characteristics that began to define a twentieth-century everyman for the African diaspora.

"Langston Hughes's ability to see the beauty in everyday Black life," suggested *Philadelphia Tribune* reporter Bobbi Booker, "is evident in every item he wrote."[1] Just as interesting, I think, was Hughes's ability to create a poetic vocabulary and establish an Afrocentric point of view that would help to shape the work of two generations of poets in the United States, the Caribbean, and Africa.

Langston Hughes began his career writing in a modernist style, having been influenced by reading Carl Sandburg's *Chicago Poems* (1916) while still in high school. Sandburg's Whitmanesque catalogs and psalm-like long lines were intriguingly matched with Midwest vernacular diction and created a seismic effect on the world of American poetry. Perhaps because of Sandburg's daily contacts as a newspaper reporter in Chicago, his poems also communicated a sympathetic interest in the experiences of immigrants and the working class. Within months of Sandburg's first appearances in Harriet Monroe's *Poetry* magazine, many poets across the country were attempting to write in his new idiom. Sandburg was a major influence on the language of American modernist poetry, but there were other important contributors. In 1919, critic Louis Untermeyer celebrated the diverse origins of the younger American poets. "Glance also," he wrote, "at the various racial colors of the names themselves: Frost, Oppenheim, Lindsay, Masters, Sandburg, Lowell, Giovannitti, Robinson, Neihardt, Benét, Pound, Kreymborg, Endicoff, Eastman, Tietjens. What a medley of clans and nationalities." (One might note that the only poet of African descent mentioned in Untermeyer's *The New Poetry* [1919] is William Stanley Braithwaite—but McKay, Cullen, and Hughes had not yet come on stage.) While Untermeyer praised Sandburg's attention to language, he was more impressed by the poet's spirit—which was precisely what appealed to ordinary readers. "Here," he wrote, "in spite of its moments of delicacy, is no trace of delicate languors, of passion extracted from songs or life that is gleaned in a library." For Untermeyer, as for the many poets who immediately began to mimic Sandburg's style, the Chicagoan seemed to be creating poetry *directly* from everyday life.[2]

In 1917, encouraged by Ethel Weimer, his sophomore English teacher at Cleveland's Central High School, Langston Hughes carefully studied and imitated Sandburg's free-verse model. In one of the poems he wrote that year, Hughes recognized Sandburg as "a lover of all the living" (*CW* 13:48). During the summers, in Cleveland and in Chicago, Hughes also got his first lessons in what racial prejudice was all about. But back at school in 1918, learning to read French, Hughes had an epiphanic mo-

---

1. Booker, "Langston Hughes's Centennial Celebration."
2. Untermeyer, *The New Era in American Poetry*, 356, 109.

ment. "I think it was de Maupassant," he wrote in *The Big Sea* (1940), "who made me really want to be a writer and write stories about Negroes, so true that people in far-away lands would read them—even after I was dead" (*CW* 13:51). It is from these inspirations that Hughes began to shape his own original voice.

As Cary Nelson usefully points out: "it is one thing to decide that poetry can help illuminate a 'real' political world," but "it is another thing to imagine that poetry is itself a terrain of political action, that what poetry does to and for people, what people do for themselves with poetry's assistance, reshapes the political arena itself."[3] It is faith in the latter possibility that energized poets of African descent during the first three decades of the twentieth century. These poets did not, however, believe that merely writing the poem was sufficient. The poem was just one aspect of an entire repertoire of actions.

Before he could become a full-fledged modernist political poet, Hughes had to reject the conventional verse of the era. As mentioned earlier, he was fortunate that he had little personal investment in the type of verse that appeared in his schoolbooks. In "Formula," published in *The Messenger* in August 1926, Hughes employed heavy irony to describe the sort of poetry he had no intention of writing:

> Poetry should treat
>   Of lofty things
> Soaring thoughts
>   And birds with wings.

According to this formula for "success,"

> The Muse of Poetry
>   Should not care
> That earthly pain
>   Is everywhere. (*CW* 1:178–79)

While Hughes was striving to become an avant-garde poet in terms of poetic style, he did not always share the avant-garde attitude toward the reading audience. Just as he avoided the formula of lofty and irrelevant sentiments, he rejected the notion of the alienated artist. Clearly, Hughes

---

3. Nelson, *Repression and Recovery: Modern American Poetry and the Politics of Cultural Memory, 1910–1945*, 127–28.

would not have subscribed to an avant-garde proclamation signed by Kay Boyle, Hart Crane, Eugene Jolas, and others, in which they declared, "The revolution in the English language is an accomplished fact." For that wing of the poetic avant-garde, expression was more important than communication and there was nothing but disdain for "literature still under the hegemony of the banal word, monotonous syntax, static psychology, descriptive naturalism, and desirous of crystallizing a viewpoint." Although Jolas was disturbed by the capitalist system's replacement of "regional particularities" with a bland mass consciousness, his remedy—worked out in the usual passionate conversations at sidewalk cafes of Paris—was an envisioned neologistic poetry that transcended nationalism and political ideology. The 1929 manifesto was purposely "insolent" and succeeded in creating an irate reaction in the international press. Hughes was as interested as were Jolas, Crane, or Sandburg in disrupting the complacent and overstuffed poetic diction of the nineteenth century, but he was also determined to *communicate* a point of view that had traditionally been ignored.[4]

If the diction and structure of Hughes's early poems reflect the influence of Sandburg, their content suggests that Hughes was familiar with the polemics of a developing militant race consciousness. In addition to his youthful study of midwestern American modernism, Hughes—as demonstrated by "Proem" and "The Negro Speaks of Rivers" (1921)—was also conversant with the vocabulary of black nationalism that was appearing in works by young writers such as Andria Razafkeriefo who published during the World War I period in militant journals such as *The Crusader*. Razafkeriefo—who later achieved fame and a considerable fortune as Andy Razaf, lyricist for jazz composer Thomas "Fats" Waller—was a frequent contributor to *The Crusader*. His 1918 poem "Why I Am Proud," says critic William J. Maxwell, "versifies race patriotism into memorizable quotations."[5] Perhaps because Razaf was also a soapbox orator on Harlem's 125th Street, his verses are seldom obscure. In one poem he denounces D. W. Griffith's racist film *Birth of a Nation* and defiantly declares

> I'm the NEW NEGRO, of much sterner stuff,
> And not the "old darkey," so easy to bluff!

4. Jerome Rothenberg, ed., *Revolution of the Word: A New Gathering of American Avant-Garde Poetry, 1914–1945*, esp. 150, xvii–xix, 107–10.

5. Maxwell, *New Negro, Old Left: African-American Writing and Communism between the Wars*, 29.

Although he moved in show-business circles, Razaf continued to write topical poetry throughout his life (some of it more ambitious stylistically than his early publications). According to his biographer, Razaf knew the emerging Harlem Renaissance writers well and formed a close friendship with Langston Hughes in the late 1920s.[6]

It is not difficult to see how Hughes's early poems reflect political ideas that might have been found in the pages of *The Crusader,* poet Fenton Johnson's *Champion Magazine,* Marcus Garvey's *Negro World* newspaper, or *The Crisis*—the journal of the National Association for the Advancement of Colored People (NAACP). Hughes's "The Negro Speaks of Rivers" offers an inventory of African achievement from antiquity to the present and mounts a poetic counterargument to what a 1918 *Crusader* editorial called "alien education." Editor Cyril V. Briggs had complained that "not only does the white man's system of education effectually cover up the ancient glories of the race when the Ethiopians . . . were looked upon as akin to the gods, but covers up as well the recent and by no means insignificant achievements of the Race in modern times."[7] Hughes's youthful yet ageless speaker demonstrates that he has not succumbed to such miseducation by pointing out that he does, in fact, know who raised the pyramids. What is notable about the "Proem" to *The Weary Blues* (1926)—sometimes reprinted under the title "Negro"—is the poet's specific evocation of an eternal presence for his protagonist. He is, for example, a worker who labored on Egypt's pyramids in 3000 B.C. as well as on New York City's splendid twentieth-century Woolworth Building skyscraper. As in "The Negro Speaks of Rivers," Hughes's persona has always been here and, we might assume, will always be. This is a trope used to good effect more recently in John A. Williams's novel *Captain Blackman* (1972), but it is not, of course, employed by Hughes solely for literary effect. The assertion of the Negro's eternal presence—and participation in the great works of many civilizations—is one of the arguments put forward by black nationalists to counter the racist charge that people of African ancestry have had no significant role in history.

If Andy Razaf (in a sense reversing James Weldon Johnson's journey) moved from being a ponderously political poet toward becoming a brilliant popular songwriter, Hughes's efforts to bring authentic Negro lyricism into the domain of literature were not always greeted with applause. In 1926, reviewing the first and only issue of *Fire!!* magazine, the *Baltimore*

6. Barry Singer, *Black and Blue: The Life and Lyrics of Andy Razaf,* 49, 51, 176.
7. Briggs, "Alien Education."

Afro-American noted that Hughes "displays his usual ability to say nothing in many words, willfully violating all the rules of poetics and still calling his work poetry."[8] Early attempts to turn the blues into literature, as in poems collected in *Fine Clothes to the Jew* (1927), also met with harsh criticism in the black press.

Others, of course, saw things differently. The way Hughes wrote poems was also, to a great extent, the way he lived his life. Beginning in the 1920s, Hughes's travels as a merchant seaman and curious aspiring journalist provided images and subject matter for his poems. When Hughes gave a reading in Houston in April 1932, *Houston Informer* editor Carter Wesley was impressed with his "purposefulness." Wesley did not see Hughes's extensive travels as wandering but as "the key to his success. He had been to Africa and to parts of the West Indies, where Negroes live. He went because he wanted to know the black man everywhere."[9] Hughes's travels put him in direct contact with writers of African descent outside the United States beginning with his sojourn in Paris in 1924. In 1930, traveling to Cuba and Haiti, he became friendly with poets Nicolás Guillén and Jacques Roumain and published translations of their work in *The Crisis* in 1931. He was reunited with them in Paris in 1937 at the Second International Writers Congress and, from there, traveled to the battle fronts of Spain as a war correspondent in the company of Guillén.

These experiences also gave Hughes a polished, debonair cosmopolitanism. "One of the main characteristics of Langston Hughes," wrote Nancy Cunard in 1937, "is ease—both of manner and of mind. The impression of one who skates over the difficulties with grace and with tact. But this charm of manner does not signify that Langston is not very much *all there*. And doubtless the particular problems which face the coloured intellectual in that strange mixture of ferocity, ignorance and, more recently, appreciation of talent which is the U.S.A., have engendered this manner—an excellent 'professionalism' in the handling of life. Add to this a lovely sense of humor and a heart that forgets never friend—nor foe."[10]

When Hughes spoke of human suffering, he was specific. "We Negroes of America," he told the Second International Writers Congress, "are tired of a world divided superficially on the basis of poverty and power—the rich over the poor, no matter what their color. We Negroes of America are

8. Quoted in Hughes, "Harlem Literati in the Twenties," 14.
9. Quoted in Lorenzo Thomas, *Extraordinary Measures: Afrocentric Modernism and Twentieth-Century American Poetry*, 194.
10. Cunard, "Three Negro Poets," 531.

tired of a world in which it is possible for any group of people to say to another: 'You have no right to happiness, or freedom, or the joy of life.'"[11]

Even more significant is the fact that Hughes's poems were quite as specific as were his political speeches. Poems written in the early 1930s, particularly "Always the Same" (1932) and "Cubes" (1934), differ markedly from the exotic and primitivist depiction of Africa found in the early "Danse Africaine" (1922). As M. E. Mudimbe-Boyi pointed out in a 1988 *Présence Africaine* essay, the poets of the Harlem Renaissance tended to view Africa as the symbol of a lost paradise, more mythical than militant.[12] The evocation of a romanticized Negro lyricism in Hughes's "Song for a Banjo Dance," for example, mimics Paul Laurence Dunbar directly, but "Danse Africaine" also effectively accomplishes Dunbar's trick of delivering slightly different messages to black and white readers. In Hughes's poem the tom-toms' beat that "stirs your blood" might mean an unleashing of libidinal impulses for the white listener as opposed to an atavistic surge of racial identification. Still, the poem's midnight bonfire and dancing girl inscribe an image that is pleasantly romantic for all audiences. While the early Hughes poem typified the view of Africa shared by many Harlem Renaissance writers, the poems of the 1930s are informed by a revolutionary, anti-imperialist political consciousness.

Viewed together, however, Hughes's best poems of the 1920s and 1930s present a model of diasporic consciousness in the persona of a black worker exploited by capitalism, but aware of being oppressed and prepared to resist. Unlike the scholars and politicians enlisted in the turn-of-the-century Pan-African movement, Hughes was not concerned with the local differences and global similarities of Europe's imperialist hegemony. Instead, he created the universal and eternal Negro whose modern situation differs from antiquity primarily in the loss of power and self-determination. As we have shown, this figure is eloquently articulated in "The Negro Speaks of Rivers" (1921) and "Negro" (1922). Such a figure, however, can encourage a backward-looking and self-deluding nostalgia as easily as it can inspire racial pride. It is necessary, then, for Hughes to present a *modern* agenda for this persona—a task fulfilled with careful specificity in "Always the Same." Hughes's speaker proclaims,

> It is the same everywhere for me:
> On the docks at Sierra Leone,

---

11. Edward J. Mullen, ed., *Langston Hughes in the Hispanic World and Haiti*, 94.
12. Mudimbe-Boyi, "Harlem Renaissance et l'Afrique: Une aventure ambiguë," 23.

In the cotton fields of Alabama,
In the diamond mines of Kimberley,
On the coffee hills of Haiti,
The banàna lands of Central America,
The streets of Harlem (*CW* 1:226)

Similarly, the sensuous, exotic depiction of an ecstatic precolonial African heritage in "Danse Africaine"—marked by the hypnotic, blood-stirring "slow beating of the tom-toms"—is given a shocking, sobering twist in 1934's "Cubes," a poem that mercilessly undermines facile notions of primitivism and European theories of racial superiority.

Before World War I, African sculptures—the plunder of imperialist campaigns—were retrieved from ethnographic museums and exhibited as art in Paris and New York. Writers such as Marius de Zayas and Alain Locke celebrated this development as a sort of cultural vindication, the influence of African artistic models serving to revitalize European art that suffered from "decadence and sterility."[13] In "Cubes," however, the intercultural contact that jump-starts the international modernist avant-garde signals dissolution and destruction for Africa's grand heritage and present society. African art might refresh the exhausted creative stream in European painting, but Africa suffers in the exchange.

Indeed, what others might laud as cultural exchange is, in the poet's eyes, merely "the old game of the boss and the bossed." The unorthodox planes of the avant-garde Cubist painting offer a fragmented view of reality. In Hughes's brutally cynical view, Picasso's world-famous *Demoiselles d'Avignon* (1909) becomes "the three old prostitutes of France—/ Liberty, Equality, Fraternity—/ And all three of 'em sick." Thus, in return for bringing his beauty and rhythm to Europe,

the young African from Senegal
Carries back from Paris
A little more disease (*CW* 1:236–37)

In the poem's most startling turn, the souvenir-bearing sailor returns from the sea to his native village to infect the beautiful "night-veiled girl" we met and admired in "Danse Africaine."

"The view from the bottom of the hill is not the same as the view from the top of the hill," said Amiri Baraka. Relationships that provide rhap-

13. Locke, "The Legacy of the Ancestral Arts," 258.

sodic opportunities for literary critics or art historians look somewhat different when recast in the milieu of the merchant seaman. The difference between a young sailor's "devil-may-care" attitude and the sardonic wisdom of the blues is experience. As an alpine skier once said, good judgment is the product of experience, but experience is the result of making mistakes. The trick is to survive mishap long enough for experience to become useful.

During his 1937 visit to Paris, Hughes was able to personally meet young writers who had been influenced by his work. These included the founders of the negritude movement—students who had been associated with the *Revue du Monde Noir* edited by Paulette Nardal—Léon Damas from Guyana, Aimé Césaire from Martinique, and Léopold Sédar Senghor from Senegal. In Paris, these young poets enjoyed the friendship of the Martinican scholar Nardal and her cousin Louis Achille Sr., a former member of the Howard University faculty. Nardal, well versed in what she termed "Aframerican literature," was a teacher of English and organizer of a literary salon. In 1931 she launched the bilingual journal.[14] It was through the *Revue du Monde Noir*—as well as Alain Locke's *The New Negro* (1925) and copies of *The Crisis* and the National Urban League's *Opportunity: Journal of Negro Life*—that the Paris-based poets encountered the poems of Claude McKay and Langston Hughes, Jean Toomer and Countee Cullen.[15] Brent Hayes Edwards has demonstrated that Paulette Nardal and her sister Jane shared Locke's view that black intellectuals from the Americas might provide leadership for Africa's reemergence from European colonial domination, an issue of extreme importance to the young poets.[16]

La Revue du Monde Noir was diasporic in scope. "The goal," wrote Janet G. Vaillant, "was nothing less than the creation of a new worldwide black consciousness." Making explicit what W. E. B. Du Bois's *Crisis* implied, the editors of the *Revue* announced their desire "to create among Negroes of the entire world, regardless of nationality, an intellectual and moral tie which will permit them to better know each other, to love one another, to defend more effectively their collective interests and to glorify their race."[17] Nardal's journal was the prototype for the postwar *Présence*

14. Janet G. Vaillant, *Black, French, and African: The Life of Léopold Sédar Senghor*, 91–97.

15. Michel Fabre, "The Harlem Renaissance Abroad: French Critics and the New Negro Literary Movement (1924–1964)," 318–19.

16. Edwards, "Three Ways to Translate the Harlem Renaissance," 294–96.

17. Vaillant, *Black, French, and African*, 92.

Africaine, and its name was revived—in English—when Johnson Publications' *Negro Digest* was renamed *Black World* in the 1960s. In Paulette Nardal's view, "the idea of race was a necessity" for people of African heritage in the United States. As Léon Damas summarized her idea, "the systematic contempt in which White Americans held Blacks forced them to look at the past of the Black race for motives of pride, historically, culturally and socially."[18] Nardal's argument was not unique. As early as 1917, this Afrocentric impulse had been eloquently expressed in Carter G. Woodson's *Journal of Negro History* by a George Wells Parker essay presenting "the African race as the real founder of civilization."[19] Hughes's "The Negro Speaks of Rivers" is a poetic reflection of Parker's thesis. Similarly, the poems of the negritude poets reflect the influence of Hughes.

Negritude poetry, as Ellen Conroy Kennedy has explained, was "strongly influenced, thematically and stylistically, by American poets of the Harlem Renaissance."[20] When Mercer Cook read Damas's *Pigments* in 1938 he was, he recalled, "enraptured. Never before had I seen such poems in French." Cook saw a similarity of approach in Damas's work to the poems of McKay and Hughes. Cook met Damas in Paris a few days later, and the poet proudly acknowledged that he had, in fact, translated poems by Hughes and "Strong Men" by Sterling A. Brown. Léopold Sédar Senghor found Damas's work marked by "absolutely Negro rhythm and it greatly resembles that of Langston Hughes." "We were determined," Damas recalled in 1974 of his own work and that of his colleagues, "to follow in the footsteps of Langston Hughes, Countee Cullen, and likewise Jean Toomer, Sterling Brown, Claude McKay."[21]

If Hughes had a direct influence on Senghor and Aimé Césaire, it would seem to be thematic, but the poems of Damas and Jacques Roumain clearly also have a stylistic affinity with the open vernacular polyrhythms of Hughes's lyrics. The excitement that Senghor, Damas, and others experienced when they discovered Hughes's work had been anticipated by Hughes himself when he encountered poets such as Roumain and Nicolás Guillén—both of whom he translated for publication in *The Crisis.* Roumain (1907–1944) was among the founders of the literary journal *La Revue Indigène* in 1927 and helped organize the Haitian Communist Party in

18. See Damas, "Négritude in Retrospect," 258–60.
19. Thomas, *Extraordinary Measures,* 12.
20. Kennedy, ed., *The Negritude Poets: An Anthology of Translations from the French,* xx.
21. Cook, "Léon-Gontran Damas: The Last Four Decades," 60, 62; Damas, "Négritude in Retrospect," 259–60.

1934.[22] Roumain's poetry indicts both white supremacy and capitalism. He also denounced the exploitation of African-based culture through tourism, looking forward to a day of reckoning "when the rhumba bands and the blues bands / in your clubs / start to play another tune." In his poem "Sales Negres" (1939), Roumain anticipated Frantz Fanon as he envisioned a revolutionary moment when "even the tom-toms will have learned the language / of the Internationale," providing a marching song for those he calls "Tous les damnés de la terre."[23] From the time they met in Haiti in 1930, Hughes remained a booster of Roumain's literary reputation and published articles defending him when Roumain's political activism caused him to be imprisoned in Haiti in the late 1930s.

In the late 1930s and 1940s, Hughes's influence would also electrify Portuguese-speaking Africans studying in Lisbon, especially the gifted Francisco-José Tenreiro (1921–1963)—a poet credited with launching the negritude movement in Lusophone Africa.

While a student in Lisbon, Tenreiro, a native of what was then the Portuguese island colony of São Tomé, studied Hughes and the Harlem Renaissance poets and became familiar with the francophone writers as well. He published *Ilha de Nome Santo*, a collection of poems, in 1942 and a critical study of North American literature three years later.[24] Tenreiro's poems combine the exotic machinery of Hughes's "Danse Africaine" with a barbed humor that resembles the work of Léon Damas. In his poem "Mestiço's Song," Tenreiro takes delight in enraging white racists because, he says,

> When I love the white woman
> I am white,
> When I love the black woman
> I am black,
> Uh-huh![25]

Here Tenreiro's mulatto speaker is more trickster than tragic; and, as Caroline Shaw notes, "espousal of a worldwide black and African culture is explicit" in Tenreiro's poems.[26] This is made especially clear in the mag-

22. Kennedy, ed., *Negritude Poets*, xxxi, 19.

23. Roumain, *Ebony Wood / Bois d'Ebene*, 35–37, 43–45.

24. Mario de Andrade, *La poésie Africaine d'expression Portugaise*, 72.

25. Russell G. Hamilton, *Voices from an Empire: A History of Afro-Portuguese Literature*, 15–16.

26. Patrick Chabal, *The Post-Colonial Literature of Lusophone Africa*, 236.

nificent poem "Negro do Todo Mundo," where Tenreiro acknowledges his debt to Langston Hughes.

According to Richard A. Preto-Rodas, Tenreiro saw his poetry as part of a movement "transcending sectional and political interests in pursuit of a Pan-African awareness which might effectively combat the complacent ethnocentrism of Occidental culture."[27] Like Césaire, Damas, and Senghor, Tenreiro was a "man of culture" (to use Césaire's phrase) who became a professor and went on to serve in his country's legislature.

Although he himself was very much aware of the worldwide influence of his work, and of his success in defining a persona of black proletarian resistance that was a model for poets writing in Spanish, French, and Portuguese as well as English, during the 1950s Hughes often seemed disappointed with the progress of what Du Bois called "the darker races."

In an astonishingly sarcastic address to a March 1959 conference of Negro writers, convened by the American Society of African Culture (AMSAC), Hughes recited one of his most popular poems:

> someday somebody'll
> Stand up and talk about me,
> And write about me—
> Black and beautiful—
> And sing about me
> And put on plays about me!
> I reckon it'll be me myself!
> Yes, it'll be me

Then, keeping it real, he added:

> Of course, it may be a long time before we finance big Broadway shows or a seven-million-dollar movie like *Porgy and Bess* on which, so far as I know, not a single Negro writer was employed. The *Encyclopedia Britannica* declares *Porgy and Bess* "the greatest American musical drama ever written." The *Encyclopedia Britannica* is white. White is right. So shoot the seven million! 7 come 11! Dice, gin, razors, knives, dope, watermelon, whores—7–11! Come 7! (*CW* 9:381–82)

In other words, though the Black Arts movement was waiting in the wings, Hughes perceived that the day Jacques Roumain had dreamed of,

27. Preto-Rodas, *Négritude as a Theme in the Poetry of the Portuguese-Speaking World*, 46.

the day when the blues bands would play a different tune, was still a long way off.

At the same AMSAC conference, poet Samuel W. Allen remarked, "Hegel has somewhere said that the slave must not only break the chain; he must also shatter the image in both his and his former master's mind before he can truly become free."[28] That perception, of course, was fully understood by Hughes and those he influenced and would become a guiding principle for many of the African American artists of the 1960s. Even though they grew up thinking that the Blaxploitation gangster movies of the 1970s are "Black classic cinema," it might still be useful to remind today's young artists that Allen's point remains true. At the end of his remarks to the AMSAC conference, Hughes returned to one of the images used in his 1926 poem "Formula." His last instruction to his audience was to "let your talent bloom! You say you are mired in manure? Manure fertilizes. As the old saying goes, 'Where the finest roses bloom, there is always a lot of manure around'" (CW 9:383).

When, in 1963, Hughes edited *Poems from Black Africa* for Indiana University Press, he was—in a very real sense—taking an inventory of a movement that he himself had a major role in launching. Assessing African poets writing in French, Portuguese, and English at the beginning of the 1960s, Hughes noted that these writers "are not so much propagandists for African nationalism, as they are spokesmen for variations of *négritude*—a word the French-speaking writers have coined to express pride in and a love of the African heritage, physically, spiritually and culturally." He noted that these poets were "modernists in style, in contrast to the older writers of colonial days who were influenced by Victorian models or by the classical French poets taught in the missionary schools" (CW 9:508).

These poets, Hughes stressed, were not cultural isolates but well educated and cosmopolitan. More important to Hughes, however, was his sense that these poets were also—as he puts it—"close enough to tribal life to know the names of the old non-Christian gods" (CW 9:510). Whether or not that assumption was accurate, it was clear that their sophistication did not mean estrangement from their people. In fact, these were poets who had gone to school to Langston Hughes. They were, like him, modernists; and, like him, they felt deeply honored to be seen as the voices of their people within a growing diasporic choir.

In notes that he scribbled to himself in 1964, Hughes stated, "A poet is

---

28. Allen, "Négritude and Its Relevance to the American Negro Writer," 16.

a human being. Each human being must live within his time, with and for his people, and within the boundaries of his country. Therefore, how can a poet keep out of politics?"[29] In Hughes's understanding of politics, as he had experienced in Spain in 1937 during the Civil War, and in his own land, we are also—in spite of national borders—all connected, as Martin Luther King Jr. said, by an "inescapable mutuality."

Langston Hughes did live for and with his people, but the influence of his poetry spread far beyond the boundaries of any country, helping to create an African diasporic consciousness that continues to flourish in many lands, in many tongues.

29. Arnold Rampersad, *The Life of Langston Hughes: Volume 2, 1941–1967, I Dream a World*, 385.

Montage of a Dream Destroyed

Langston Hughes in Spain

Michael Thurston

It is hard to complain about how Langston Hughes is remembered, how his work is preserved in the canon of American writing, when we think of all the writers who have been forgotten and whose work does not appear in our anthologies or course syllabi. Complain we should, though, when the same three or four standards continue to represent the rich and complex work of this important poet. I do not wish to dispute the excellence of Hughes's most often anthologized poems ("The Negro Speaks of Rivers" and "Mulatto" are anthologized for very good reasons, after all, including their excellence). The narrow view these poems provide of Hughes's career, however, misses much of the complexity—of formal technique, of philosophical and political insight—that makes the career worth preserving in the first place. Hughes's writing about the Spanish Civil War is a particularly revealing example of that complexity in action.

My title refers to Hughes's late masterpiece, "Montage of a Dream Deferred," but for this exploration of Hughes's Spanish Civil War writing I want also to invoke more directly the cinematic technique that juxtaposes contrasting shots in order to achieve meanings different from those that arise from any of the shots seen independently. Montage is most directly associated with the work of Russian director Sergei Eisenstein, who theorized, as Geoffrey Nowell-Smith explains, that "meaning in the cinema was not inherent in any filmed object but was created by the collision of two signifying elements."[1] Montage has an earlier theoretical and practical life, however, and even in its pre-Eisenstein iterations the term has meanings of some utility for a revisionist reading of Hughes's career. The word *montage* (in Russian *montazh*, from the French *montage*) carries as one of its original meanings the sense of machine assembly (one mounts an engine, for example). David Bordwell grounds Eisenstein's theory in this meaning of montage and in the Russian Constructivists' application of this notion to the creation of artistic work. Of particular importance, Bordwell argues, was the Constructivist idea of "assembling materials in a way that generates a degree of friction among them." Montage creates a unified impression through the collision of different shots; it combines "parts" so that they rub against each other to create frictional heat. Behind both meanings stands the artist as engineer, building a mechanism intended to produce specific effects upon the spectator.[2]

I want to suggest that when we look with montage in mind at Hughes's writing and other actions in, around, about, and for the Spanish Civil War (fought between 1936 and 1938 but reverberating through the rest of the twentieth century), we can see these actions as parts of a unified project with meanings beyond those suggested by any text or act taken on its own. Hughes's activities and writing in support of the Spanish Republic are of different types. They occurred in a variety of locations and under a variety of conditions. When combined, though, they produce a coherent effect (and some significant and useful friction). Furthermore, I want to suggest that the notion of montage is useful for understanding Hughes's own interpretation of Spain's significance. The Civil War, too, comprises quite different shots that, when juxtaposed, give rise to meanings not contained by any in isolation. Finally, reading Hughes in Spain as a montage alerts us to the similarly multivalent character of Hughes's work (especially his explicitly political writing) throughout his long career.

The Spanish Civil War began as a rebellion against the government elected in 1936. That government, a coalition of socialists, communists, anarchists, and liberals, undertook a series of reforms that threatened the entrenched power of landowners, the Catholic Church, and the army.

1. Nowell-Smith, "Eisenstein on Montage," in *S. M. Eisenstein, Selected Works Volume Two: Towards a Theory of Montage*, xiii–xx, xiv.
2. Bordwell, *The Cinema of Eisenstein*, 120–21. Bordwell notes that "Eisenstein conceives of the spectator as his material, with the techniques of theatre furnishing the tools for working on it . . . techniques selected for their power to stimulate strong perceptual and emotional reactions" (ibid., 120).

When Gen. Francisco Franco led an insurgent army against the government, conservative and reactionary elements in the country threw their support behind him and the country was torn apart. Government forces were quickly driven out of much of the country, retreating to strongholds in Barcelona and Madrid. Siege lines were drawn, and the armies settled into a trench war that lasted more than two years.[3]

The fascist governments of Germany and Italy supported Franco's forces with money, matériel, and military advisers. The European democracies, fearful of upsetting delicate diplomatic balances, declared themselves neutral. Support for the Spanish Republic came from the Soviet Union and the Communist International (Comintern); the latter organized groups of volunteers as the International Brigades. These volunteers came from all over Europe (supported by the Comintern and by the Communist parties of various countries), from Canada, and from the United States, where they were assembled and financed by the Communist Party of the United States of America (CPUSA).[4]

Throughout the 1930s, Langston Hughes had been active in politics along both racial and international Left/Right lines. He wrote, read, and agitated on behalf of the Scottsboro defendants, on behalf of the imprisoned International Workers of the World (IWW) leader Tom Mooney, and on behalf of the Soviet Union. Hughes's work around these causes ranged from his thematic treatment of them in his poetry and drama to public identification and fund-raising. He wrote poems and plays that connected racial struggle with international politics, concluding his 1931 one-act play *Scottsboro Limited* with the waving of a red flag and the singing of the Internationale (the Communist Party anthem). At the same time, Hughes participated in more direct modes of political engagement. He addressed the 1935 International Writers' Conference and traveled to the Soviet Union. While Hughes seems never to have joined the CPUSA, he published frequently in the party's magazine, *New Masses;* he produced a pamphlet to be sold in support of the International Labor Defense, the CPUSA-related organization that handled the appeals of the Scottsboro defendants; and he alienated himself from patrons (Charlotte Osgood Mason and Loren Miller) by refusing to temper his political attitudes and acts.

The summer of 1937 offered Hughes yet another chance to live as well

3. The best single-volume work on the Spanish Republic and the Civil War is Gabriel Jackson's *The Spanish Republic and the Civil War, 1931–1939.* On the beginnings of the rebellion, see 218–30. On the early military action, see 262–75 and 310–32.
4. Ibid., 247–61.

as write his political vision. When the Left-leaning Republic in Spain was threatened with destruction by right-wing forces within and surrounding the country, Hughes paid attention. He wrote "Song of Spain," and early in 1937 he sent it to Nancy Cunard when she wrote to ask him for a poem to include in a collection she hoped to assemble with Pablo Neruda. Cunard published the poem along with a poem by Federico García Lorca as the third in her series of six poetry leaflets, *Deux poèmes par Federico García Lorca et Langston Hughes: Les poètes du monde defendant le peuple espagnol.*[5] The poem stages an awakening from cultural stereotype ("*Flamenco* is the song of Spain") to historical reality ("A bombing plane's / The song of Spain" [*CW* 1:142]), which culminates in a final resolution to take action:

> I must drive the bombers out of Spain!
> I must drive the bombers out of the world!
> I must take the world for my own again (*CW* 1:144)

When André Malraux and Louis Aragon invited him to attend the Second International Writers' Congress that was to meet in Spain and Paris, Hughes hesitantly decided to attend. He then arranged with the *Baltimore Afro-American* and the *Cleveland Call and Post*, two African American newspapers, to serve as their special correspondent from Spain. At the end of June, he sailed for Europe, where he would spend four months in the wartorn Spanish Republic.

A montage of Hughes's Spain-related work would consist not only of the different kinds of writing he did during, after, and about those four months (poetry, reportage, lectures, essays, and autobiography), but also of the kinds of actions he participated in. Like the texts, the acts seem quite disparate on the surface: going to dinner or a party, visiting the front. The montage, then, might look something like this:

> Shot 1: "Air Raid: Barcelona"
> When the first BOMBS fall
> All other noises are suddenly still
> When the BOMBS fall.
> All other noises are deathly still
> As blood spatters the wall
>
> . . . .

5. Arnold Rampersad, *The Life of Langston Hughes: Volume 1, 1902–1941, I, Too, Sing America,* 338; Anne Chisholm, *Nancy Cunard: A Biography,* 238.

With wings like black cubes
Against the far dawn,
The stench of their passage
Remains when they're gone.
In what was a courtyard
A child weeps alone.

Men uncover bodies
From ruins of stone. (CW 1:262–63)[6]

Shot 2: Hughes walks the streets of Madrid with Nicolás Guillén. We see the city's plazas and facades. The two enjoy a meal whose quality resembles that of a dinner in Madrid before the war, only the limited choices on the menu indicate the deprivations suffered by a city under siege. Then they go to the Mella Club, where Hughes witnesses a scene of interracial utopia:

> We were invited to a dance that afternoon given in honor of the soldiers on leave, and here we met a number of Cubans, both colored and white, and a colored Portuguese, all taking an active part in the Spanish struggle against the fascists.
> And all of them finding in loyalist Spain more freedom than they had known at home. . . .
> In Spain, one could see at the dance that afternoon, there is no color line, and Catalonian girls and their escorts mingled gaily with the colored guests. (CW 9:159)[7]

Shot 3: Hughes travels to Brunete, the site of a disastrous Republican defeat, with war correspondents Leland Stowe and Richard Mowrer. At the nearby town of Quijorna, he first witnesses battlefield carnage: the sight of trees destroyed by shells, the stench of rotting flesh from disembodied limbs lying where they had fallen, and the chirping of birds. Birds?

"There's no birds. Those are sniper bullets whistling by."
"Firing at *us*?"

6. The poem was first published in *Esquire* (October 1938).
7. First published in the *Baltimore Afro-American*, October 23, 1937, p. 1. See also Rampersad, *Life*, 1:345–46. Hughes's reportage from Spain is collected in two convenient sources: Edward J. Mullen, ed., *Langston Hughes in the Hispanic World and Haiti*, which also gathers Hughes's poems about Spain and his writings about Mexico, Cuba, and Haiti; and *The Collected Works of Langston Hughes*, vol. 9.

"Certainly. . . . There's nobody else on this road to fire at."
"I never knew bullets sounded like birds cheeping before."
"Well, now you know." (CW 14:336)[8]

Even in Madrid, of course, Hughes is not safe from sniper fire. "Several times in Spain," he would later write, "I thought I might not live long" (CW 14:345). He accompanies a group of visiting "do-gooders" to Madrid's University City, an urban front line divided by trenches and patrolled by snipers. There, as he looks through a sandbagged opening toward the Fascist trenches, he is nicked by an explosive bullet (CW 14:348).

Shot 4: At the Alianza des Intelectuales Antifascistas in Madrid, Hughes sits at his typewriter, the jazz records he has brought with him playing in the background, translating poems from Lorca's *Romancero Gitano* into English and poems by Edwin Rolfe, the International Brigades' political commissar for Madrid, into Spanish. "Ahora monta cruz de fuego, / Carretera de la muerte," he reads, then types a draft translation of the lines: "Now a cross of fire / Flames on the road of death." Hughes leaves his typewriter to go to dinner with Rolfe, who described the evening:

> We discovered that it was Antonio La Sierra's 20th birthday, & we had a swell spontaneous party, till midnight. Cognac & coffee—speeches in Italian, German, Spanish, French & English by Langston Hughes. Then songs and toasts.[9]

Hughes had arrived at the Alianza with a letter of introduction addressed to Rolfe from Bill Lawrence, chief American commissar in Spain:

> The bearer Comrade Langston Hughes will remain in Spain for some time to write especially about the work of some Negro Comrades.[10]

---

8. See also Rampersad, *Life*, 1:349.

9. Cary Nelson and Jefferson Hendricks, *Edwin Rolfe: A Biographical Essay and Guide to the Rolfe Archive at the University of Illinois at Urbana–Champaign*, 31. The letter is in the Edwin Rolfe archive at the University of Illinois.

10. The note, which is in the Edwin Rolfe Archive at the University of Illinois, is reproduced in ibid., 30. Nelson and Hendricks note that "it adds a specific political dimension to Hughes's passionate work on behalf of the Spanish Republic that hasn't been acknowledged in Hughes scholarship to date. Hughes was receiving Party cooperation in Spain and thus at the very least the Party considered him to be working on common interests" (31).

With Rolfe's help and coordination, Hughes visits the Brigades in the field, broadcasts poems on the radio, and publishes in the International Brigades' English-language magazine, *Volunteer for Liberty*.

Shot 5: In Madrid, in Valencia, in Brunete and Quinto, Hughes meets African Americans who have come to fight for the Spanish Republic. For the *Afro-American* he writes dispatches about Abraham Lewis, a quartermaster in the International Brigades; about Ralph Thornton, a former newsboy from Pittsburgh who led a group of Internationals to take a Fascist bastion in Belchite; about Thaddeus Battle, a Howard University student serving in the Fifteenth International Brigade; about Basilio Cueria, a Cuban baseball player who left Harlem to captain a machine gun company for the Internationals. On his first visit to the front at Valencia in October 1937, he hears about the heroic death of Milt Herndon, brother of labor organizer Angelo Herndon and one of the African Americans who had risen to command posts in the International Brigades. "He died like this," Herndon's comrades tell him:

> "He was taking the second machine-gun over the top. He was the sergeant, the section leader. He had three guns under him. He was taking the second gun over the top with his men. We went about three hundred meters up a little rise—when all of a sudden the Fascists opened up on us. We had to stop. A regular rain of bullets.
>
> "They got one of our comrades, Irving, and he fell just ahead of us on top of the ridge in full view of the Fascist fire. He was wounded in the leg and couldn't move. The man nearest to him, Smitty, raised up to drag him back aways, and a bullet got Smitty in the heart. Got him right in the heart. Then Herndon crawled on up the slope to rescue the wounded boy. They got Herndon, too." (*CW* 9:183–84)[11]

While in Spain, Hughes visited a prison hospital and saw wounded "Moors," North Africans from Spanish colonies conscripted into Franco's army and forced to fight on the front lines. Before he arrived in Spain he had read about these "colored troops in the service of white imperialists" who had "been put in the front lines of the Franco offensive . . . and shot down like flies" (*CW* 9:164).[12] Now he notes the contrast between these soldiers and the mostly civilian conscripts now that the "regular Moorish cavalry and guard units" (*CW* 9:164) have been wiped out. While blacks in the International Brigades rise to command positions and give un-

---

11. First published in the *Baltimore Afro-American*, January 1, 1938, pp. 1–2.
12. First published in the *Baltimore Afro-American*, October 30, 1937, p. 1.

questioned orders to white soldiers beneath them, these "illiterate African colonials [are] forced to obey the commands of the Fascist generals" and "spurred on by promises of loot" (*CW* 9:178–79).[13]

There are numerous scenes we could add, numerous juxtapositions we could construct of these contrasting shots. The montage could be extended far beyond the end of the war itself. Hughes lectured on Spain for the Friends of the Abraham Lincoln Brigade upon his return to the United States. As late as 1954, he contributed two elegiac poems on Spain to Alvah Bessie's *Heart of Spain* anthology.[14] But this sample suffices, I think, to show how Hughes, in a variety of sites and circumstances, in a wide range of voices and venues (from the *Volunteer* to the *Nation* to *Esquire*, which published "Air Raid: Barcelona"), invested in the Spanish Republic all the cultural capital he had accumulated as a black poet, a social poet, a cultural commentator, a fellow traveler in Communist circles, and an international man of letters.

The montage illustrates not only the variety of work Hughes did on behalf of the Republic but also, and more important, the many personae in which he worked on behalf of the Spanish Republic. Indeed, it was only as this multifaceted political poet that Hughes could work as effectively as he did for the internationalist cause. Without his racial identity and the literary reputation he had built on poems exploring the consequences and opportunities that identity entailed, Hughes would not have had the backing of the African American newspapers that sponsored his travel to Spain. Had his literary reputation been smaller, he would not have been invited to the Writers' Congress from which he traveled to Spain, nor would he have had access to the literary community of Madrid and the Alianza. The political credentials he had earned by publishing frequently in *New Masses* and other Left magazines and by traveling to the Soviet Union to work on a documentary film project about race in that Communist country gained Hughes the cooperation of the International Brigades and the access to battlefields, hospitals, and black troops that he enjoyed. Once Hughes was in Spain, his meaning for the struggle depended on the intersection of these identities, both received and achieved. His significance for Spain arose from the juxtaposition of dinners with Guillén and Rolfe with the visits to battlefields, the endurance of bombardment, and

13. First published in the *Baltimore Afro-American*, December 18, 1937, p. 1.

14. "Hero—International Brigade" and "Tomorrow's Seed." See Bessie, ed., *The Heart of Spain: Anthology of Fiction, Non-fiction, and Poetry*, 325–26. See also Hughes, *CW* 3:201.

the interviews with soldiers. It was through a montage of roles, capacities, actions, and texts that Hughes could serve the Republic.

More important, it was as a montage of sorts that Hughes understood the significance of the Spanish Civil War, a significance that drove him to go to Spain in the first place. That complex conflict has been flattened in many recent accounts, reduced to the suppression of non-Communist groups by the Stalinist Communist Party and its International Brigades. On the ground in 1937 and 1938, of course, the war presented many different faces. From one angle, the Civil War appeared to be a conflict between a Left-leaning coalition government and the forces of reaction led by Franco to prevent and reverse reforms the government had begun to implement. It was a microcosmic conflict between the international Left and the Right, or between democracy and autocracy. From another perspective, though, the war was about colonialism. The disastrous neutrality of Europe's democracies during the conflict (a neutrality not matched by the continent's fascist governments—it was from German and Italian planes that bombs fell on Guernica) was partially attributable to concern for their own colonies (or, more properly, their grasp on those colonies). In yet another view, the war was about race; it represented a conflict between a government and an army that were fully integrated and an army whose conscripted "Moors" were deployed as cannon fodder and then paid off in German marks they could not spend.

Out of the juxtaposition of these views arose a meaning for the conflict that motivated Hughes. When viewed alongside one another, fascism abroad looked a lot like racism at home, as Hughes remarked in his address to the Writers' Congress in Paris. There, Hughes called himself "both a Negro and poor," a member of "the most oppressed group in America, that group that has known so little of American democracy," and he wrote, "We are the people who have long known in actual practice the meaning of the word Fascism—for the American attitude towards us has always been one of economic and social discrimination: in many states of our country Negroes are not permitted to vote or to hold political office" (CW 10:221).[15] He went on to argue that the plight of southern sharecroppers, the segregation of the races in public facilities, the treatment of the Scottsboro defendants, race riots, and lynchings all demonstrated "Fascism in action." Out of the montage, in other words, Hughes saw in Spain an important intersection between black and red interests. Spain

15. "Too Much of Race" first published in *Volunteer for Liberty*, August 23, 1937, pp. 3–4.

was for Hughes, as Robin D. G. Kelley notes that it was for many African Americans, "the place where it all came together."[16]

Although far from exhaustive, recent Hughes scholarship has provided a useful focus on Hughes's multiple cultural identities and roles. Particularly in the last decade, Hughes criticism has presented the political Hughes in compelling terms. Cary Nelson brought attention to Hughes's poetry on poverty and politics in *Repression and Recovery: Modern American Poetry and the Politics of Cultural Memory, 1910–1945* and set Hughes's poems about Spain in the context of American poetry arising from that war in *Revolutionary Memory: Recovering the Poetry of the American Left.* Maryemma Graham attended to Hughes's politically activist writing in "The Practice of a Social Art." Karen Ford's "Do Right to Write Right: Langston Hughes's Aesthetic of Simplicity" and "Making Poetry Pay: The Commodification of Langston Hughes" effectively complicate Arnold Rampersad's blithe dismissal of Hughes's leftist poems ("A generation later, not one of these pieces would appear in Hughes's *Selected Poems*").[17] William J. Maxwell, in *New Negro, Old Left: African-American Writing and Communism between the Wars,* and James Smethurst, in *The New Red Negro: African American Writing and Communism,* have illuminated and explored Hughes's many contributions to the American Left in and after the 1930s. Robert Shulman, in *The Power of Political Art: The 1930s Literary Left Reconsidered,* devotes a chapter to Hughes's poetry for and about the Left, including his writing about Spain. The present author has treated Hughes's political poetry and his writing about Spain in previous publications.[18] This work has enhanced not only our understanding of Hughes and his cultural work but also the important nexus of racial and class politics in the 1930s and beyond.

Widespread change in the understanding of Hughes, though, cannot happen until the montage of his work is more fully represented in those powerful technologies, the anthology and the course syllabus. On one hand, the representation of Hughes in some anthologies (notably, the *Heath Anthology of American Literature,* the *Oxford Anthology of Modern American Poetry,* and the new *Houghton Mifflin Anthology of Literature*) has

---

16. Kelley, "'This Ain't Ethiopia, But It'll Do,'" 18.

17. Rampersad, *Life,* 1:358.

18. Thurston, *Making Something Happen: American Political Poetry between the World Wars* and "'Bombed in Spain': Langston Hughes, the Black Press, and the Spanish Civil War."

become both larger and more comprehensive.[19] To the typical anthology selections ("The Negro Speaks of Rivers," "Mulatto," "Theme for English B"), the Heath anthology adds not only a wider variety of Hughes's racially focused poems but also his 1926 essay "The Negro Artist and the Racial Mountain" and a handful of his poems devoted to Left politics ("Goodbye Christ," "Come to the Waldorf-Astoria," and "Air Raid over Harlem"). Moreover, while the bulk of the Hughes selections appear in a section titled "The New Negro Renaissance," alongside work by Alain Locke, Jean Toomer, Countee Cullen, and others, the three poems I name above appear in a separate section titled "A Sheaf of Political Poetry in the Modern Period." Hughes's poems here are surrounded by the work of Kenneth Fearing, Tillie Olsen, Kay Boyle, and others. This very different group of writers provides a quite different context for Hughes.

The web site associated with the Oxford anthology and the CD-ROM that accompanies the Houghton Mifflin anthology also serve to re-create the very different communities of discourse through which Hughes circulated. The Oxford anthology's web pages on Hughes (compiled and prepared by Cary Nelson) include not only the biographical background and critical readings typical of this technology but also readings on lynching, on the Spanish Civil War, and on Hughes's activism in the 1930s, as well as "The Negro Artist and the Racial Mountain" and Hughes's essay "Negroes in Spain." One page is devoted to a reproduction of a Spanish Civil War broadside on which appear three Hughes poems ("Dear Folks at Home," "Love Letter from Spain," and "Dear Brother at Home" [later published as "A Letter from Spain Addressed to Alabama"]) with illustrations that visually link a sharecropper hoeing cotton and a rifle-bearing soldier on patrol.[20]

On the other hand, the literary taxonomies that nominate Hughes simply as a "Harlem Renaissance poet" continue to dominate most anthologies, syllabi, and classrooms. The Norton anthologies most often adopted for courses on American and African American literatures present students with the usual choices. The *Norton Anthology of American Literature* (sixth edition, volume D) provides a substantial Hughes offering: "The Negro Speaks of Rivers," "Mother to Son," "The Weary Blues," "I, Too," "Mulatto," "Song for a Dark Girl," "Vagabonds," "Genius Child," "Ref-

19. Full disclosure: the author is a member of the Oxford anthology's editorial advisory board.
20. http://www.english.uiuc.edu/maps/poets/g_l/hughes/hughes.htm.

ugee in America," "Madam and Her Madam," "Madam's Calling Cards," "Silhouette," "Visitors to the Black Belt," "Note on Commercial Theatre," and "Democracy." Only the latter suggests a politics other than one based on racial identity in isolation from issues with which race might be imbricated (and with which race is imbricated in much of Hughes's other writing). Hughes's fiction, drama, criticism, reportage, and autobiography are not included. The second edition of the *Norton Anthology of African American Literature*, as we might expect of a more narrowly focused anthology, gives Hughes a fuller representation. Most of the poems that appear in the sixth edition of the *Norton Anthology of American Literature* are provided here as well, along with twenty others. The short story "The Blues I'm Playing," three excerpts from the autobiography *The Big Sea*, and "The Negro Artist and the Racial Mountain" are also included. Even this selection, though, keeps the focus intently on Hughes's racially engaged work and on his valuable experiments with black vernacular forms and traditions. It is not only older, established anthologies that perpet-uate this limited Hughes. The selections in both Norton anthologies are better than what confronts the reader in the McGraw-Hill anthology, *Twentieth-Century American Poetry* (2004), edited by Dana Gioia, David Mason, and Meg Schoerke. This collection leaves Hughes uncomplicatedly resident in the Harlem Renaissance and reproduces the same selections readers have come to expect (from "The Negro Speaks of Rivers" to "Theme for English B").

Because Spain offers an effective microcosm that illustrates Hughes's multiplicity, flexibility, and capacity, course units that explore his Spanish Civil War writing and activism (in classes, for example, on twentieth-century American literature, American poetry, or African American literature) might help to enrich and complicate students' sense of Hughes. Such a unit might comprise the poems Hughes wrote about the conflict, his reportage, his essays, and his autobiographical ruminations on Spain. This combination of texts includes the Hughes deeply devoted to racial equality and the Hughes committed to a broader revolutionary politics. More than this, it shows that these two sides of Hughes were inextricable.

Perhaps even more effective would be textual montages that draw their discrete shots from more widely disparate realms, montages that use Spain to ground Hughes's utopian imagination in concrete political work. Students might read "Harlem Night Club," a poem published in *The Weary Blues* in 1926, alongside Hughes's account of the Mella Club dance in Madrid. The poem, a familiar and canonical choice typical of Hughes's mid-1920s work, imagines the dissolution of racial barriers in the sexually charged atmosphere of a nightclub:

White girls' eyes
Call gay black boys.
Black boys' lips
Grin jungle joys.

Dark brown girls
In blond men's arms. (*CW* 1:28)

The racial mingling in the poem is mediated by jazz, characterized as "joy," and seen as momentary, provisional, and ultimately doomed: "Tomorrow . . . is darkness. / Joy today!" (*CW* 1:29). In the Madrid club, on the other hand, the interracial community is built on the foundation of political commitment; the "color line" is erased by common cause. Hughes's tone is much less gloomy because the ground here for racial unity is solid where the poem's is ephemeral. These two scenes generate productive interpretive friction: Does the newspaper article amount to a rejection of black vernacular culture as a mechanism for change? Does it highlight a pessimism lurking in the earlier poem's evocation of an end to the night's joy? Alternatively, does the poem offer the libidinal energies released by popular culture, especially black vernacular forms, as a revolutionary resource that should be recovered from the grim circumstances that bring the races together in Madrid? At the same time, these perspectives contribute to a unified impression that might be elaborated with reference to Hughes's 1935 address to the American Writers' Conference, "To Negro Writers":

> Negro writers can seek to unite blacks and whites in our country, not on the nebulous basis of an inter-racial meeting, or the shifting sands of religious brotherhood, but on the *solid* ground of the daily working-class struggle to wipe out, now and forever, all the old inequalities of the past. (*CW* 9:132)

The two scenes share the character of the provisional; they represent spaces in which blacks and whites can be momentarily and joyfully united (helped by the medium of jazz), but spaces clearly surrounded by forces hostile to the utopia they image. Certain widely popular means advocated for the achievement of the goal—"religious brotherhood," an emptily isolated "inter-racial meeting"—are disavowed in both scenes. At the same time, the goal—to "unite blacks and whites in our country"—remains unchanged.

Spain, of course, is not the only site where we find Hughes working through, and as something of, a montage. Harlem in the 1920s, California,

North Carolina, the Soviet Union in the 1930s, and the very different Harlem of the 1950s offer interesting settings as well. Wherever we find the shots, though, we do greater justice to Hughes's talents if we juxtapose the discrete images to show how they contribute to a multifaceted but unified careerlong effort to address through literature the suffering wrought by intertwining oppressions on the basis of race and class.

The Russian Connection

Interracialism as Queer Alliance
in *The Ways of White Folks*

Kate A. Baldwin

> The blood of Pushkin
> Unites
> The Russian and the Negro
> In art.
> Tomorrow
> We will be united anew
> In the Internationale.
>
> —Julian Anissimov, "Kinship"

The gentlemen who wrote lovely books about the defeat of the flesh and the triumph of the spirit . . . will kindly come forward and Speak about the Revolution—where flesh triumphs . . . and the young by the hundreds of thousands are free from hunger to grow and study and love and propagate, bodies and souls unchained without My Lord saying a commoner shall never marry my daughter or the Rabbi crying cursed be the mating of Jews and Gentiles or Kipling writing never the twain shall meet—For the twain have met.

> —Langston Hughes, "Letter to the Academy"

In June 1932, Langston Hughes posted a telegram to his friend Louise Thomspon that read, "hold that boat 'cause to me it's an Ark."[1] The boat in question was the *Europa*, bound for Berlin, and beyond that for Leningrad and Moscow. Scheduled on board were Thompson and the group of would-be actors she had organized to participate in a proposed Soviet-funded project for a film titled *Black and White*. The image of an "ark" that Hughes proposes in his description of the steamship illustrates his eagerness to depart U.S. shores, excited about the artistic and social potential a Soviet adventure might bring.

Hughes's sojourn to the Soviet Union, a trip that ended up covering a year, from June 1932 to June 1933, has been acknowledged in biographical accounts. Indicating the significance of this experience to Hughes's development as a writer, Faith Berry described the Soviet period as "among the most productive of his literary career."[2] While in the Soviet Union, Hughes produced poetry, essays, and fiction, including the poem "Letter to the Academy," the Soviet-published "A Negro Looks at Soviet Central Asia," and several of the short stories later published in the collection *The Ways of White Folks*, including "Cora Unashamed," "Slave on the Block," and "Poor Little Black Fellow."[3] Despite Hughes's prolific output during his Soviet experience, the specific ramifications of this journey in relation to his writing from the early thirties, particularly the stories that were written in Moscow and immediately following his return to the United States in 1933, have remained virtually unexplored.[4]

While in the Soviet Union, Hughes was exposed to the exhilarations of a society in progress, the reconstruction of the Soviet citizen, and the Leninist conception of internationalism. Combined, these interventions into the Russian social status quo created a heady atmosphere of possibility, of subjectivity under formation. The *novyi Sovetskii chelovek* (new So-

---

1. Quoted in Arnold Rampersad, *The Life of Langston Hughes: Volume 1, 1902–1941, I, Too, Sing America*, 241.
2. Berry, *Langston Hughes: Before and beyond Harlem*, 189.
3. Attesting to the validation of his writing career he found in the USSR, and significantly contrasting this validation with his struggles as a writer in the United States, Hughes recalls, "I made more from writing in Moscow in terms of buying power than I have ever earned within the same period anywhere else" (*CW* 14:205).
4. See my *Beyond the Color Line and the Iron Curtain: Reading Encounters between Black and Red, 1922–1963*, in which I focus on Hughes's negotiation of interstices between Du Bois's black masculine veil and the feminine, Orientalist veil of Central Asia in his writings about Soviet Central Asia, and the way the feminine veil enabled Hughes to theorize an alternative black masculine subjectivity through feminine identification and the Soviet project of unveiling.

viet person) augured a reconfiguration of the family, and Lenin's internationalism promised interracial alliances in the name of global solidarity. As the poem "Kinship," written by Julian Anissimov and translated by Hughes, suggests, partnerships between "the Russian" and "the Negro" promised a shift from biologically determined links (that is, those fabricated through blood) to politically determined ones.[5] The idea of reconstructed kinships emerges with equal force in Hughes's Moscow-composed "Letter to the Academy" in which cross-racial unions beget a heretofore taboo meeting of the "twain." The influence of these interventions into conventional mappings of the familial and the racial can be traced throughout the prose pieces that Hughes produced during this period. The Soviet project provided an impetus for rethinking the intimacies associated with family and race as given demarcators of an inherent connection between group members and for skewing these naturalized categories. In their place, Hughes's stories offer interracial and reconfigured kinship structures as alliances and formations through which to suggest a differently affiliated black masculine subjecthood. In these stories, many of which were collected into *The Ways of White Folks*, interracial coalitions between "black" and "white" promoted by the ethos of the "Internationale" are reformed to explore and trouble sexually proscriptive boundaries between blacks and whites in the defiantly anti-Internationale zone, the United States.[6]

As Siobhan Somerville has elaborated in her work on the complicities between racial and sexual-oriented ascriptions of identity, "the often unstable division between homosexuality and heterosexuality circulates as part of [the] exploration of the barriers to desire imposed by the color line."[7] Drawing on Somerville's pioneering work, I am interested in how,

5. Hughes partnered with other Russian authors, most notably in his translations of Vladimir Mayakovsky and Boris Pasternak. See, for example, his translation of Pasternak's "Beloved" in *I Wonder As I Wander* (*CW* 14:206), as well as of (with the assistance of Lydia Filatova) Mayakovsky's "Black and White," "Syphilis," and "Hygiene" (the latter in *CW* 14:207). The originals are at Special Collections, Fisk University Library, Nashville, Tenn.

6. As Michael Uebel notes, "crossing racial, class, and national boundaries, and most significantly, the lines imposed by normative sexuality and erotic practice, is a vital, empowering act of social critique" ("Men In Color: Introducing Race and the Subject of Masculinities," 8), but little scholarly attention has been focused on linking identificatory boundary crossing to the specific national borders crossed in work such as Hughes's.

7. Somerville, *Queering the Color Line: Race and the Invention of Homosexuality in American Culture*, 11.

in Hughes's work from this period, an unstable division between black and white, exemplified in the rhetoric of Soviet internationalism, functions as part of his exploration of the barriers to desire and identification imposed by sexual ascription. Reclaiming a slighted portion of the historical background of Hughes's oeuvre is key to resituating his work from the 1930s and to thinking through how this work articulates alternative modalities of desire. Rather than approaching this project with a retrospective eye toward pinning down Hughes's sexuality through empirical evidence or ascribing to his texts a correlated identity, my methodology follows the advisory articulated by Kaja Silverman, who asks us "to approach history always through the refractions of desire and identification, and to read race and class insistently in relation to sexuality."[8] Hughes's experiences in the Soviet Union—his encounters with new modes of subjectivity and, with the impetus of authors such as Anissimov and D. H. Lawrence, his explorations of the familial—promoted a rethinking of interracial alliances, kinship structures, and black American masculinity: these formative restructurings emerge in his work as the Russian connection.

The Souls of Black Men

At the time of Hughes's arrival in Moscow in 1932 the preeminent paradigm for understanding black American consciousness was that of "double consciousness," a concept articulated powerfully by W. E. B. Du Bois in his 1903 *The Souls of Black Folk*. For Du Bois, double consciousness arises out of an awareness of an irresolvable twoness, a sense of being both American and black, categories that remained institutionally and ideologically mutually exclusive. As I have discussed elsewhere, in *Souls*, Du Bois's revelation of a veil that signifies double consciousness establishes straightaway a representative means of thematizing not only African American consciousness but more precisely black male consciousness.[9] Although this is one of the most-often cited passages from Du Bois, what Henry Louis Gates Jr. has termed the "ur-text of the African American experience,"[10] the fact that this revelation comes about through a specific

8. Silverman, *Male Subjectivity at the Margins*, 300.
9. The argument elaborated here is a reformulation of the one I make in *Beyond the Color Line and the Iron Curtain*.
10. "Introduction: Darkly as through a Veil," xvii. The passages from *The Souls of Black Folk* quoted here are from p. 2 of the 1989 Bantam edition containing Gates's introduction.

configuration of aborted interracial desire is often overlooked. A young girl's refusal to exchange visiting cards with Du Bois provokes the narrator's sense of difference "from the others, or like, mayhap, in heart and life and longing, but shut out from their world by a vast veil." In this seminal scene, desire operates in at least a twofold manner: it is depicted as both cross-racial and heterosexual. Both of these desires are simultaneously proffered and denied; both are structurally mandated and disavowed ("I had thereafter no desire to tear down that veil, to creep through"). They seem to accord to one another a reciprocal degree of necessity, of compulsion, so that both are mutually constituting.

Black masculine desires for sameness, recognition by, and equality to the privileged space implied by the absent but constitutive presence of white male heterosexuality, by which citizenship and national belonging are defined, are meted out across the figure of white femininity.[11] In affixing black masculinity to the body of white femininity, Du Bois reiterates a social logic wherein the coupling of black man/white woman is inherently and always about a specific kind of desire—for a black man to have commerce with a white woman who denies him recognition and likewise access through a sense of social propriety or taboo. The normativization of this illicit desire is related to its larger social proscription in that prohibition creates the ground for its instantiation as a regulatory force. In the 1896 ruling of *Plessy v. Ferguson,* the majority opinion found that the object of the Fourteenth Amendment "could not have been intended to abolish distinctions based upon color, or to enforce social, as distinguished from political, equality, or a commingling of the two races."[12] In barring social from political equality in terms of a fear of racial "commingling," this ruling revealed the extent to which white anxiety about black male desire was inherently couched in a heteronormative paradigm. Du Bois's pattern echoes the larger cultural taboo of racial commingling, using proscription as the generative source for its normativizing compulsion and likewise taking up not only its interdiction but also its terms of heteronormativity. In Du Bois's configuration, heterosexuality is the tacit binding agent, an organizing structure of social membership, albeit in this case a denied membership, based in mutual recognition.[13]

---

11. On the privileges of white masculinity as a disembodied entitlement of citizenship and the correlative ways in which black masculinity is forced to embody otherness, see Robyn Wiegman, *American Anatomies: Theorizing Race and Gender.*

12. Henry Billings Brown, "Majority Opinion in *Plessy v. Ferguson,*" 50.

13. As others have noted, Du Bois's example is based on a Hegelian model of dialectical recognition. See, for example, Gilroy, *The Black Atlantic: Modernity and Double Consciousness,* 50–58.

By repeatedly querying and rewriting this primal scene of identification, in *The Ways of White Folks* Hughes taps into the ways in which, within the very structure of representative black masculine desire, slippage offers a possibility for difference.[14] By constantly replaying and reshuffling the Du Boisian frames of black masculinity, Hughes's work detects in Du Bois's enumeration of the barriers to intimacy a foregrounding of desire as an expression not of a private selfhood but of a publicly ordained one. Hughes's work reveals the constitutive scene of double consciousness as a mediation between private and public displays of the heteronormative impulses behind the Du Boisian formation of a black masculine consciousness. In this light, the black male/white female coupling is always about the public nature of this dyad—how the private voicings in Du Bois (such as "heart and life and longing") are the expression of social mandates. Varied formations of cross-racial desire emerge in several of Hughes's short stories to summon a possibility of rearticulating the heteronormative impulse of the Du Boisian interracial dyad. Drawing on the energizing reformulations of the Internationale, interracial alliances structurally haunt Hughes's stories as a kind of queer presence.[15]

Getting Between

In order to more fully explain the ways in which Hughes's work performs this rearticulation of Du Bois, it is necessary to reiterate the impor-

14. Judith Butler argues that heterosexuality secures its success by eliciting and simultaneously disavowing its abject, interiorized, and ghostly other, homosexuality. In a similar fashion, Hughes's stories reread the compulsorily heterosexual in the Du Boisian dyad to summon key links between the aberrance of interraciality and the aberrance of nonhetero desire that remain otherwise under erasure. See her *Bodies That Matter: On the Discursive Limits of "Sex,"* 106.

15. My use of *heteronormative* here and elsewhere is informed by the work of Lauren Berlant and Michael Warner, who underscore the elasticity and divergence within the category of heterosexuality even as the category works as a unifying and privileged location for a national idiom of "rightness." They write, "by heteronormativity we mean the institutions, structures of understanding, and practical orientations that make heterosexuality seem not only coherent—that is, organized as a sexuality—but also privileged. . . . It consists less of norms that could be summarized as a body of doctrine than of a sense of rightness produced in contradictory manifestations—often unconscious, immanent to practice or to institutions" ("Sex in Public," 548). The term *queer* here suggests ruptures of "normalcy" often associated with heteronormativity, spaces in which interventions into the heteronormative provide the possibility for inhabiting a differently configured black masculine subjectivity.

tance of the Russian connection. Upon his return to Moscow after several months' travel in Soviet Central Asia, Langston Hughes received a copy of D. H. Lawrence's collection of stories *The Lovely Lady* from his friend Marie Seton. In his autobiographical *I Wonder As I Wander,* Hughes recalls that the Lawrence stories affected him deeply:

> I had never read anything of Lawrence's before, and was particularly taken with the title story. . . . The possessive, terrifying elderly woman in "The Lovely Lady" seemed in some ways so much like my former Park Avenue patron that I could hardly bear to read the story, yet I could not put the book down, although it brought cold sweat and goose-pimples to my body. . . . I had been saying to myself all day, "If D. H. Lawrence can write such psychologically powerful accounts of folks in England, that send shivers up and down my spine, maybe I could write stories like his about folks in America." (*CW* 14:220)

Before exploring the specificities of Hughes's enthrallment with Lawrence's stories, I want to pause and draw attention to the ways in which from their very inception the Moscow-influenced stories collected in *The Ways of White Folks* can be read as reconfiguring the bonds between the interracial and the heterosexual in the Du Boisian dyad.

I Wonder As I Wander introduces Lawrence with a section titled "D. H. Lawrence between Us." This positioning of Lawrence underscores the way in which Hughes's "us"—a liaison with a woman he calls Natasha—is altered by the incursion of Lawrence's stories into their affair. *The Lovely Lady* effectively triangulates the circuit of desire between Natasha and Hughes, interrupting their programmatic interracial, male-female affair, as Hughes's words (deceptively?) describe it. Emphatically unlike the fantasy of white femininity fulfilled that might be suggested superficially by Hughes's relationship with Natasha, his experiences with cross-racial alliances in the Soviet Union did not serve as a means to simply refute the socially constrictive boundaries and laws against miscegenation that provided the building blocks for black male exclusion from the entitlements of citizenship in the United States. His memoir does not decorously celebrate unmediated access to white women as the driving credential of internationalism's potentialities (although certainly for some this was a hallmark of Soviet difference).[16] Rather, what the setting provides is a repositioning of this very circuit of desire as mandatory, an opportunity

16. In his manuscript "Russia and America: An Interpretation," one of the first things W. E. B. Du Bois notes about Russia is that "women sit beside me quite confi-

to rub against and articulate a space between the routes of desire paradigmatic of the black male / white female coupling.

Natasha, whom Hughes describes in *I Wonder As I Wander* in clearly ambivalent terms as "buxom," "Slavic—not beautiful, not ugly" (*CW* 14:210) and "fun and as wholesome in body as an apple" (*CW* 14:220), appears briefly as the subject of Hughes's "Moscow Romance." Defying the Du Boisian convention of the desirous yet spurned male suitor, Hughes clearly delineates her as the aggressor with "a one-track mind. Without advance warning, Natasha simply came to my room in the New Moscow Hotel one night when I was out—and was in bed when I got back" (*CW* 14:210). What is more interesting than seeking out the empirical details or authenticity of this intimacy between Hughes and Natasha is examining how this relationship and its foreclosure provide a frame for reading Hughes's stories. As Hughes recollects, he was so caught up in the reading of Lawrence and the composition of his own stories that he "really did not want to be bothered with an almost nightly female visitor." The plenitude implied here (and denied Hughes in the United States)[17] is cut short, its potential pleasures disavowed by more pressing investments: Hughes continues, "[A]nother and more possessive 'Lovely Lady' from D. H. Lawrence's stories had come between us" (*CW* 14:221). Hughes illustrates how a willful femininity provides the impetus and charge to disrupt a cross-racial, heterosexual bond, and Hughes's authorial fascination with the displays of feminine willfulness elaborated in Lawrence's "The Lovely Lady" becomes a stepping stone to his rearticulation of this lure in *The Ways of White Folks*. Irreverent and uncouth exhibitions of femininity create a magnetic force that enables a commingling of cross-gender identification and desire that proves more compelling than the cross-racial, heterosexual configuration proffered by Natasha.

---

dently and unconsciously" (27). Many African American men (including several from the "Black and White" troupe) who ventured to the Soviet Union in the 1930s because of the job opportunities there had affairs with and / or married Soviet women.

17. In "Moscow and Me," Hughes makes the comparison explicit: "to dance with a white woman in the dining room of a fine restaurant and not be dragged out by the neck—is to wonder if you're really living in a city full of white folks" (*CW* 9:60). Noting the difference between white attitudes toward blacks in the United States and the USSR, Hughes then queries the adequateness of a term like *white* to describe Moscow's residents, "But then the papers of the other lands are always calling the Muscovites red" (60).

The Lady's Possessions

What was it about Lawrence's stories that Hughes found so compelling? Let us first consider the "possessive" femininity outlined in the character of Mrs. Pauline Attenbourough, the character from whom the story, as well as the collection, takes its title. Part of Hughes's strong identification with this story may be due to the ambiguously charged relationship Lawrence depicts between an elderly dowager and her younger, impressionable protégé. Although the relationship detailed in "The Lovely Lady" is between a mother and son, as Hughes himself notes, the resonances with Hughes's own relationship to Charlotte Osgood Mason, his benefactress with whom he had severed ties shortly before leaving for Moscow, ring clearly. Commenting on a power structure in which monied age beguiles and renders hapless dependent youth, and the ways such structural inequities comingle desire and its disavowal, Lawrence zeros in on what he portrays as the terrifying, seductive powers of a financially empowered matriarchal femininity.

In fact, the maternal possessiveness outlined in "The Lovely Lady" veers into the destructive. Pauline Attenborough is described as "a mother murdering her sensitive sons, who were fascinated by her: the Circe!" Robert, the younger of these two sons, sums up Pauline in the following manner: "She fed on life. She has fed on me as she fed on [my brother] Henry. She put a sucker into one's soul, and it sucked up one's essential life."[18] Awestruck by such all-encompassing matriarchal power, to which men are mere casualties, Robert is "sucked" dry of his vitality. In inverse relation to Robert's increasing vapidity, Pauline seems to grow more and more enlivened. Mrs. Attenborough is so thorough in her possessiveness that she inhabits not only her own identity but also the identities of everyone around her. In this sense, Pauline's feeding on her children is cannibalistic, an act of consumption that repeatedly seeks to satisfy the demands of an ego for more. But, unlike the popular 1930s Freudian interpretation of strong mothers who dominate their sons into weak-willed automatons (an account that clearly drew upon Freud's theorizations of connections between orality and cannibalism), Pauline's appetite lacks the requisite desire to become the other through its incorporation. Instead, we can think of Pauline as more akin to a structure of desire and identification outlined by Diana Fuss. Fuss describes the vampiristic as a cultural figure for identification that differs from cannibalism in that, rather

18. D. H. Lawrence, *The Lovely Lady*, 23, 40.

than simply incorporating the other, the vampire transforms her victims into fellow vampires.

> Vampirism works like an inverted form of identification—identification pulled inside out—where the subject, in the act of interiorizing the other simultaneously reproduces itself in that other. Vampirism is both other-incorporating and self-reproducing; it delimits a more ambiguous space where desire and identification appear less opposed than coterminous, where the desire to be the other (identification) draws its very sustenance from the desire to have the other.[19]

The characterization of Mrs. Attenborough enables us both to draw connections with Fuss's elaboration of vampirism and to designate differently configured modalities of desire. To be sure, Mrs. Attenborough thrives on the lifeblood of those around her, incorporating their vitality into her own and fortifying the illusion of agelessness through her acts of ingestion: "at seventy-two Pauline Attenbourough could still sometimes be mistaken, in the half light, for thirty."[20] Yet her identification with (desire to be) these others is more ambiguous. The reproductions of self that her fits of appetite enact are less imperfect replications of herself—the reflection of the vampiristic within Robert—than partial failures to create the dialectical processes that would ensure Robert's own vampirism. Robert seems poised to rebel against his mother, an indication that he might, indeed, be like her, but throughout the story he is constrained to tired and effete ineffectuality. Rather than being an invigorating bite, his mother's mouthwork has produced stasis, paralysis "in a lifelong confusion."[21] Mrs. Attenborough's suggestive affiliation to but divergence from Fuss's powerful model of vampirism is the result of her excessive acquisitiveness, her incorporation of the other as self-fulfilling, and an inability to allow for any trace of the otherness of the other.

Mrs. Attenborough's preying powers are depicted as sufficient to unhinge the conventional heterosexual plot, to come between characters seemingly destined to be partnered. Her position between Hughes and Natasha structurally parallels her abutting between Robert and his female suitor, Cecilia. Rather than being an altruistic intervention, this interruption hinges on a possessive relationship to identity: a desire to have in order to assert transcendent being. According to Robert's description of her,

---

19. Fuss, "Fashion and the Homospectorial Look," 730.
20. Lawrence, *Lovely Lady*, 11.
21. Ibid., 18.

for Pauline there is no difference between being and having. Partial ful-
fillments of one another, they run in seamless continuity. Her sense of self
extends beyond the body and merges with the rich appointments with
which she has surrounded herself. As Lawrence describes her, Pauline
was "a devoted collector of beautiful and exotic things," who "really had
a passion and a genius for loveliness, whether in texture or form or colour,
[and] had laid the basis of her future on her father's collection. She had
gone on collecting, buying where she could, and selling to collectors and
to museums. She was one of the first to sell old, weird African wooden
figures to the museums." These descriptions elaborate on Pauline's predilection for possessing objects, depicting her relationship to identity as
also implicitly one of (imperialist) plunder: "all collectors' pieces—Mrs.
Attenborough had made her own money, dealing privately in pictures
and furniture and rare things from barbaric countries."[22] She has cultivated a self in which "being" equals "having," and the violence of this
possessiveness demeans others to furniture, decor, or accoutrements
arranged to set off her supreme subjecthood. A fantasy of the other as aestheticized, pliable object enables the superiority of the mother as peerless
subject. In fact, by having so much, Pauline is constantly in excess of being: this is a point reiterated at the story's end when Pauline leaves her
fortune not to her son but to the endowment of the Pauline Attenborough
Museum, a denouement that befits her identificatory apparatus.

On the other hand, Robert's lack—of resources, of resourcefulness, and,
significantly, of heterosexual desire—appears to be experienced as a
complete deficit of identity, of selfhood: he is thoroughly dependent and
libidinally effaced in contrast to Pauline's voracious displays of self-
ownership. For example, when Robert is confronted by Cecilia, who desires to marry him, Robert admits, "I know that I am no lover of women."
He makes the comment "with sarcastic stoicism . . . but even she did not
know the shame it was to him. 'You never try to be!' she said. Again his
eyes changed uncannily. 'Does one have to try?' he said." Although the
story may suggest that Pauline Attenborough's tenacious grasp has left
Robert tellingly bereft of agency, it also gives us reason to believe otherwise. Robert's subjectivity is not a replication of his mother's willful performance of self, the transformation wrought by "the mysterious little
wire that worked between Pauline's will and her face."[23]

As the object of his mother's drive to become "lovely," Robert is neither

22. Ibid., 25, 16.
23. Ibid., 29, 12.

possessive nor object-oriented. For this reason his mother remains peripheral to the locus of his identity. Juxtaposed to Mrs. Attenborough's sense of fulfillment through objects is Robert's fascination with *process.* Robert, a barrister, delights in the "weird old processes" of litigation and legal intricacies. This interest seems to offer some kind of orientation for his "habitual feeling that he was in the wrong place: almost like a soul that has got into the wrong body."[24] Robert finds solace in the law—not the easily defined options between right and wrong, but rather the nuances, awkwardnesses, and slippages, the processes akin to those at work in the flux of desire, of identity in formation, of a self dispossessed. In spite of Robert's protestations, the story of his relationship with his mother is not simply about Mrs. Attenborough usurping his desire, but about Robert's fascination with his mother to the point of abandon, that is, the conflict between her "having" and his penchant for forgoing identity as an achieved object.[25]

The idea of Robert as a character who defies Mrs. Attenborough's imperatives for subjecthood is substantiated toward the end of the tale when we learn that Robert is the illegitimate son of Pauline and an Italian priest. In fact, this strand of illegitimacy seems to course throughout "The Lovely Lady." It is the specter that subtends Robert's "shame" over not being a "man": "He was ashamed that he was not a man. And he did not love his mother."[26] Robert's refusal of familial intimacy and his refusal to reiterate his mother's model of self-possession figure him multiply as the "miscegenated" or "queer" offspring of a socially forbidden coupling. This layered contravening of social sanctions resonates with the implicit taboo of the Du Boisian dyad, while suggestively insinuating a means of rewriting that configuration.

The idea of powerful femininity that so captivated Hughes in the title story runs throughout the *Lovely Lady* collection, in which women are depicted as possessing "a strange muscular energy" that annihilates men. Bringing together the shame associated with a lack of normative hetero-

---

24. Ibid., 14. A parallel between Robert's self-description and that of the "invert" further underscores the queer contours of Robert's subjecthood. Robert's words echo the model of the invert that emerged in the late nineteenth century and reduced complex gender identifications to binary structures so that an "invert" identified a person as a woman's soul trapped in a man's body or vice versa. See Lisa Duggan, "Theory in Practice: The Theory Wars, or Who's Afraid of Judith Butler?" And in the 1920s and 1930s Freudian theory popularized the idea of homosexuality as inversion. See Freud, *Three Essays on the Theory of Sexuality,* esp. 2–14.

25. Lawrence, *Lovely Lady,* 14.

26. Ibid., 18.

sexual desire and the driving force of a "strange female power that had nothing to do with parental authority,"[27] "The Lovely Lady" provides an impetus for rethinking the routings of desire and identification within the family: for defamiliarization, as it were, making strange the familial.

Recoding the Familial

Questions of literal defamiliarization were at the heart of the unprecedented social transformation and artistic experimentation that characterized the Soviet Union in the 1920s. Much of this activity was connected to the New Economic Policy, or NEP (1921–1928), which came to distinguish an era in which bold challenges were made to strict Bolshevik doctrine and a modified capitalism was reintroduced to jump-start the nation's economy. Caught up in this flurry of reconstruction was the idealized citizen—*the novyi Sovetskii chelovek*—the Soviet worker cum proletariat, and a utopian aspiration for the abolishment of petty bourgeois individualism. Even beyond the era of NEP, Stalin recognized that a reconstituted nation required a reconstituted citizen, and his hope was that emphasizing a new iconography of the depersonalized subject would allow a new Soviet citizen to emerge, one that supported and represented the collective interests of the people. One of the ways that individualist bourgeois tendencies were purportedly subverted was through the reconstruction not only of bodies but also of urban topography—the creation of new parks, public thoroughfares, and high-rises.[28] The latter were to be dwelling spaces that undermined "the structure of the bourgeois family," in its place "instituting the relationships of proletarian comradeship."[29] In fact, much emphasis was placed on the family as the locus of the reproduction of individualism and thus as the necessary site of intervention.[30] In 1926 a new Family Code was introduced, a document that espoused radically reformulated conceptions of the family and its social counterpart, marriage. Although not all bureaucrats or intelligentsia agreed on the proper place of family in the emergent society, most rejected what they termed

27. Ibid., 97, 92.
28. See Lynne Attwood and Catriona Kelly, "Programmes for Identity: The 'New Man' and 'New Woman.'"
29. Svetlana Boym, *Common Places: Mythologies of Everyday Life in Russia*, 127.
30. Examples of artistic renditions of the new family include Evgeni Zamiatin's *We* (1920), Yuri Olesha's *Envy* (1927), and Abram Romm's *Bed and Sofa* (1927). See also Olga Matich, "Remaking the Bed: Utopia in Daily Life."

"bourgeois piety." As Richard Stites has commented, "In comparison with both Roman and Anglo-Saxon legal traditions, the code was truly radical. Western family law was generally designed to penalize extra-marital unions by means of property, inheritance, legitimacy, and even fornication laws. The Soviets, on the contrary, recognized them as an established and by no means repugnant fact."[31]

By subtending the existence of extramarital liaisons, the Soviet Union implicitly challenged compulsory monogamy and left open the possibility for intimacies outside the bounds of the conjugal bedroom. Similarly, in granting full freedom of divorce to either partner, the Soviets abolished "the concept of guilt, the humiliating delays, and the publicity," elsewhere associated with the procedure.[32] In a characteristically ambiguous summation of the era, Lynne Attwood and Catriona Kelly describe the reformulation of family in the 1920s as an experiment "which sought to socialize family functions and explore new modes of personal relationships."[33] Although neither of these scholars makes this connection, these interventions into the structures subtending marriage produced a correlative intervention into the affective emotions conventionally associated with matrimony; by releasing the "guilt" and "shame" commonly paired with its dissolution, they also provided a release for those similarly inflected emotions associated with "unconventional" erotic drives and impulses. As Stites notes, "The measure won the general approval of the Russian urban intelligentsia, Bolshevik and otherwise, who despised the hypocrisy of tsarist and western bourgeois marriage laws."[34] While Soviet Russia was not a promised land for libidinal drives that did not conform to a norm, it is possible that within the language of societal reconstruction spaces for nonnormative identities were articulated alongside the prescripted ones.

As families were confined to *kommunalkas*, the communal apartments for which the Soviet era is renowned, the reworking of familial intimacy became standard-issue: the very idea of privacy was undermined through the assertion of privacy's public display. Forced into "unnatural" alliances with one another, previous strangers became aunts, uncles, cousins. The paradigm of family was extended and distended to move beyond a rote association with genealogy and blood heritage. Similarly, a reconstruction

31. Stites, *The Women's Liberation Movement in Russia: Feminism, Nihilism, and Bolshevism, 1860–1930*, 370.
32. Ibid., 369.
33. Attwood and Kelly, "Programmes for Identity," 71.
34. Stites, *Women's Liberation Movement*, 369.

of the national family was underway. The grouping of unindustrialized, economically dispersed republics into a multifederated union of Soviet "peoples" produced an "integration of nations and nationalities into a single community and thus, for the first time in history, creat[ed] a truly multinational culture."[35] Theoreticians gauged that the success of multinationalism within the socialist Union was possible, as traits and cultural norms formerly seen as innately divisive were reconfigured into potentialities for future federation. In his work on materialist theory and heredity, for example, N. F. Posnanski claimed that "even naturally caused differences of birth, e.g. racial, can and must be abolished by a new historical development."[36] While we must remain skeptical of the presuppositions and logic of the "natural," we can at the same time register in Posnanski's terms a desire to unseat tired theories of the natural, and of race, as strictly biological: an attempt to reconfigure alliances through material processes as agent of and product of the Internationale. Even though far from an explicit endorsement of alternative sexualities, the Internationale provided a space for queer identifications coded through interracial, differently familial, heretofore unimagined and unimaginable alliances across previously proscriptive boundaries.

The Lawrence Connection

Bringing together Lawrence's exploration of possessiveness and a Soviet reordination of selfhood, Hughes's stories, in their exploration of the interracial, offer a theory of self-dispossession as a response to the stultifying constraints of white supremacy and as a means of refiguring the bonds of Du Boisian black masculinity. If we see in Lawrence's story a preoccupation with strong femininities, it is to be sure equally a preoccupation with feminine possessiveness, that is, with the concept of self-possession as a condition of subjecthood. As discussed above, Hughes pinpoints his fascination with "The Lovely Lady" as located in the vicinity of such "possessive" femininity. That this feature of Lawrence's story should have stood out for Hughes in Moscow in 1933 makes sense: self-possession, or more precisely self-ownership, as a means of articulating autonomy was precisely at issue in Bolshevik theorization of subjectivity in which the collective was prized over the individual. Such theorization

35. Catriona Kelly et al., "Why Cultural Studies?" 10.
36. Quoted in Attwood, "The New Soviet Man and Woman," 59.

offered a critique of liberal notions of the self in which self-ownership was the goal. A disbanding of personal property and its ideologies was especially salient to a critic, like Hughes, of the residual slaveowning structures underlying U.S. attitudes toward property and likewise citizenship. Given the historical property status of blacks in the United States, a goal of self-ownership would seem the obvious and necessary counter to the delimitations of property laws subtending the national ideology of citizenship. Thus, to explore a theory of self-dispossession as counter to the goal of self-ownership challenges expected avenues of retribution.[37] Hughes explored this dilemma, refusing to supply a definitive answer but gesturing toward a rebuttal of liberal notions of selfhood that subtend whiteness as the standard bearer of subjecthood and belonging. Thus what emerges in Lawrence as a preoccupation with strong femininities reappears in a highly altered form in *The Ways of White Folks*.

Although the Russian connection has been largely occluded from Hughes scholarship, two critics have commented on Hughes's Russia-originated relationship to Lawrence. Both, however, have summarily dismissed the dynamics of influence at work in Hughes's stories that emerged in response to his reading of Lawrence. Faith Berry concedes that Hughes was "overwhelmingly influenced by D. H. Lawrence" but later qualifies this influence as "more emotionally than stylistically" important. In the end, for Berry, Hughes's work "bears little resemblance" to that of Lawrence. Similarly, Leo Hamalian, whose exploration of the authorial relationship is more extensive, reduces the significance of Lawrence's work to a concern with "domineering, hateful parents" and the ways that "our revered authority figures, representing a society run on a money ethic, can best educate the younger generation in violation and murder."[38] While acknowledging a terrain of contiguity, Berry and Ha-

---

37. In *The Possessive Investment in Whiteness: How White People Profit from Identity Politics*, George Lipsitz uses the phrase *possessive investment* to demarcate both literal and figural advantages afforded whites by the social fact of whiteness as profit-bearing: "whiteness has a cash value: it accounts for advantages that come to individuals through profits made from housing secured in discriminatory markets, through the unequal educations allocated to children of different races, through insider networks that channel employment opportunities to the relatives and friends of those who have profited most from present and past racial discrimination, and especially through *intergenerational transfers of inherited wealth* that pass on the spoils of discrimination to succeeding generations" (vii; emphasis added).

38. Berry, *Langston Hughes*, 18, 188; Hamalian, "D.H. Lawrence and Black Writers," 587–88.

malian overlook the subtle dynamics of desire and identification within the familial, the exploration of nonnormative female/male relationships, the specters of illegitimate offspring, and the ways Hughes implicitly connected these narrative circuits to the querying of relationships between black and white underway in the Internationale.

Hughes admitted that in his stories he was aspiring to the "same hair-raising manner" of character and situation found in Lawrence's stories (CW 14:221). To accomplish this effect while focusing not on Britain but on the United States, Hughes strayed from the standard shorthand used to describe black American masculine consciousness. Two of the most pointed reconfigurations of interracial alliances that bear on a rearticulated black masculinity emerge in "Slave on the Block" and "Home." "Slave on the Block" was written in Moscow in 1933, and "Home" was written shortly after Hughes's return to the United States. Invoking the constraints of Du Bois's interracial dyad, and the reconfigured "queer" contours of feminine identified masculinity insinuated by Lawrence, these stories establish their Russian connection through explorations of the interracial. Each story offers a different eroticized bond between the members of an interracial couple, suggesting emotional alliances through aberrant sexual behavior, and toys with this filiation as an expression of reconfigured black male subjectivity.

In "Slave on the Block," Anne is an artist who thinks "in terms of pictures," an indication that she cannot get outside visual representation as a means of mapping identity. Indeed, when she first meets Luther, she can "hardly see the boy, it being dark in the hall, and he being dark, too." Luther's presence establishes a critique of modernity's insistence on the immediate readability of the racialized body, but it also enables this episteme's (unjust) elaboration through Anne's persistent inability to "see" Luther. "[C]ome in . . . and let us see you," Anne pleads, an indication that she will remain affixed to a modern means of extrapolating and producing meaning through surface, visible signs. What Anne and her husband do see is that Luther is "[t]he essence in the flesh" of Negro-ness (CW 15:31), and in their excitement to bring this essence into proximity to them, they make "a place for him to sleep in the basement by the furnace" (CW 15:32). This mingling of the desire for proximity with the barriers to it erected by racial stereotypes produces the story's key tension: the dialectic between Anne's mounting erotic attachment to Luther and her attempt to produce his image as a warding off of this illicit desire. We see these proclivities at work when Anne summons the courage to ask Luther to undress:

Anne could stare at him at leisure when he was asleep. One day she decided to paint him nude, or at least half nude. A slave picture, that's what she would do. The market at New Orleans for a background. And call it "The Boy on the Block."

. . . She wanted to paint him now representing to the full the soul and sorrow of his people. She wanted to paint him as a slave about to be sold. And since slaves in warm climates had no clothes, would he please take off his shirt. (CW 15:32–33)

Anne uses artistic license to access an idealized image as an excuse to disrobe her subject. At the same time, this very image of Luther—the slave on the block—provides both a partial barrier to Anne's increasing desire and a means of further incitement. "It's too marvelous!" (CW 15:33) Anne delights when she sees Luther's naked torso, and thereafter Luther is allowed to neglect his houseboy duties and simply pose for Anne's delectation.

Anne's fantasy of Luther as her self-fulfilling spectacle of desire comes crashing down when Luther explicitly directs his own erotic arrows. When Anne learns that Luther is sleeping with the maid, Mattie, her jealousy is tempered by rationalization. She "condoned them" because "it's so simple and natural for Negroes to make love," and the Carraways "prided themselves on being different; artists, you know, and liberal-minded people." Anne decides to "keep" Luther in spite of his libidinal truancy. However, when Luther's erotic attachments bar her completion of "The Boy on the Block," she grows frustrated. She notes that Luther "had grown a bit familiar lately" (CW 15:34), an indication that Luther has become too proximate within this "different"-oriented household. It is clear not only that Luther has transgressed the limits of Anne's fantasized image of blackness but also that this image relies on a possessive relationship between the artist and her object. Mattie is a source of comeuppance for Anne, who must temper her desire for Luther through the knowledge that he desires not her but the black maid. In order to stave off this threat to white femininity, Anne indulges in a fantasy of blackness as proximate, as "familiar," by welcoming Luther into her home. But she simultaneously asserts the superiority of her whiteness, her model of self-ownership, through the act of aestheticization.

Unlike the "ur"-bond between black male/white female as contingent on denied male access, Luther's attitude toward Anne can be interpreted as disinterest. He is unmoved by her advances, disengaged from her model of desire as acquisitiveness. Indeed, Luther construes Anne's desire—

which can only be expressed as possessiveness—as "too strange": "They is mighty funny," he comments. The modality of Anne's fascination with, indeed fetishization of, Luther's body is odd to Luther, who remains impermeable to her (socially mandated) structures of representation and desire. Hughes notes that "they didn't like the Carraways. . . . They didn't understand the vagaries of white folks, neither Luther nor Mattie, and they didn't want to be bothered trying" (*CW* 15:33). As this passage exemplifies, throughout the story Luther is accorded a kind of false simplicity, a seeming unawareness of and apathy toward the "vagaries of white folks." However, Luther's lackadaisical attitude toward Anne can be read at the same time as a reflection of a subjecthood that knows these "vagaries" all too well. In other words, Luther's indifference both reads as a refusal to cohere to a pattern that turns on the vagaries of desire and identification implicit in a verb such as "like"—"They didn't like the Carraways"—and structurally reiterates the prohibition against interracial desire and its sanctioned reinforcement through law and violence. While Luther's disinterest demonstrates his ex-centric position vis-à-vis a Du Boisian pattern of black male subjectivity, it also places him precariously within the larger cultural proscription endorsed through lynching and antimiscegenation laws. But, at the crossroads of these related but far from isomorphic forces, Luther presents the possibility of aberration, of sexual transgression from the bond of interracial heteronormative desire that reads, only superficially, as complicit with the strictures of white supremacy. His disinterest is a calculated strategy to deflect social taboos and reflects the structural inequalities that exist between white women and black men.

Luther's interventions into the familial reveal further aberration from white imperatives. As if sensing Luther's refusal to conform to a presupposed model of filiation, the Carraways with their liberal attitudes toward a reworked familial unit establish limits. This is made starkly clear through the imposition of Michael's mother into their household. Mrs. Carraway Sr. accuses Luther of overstepping implied boundaries: "I never liked familiar Negroes," she declares (*CW* 15:35). Her objection to Luther as too familiar initiates Luther's eviction from the family. The story depicts the limits of familiarity accorded objects of desire, thereby remarking on the contiguous yet asymmetrical relations between positions accorded "black men" and "white women" in the spectrum of a model in which subjectivity is based on self-possession. At the same time, the story reads against these constraints, not only by portraying Luther's disinterest in such models but also through Anne's response to Luther's exit, which can only be read as melancholic: her plea to have Luther stay reveals itself as the fear of losing an object of desire through which she orients her own subjectivity. Anne is tongue-tied:

> She looked at Luther. His black arms were full of roses he had brought to put in the vases. He had on no shirt. "Oh!" His body was ebony. . . .
> "Oh," Anne moaned distressfully, "my 'Boy on the Block'!" (*CW* 15:36)

Anne's lost object of fantasy (based as it is on demoralizing representations of the black other) threatens to unseat a racial superiority inextricably bound to her sense of self; the loss of Luther is experienced as a potential loss of self, of a self dispossessed.

In the fall of 1933 Hughes had returned to the United States and taken up residence in Carmel, California, where he worked assiduously to complete the stories triggered by his Soviet journey. Arnold Rampersad comments that "the whirlwind of fiction that started in Moscow with his reading of D. H. Lawrence carried Hughes through long sessions at his typewriter during the fall in Carmel."[39] By December, Hughes had completed a manuscript draft of what would become *The Ways of White Folks*, which included the Moscow stories in addition to several that up to that time he had been unable to publish stateside.[40] Among these stories, "Home" signals Hughes's interest in thinking through the complexities of returning to the States after his encounters abroad, taking up the idea of self-dispossession to forward it as an alternative model of subjectivity. This story summons the Du Boisian black male/white female dyad as a site of intimate negotiation between self and other to elucidate a disavowal of possessive subjecthood. In reframing this coupling, the story refuses the recognition-based model as linked to heteronormative bonds articulated as the improperly interracial. "Home" is the story of a young violinist, Roy, who, stricken with a mortal illness, returns home from Europe. Upon his arrival he is immediately marked as different, foreign, unreadable: "When the boy came back, there were bright stickers and tags

---

39. Rampersad, *Life*, 1:282.

40. "Home" was rejected by *Harper's, American Mercury, Atlantic Monthly, Scribner's,* and *Forum.* When it finally was accepted for publication by *Esquire* in 1934, one reviewer commented, "Why is it that authors think it is their function to lay the flesh bare and rub salt in the wound? . . . [M]ost people read for pleasure, and certainly there is no pleasure here" (quoted in Rampersad, *The Life of Langston Hughes: Volume 2, 1941–1967, I Dream a World,* 2:282).

in strange languages the home folks couldn't read all over his bags" (*CW* 15:37). This unreadability becomes the mirror of Roy's articulation of selfhood in which recognition is always under erasure. The story is filled with abstract hallucinatory moments that break from the third-person narrative to introduce a first-person stream of consciousness in which people and objects mingle and merge and cross-gender identifications circulate with racial taboos. Commissioned to play a concert for his hometown, Roy fantasizes deliriously while onstage:

> This is the *Meditation from Thaïs* by Massenet. . . . This is the broken heart of a dream come true not true. This is music, and me, sitting on the doorstep of the world needing you . . . . O, body of life and love with black hands and brown limbs and white breasts and a golden face with lips like a violin bowed for singing. . . . Steady, Roy! It's hot in this crowded church, and you're sick as hell. . . . This, the dream and the dreamer, wandering in the desert from Hopkinsville to Vienna in love with a street-walker named Music. . . . Listen, you bitch, I want you to be as beautiful as the moon in the night on the edge of the Missouri hills. . . . You sure don't look like Thaïs, you scrawny white woman in a cheap coat and red hat staring up at me from the first row. . . . What is it you want the music to give you? What do you want from me? . . . This is Hopkinsville, Missouri. . . . Look at all those brown girls back there in the crowd of Negroes, leaning toward me and the music. First time most of them ever saw a man in evening clothes, black or white. First time most of them ever heard the *Meditation from Thaïs*. First time they ever had one of their own race come home from abroad playing a violin. See them looking proud at me and music over the heads of the white folks in the first rows, over the head of the white woman in the cheap coat and red hat who knows what music's all about. . . . Who are you, lady? (*CW* 15:41–42)

Roy's first-person hallucination distinguishes itself from the narrative that has preceded it, creating a private space by calling attention to itself as such. This formal abruption of the third-person narrative reveals the extent to which Roy's private musings are simultaneously a public iteration. The provenance of Roy's thoughts as public is reinforced not only by their location as part of his performance in the music hall (where the hallucination could itself be seen as constitutive of the self-constituting performative) but also through the larger plot. Closing with the violent realization of white presuppositions about a black male/white female dyad—that such a couple can only and always will be interpreted as about masculine voraciousness and feminine fear—reconfirms the inseparability between private and public enactments of black masculine selfhood. In spite of his desires to create a space unimpeded by public mandate, voiced powerfully in his delirium, Roy is all too aware of this interpretive model: it has come to structure what he calls "home" and thus structures Hughes's story of the same name. Roy's mortal illness, the fact that we are told that he is doomed to die from the outset of the story, becomes an expression not so much of mysterious ill health as of the inescapability of public intervention into, and regulation of, his "private" life. Roy's glance into the mirror before he leaves for his ill-fated evening stroll becomes an expression of his accepting the destiny of his racial bearing, even as the face staring back at him poses a strong countermodel to this interpretation: "Roy lighted the light, the better to see himself in the warped mirror of the dresser. Ashy pale his face was, that had once been brown. His cheeks were sunken" (CW 15:43). The image looking back at Roy from the "warped mirror" has been distended, retaining only a faint resemblance to the white fantasy of its racialized counterpart. His hallucinations offer an alternative narrative, but one that Roy, set on a course to encounter a violent death, seems resigned to renounce.

In the delirious musings cited above, Roy's thoughts offer glimpses of an alternative model of black masculine selfhood. In the first part of the hallucination, the word *this* works as a transitional term to indicate the contiguities among music, Roy, and the "scrawny woman in a cheap coat and red hat." The bonds created suggest the enticement and risk imbedded within interracial coupling, but these inducements are charged with a flux of identity and desire, creating a scene in which the dream becomes the dreamer, the music the prostitute, the music the dream, Roy the streetwalker, and so on. In order for these connections to proceed, Roy summons another visual point of contact: "all those brown girls back there in the crowd of Negroes . . . looking proud at me." The collective gaze of brown girls marveling at Roy, who hails "from abroad," recalls the recognition under erasure poised by the story's opening scene in which white people "wonder about the brown-skinned young man" with the "stickers and tags in strange languages the home folks couldn't read." Whereas within white disdain there lurks a specter of violence against black males who appear different, who are not immediately or transparently readable, within the gaze of the brown girls (who are, as Roy admits, equally unable to "read" him) there remains a sense, however superfluous, of racial connectedness that soars "over the heads of the white folks."

In this vein Hughes introduces into the Du Boisian dyad of black male /

white female the interloping gaze and presence of black femininity, a presence remarkably absent from the scene of Du Bois's production of black masculinity. Rather than posing the insinuating look of violence proffered by the implied white masculine overseer in Du Bois's configuration, these girls offer mute pride. It is as if the girls are necessary collective witnesses to the transformation underway here: witnesses whose "look" is full of pride, albeit based in partial misrecognition.[41]

Roy's hallucinatory meanderings cut short any material connection between himself and the brown girls by focusing his identificatory gaze on the white woman in the front row. The girls may swell with possessive pride at the thought of one of "their own" dressed in a tuxedo and playing classical music, but this sense of affiliation is unmoored by their inability to comprehend anything other about Roy than the fact that his skin looks, like their own, brown. This filiation, based as it is on "looking," turns out to be an insufficient basis for identification. The inadequacy of visual mechanisms to determine connections in "Home" recalls Hughes's critique of Anne's dependency on this episteme in "Slave on the Block." When Roy figuratively addresses Mrs. Reese to say, "You don't look like Thaïs," he underscores the unreliability of visual sources of association. Thaïs, the heroine of Massenet's opera of the same name, was an Egyptian dancer of questionable reputation, and Roy's depiction of Mrs. Reese as both proximate to but different from Thaïs insinuates the instability of the category of looking. She may not look like Thaïs, if Roy imagines that Thaïs has brown skin, but she is associatively linked through music to the prostitute, who links back to Roy, the music's source. This association proves more powerful than the one between Roy's brown skin and that of the girls. The addressee, "you," here remains the white woman, who together with Roy is constitutive of an "us," whereas the brown girls become the "them": "See them looking proud at me."

Thus the negotiation of intimacy finally at play comes to be about the decidedly nonpossessive relationship between Roy and the woman who stands out, who seems, unlike the others, to know what it's "all about." Elizabeth Povinelli's work on intimacy is helpful here. In her tracing of the links between personal and social filiations, between intimacy as a

41. In *Beyond the Color Line and the Iron Curtain,* I explore the importance to Hughes's work in *The Ways of White Folks* of asserting black female agency as key to the reconstruction of black masculinity. In "Home" and "Slave on the Block" this can be seen in the presence of Mattie and the "brown girls" in Roy's audience, all of whom structurally intervene in the absenting of black femininity from Du Bois's representative paradigm of black masculinity.

form of recognition that validates the self and as a form of recognition that validates one's relationship to others within a given community (a "We the People"), Povinelli explains how intimate love came to be based on intimate recognition.

> [T]o assert the bond of love was to assert simultaneously a rejection of social utility. . . . Along with being a form of orientation and attachment, intimacy is the dialectic of this self-elaboration. Who am I in relation to you? This question and its cognates lift up a reflexive ego in the act of asking and stitch it to a world of others. The question is performative in the strict sense. In the act of asking Who Am I, the I is constituted.[42]

The codependency between "private" longings and social recognition that Povinelli describes is, again, reinforced in Du Bois's model. In the scene of Roy's performance of Thaïs, however, Roy turns the tables on Du Bois's recognition-based model of subjectivity. Rather than asking "who am I?" Roy asks, "Who are you, lady?" This question is, to be sure, self-constituting, but in a backward fashion: the "who am I" is constituted in the moment of asking not simply "who are you," but "who is *she*?" There is a merging of subjectivities here, a flux of identificatory objects and desires, punctuated only intermittently by Roy's attempt to remain "steady." She, it turns out, is the one who knows music and, correlatively, represents a differently identified sense of subjectivity, as suggested by language such as "bitch" and "cheap." In its emergence, this lyrical, delirium-based selfhood recalls Robert's objectless identity. Selfhood is identified as Roy's difference, his "red" internationalism, his unreadableness, and his refusal of recognition through prescribed models of gender, racial, and sexual ascription. The intimate space carved out here between Roy and Mrs. Reese defies Du Bois's ideal of intimate, heteronormative recognition as key to black masculine selfhood. In the same way that he refuses self-possession as a key to subjecthood, Hughes bars intimacy as recognition.[43] Hughes disentwines the subjective I based on intimacy (Du Bois's model) from the I of a self dispossessed. The latter, in the character of Roy, navigates differently this relationship between self and other, allowing for commingling and cross-identification, a "knowing" without mutual

---

42. Povinelli, "Notes on Gridlock: Genealogy, Intimacy, Sexuality," 230–31.

43. Perhaps this is one of the reasons Hughes's stories are generally read (and critically dismissed) as overly simple—a means of signifying that is impersonal and thus expendable.

recognition or a desire to possess. This formulation offers a powerful critique of the model of white citizenship as based in a relationship to selfhood in which self-possession and recognition by the other create mutual consensus of the "we" in "We the People." Hughes disbands this idea / model by challenging it through differently configured intimacies, problematizing this formative Du Boisian moment in which the narration of black masculinity organizes a structure of social membership based in heteronormative impulses voiced as a desire for recognition. Hughes's intervention into the familial arrives here in the middle of Roy's delirium. The introduction of Ma into the flux of hallucinatory language promises a place for the maternal bond: "You remember, Ma, . . . you remember that Kreisler record we had on the phonograph with the big horn when I was a kid? Nobody liked it but me, but you didn't care how many times I played it, over and over. . . . Why did you pray all night when I told you we had a contract to go to Berlin and work in a cabaret there? . . . And didn't I send you money home?" (CW 15:41). In the process of defamiliarizing Ma, the narrative usurps her space or overwhelms it with a more enticing association, that between Roy and Mrs. Reese, one that suggests an emotional alliance created through aberrant sexual behavior, a refusal to conform to "white" ways of recognizing interracial desire.[44]

As I mention above, a kinship between Roy and Mrs. Reese becomes cruelly, violently reinforced at the story's end when the two exchange partial greetings on the street and Roy is subsequently lynched for a purportedly errant display of black male desire. In depicting this denouement, the story offers a key rereading of the Du Boisian dyad of black man / white woman as based on a misrecognition of desire. What the white folks see when they observe Roy and Mrs. Reese takes on a life of its own. Consider how Hughes's language here escalates to make this point through the use of voice, point of view, and speculation. A seemingly unmediated flow of opinion gathers momentum, transforming the benign act of talk in the following spectrum: talking / insulting / attacking / RAPING. In operation there is a need to turn the unreadable Roy into a codifiable (and forbidden) display of black masculinity as sexual aggressor, to fulfill the larger cultural mandate that promises violence as ret-

---

44. In the story "Cora Unashamed," Hughes pursues the idea of interracial bonds created through sexual transgression. Between the protagonist Cora (who is black) and the daughter of the family Cora works for (who is white) he creates structurally parallel tales to forge an "interracial" alliance based on their aberrant sexual behavior (both have interracial affairs) that challenges the conventional basis of the familial bond.

ribution for fantasized desire.[45] Likewise, his punishment is the eviscera-
tion of his corporeality, the "feminization" of his body, so that it "hung . . .
like a violin for the wind to play" (*CW* 15:45). Rescue from the purported
danger posed to Mrs. Reese by Roy signals a mode by which white concerns about preserving white femininity summon a familiar Lacanian paradigm. As Slavoj Žižek rephrases it, "Lacan's thesis that 'there is no sexual relationship' means precisely that the structure of the 'real' sexual act
(of the act with a flesh-and-blood partner) is already inherently phantas-
matic—the 'real' body of the other serves only as a support for a phan-
tasmatic projection."[46]

In replaying this compulsory projection of white male fantasy, and its
counterprojection articulated by Du Bois, Hughes offers a renarration of
African American masculinity, a disarticulation of the bonds of phantasm-
matic projection, and a rewriting of interracial, cross-gender desire as a
site for alliances through aberration from the norm. These stories offer a
"bond" of sexual transgression, a means of articulating queer emotional
alliances through the identifications that emerge therein. Drawing on the
utopian impulses of Soviet society in the 1930s, Hughes's stories unite the
urges behind reconfigured subjectivity announced by the *novyi Sovetskii
chelovek* with the queer contours of a feminine-identified masculinity suggested by Lawrence to offer a differently affiliated black American masculine subjecthood. Political coalitions between blacks and whites proposed by the Internationale are adjusted to explore the interdictions of
sexual boundaries between black and white in the United States. As readers of these stories, we are invited to explore the different modalities of
desire and identification that Hughes's characters bring to life, to investigate the ways in which Hughes's depictions of interracial alliances, in-
fused with the possibilities of the Internationale, enable a vocabulary for
meditating upon queer desire and its social disavowal.

45. In some ways Roy's story offers a parable for what Judith Butler has described
as the mechanism of heterosexuality's "success." Seen in this way, heterosexuality (or,
in the case of "Home," white consensus) secures this success by summoning and simultaneously erasing its abject other, homosexuality (in this case Roy). See Butler, *Bodies That Matter*, 106.
46. Žižek, "Introduction: The Spectre of Ideology," 21.

V

Langston Hughes and the Boundaries of Art

Langston Hughes and the
Children's Literary Tradition

Giselle Liza Anatol

I have to wonder is it possible that Black children's literature has been ignored because today's Black literary scholars did not have it as children? Or is it because they cannot face their own childhood experiences? . . . Can we afford to ignore our children's exposure to prejudice, ignorance and injustice that are focused upon them through the omission of books that do not portray their images?

—Nancy D. Tolson

The poetic works of Langston Hughes have received much attention over the years, and even more so in light of the worldwide celebrations honoring the centennial of his birth on February 1, 1902. However, comparatively little study has been done of Hughes's writing for children. Literature for young people has long been deemed undeserving of analytical pursuit: it is often considered to be empty of serious content; a vehicle for lighthearted "fun" and pure entertainment; a means of keeping children occupied while adults get down to the serious business of living. In truth, however, as those who write for children and those who study this body of literature can attest, these works are a potent means of inculcating social roles and behaviors, mapping out a moral framework, and suggesting and validating particular desires and fears. Black children's literature scholars such as Dorothy Broderick, Bernice E. Cullinan, Donnarae MacCann, and Nancy D. Tolson have asserted that because juvenilia can function as a reference point for developing values, solving problems, making decisions, and establishing a conception of self, children of color need works that mirror their own family structures, lifestyles, and cultures. They can then develop a proud and healthy self-image and sense of their own identities within the world in which they live.

Tolson notes that prominent black writers such as Carter G. Woodson, Arna Bontemps, Countee Cullen, and Langston Hughes published children's works, but few contemporary readers are familiar with them: "With the help of these writers and many others Black children were able to know the historical backgrounds as well as the heroic figures who set down monumental tracks in the progressive movement for Blacks in America and the world."[1] Tolson's use of the past tense emphasizes the crucial point: while child readers of these writers' generation might have been able to discover the glories of African-diasporic achievement, today's children (and adults) have little to no exposure to these writings.[2]

In the past, members of the literary establishment critiqued Hughes's writing as too elementary to be taken seriously. The fact that the poems of Hughes's *The Dream Keeper* (1932), a collection for young people, were selected from previously published "adult" verse only supported their argument. Similarly, when asked to submit work for *Golden Slippers: An Anthology of Negro Poetry for Young Readers*, compiled by Arna Bontemps, Hughes forwarded a group of poems along with the following note:

> Some of these for children,
> And some for older fry.
> You may take your choice
> Since you're as old as I.[3]

1. Tolson, "Introduction," 10.
2. Hence contemporary projects such as Wade Hudson's *Pass It On: African-American Poetry for Children*, which features three poems by Hughes, and Tom Feelings's *Soul Looks Back in Wonder*. In his preface, Feelings describes *Soul* as his attempt "to connect the ancient with the new, the young with the old, the unborn with the ancestors." He posits the book as one way "for young people to see their own beauty reflected in our [African diasporic] eyes, through our work." Hudson similarly cites a "rich literary legacy" that many children fail to access.
3. Bontemps, ed., *Golden Slippers: An Anthology of Negro Poetry for Young Readers*, 210.

Bontemps ended up including at least one Hughes poem in each section of the collection ("Waking Up," "Hard Work," "Big Cities," and so on). Rather than reflecting the facile nature of his writing, Hughes's refusal to make a definitive age distinction in his readership suggests his respect for children's abilities to absorb mature topics. One might refer to *Black Misery*, a manuscript on which Hughes was working when he died in 1967. When it was reissued by the Opie Library of Children's Literature in 2001, some reviewers remarked on its incompatibility with contemporary ideas of children's materials: although there is quite a bit of dry humor involved, the one-sentence captions, presented with understated elegance, can evoke distress over social conditions such as racist ignorance. Consider the proximity of the lines "Misery is when your pals see Harry Belafonte walking down the street and they holler, 'Look, there's Sidney Poitier'" and "Misery is when somebody meaning no harm called your little black dog 'Nigger' and he just wagged his tail and wiggled" (*CW* 11:173). I would argue that, in the spirit of many vernacular traditions, Hughes did not segregate his audiences by age—everyone in the community had something to bring to his art. In fact, the writer asserted that children make the best readers of poetry: "Children are not nearly so resistant to poetry as are grown-ups. In fact, small youngsters are not resistant at all" (*CW* 9:363).

I hope to demonstrate that, by examining Hughes's pieces for children, contemporary scholars can observe the complex themes and images present in his adult writings in a more distilled form—particularly his celebration of African American culture and accomplishments despite racial injustice. As a "poet of the people," especially the poor and dispossessed, what better forum than through works for children—often the most disempowered members of our society in their lack of independent agency—could Hughes use for expressing his ideas? As Steven C. Tracy, editor of children's biographies volume of *The Collected Works of Langston Hughes*, inquires: "And why not tell [the history of African American people] in a variety of genres, in a number of ways, across a series of decades, not only to adults needing to know the full history of their country, but also to children who craved its spiritual and intellectual nourishment and its social and political motivation?" (*CW* 12:1)

What I find most striking about Hughes's juvenilia is how, in addition to the pride he evoked in African American progress, his deep desire to encourage "interracial good will" (*CW* 12:307) for the true success of the U.S. democracy often made his writing fraught with tensions. Reading many of his children's works, one witnesses Hughes's lifelong battle between a staunch patriotism and a bitter condemnation of American injustice and hypocrisy.

Hughes's essay "Children and Poetry" sets out to explain to young readers why people compose poetry. Reasons include helping people to recall words or events, sharing vivid scenes or moving personal experiences, and identifying with and connecting to the world around one. All three notions point to the establishment of a strong community—both local and global. When Hughes discusses poetry and memory, for instance, he specifies remembering the words and experiences of others instead of only self-generated, localized ideas—"poems need not always be about what one sees or thinks or feels oneself" (CW 9:365). When he states that "poetry helps people to remember" (CW 9:363), one is reminded of the myriad narratives within African American literature that stress the importance of memory—both individual and communal—for the African-diasporic subject: Toni Morrison's *Beloved*, Gayl Jones's *Corregidora*, Jamaica Kincaid's *My Brother*, Edwidge Danticat's *Breath, Eyes, Memory*, Kasi Lemmons's film *Eve's Bayou*. Additionally, Hughes's example of a verse to help him remember to buy peas instead of corn for his mother brings poetry and art into the realm of everyday thoughts and experiences; it also counters traditional notions of poetry as a formalist aesthetic and presents it as utilitarian.

Likewise, employing poetry to share experiences beyond the range of one's easily accessible neighbors emphasizes an extended community and the need for communication beyond familiar borders. This parallels Hughes's express desire to use poetry "to help us remember to walk together" (CW 9:366). His example of feeling deeply moved by the situations of people suffering under Nazi rule in Germany and being prompted to write the poem "Refugee in America" encourages selflessness and a heightened awareness of a world community, as opposed to one's local geographical, racial, national, religious, or cultural community. His choice of words at this point in the essay is telling: he describes people "mistreated and enslaved by the Nazis" and proclaims:

> There are words like *Liberty*
> That almost make me cry.
> If you had known what I knew
> You would know why. (CW 9:365)

By referring to "mistreated and enslaved" Europeans and the experiences that the speaker of the poem knows but the reader might not, Hughes highlights some poignant connections and potential alliances between African American and Jewish people. He simultaneously calls attention to past and present injustices that occur within U.S. borders while those in power choose to look away and focus on foreign atrocities.

Hughes's "18 Poems for Children," originally published in *The Langston Hughes Reader* (1958), can be broken down into seven loose and interrelated categories: the Nativity poems;[4] poems about simple, everyday events, including "Poor Rover," "Silly Animals," and "Old Dog Queenie"; responsibility poems, such as "Brand New Clothes" and "Grocery Store"; nature poems, such as "Country," which celebrates the openness and beauty of rural landscapes in comparison to the growing urban sprawl where buildings hide the sky;[5] family poems, including "Grandpa's Stories," "Piggy-Back," and "Not Often"; poems validating African American culture and traditions, such as "The Blues" and "Problems," which features riddles, very much in the African oral tradition; and poems describing a larger cosmopolitan community, such as "Little Song," which presents children of many races and ethnicities—implied primarily through names: Carmencita and Miguelito (Latina/o), Patrick (Irish), Si Lan Chen (East Asian), Lucienne (French), Xenophon (Greek), Giovanni (Italian), and Hildegarde (ostensibly German)—dancing around a maypole. One might argue that the poet's choice of May Day as the holiday where interracial, international harmony can be celebrated subtly calls holidays such as Independence Day into question: July Fourth did *not* mark independence for enslaved Africans in the United States; nor did it mark true independence and equality for women or non-landowning men. This ambivalence, both commemorating the multiplicity of American identity and harmonious interaction of races and casually revealing social tensions and inconsistencies, comes through even more aggressively in Hughes's biographical works from the 1950s, as I will show.

4. Reprinted with new illustrations by Ashley Bryan in *Carol of the Brown King: Nativity Poems by Langston Hughes.*

5. Hughes's *The First Book of Rhythms* (1954) deserves additional comment here because of its striking attention to the natural world. The poet begins, "Your rhythm on this earth began first with the beat of your heart" (CW 11:257), and thus casts rhythm not only as natural, and deep inside each living thing's body, but also life-sustaining. Rhythm is linked to geographical wonders, such as the Niagara Falls; physical forms like leaves and snowflakes; biological rhythms, such as nest shapes and behavioral instinct; and rhythmical patterns of movement, from the flight of a gull to the paths of the planets. The book is as much—if not more—about teaching an appreciation of the natural world as it is about rhythm. I wonder, however, if this focus ends up alienating the urban child reader who has little to no exposure to the images Hughes describes.

That the serious elements are not left out of writing for children, giving them only happy pictures of life, can be witnessed in much of the "18 Poems" series. In "Piggy-Back," the speaker says his grandmother will not give him a ride because her back "Has had enough to do" (*CW* 11:104). That the grandmother has done a good deal of backbreaking labor is obvious—whether in the fields, in the factories, or as a domestic in the house of a white family, readers cannot know but can certainly infer. One of Hughes's major goals in his writing for children was to acknowledge and celebrate the contributions of African Americans to the larger American society without being naive as to the racial and class discrimination they had suffered. Thus, although the grandmother's time for working is finished, she is physically broken and cannot engage in strenuous play with her grandson.

In "Piggy-Back," a father and mother are present in addition to the grandmother, conveying a traditionally nuclear as well as extended family. Strikingly, this situation was quite contrary to Hughes's own lived experience. The contrast is interesting to note when perusing "Grandpa's Stories" alongside "Piggy-Back," given that Hughes's grand*mother* is the renowned storyteller of his childhood. It would seem that Hughes wrote out of a certain sense of desire, a situation of lack and longing. In his introduction to the biographies, Steven Tracy remarks on this dynamic, citing Hughes's quotation of a Paul Laurence Dunbar poem and proposing a vision of "a Langston starved for parental love" and perhaps seeking "a playful father's nurturing presence in his child's life" (*CW* 12:4).

In "Not Often," Hughes repeats the theme of the strength of the black family and the presence of male figures despite their apparent absence. The speaker claims never to have seen his great-great-great-grandfather: he supposes the man "must've been / A family fixture, / But there's no / Picture" (*CW* 11:106). The poet thus speaks to issues of family history and counters the stereotype of the weak and lazy African American father figure with a comment on the absence of records and the lack of "official" existence and personhood for African Americans in white mainstream society.

Hughes's Nativity poems are perhaps the most explicit in their recognition and celebration of black peoples. "Carol of the Brown King" describes the three wise men, one of whom "was a brown man, / So they sing." The line "One was a brown king" reemphasizes the character's race and complexion, and a connection is made between past and present generations when the man is described as "dark *like me*" (*CW* 3:232, emphasis added). The poem thus attempts to instill a sense of racial pride in black children, providing little-seen images of prosperity and respect for an African character: royal, wealthy, wise, and reverent, bowing his head "in Jesus' name" at the manger. Perhaps most important for Hughes's project of, in Tracy's words, "refocus[ing] the lens of history and culture on significant African [diasporic] contributors to American and world history" (*CW* 12:2), as part of the Nativity this brown man is included and recognized in a momentous religious and historic event rather than as a member of an excluded, segregated, and demeaned population.

Representations of the "lowly" are not omitted, however; in striking contrast to the proud king, the speaker of "Shepherd's Song at Christmas" is "among the least." His social position parallels not only that of African Americans during the time of Hughes's writing but also that of the economically poor and dispossessed of all races and, as we have seen, that of children, who are often disempowered because of their age.[6] The youth explains, "I'm *just* a shepherd boy, / Very poor I am— / But I know there is / A King in Bethlehem" (*CW* 11:109, emphasis added), and the reader's attention is drawn to his lack of material wealth, social status, prestigious job, and formal education. At the same time, one is encouraged to see that these things have no connection to the presence of intelligence and knowledge; the boy *knows* about the birth of Jesus as king and will be welcomed at the site of his birth.

Tracy identifies Hughes's purpose in creating an oeuvre of children's literature that ranged over twenty years as continuing "to appreciate and celebrate the contributions of African Americans to the American enterprise and the human spirit while acknowledging the tortuous path they had traveled, and continued to travel" (*CW* 12:2). Looking at Hughes's biographical works for children after viewing much of the earlier poetry, one notices that this pride in "the American enterprise" became increasingly pronounced in the prose. One must wonder how effectively Hughes was able to maintain a balance between his own personal and political values and the capitalistic desires of editors at mainstream presses whose approval was needed for him to get published and survive as a writer. Arna Bontemps, fellow poet and children's book collaborator with Hughes, composed a telling letter about these pressures on March 28, 1937:

6. This celebration of the "lowly" in a Eurocentric patriarchal American society might partially account for the proliferation of woman-voiced poems in Hughes's writing.

[Houghton, Mifflin] are having the best of luck with *Sad-Faced Boy*. . . . [T]hey anticipate a royalty for me of $1,200. . . . They have offered . . . to give me an advance on a new [children's book] before I put paper in the typewriter. So you see it's worth while to write for the Rosenwald libraries . . . . And they still want you terribly, and they keep hinting as much to me. As a tip off, if you can use it, they want a plantation story—with lots of plot and many sharecropping problems, wicked enemies, etc.—for the teen age readers—say about sixteen. Better if it had a mystery like a lost deed to property or something like that.[7]

One must also wonder how intensely Hughes felt the need to prove his loyalty to the United States after: (1) the FBI began surveillance of him in 1944 on the grounds of prior radicalism; (2) being denounced as a communist by the Senate in 1948; and (3) being compelled to testify in front of Sen. Joseph McCarthy's subcommittee on subversive activities in 1953. Was Hughes's commitment to, in Tracy's words, "letting 'America be America again' by reaffirming the principles of democracy through his writings" entirely sincere (*CW* 12:2), or was it, in effect, further testimony to his doubted patriotism? Could the resolute integrationist theme in his work have been influenced by the committee's exoneration of the poet after he repudiated his past revolutionary ideas?

Richard K. Barksdale reads Hughes's Harlem Renaissance–era poetry as part of a "literary insurrection" against conventions that pronounced that "whatever literature the Black man produced must not only protest racial conditions but promote racial integration. There was little or no place in such a literary tradition for the celebration of the Black lifestyle for its own sake."[8] It is clear that this "rebellion" shifted, however, in Hughes's writing for children published in the 1950s, when integration became one of his most prominent themes. Possible reasons for the ideological transformation abound: a true conversion in beliefs about what literature should accomplish; increased political conservatism; support for the principles behind the 1954 *Brown v. Board of Education* Supreme Court decision (which, incidentally, Zora Neale Hurston, whose once-close relationship with Hughes had soured, opposed); an attempt to avoid further political controversy and prove his "true" American-ness; a desire to keep alive children's hope for justice and a more positive future.

Maryemma Graham's analysis of several of Hughes's short stories serves as a lens through which to interpret these changes. Graham points

---

7. Charles H. Nichols, ed., *Arna Bontemps–Langston Hughes: Letters, 1925–1967*, 26.
8. Barksdale, "Hughes: His Times and His Humanistic Techniques," 94.

to Hughes's repeated efforts to wrestle with contradictions between concepts, including national literature versus revolutionary literature; bourgeois values versus proletarian ideals; traditional black folk culture's fabulist nature versus a Marxist emphasis on realism; artistic individualism versus collective responsibility.[9] All of these issues are raised again and again in the prose juvenilia. I will illustrate how the apparently antithetical esteem for *and* bitterness toward the nation that produced great African American talents make it possible to interpret the texts as both deferentially conventional and simultaneously quite radical.

Hughes produced an enormous amount of children's literature: he contributed to *The Brownies' Book* in 1921; *The Sweet and Sour Animal Book,* a poetic alphabet book, was copyrighted in 1932 (although not published until 1994), and *The Dream Keeper and Other Poems* and *Popo and Fifina: Children of Haiti* were also published that year; *The First Book of Negroes* was released in 1952; *Famous American Negroes* in 1954 (in which year the writer also published *The First Book of Rhythms*); *Famous Negro Music Makers* in 1955 (also the publication year of *The First Book of Jazz*); *A Pictorial History of the Negro* in 1956 (along with *The First Book of the West Indies*); *Famous Negro Heroes of America* in 1958; and *The First Book of Africa* in 1960. *Black Magic: A Pictorial History of the Negro in American Entertainment* was released by Prentice Hall in 1967, shortly after Hughes's death; *Black Misery* and *The Pasteboard Bandit* were also published posthumously, in 1969 and 1997, respectively.

The First Book of Negroes begins with the biography of Estevan, a sixteenth-century Spanish explorer. Significantly, even before readers learn what claim to fame, the first line provides an explicit reference to his racial identity as "a black man" (*CW* 11:227). The "very dark Negro born in Morocco" is then described as "fearless and full of the spirit of adventure," as well as incredibly strong and resourceful. He was one of only four men to survive out of a crew of five hundred sailing from Spain to Florida; he later learned to speak several American Indian languages and served as a guide to the Spanish in the Americas.

The contradiction between pride in the achievements of a man of African descent who was invaluable to the Spanish empire and disgust for the European system for which he worked—a system that continued to oppress thousands of people—becomes clear when Hughes depicts the Moroccan's death: Estevan is killed by the Zuni Indians, who fear that other foreigners will follow Estevan and take their land. "And that is exactly

9. Graham, "The Practice of a Social Art," 213–20.

what happened in the end. The Spaniards claimed it in the name of the King of Spain, and it became a part of the New World—now Arizona and New Mexico" (*CW* 11:228). The black body was destroyed (and, as we find out in *Famous Negro Heroes of America*, severely mutilated), and Spain, and later the United States, gained valuable territory for which it never acknowledged the labor of people of color. Notably absent from the passage, however, is any allusion to Estevan's complicity in the imperialistic enterprise, or the position of the United States as a neoimperial power that took over where the Spaniards left off.

The same can be said of Hughes's biography of Paul Cuffe in *Famous Negro Heroes of America*. Cuffe is cast in the table of contents as "seaman and colonizer" (*CW* 12:203). The prosperous ship owner and trader traveled to Africa during early colonial history in order to explore the possibilities of settling African American families in Sierra Leone. As with his depiction of Estevan, Hughes's choice of words, linking Cuffe's investigation to "colonizing" Africa (*CW* 12:223), reveals the poet's potential blindness when it comes to U.S. colonialism and the ways in which these political and cultural imperialistic tendencies have been repeated over time.

Hughes's presentation of slavery in the Americas in *The First Book of Negroes* also proves to be complicated. He struggles between an accurate representation of the injustices perpetrated against African peoples and a desire to stress the ties and collaborations between black and white subjects, necessary for his emphasis on integration for his 1950s audience. For example, he creates a direct parallel between indentured servitude and slavery, briefly mentioning the Africans brought to Virginia and sold as slaves before writing that other ships brought "white men and women to work as slaves, too. These were called 'indentured servants'. . . . [T]hey had to work for nothing until they had paid the fines and bought their freedom" (*CW* 11:229). The impulse can be read as an equalizing measure, attempting to raise the status of African Americans by preventing contemporary whites from believing in an innate superiority that kept their ancestors from being reduced to slavery. The effect, however, weakens Hughes's cry against racial injustice by failing to concretely acknowledge the disparity of treatment between indentured servants and slaves: white *people* versus black *chattel*. Along the same vein, when Hughes informs his reader about the Haitian slaves who were treated exceptionally cruelly by their French owners, and who "*freed themselves* long before American slaves *were freed*" (*CW* 11:235, emphasis added), his use of active and passive voice suggest agency for the Haitians in contrast to the passivity of U.S. African Americans. The reader might conclude that U.S. slavery and North American masters were not quite so bad: these slaves were content and remained submissive until liberated by some outside force.

The ideological contradictions in *The First Book of Negroes* are perhaps most evident in Hughes's portrait of Terry Lane, the fictional character with whom any child can identify, but who stands as an exceptionally positive role model for young black readers who did not see themselves in the standard children's texts of the time, such as the ubiquitous *Dick and Jane* primers. Terry is a young resident of New York City, "whose skin is brown as a walnut and whose hair is black and beautifully crinkly" (*CW* 11:230). Hughes presents blackness as desirable in an effort to instill racial pride. This message is accentuated in the book's section on "the brown kings and queens in ancient lands" (*CW* 11:233). The emphasis on these stories as "true"—unlike the make-believe fairy tales of princess and princess-to-be Snow White and Cinderella—serves a similar purpose to "Carol of the Brown King": it provides a long-standing history of wealth, royalty, respect, art, and learning for people of African descent. In this section of *The First Book of Negroes*, references to the Ethiopian civilization that "spread into Egypt where brown-skinned Pharaohs were building gigantic pyramids" (*CW* 11:233) challenge the idea of Egyptians as the white (non-African) source of all civilization. Similarly, the depiction of the University of Sankoré in Timbuktu, where "scholars from all over the ancient world came to study medicine, geography, literature, or law," inverts traditional beliefs in Europe as the center of culture and learning. All of these details serve to instill racial pride in the black reader.

Terry's socioeconomic class seems to be intended to function as another source of pride and to challenge mainstream stereotypes of the economically struggling black family. Terry's mother *and* father have the leisure time and financial resources to take their son to Broadway and Radio City Music Hall performances and to "fine" restaurants (*CW* 11:230). Terry's grandmother graduated from Fisk University, "so she does not say 'ain't,' or use bad grammar, except when she is reciting folk poems or telling stories" (*CW* 11:232). Terry's father is highly educated; fluent in French, Spanish, *and* Italian, he works at the United Nations as a translator.

The celebration of this solidly middle-class existence would appear to run counter to the antibourgeois values that Hughes proposed earlier in his career. However, Hughes is sure to show that Terry's grandmother is not alienated from her race and culture: she still embraces a vernacular tradition, sharing folk stories and poems with her grandson. Additionally, Hughes mentions that, despite the contemporary successes of the Lane family, Terry's great-grandfather was a slave, and that painful history is not to be forgotten. Rather than employing this device fully in service of the rags-to-riches ideal of the American Dream, which falsely promises that *anyone* who works hard enough can succeed, Hughes uses it to critique the racial politics of his time:

> If Terry lived in the South where his great-grandfather was once a slave, he could not go into a downtown theater or restaurant, since it is against the law in Southern cities for colored people to sit next to white people or eat with them in public. . . . This is legal segregation, but Negroes . . . do not believe it is legal because it does not follow our Constitution or the Declaration of Independence. (*CW* 11:230–31)

Hughes's political agenda is explicit here. He constantly references specific disparate practices of segregation, such as describing separate water fountains for whites and blacks, whites-only parks, and how African American children were permitted to enter the zoo "only on Mondays" (*CW* 11:239). The poet builds on the sense of injustice and arbitrariness in the Jim Crow South, a subject that would be especially poignant for young readers, who are often consumed with the idea of fair and equal treatment once they leave the egocentric stage of development and begin to be curious about other people and their relationships with them. By remarking that these practices "seemed very silly to Terry" (*CW* 11:239), Hughes ridicules the logic that even a young child can see through and deride.

When the poet states, "If Terry lived in the South he could not go to school with white children, *nor could they go to school with him*" (*CW* 11:231, emphasis added), his wording places the desire to be with another group on *both* sides, rather than exclusively in the striving of African Americans to be among whites. For Hughes, the integrationist project must be a shared one, with everyone working together for the good of the larger society. Rather than cast these alliances as part of the new and unfamiliar process of the 1950s civil rights movement, however, Hughes chooses to refer to examples of collaboration from past centuries: "Terry's grandmother said, there have always been white people in America who wanted Negroes to live happily and have the same rights as other Americans" (*CW* 11:240). Harriet Tubman's story, with reference to the assistance of "many kind white people" (*CW* 11:240), serves a similar integrationist purpose.

Hughes also takes pains to identify Phillis Wheatley's masters as a nurturing presence in the young girl's life: Mrs. Wheatley is described as "gentle" and, "seeing that [Phillis] was a bright child, soon taught her to read and write," although this went against social convention and the law (CW 12:21). Hughes repeatedly strives to undercut the stereotype of the bigoted white American, and especially the heartless white slaveholder. This attempt on behalf of the mainstream majority, however, simultaneously appears to serve a secondary purpose—easing the guilt of the writer's twentieth-century white audience and making his text less controversial. Thus, when he writes, "To a sensitive little African girl, under the circumstances of slavery, fate could hardly have been more generous. The Wheatleys were good people. But in spite of their kindness, as a child, . . . Phillis must have wept for her own mother" (CW 12:25), Hughes undermines his own subversive message about the flawed practice of American democracy. He essentially excuses the practice of slavery if the master is kind. By focusing on Phillis's emotional distress as a motherless child, and not as an enslaved woman, he fails to condemn the practice of owning other human beings. He ends up being much more critical of Wheatley's husband—"jack-of-all-trades and a master of none," who might have married her because of her fame—than he is of her masters (CW 12:24).

In the story set in Hughes's present, the writer highlights the diversity of various racial groups, positive interactions between them, and how working toward a common goal solidifies their ties. Terry's friends "are children of all nationalities" (CW 11:239), and Hughes is careful to mention that "[a]ll of these different people get along all right." In the subway station, Terry and his family see black and white guards, "all working together on the same train," and when the protagonist and his cousin Charlene visit the United Nations they note that "[t]hey had never seen so many different nationalities before, colored and white, working together" (CW 11:247). The children receive a children's copy of "The Universal Declaration of Human Rights," which informs people about "how many nationalities can work together to make our world a happy place for everyone" (CW 11:248). The reiteration of "working together" not only emphasizes the importance of interracial collaboration but also taps into a mainstream belief in the Protestant work ethic. The focus on labor as a means to progress is reinforced with the biographies of Satchel Paige—"Satch is a great example of what a man can do who keeps on trying" (CW 11:244)—and Booker T. Washington, who is described as being admitted to Hampton Institute for cleaning a room until it is spotless. The benefits are also stressed in Famous Negro Music Makers, where, as Tracy notes in his introduction, recurring ideas of "dedication to craft, sense of mission, hard work, and catholic tastes of many of the performers" (*CW* 12:6) allow Hughes to combat stereotypes of lazy and immoral blacks, and licentious musicians in particular, while revealing how their strong work ethic makes them worthy of being a part of the U.S. enterprise. Here again, Hughes divulges a contradictory ideology. The frequent references to diligent labor reinscribe a strongly nationalist, "pull yourself up by your bootstraps" notion, suggesting that race and color are unimportant when ambition and determination come into play.[10]

In the concluding paragraph of *The First Book of Negroes*, Terry's father extols:

> [I]t is good to live in America. . . . Our country has many problems still to solve, but America is young, big, strong, and beautiful. And we are trying very hard to be, as the flag says, 'one nation, indivisible, with liberty and justice for all.'[11] Here people are free to vote and work out their problems. . . . [A]ll of us are a part of democracy. By taking an interest in our government, and by treating our neighbors as we would like to be treated, *each one of us* can help make our country the most wonderful country in the world. (*CW* 11:250)

Hughes calls on his readers to engage actively in their civic duty—making the United States "the most wonderful country in the world" by participating in the integrationist project. Like George Washington Carver, true patriots will give to the nation "out of love, not for profit" (*CW* 11:238). While encouraging young African American readers to become involved in the political process instead of accepting the injustices of the establishment, the nationalist focus privileges the United States above all other nations and thus allows Hughes to depict Nobel Prize–winner Ralph Bunche as a man "of service to his country" (*CW* 11:238), rather than to the world at large.

Hughes's *Famous American Negroes* repeats some of the information furnished in *The First Book of Negroes* but provides more extensive biographies on the figures it represents. As in *The First Book of Negroes*, these people—two poets, a painter, an actor, two musicians, a religious leader, two slave resistors, an educator, a surgeon, an agricultural chemist, a journal-

---

10. It should be noted, too, that Booker T. Washington's well-accomplished task in *The First Book of Negroes* also rewards African American servitude and domesticity.

11. The book was written before the "under God" addition was passed by Congress.

ist, a businessman, a labor leader, a political scientist, and an athlete—can be read as key figures in the process of integration and participants in a movement toward peace. Hughes lauds Booker T. Washington as a man who "sought a way to make peace between the races in the South" (*CW* 12:51). Ralph Bunche is noted to have won the Nobel Peace Prize, and Hughes includes a quotation in which the political scientist remarks on his struggles to bring about "a world at peace . . . a world in which all men shall walk together as equals and with dignity" (*CW* 12:98). *Chicago Defender* founder Robert S. Abbott is also quoted respecting the peaceful coexistence and full integration of black and white Americans: "We are Americans and *must* live together, so why not live in peace?" (*CW* 12:68).

Each story praises the drive of the African American who succeeds in achieving the American Dream and paving the way for others to find "true happiness" in American society. At the same time, by enumerating the battles each one had to fight, Hughes calls the actual *practice* of American democracy into question.

> The careers of the famous American Negroes in this book were achieved, not only in the face of handicaps which any other American might have, but *in spite of* the additional difficulties which Negro Americans have known—beginning with slavery . . . [and] continuing with such varied racial discriminations as not being permitted to vote. (*CW* 12:20)

Hughes then claims that the biographies are emblematic both "of personal effort and of democratic possibilities." Again readers witness the push and pull of impulses. The acknowledgment of racial injustices and psychological brutality is coupled with the celebration of U.S. greatness and democratic ideals.

The absence of figures such as Paul Robeson, Marcus Garvey, and W. E. B. Du Bois is striking in the collection, as it is in *Famous Negro Heroes of America,* especially given that, as Tracy notes, in *Ebony* magazine in 1949 Hughes had called Du Bois "the figure he admired the most in literary race relations" (*CW* 12:5). When Marcus Garvey finally *is* mentioned in the biographies, he is essentially relegated to a side note on Hugh N. Mulzac, who is introduced as the captain of one of Garvey's Black Star Line ships but is featured as a U.S. war hero: "[I]t was during World War II as the master of the Liberty Ship *Booker T. Washington* that Captain Mulzac became famous. Dodging submarines, his ship transported safely across the Atlantic 18,000 soldiers and prisoners, as well as thousands of tons of war material, without the loss of a single man" (*CW* 12:290). Tracy calls further attention to the point when he notes: "except for crusader Ida B. Wells, whose career straddled the nineteenth and twentieth centuries, none of the twentieth-century figures are political agitators or race leaders" (*CW* 12:8).

Tracy attributes the absence of these notable twentieth-century figures to their leftist political beliefs, to which one can add that, as a woman, Wells would have been less threatening to readers of Hughes's era. However, the scholar observes an apparent ideological discrepancy in Hughes's inclusion of A. Philip Randolph, founder of the socialist magazine *The Messenger*. Indeed, *The Messenger* denounced the World War I slogan "Making the World Safe for Democracy"—and, by extension, U.S. democracy in general—because "Negro citizens were disfranchised, segregated, and lynched throughout the South." Hughes also notes that Randolph was called "the most dangerous Negro in America" by some mainstream newspapers as he was "agitating for the fulfillment of our Constitutional guarantees for *all* citizens and the protection of the law for everybody" (*CW* 12:90). This biography challenges the simplistic assertion that Hughes sought to create a purely accommodationist text, once again highlighting the contradictions in Hughes's philosophies.

The entries in *Famous Negro Heroes of America* shift the focus of *Famous American Negroes* from peacekeepers and pacificist integrationists working within U.S. bounds to those who served by fighting for the United States in a larger world context. Of the thirteen heroes featured, over half participated in what might be called "the American enterprise" by their engagement in U.S. war efforts and a marked patriotism. One is reminded of Hughes's biography on Robert S. Abbott in *Famous American Negroes*: in that work, Hughes reports how the journalist urged African Americans to pursue their democratic rights while engaging in "their full civic and national duties, to keep their neighborhoods clean, be thrifty and self-respecting, buy bonds, aid the [World War I] effort, and in general be good citizens" (*CW* 12:68). Participation in the capitalist economy is closely identified with one's patriotism and worthiness for citizenship. Significantly, Hughes goes on to recount how the U.S. Maritime Commission later named a Liberty ship the USS *Robert S. Abbott* in honor of the journalist's efforts to get the Chicago African American community to buy two million dollars' worth of war bonds. Emphasizing the idea of national pride that results from supporting the military and the U.S. economy, Hughes quotes a *Defender* editorial that appeared several years after Abbott's death:

Regardless of how deeply we may resent numerous injustices perpetrated against us and how hard we may fight against them, we must admit that this is our war too. Our boys are fighting overseas, facing a dangerous, murderous enemy who will destroy them and us as quickly as he will our white brothers. . . . Participation in this Fourth War Loan drive is not only a patriotic act, but is a matter of self interest. (*CW* 12:68)

The question remains: is Hughes praising and celebrating this obviously anti-Marxist project, or merely celebrating the initiative, success, and long-lasting legacy of a great man? The ambiguities send the critic down the proverbial rabbit hole in search of a clear political agenda.

Among the other "patriots" discussed in *Famous Negro Heroes of America* are African Americans who participated "in every war since the colonial period" (*CW* 12:272). The Revolutionary War is exceptionally well represented, given the absence of mention of these figures within mainstream history and the poet's desire to right/write this wrong. Hughes wrote about Crispus Attucks, named "martyr for American independence" in the table of contents; Oliver Cromwell and Prince Whipple, who crossed the Delaware with George Washington, making them right-hand men to the so-called father of the U.S. democratic nation; Tack Sisson, who helped raid British headquarters at Newport in 1777; "Black Samson, a giant Negro armed with a scythe," who, also in 1777, "swept through the ranks of the Redcoats" (*CW* 12:272); and Deborah Gannett, who fought for a year and a half with the Fourth Massachusetts Regiment disguised in a man's uniform. Hughes takes great care to detail African American participation in the very origins of the U.S. democracy.

He goes on to record African American military service in the War of 1812, the Civil War, the Spanish-American War, World War I, and World War II. Hughes relates important events in the life of Robert Smalls, the Civil War hero who stole a Confederate vessel, sailed his enslaved family into Northern waters—for which he gained *national* acclaim—and went on to supply Union officers with information garnered from being impressed by the Confederate Navy. Like the figures from the Revolutionary period, Smalls is included to highlight African American involvement in the critical formation of the democracy—this time the manifestation of a newly united country that emerges after the War between the States.

Also included among Hughes's "patriots": Henry Johnson, a member of the 369th Infantry, the first group of African American combat troops to land in Europe in World War I, and Charles Young, an 1889 West Point graduate who proceeded to become a colonel in the U.S. Army, making him the highest-ranking African American up to that time. Hughes describes how, whereas Johnson could fight as a private, racism kept Young from advancing. "[H]is failure to see active duty proved a great disappointment to Negro Americans. They felt that the then existing race prejudice in our defense system prevented Colonel Young from being given service commensurate with his rank" (CW 12:275). Interestingly, Hughes separates himself from this accusation of American racism by associating racism not only with "they" and "them" rather than "we" but also with *feeling* instead of *knowing*. Remaining in a safe space, perhaps one necessitated by his experiences with McCarthy's Senate committee, Hughes raises the specter of injustice without being able to be held accountable for it. Similarly, when he rehearses hero Dorie Miller's skill with a gun during the raid on Pearl Harbor—even though, as a messman, he was not allowed to participate in actual combat—Hughes calls attention to the irony of the situation but fails to explicitly critique the system that sends Miller "back to being a messman again" after felling four Japanese bombers (CW 12:302).

The story of Hugh N. Mulzac, "master mariner," might be interpreted as emblematic of Hughes's increasingly accommodationist policies toward white society and the balance sought between integration and patriotism. Mulzac was at first denied a ship to captain during World War II, even though the armed forces were desperate for officers. Eventually offered a position, he refused it because he was required to hire an all-black crew. He finally won his case and took on a crew of white and black seamen in 1942. Hughes notes how the greater New York Council of CIO Unions hailed the ship—significantly named the *Booker T. Washington*— "as an inspiring example of the fact that whites and Negroes could easily . . . 'live and work together in harmony and concord and fight together for a world free from intolerance and oppression'" (CW 12:293). However, despite this and many other idealistic entries, the piece that concludes the collection—the biography of Benjamin O. Davis Jr., a brigadier general of the Air Force—leaves the reader unsettled rather than content. Instead of ending on a perfectly harmonious note, this chapter starkly reveals the tensions among the writer's belief in patriotic military service, a call to resist the unfair practices of American segregation, and a more subversive bitterness about the possibilities of true integration.

The entry details the military experiences of both father and son— Davis Senior, an "army career man . . . [who] worked himself up from the ranks" (CW 12:303), and Davis Junior, who followed in his father's footsteps but began in an elite officer's training program at West Point. The younger Davis commanded the all-black Ninety-ninth Pursuit Squadron in World War II, flying more than three thousand missions. Hughes remarks that these African American aviators were not only fighting for world democracy but also seeking "a greater share of democracy for themselves and their race . . . in civilian life on the home front. . . . [T]he contributions which the heroism and daring of these colored aviators made to the cause of interracial good will was invaluable" (*CW* 12:307). Where the specter of discontent is raised, Hughes appears to stifle it with his commentary on "good will." However, he raises the specter again when he reports that Davis Junior's eventual assignment to an integrated air base was met with "considerable opposition" from whites (*CW* 12:308). The "invaluable contributions" were obviously not enough to quell the racist tendencies of the soldiers who fought with these men. The very last line of the book subtly undercuts any tendency toward idealistic hopefulness: "The two Davises have served their country, militarily speaking, for a long time. And they have served it well" (*CW* 12:309). By pointing out the racism and resistance they must constantly battle, Hughes effectively calls their *ability* to fully serve, despite patriotic desire and intellectual skill, into question. Once again we see his contradictory impulses toward celebrating and denigrating the country in which he lived.

Finally, I would like to turn to several excellent picture books about Hughes that have been marketed for young audiences, especially those released in the centennial year 2002. *Langston Hughes: American Poet*, written by Alice Walker and first published in 1974, was rereleased in 2002 with an afterword by the author and paintings by Catherine Deeter. In this text, Walker focuses on Hughes's grandmother's storytelling, highlighting the importance of the oral tradition in African American cultures and women's active participation in this tradition.

Walker's book identifies Hughes's favorite tale as the one about his grandfather, Sheridan Leary, who had been killed fighting at Harpers Ferry with John Brown, and also describes his other grandfather, Charles Langston, as "a politician whose fiery freedom speeches brought tears to his eyes when Langston read them."[12] Coming soon after a description of young Langston learning not to cry about most things, the image of Charles Langston's oratory power, bringing tears to the boy's eyes, is

---

12. Walker, *Langston Hughes: American Poet*, 15. According to Arnold Rampersad, Lewis Sheridan Leary was Mary Langston's first husband; her second husband, Charles Langston, was Langston Hughes's biological grandfather (*The Life of Langston Hughes: Volume 1, 1902–1941, I, Too, Sing America*, 6–7).

striking. Walker effectively places Langston Hughes in the direct line of descent of skilled orators who pass down not only a talent with spoken words but also a legacy of greatness. This point is further emphasized with information about Hughes's grandfather's brother, John Mercer Langston—a Virginia congressman after the Civil War, minister to Haiti, and dean of Howard University's law school. Knowledge of these men is crucial for today's children, who so often fail to learn about prominent African Americans in U.S. history. Walker's project thus falls firmly in line with Hughes's own. Particularly important, I would argue, is Walker's focus on all of the figures' deftness with language, counter to predominant contemporary images where *illiterate, uneducated, poorly spoken,* and *black* all come to mean the same thing.

Tony Medina's *Love to Langston,* illustrated by R. Gregory Christie, follows the trend of highlighting the importance of Hughes's grandmother. The first poem in the collection gives an account of the young Hughes's "blues": he cannot go out and play because his grandmother wants to protect him from being chased and beaten by white children. The second poem, "Grandma's Stories," details Grandma's escape from an attempted abduction and probable slavery as well as history of her husband's death at Harpers Ferry.

> Grandma has a head full of stories. . . .
> Oh, I know Grandma's stories are true
> they didn't come from school or any book
> Grandma was there fighting for freedom too![13]

In comparison to many other writers, Medina emphasizes this remarkable woman's participation in struggles for freedom and rights, not just her husband's involvement with John Brown. Notions of gender equality can be read into these details, as well as the strong theme of fighting for one's rights at a young age. Medina fosters the latter idea in another of his poems, which describes the protest Hughes started in 1914 while in the seventh grade, demanding true classroom integration and fair treatment for black children in his school. The lesson of being able and willing to stand up for oneself, at no matter what age, could have significant influence on the contemporary child, and Medina therefore becomes another writer who follows in Hughes's footsteps, encouraging social awareness in his readers.

13. Medina, *Love to Langston,* 3.

Willie Perdomo's *Visiting Langston* also points to Hughes's grandmother's storytelling as crucial to the young poet's development. The prefatory note states, "If you asked him why he started writing he would say that it started when his grandmother used to sit him in her lap and tell him stories." The end of the book focuses not only on children's ability to appreciate reading or listening to poetry but also on the young female protagonist's love for writing poetry and the importance of self-expression. In her poems, she proudly announces who she is—"I'm a Harlem girl"— and where she is from—"I'm from . . . Harlem world." She conveys a strong sense of self in the larger world, pride in her community and culture, her personal tastes (hip-hop, for example), and her love for "mommy" and "daddy."[14]

In this way, *Visiting Langston* brings together some of the major themes of its namesake's work. The book also contains the subtle embodiment of Hughes's style and lyricism in its text and illustrations. *Visiting Langston* employs jazz and blues rhythms and structures in its telling of the story: "Langston / Langston / Langston Hughes / Wrote poems / Like jazz . . . / Cried like blues." The short lines, repetition, and rhymes mirror Hughes's interest in combining his poetry with popular musical forms like jazz and blues. In addition, titles of and lines from Hughes's significant works are woven into Perdomo's text. The narrator describes Hughes sitting by a window and writing about his travels "Across *the big sea* / He could tell you / *What Africa means to me* / He can tell you why my / *Dreams run wild* / Why Daddy says I'm like / Langston's *genius child*."[15]

Bryan Collier's artwork reinforces Perdomo's style by incorporating lines from Hughes's poetry and visual images of significance in Hughes's life in collaged form. In one spread that contains the image of a typewriter, a bit of typewritten Hughes text is cut out and pasted onto the typewriter's page; the phrase "Hold fast to dreams" can be found in a huge banner declaring "Langston's"; Collier includes the image of a plaque made by Hughes for the neighborhood children's flower garden in one of his paintings.

Besides the illustrations themselves, which blur conventional boundaries between written text and visual image and between "found" and

---

14. Perdomo, *Visiting Langston*, n.p.
15. Ibid. (emphasis added). In contrast, Robert Burleigh's *Langston's Train Ride*, illustrated by Leonard Jenkins, focuses less on the communal and the oral and more on Hughes's individual, intellectual, and artistic processes. The story charts the creation of a single poem, "The Negro Speaks of Rivers," which is quoted in its entirety at the end of the book.

"created" art, Collier's dedication at the start of the book further stresses the theme with which I began. He gives the book "to both children and adults. I point you all to the artistry of Langston Hughes because in it there is a mirror, a place for you." His words eliminate the strict division and ensuing hierarchy between work for adults and work for children—a worthy project for anyone who seeks true understanding of the artist's oeuvre.

Circles of Liberation and Constriction

Dance in *Not without Laughter*

Joan Stone

[W]here people live closer to the earth and much nearer to the stars, every inner and outer act combines to form the single harmony, life. Not just the tribal lore then, but every movement of life becomes a part of their education. They do not . . . neglect the truth of the physical for the sake of the mind.

—Langston Hughes, *The Big Sea*

Aware of his distance from a society "where people live closer to the earth and much nearer to the stars" (*CW* 13:233), Langston Hughes nevertheless tried to find society's wholeness in modern terms. He searched for an ethos that would bring people together within themselves, with each other, and with nature, and dance was important to that search. He once said that ballet and bullfights were very hard to describe (*CW* 13:76), but he discovered ways of describing dance and embodying its rhythms and gestures in his prose and poetry. Although he himself didn't dance, he observed dance from his childhood on, with an attention to form and context worthy of a dance scholar. He has left us observations of dance from his childhood in the Midwest, his long residency in New York City, and his travels around the world, which dovetail with historic accounts.

He turned historian for one of his last books, *Black Magic: A Pictorial History of the Negro in American Entertainment* (1967), which he coauthored with Milton Meltzer. As a historian, Hughes honored the scholarly pattern of isolating dance from everyday life in order to analyze its special characteristics, but as a novelist, autobiographer, and poet, he revealed the personal, social, and philosophical significance of dance by writing about it as part of everyday life, as part of the human story of growth and change.

In *Not without Laughter* (1930), Hughes gives us remarkably particularized glimpses of the vernacular forms danced by African Americans in the early twentieth century and how they were learned and passed on. He tells us about the kinds of professional dance acts that came through Kansas and how a person could emerge from the backyards and dance halls and pursue a professional career. He makes us aware of the ways in which dance functioned to stereotype African Americans in the dominant society, but above all he gives us a vision of the role of dance in creating individuals and community.

The dance scenes in *Not without Laughter* can be seen as a progression of circles that liberate and constrict. As the characters move from the safe circles of a backyard and dance hall to the dangerous circle of a segregated hotel lobby to the problematic circles of a carnival and Chicago theater, Hughes conveys the importance of dance in the lives of African Americans. Although the characters suffer setbacks, they keep on dancing because Hughes insists on overcoming the circles that limit and victimize while widening those that protect and permit.

Backyard

In the early twentieth century, African American vernacular dance forms were beginning to emerge from the sites in the black community where they were learned. Dancers joined medicine shows, carnivals, circuses, and minstrel shows, which traveled from town to town, stopping and putting up a platform or a tent for a performance wherever possible. The road show on a touring circuit was the next step. By this route, dance acts could play on real stages in real theaters in larger cities, such as Kansas City, St. Louis, and Chicago. From Chicago, the goal—the dream—was to go to New York and dance on Broadway.[1]

1. The most extensive research on the path to professionalism for an African Amer-

Harriett, the aunt of Sandy, the central character in *Not without Laugh-ter*, makes her way along this path of the professional entertainer, as the novel progresses, with her young nephew watching every step. We first find Harriett in her backyard, learning the buck and wing from Jimboy, her brother-in-law and Sandy's father. Buck is one of the earliest forms of tap dancing, the name given to "low" dancing—the stomps, flaps, hops, steps, and shuffles that stay in the feet and close to the ground. Wing, as the name indicates, means getting into the air. The basic wing involves hopping off one foot while flinging the other out to the side and flapping the arms like the wings of a bird. In learning the buck and wing, Harriett is learning the rudiments of tap dance in the feet and early jazz dance moves in the torso and arms, and it isn't long before she's improvising her own steps, finding "two mo' ways to do de Buck" (*CW* 1:25) and wing. As Jimboy plays the guitar and sings, Harriett prances and dances, "her hands picking imaginary cherries out of the stars, her hips speaking an earthly language quite their own." Jimboy tells her: "You got it kid. . . . You do it like the stage women does." He goes further than a compliment. He offers her a challenge: "You'll be takin' Ada Walker's place if you keep on" (*CW* 4:48).

Ada Overton Walker was one of the first African American women to dance on Broadway. She was known as an "eccentric dancer," a catchall term for someone who developed nonstandard movements of the torso and legs into a distinct individual style.[2] The few descriptions of Ada's dancing note her fluid, flexible, "loose" moves and her "neat graceful-ness." Hughes and Meltzer in *Black Magic* point out that in addition to mu-sicals, she appeared in a modern dance solo interpretation of *Salomé* at Hammerstein's Theatre in 1910.[3]

---

ican dancer is found in Marshall Stearns and Jean Stearns, *Jazz Dance: The Story of American Vernacular Dance*, and Lynne Fauley Emery, *Black Dance from 1619 to Today*. Hughes is used as a source on African American dance in both works. Now we look to them to verify the accuracy of his observations, which he started recording in prose and poetry more than thirty-five years before scholars began their research.

2. Stearns and Stearns, *Jazz Dance*, 232.

3. Hughes and Meltzer, *Black Magic: A Pictorial History of the Negro in American En-tertainment*. This was the period of the *Salomé* craze when modern, ballet, and vaude-ville dancers performed interpretations of the dancing biblical seductress. It seems likely that Ada learned the role from Gertrude Hoffman, who was both a modern and a vaudeville dancer. Hoffman scored a hit with her *Salomé* at Hammerstein's Theatre in 1908 and coached other dancers to perform the role. One can speculate that Ada's fluid and flexible eccentric dancing would have lent itself well to the "curling lines, organic spirals, and curves" expected of *Salomé* (Elizabeth Kendall, *Where She Danced*, 55).

Ada was the wife of George Walker, who, like Hughes, grew up in Lawrence, Kansas. Born in 1873, Walker left Lawrence in his late teens to sing, dance, and play the tambourine and bones with medicine shows. His travels took him to San Francisco, where he and Bert Williams met and formed their legendary partnership. They danced their way across the country in the 1890s, eventually making it to Broadway. Williams did a lazy grind or mooche with rotary hip-slinging and occasional hops and shuffles, while George Walker was the greatest of the strutters. He turned the promenade and prance of the strut into a stage version of the cake-walk, which he introduced in 1896 to Broadway and in 1903 to London, whence it became an international fad.[4]

Ada added much to the Williams and Walker productions as a per-former of buck and wing, cakewalk, and eccentric dancing and as the cre-ator of much of the company's choreography.[5] More than fifty years after seeing the Walkers, Carl Van Vechten, a longtime friend of Hughes's and one of the first American dance critics, reminisced about their dancing of the cakewalk as "one of the great memories of the theatre. The line, the grace, the assured ecstasy of these dancers, who bent over backward un-til their heads almost touched the floor, a feat demanding an incredible amount of strength, their enthusiastic prancing almost in slow motion, have never been equaled in this particular revel, let alone surpassed."[6]

In his autobiography, *The Big Sea*, Hughes remembered George Walker:

> The great Negro actor, Nash Walker, of "Bon Bon Buddy, the Chocolate Drop" fame. . . . My Uncle Nat . . . taught him music, long before I was born. I saw [him] only once, because he was off in the East with the great Williams and Walker shows . . . but I often heard the local people speak of him. . . . [M]y mother said she had had dinner with Nash and his mother, while he was ill, and that they ate from plates with gold edging. Then [he] died and there was a big funeral for him and I got my hand slapped for pointing at the flowers, because it was not polite for a child to point. (*CW* 13:44)

Thus the reference to Ada Walker had significance for the real Hughes as it has for the fictional Jimboy and Harriett. In encouraging Harriett to fol-low in the footsteps of the successful Ada, Jimboy is thinking back to his own missed opportunity. As a lad in Memphis, W. C. Handy—again

4. Stearns and Stearns, *Jazz Dance*, 117–24.
5. Jacqui Malone, *Steppin' on the Blues*, 73.
6. Paul Padgette, ed., *The Dance Writings of Carl Van Vechten*, 5.

Hughes uses a historical name—had told him that he ought to make a living playing the guitar, but Jimboy hadn't followed the advice. For him, there were "too many things to see, too many places to go, too many other jobs" (*CW* 4:51).

Jimboy has become a traveling man, coming home occasionally to stay with the family, but then taking to the road in search of adventure and jobs. In the course of his travels, he picks up dance steps from different parts of the country, and Harriett is hungry to learn them. He teaches her "the *parse me la* . . . peculiar to Southern Negro dancing" (*CW* 4:49). It seems likely that Hughes is using a variant name for the pasmala, a southern dance with instructions found in a dance-song published in 1895:

> Hand upon yo' head, let your mind roll far,
> Back, back, back and look at the stars,
> Stand up rightly, dance it brightly,
> That's the Pas Ma La.[7]

A veteran of the Georgia Minstrels recalled the dance: "You walked forward and then hopped back three steps with knees bent . . . back, back, back."[8] One can imagine Harriett in her backyard doing just those kinds of moves—walking, hopping, clapping, and gesturing, while saying or singing the words of the song, which gave the dance a structure but allowed room for improvisation.

During the period from 1910 to 1920, songwriters revived an old tradition of writing lyrics that included dance instructions. The most popular and enduring dance-song was "Ballin' the Jack" by Chris Smith and Jim Burris:

> First you put your two knees close up tight
> Then you sway 'em to the left, then you sway 'em to the right
> Step around the floor kind of nice and light
> Then you twis' around and twis' around with all your might
> Stretch your lovin' arms straight out in space
> Then you do the Eagle Rock with style and grace
> Swing your foot way 'round then bring it back
> Now that's what I call "Ballin' the Jack."[9]

---

7. Stearns and Stearns, *Jazz Dance*, 100–101.
8. Ibid., 101.
9. Ibid., 98–99.

The well-known dance-song makes two fleeting appearances in *Not without Laughter*. Harriett balls-the-jack in the backyard, "arms flapping like the wings of a headless pigeon" to the "glides, groans, and shouts" and "whining in ecstasy" of Jimboy's guitar (*CW* 4:53). Later in the novel, Hughes gives us a more somber glimpse of "two nappy-headed little yellow kids . . . solemnly balling-the-jack" on their front doorstep in the Bottoms section of town, with a piano tinkling and someone singing softly in the shabby house behind them (*CW* 4:156).[10]

When Jimboy and Harriett are singing and dancing in the backyard, they have an audience of family and neighbors. Aunt Hager, Harriett's mother and Sandy's grandmother, is the most vociferous and disapproving observer. "Here, madam! Stop that prancin'! Bad enough to have all this singin' without turning de yard into a show-house." Aunt Hager is concerned about alarming the white neighbors, but she's also concerned about the watching children. "Unhuh! Bound straight fo' de devil . . . singin' an' dancin' this stuff befo' these chillens here. . . . It's a shame!" "I likes it," says Willie Mae, and young Sandy agrees with her (*CW* 4:48).

Aunt Hager is not alone in her condemnation of dancing. *From the Ballroom to Hell* is the title of an anti-dance book by an ex-dancing master published in 1892, with chapters such as "Abandoned Women the Best Dancers" and "Equally a Sin for Both Sexes." Many towns in Kansas and Missouri passed legislative bans on dancing. For example, Purdy, Missouri, had a ban that lasted from 1888 to 1988, when a district court judge, after a long campaign by pro-dance forces, declared the ban unconstitutional because it "promoted the values of those who oppose dancing for religious reasons."[11]

Reverend Whitman, a Methodist bishop in Lawrence, disowned his daughters when they went into show business. The Whitman sisters—Mabel, Essie, Alberta, and Alice—who were neighbors and friends of George Walker's, formed a troupe, which was "by far the greatest incubator of dancing talent for Negro shows." Hughes mentions Alice Whit-

---

10. In 1922, eight years before the publication of *Not without Laughter*, Hughes himself tried his hand at a dance-song, titled "Song for a Banjo Dance." It includes instructions to "shake your brown feet," "get way back," "do that low-down step," "come out with your left" (*CW* 1:30). Composer John Alden Carpenter (1876–1951) wrote a raglike setting for the song, which was recorded in 1928 by the Metropolitan Opera star Lawrence Tibbett. Carpenter and Tibbett, however, chose to emphasize the sadness of the lines "The sun's going down this very night— / Might never rise no mo'" rather than the liveliness of the exhortations to dance.

11. Elizabeth Aldrich, *From the Ballroom to Hell: Grace and Folly in Nineteenth-Century Dance*, 215; "Alumni Will Be Banned When Band Plays at First-Ever Dance," *Lawrence Journal-World*, December 10, 1988.

man, the tap dancer, in *Not without Laughter* when Sandy sees her picture in a newspaper where he finds an article about his Aunt Harriett's successful run in a St. Louis theater (*CW* 4:178). Ironically, Reverend Whitman taught his daughters the double shuffle when they were children but insisted that "it was just for exercise."[12]

Harriett and Aunt Hager represent the pro-dance and anti-dance forces, the sinners and saints, the body and soul, respectively, in the African American community. Sandy, like Hughes, searches for a reconciliation of the oppositions, for an ethos that does not divide people from each other and from themselves, and dance plays an important role in this search.

Annjee, Sandy's mother, is also an observer of the backyard singing and dancing of her husband and sister. Although Jimboy invites her to participate, she demurs. She is not overtly opposed like Aunt Hager, but she prefers to perform in a more formalized event with scheduled rehearsals and organizational backing. With a deep sense of irony, Hughes presents black Annjee—both Hager and Annjee herself comment on her darkness (*CW* 4:29, 39)—rehearsing to represent Sweden in a "Drill of All Nations," which is being prepared for an Emancipation celebration by the Royal African Knights and Ladies of King Solomon's Scepter. Whereas Harriett performs to confront and understand who she is, Annjee performs to pretend she is someone else.

Among the neighborhood observers of Jimboy and Harriett are two members of Aunt Hager's generation, who are much more positive about the backyard entertainment. One shouts compliments, and the other says the singing and dancing remind her of the plantation. Dance scholarship since the 1960s has been tracing the history of twentieth-century African American vernacular dance back to the fragments that survived on the plantation and further back to their roots in Africa. The Stearnses have pointed out six characteristics of African dance that help to identify its influence in the United States. Robert Hinton summarizes them as follows: "African dance (1) is danced on the naked earth with bare feet, often flatfooted, favoring gliding, dragging or shuffling steps; (2) is frequently performed from a crouch, knees flexed and body bent at the waist; (3) imitates animals in detail; (4) places great importance upon improvisation, allowing for individual expression; (5) is centrifugal, exploding outward from the hips; and (6) is performed to a propulsive rhythm, which gives it a 'swinging' quality."[13] Traces of African dance characteristics are apparent in Harriett's backyard dancing: earth-oriented buck steps, birdlike

---

12. Stearns and Stearns, *Jazz Dance*, 85–86.
13. Ibid., 14–15; Hinton, "Black Dance in American History," 4.

movement of the arms, improvisation to find a personal style, motivation from the hips, and "swinging" rhythm. In the subsequent dance descriptions of *Not without Laughter*, these African characteristics recur more or less prominently, indicating how fundamental they are to African American dance.

Thus Hughes introduces dance into *Not without Laughter* as a vehicle of memory, education, and community. The safe circle of the backyard allows Jimboy to act as a mentor to Harriett, teaching her dances he has picked up in the course of his travels, especially through the South, where the plantation dances with their echoes of African dance would have been remembered and practiced in the early decades of the twentieth century. Harriett has the freedom not only to learn the forms but also to begin to develop her own style by improvising on them, while the children of the neighborhood watch and learn along with her, and the adults watch and remember with approval or disapproval. In the next and most developed dance scene of the novel, Hughes creates another safe circle of dance for African Americans, a communal dance at a small local hall.

Dance Hall

The circular or ring dance with simple walking steps is found in the earliest records of African and European dance. While the Africans stepped in single file without bodily contact, the Europeans circled with hands linked from as early as the time of the Minoans (1400–1200 B.C.). When courtly love entered the realm of European ideas around the twelfth century, the dancers began to promenade in couples, side by side, with inside hands joined. It wasn't until the French Revolution (1789) that the partners made the revolutionary change of facing each other, linking both arms, and performing a dance from start to finish in the closed-couple position. The dances performed by the couples in *Not without Laughter*, circling the hall in a closed-couple position but often breaking apart to allow solo improvisations, are a syncretism of European and African elements. With the skill of a choreographer, Hughes creates a circle that protects and permits, within which motion joins motion, building to a dance of ecstasy.

From the first descriptions of dancing at the hall, Hughes makes us aware of the crowd, of the couple, and of the individual, and how they all move in relation to each other and to the larger universe. Harriett, who was supposed to stay at home and take care of Sandy, defies her mother, dresses up, joins her boyfriend, and goes to the dance with young Sandy tagging along. As the three arrive at the hall, Benbow's Famous Kansas City Band is filling every cubic inch of space with the "hip-rocking notes" of "Easy Rider." Harriett and her boyfriend are soon lost in "the crowd [moving] like jelly-fish dancing on individual sea-shells . . . each couple [shaking] in a world of its own" (*CW* 4:72).

In the Midwest of this period, a dance in the white community usually began with a grand march, followed by waltzes interspersed with two-steps, polkas, schottisches, and perhaps a galop or quadrille. A dance for members of the black community in the professions, business, and government service was likely to have similar dances, none of which incorporated hip rocking, undulating, or shaking. Hughes, however, immediately establishes the communal dance in *Not without Laughter* as an event where torsos and music are going to rock, roll, and shake without restraint from white, higher-class black, or religious onlookers.

In the dance hall program of *Not without Laughter*, a "Lazy River One-Step" follows "Easy Rider." Carol Téten, a dance historian of the ragtime era, says that the one-step derived from the "animal dances," such as the turkey trot, kangaroo hop, and grizzly bear, with the hops eliminated.[14] The one-step without hops was therefore a walking dance, which a couple in *Not without Laughter* performs to mark the boundaries of the dancing floor. From the crowd, Hughes singles out "a tall brown boy" walking his "partner" down the whole length of the floor, and when they reach the corner they turn in one spot. Then they walk across the room and turn in the corner. Round and round they walk, revolving at each corner with eyes uplifted, while the music speaks of a river, mountains, clouds, and the earth (*CW* 4:72). Through the couple, in harmony with each other and with nature, circling the hall with simple walking steps, Hughes claims the space as a safe circle for dance.

After finishing the first one-step, the orchestra strikes up another. Harriett has found a new partner, Billy Sanderlee, who reappears at the end of the novel as her piano accompanist in St. Louis and then in Chicago. Like Harriett, he is headed for a career as a professional entertainer, but for the moment the two are impressing the local crowd with intricate improvisations and variations on the one-step.

Hughes turns to images of weaving for the description of this dance. We picture the dancers going "like shuttles across the floor" with Harriett and Billy "winding" through the crowd from one end of the hall to the other (*CW* 4:73). Work gestures, such as these, were very much part of the

---

14. Téten, *Dances of the Ragtime Era, 1910–1920*.

ring shout, a survival of the African circle dance, performed by slaves on the plantations. As they circled counterclockwise, the dancers inserted among the more abstract stepping patterns phrases of digging potatoes, picking cotton, picking fruit, plowing. The words *digging, plowing, grinding, shaking, getting down, weaving, winding* refer both to work gestures (with sexual overtones) and to dance motions.

After the one-step dances comes a slow drag. "'Ever'body shake!' cried Benbow, as a ribbon of laughter swirled round the hall." First with the one-step and now with laughter, Hughes defines the safe circle, within which the dancers can shake, sway, and rotate their hips. The girls snuggle close, and some "boys put both arms tightly around their partners' waists and let their hands hang down carelessly over female haunches" (*CW* 4:74). Hughes's description complements the fragmented description by dance historians Marshall and Jean Stearns of the slow drag: "Congo hip movements . . . plenty of grinds . . . a shuffle . . . close couple dance . . . undulating . . . slow sensual deeply felt rhythms."[15]

A dance of the white community or the higher-class black community between 1910 and 1920 would not have included the slow drag. Historians of vernacular forms have noted a pattern of development for dances like the tango and the slow drag. Invented on street corners or in out-of-the-way clubs and dance halls, vernacular dance forms had to go through a process of acceptance by upper-class people in Paris, London, and/or New York before they were accepted by the general populace. When the slow drag was first seen on Broadway in 1929 in the play *Harlem* by Wallace Thurman and William Rapp, the critics called it "barbaric," "steaming," "orgiastic," "unholy," "violent." Unlike most musical comedy dancing, the slow drag gave a glimpse of the authentic roots of African American dance. When the Aunt Hagers of Harlem joined the white authorities in voicing objections to the dance, it was toned down, and the play had a short run. It wasn't until the 1960s that the hip shifts and pelvic grinds of the slow drag entered the mainstream of stage and social dancing.[16]

The dancers in *Not without Laughter*, slow-dragging within the permissive circle of the community, are drawn ever deeper into the power of the dance. Couples begin to split apart momentarily for improvised solos: "a gal . . . adjusted her hips, and did a few easy, gliding steps all her own"; another gal has "switching skirts"; a guy goes "grinding down the center of the floor" (*CW* 4:74–75). The breakaway or temporary separating of partners, which allows each dancer to improvise his or her own steps, one

15. Stearns and Stearns, *Jazz Dance*, 13, 67, 108, 153.
16. Ibid., 153.

of the characteristics associated by the Stearnses with African dance, is not found in social dances descended from the European tradition. Hughes adds new information to the historic picture by showing the breakaway, usually associated with the lindy and its forerunner, the Texas tommy, as part of the slow drag. He uses the improvisations to intensify the action on the dance floor: "Two short prancing blacks stopped in their tracks to quiver violently. A bushy-headed girl threw out her arms, snapped her fingers, and began to holler. . . . All over the hall, people danced their own individual movements to the scream and moan of the music. . . . [T]he hall itself seemed to tremble." All these are signs of "ecstatic dancing." Hughes himself uses the word to describe Benbow, who leaves the band and comes out on the floor "to dance slowly and ecstatically" (CW 4:75).

Hughes pushes further into the ecstatic realm. Under the "spell of its own rhythm the music had got quite beyond itself." The beat makes the dancers move "like pawns on a frenetic checker-board." In keeping with the ecstatic dance, Hughes constructs mythic partners—female earth and male sun—who appear and dance an overtly sexual dance. His language at this ecstatic moment exemplifies the quintessence of poetic expression and philosophical exploration:

> body of a ravished woman on the sun-baked earth . . .
> giant standing over his bleeding companion in the blazing sun . . .
> the odors of bodies, the stings of flesh,
> and the utter emptiness of soul when all is done . . .
>
> the earth rolls relentlessly,
> and the sun blazes for ever on the . . .
> Rolling and breeding, earth and sun . . .
> Who understands the earth? . . .
> Who understands the sun?
> Do you, Harriett? (CW 4:75)

Hughes breaks the spell, bringing us back to Harriett and an intermission in the dance hall for the musicians and dancers to drink and talk. Harriett buys Cracker Jacks and soda for Sandy, who has already been eating and drinking. There is no mention of him dancing. He shares food with a little girl his age, but then she runs away. When it comes to dancing, Sandy, like Hughes, observes rather than participates.[17]

17. In his two-volume biography, Arnold Rampersad makes reference to a few of Hughes's vain attempts to dance. When his fraternity brothers at Lincoln University were looking for an excuse to punish Hughes at his initiation, they insisted that he

When the dance resumes after the intermission, Sandy goes up to the narrow balcony, which runs the length of one side of the hall, and looks down on the dancing couples, who have picked up where they left off. He starts to fall asleep, which adds to the trancelike atmosphere of the scene. The couples are circling and turning with a slow shuffle. Hughes doesn't name the particular dance this time but uses the term *shuffle*, going back to the African roots of American vernacular dance.

Meanwhile the drummer is eagle-rocking with staccato regularity. The eagle rock was named after the Eagle Rock Baptist Church in Kansas City, where it was danced during religious services in the years following the Civil War. It incorporated the high arm gestures and body rocking from side to side associated with evangelical dances and religious trance. As the drummer pumps his arms and rocks his body, the slow shuffle gains in intensity. For Sandy, looking down, "the men and women, the boys and girls" have become "a vast confusion of busy heads on swaying bodies," and the room seems to be "full of floating balloon faces" (*CW* 4:76).

To the "St. Louis Blues," which follows the shuffle, "the dancers moved in a dream that seemed to have forgotten itself" (*CW* 4:77). Their hips roll like the Mississippi at St. Louis, "deep and wide, deep and wide"—or is it the Euphrates, the Congo, or the Nile? *Rolling, flowing, undulating* are Hughes's words, which speak equally of rivers and of dance.

After the "Saint Louis Blues," the musicians switch to "just the plain old familiar blues, heart-breaking and extravagant," which deepens the trance-like state for the dancers.

> Bodies sweatily close, arms locked, cheek to cheek, breast to breast, couples rocked to the pulse-like beat of the rhythm, yet quite oblivious each person of the other.... men and women were dancing together, but their feet had gone down through the floor into the earth, each dancer's alone—down into the center of things—and their minds had gone off to the heart of loneliness. (*CW* 4:77)

---

show them "two mo' ways to do de' Charleston," forcing him to buck and heave to unheard music (*The Life of Langston Hughes: Volume 1, 1902–1941, I, Too, Sing America*, 127). Rampersad tells us that Hughes at a later date went to the Savoy Ballroom in Harlem and tried valiantly to learn the lindy, but never got beyond a shuffling two-step (ibid., 1:174). Hughes himself writes in his autobiography *I Wonder As I Wander* about his experience at a dance in Cuba in 1931: "Several pretty girls did their best to teach me to rumba. Cuban dancing is not as easy as it looks, but I had a good time trying to learn" (*CW* 14:45).

Hughes emphasizes the separation of individuals in the midst of the community. The European couple form is there but less important than solo and group movements, making the scene truer to trance dance in Africa.

For the final round of dancing, "the music whipped itself into a slow fury. . . . nothing was heard save the shuf-shuf-shuffle of feet and the immense booming of the bass-drum like a living vein pulsing at the heart of loneliness" (*CW* 4:79). From the perspective of Africa, Frantz Fanon suggests:

> The circle of the dance is a permissive circle: it protects and permits. At certain times on certain days, men and women come together at a given place and then, under the solemn eyes of the tribe, fling themselves into a seemingly unorganized pantomime which is in reality extremely systematic in which by various means—shakes of the head, bending of the spinal column, throwing the whole body backwards—may be deciphered as in an open book the huge effort of a community to exorcise itself, to liberate itself, to explain itself. There are no limits—inside the circle.[18]

Based on his remembrance of dance when he was growing up, Hughes creates such a circle in "a hot, crowded little dance-hall in a Kansas town on Friday night" (*CW* 4:78). Rocking, undulating, shaking, winding, grinding, plowing, swaying, rotating, quivering, trembling, shuffling, rolling (to paraphrase Hughes), somehow the dancers have saved in their bodies—after all the centuries of slavery and through all the miles and miles from Guinea—the dancebeat and heartbeat of Africa (*CW* 14:42).

In *Not without Laughter* Hughes places the chapter "Dance" after "White Folks," a discussion of the difficulties of surviving, let alone thriving, in a racist society, and before "Carnival," in which Harriett leaves home to seek a career in show business. He thereby gives dance a significant role in exorcising the evils of racism, on one hand, and in awakening and reinforcing the strength to leave the safe circle of the black community, on the other.

Carnival

The carnival described by Hughes recalls the large carnivals that traveled throughout the United States during the early decades of the twen-

---

18. Fanon quoted in Paul Gilroy, "Exer(or)cising Power: Black Bodies in the Black Public Sphere," 21.

tieth century. Swank's Combined Shows, the World's Greatest Midway Carnival, had animal acts, rides, sideshows, games of chance, a small-scale circus, and a minstrel show. According to the Stearnses, "tent shows nurtured great dancers . . . in the teens . . . who blended struts, shuffles, grinds, spins, twists and what-not into endlessly new creations."[19] Consistent with the historic account, Hughes gives us images of acrobats twirling in front of a tent; Dancing Jenkins, the dark strutter; men dropping into a momentary clog dance; a woman singing a ragtime song and doing the eagle-rock; and a minstrel finale of furious, vigorous, agile, distorted, amazing dancing (CW 4:86–87). If someone in the Midwest like Harriett wanted to become a professional entertainer, she could see the newest dances done by the best dancers at the carnival and begin her own career by joining the carnival, which is exactly what Harriett does.

When Harriett and Sandy come back from the dance hall at dawn, Aunt Hager is waiting for Harriett with the Bible on her lap and switches at her feet. Mother and daughter stop talking to each other after the confrontation, and the breach widens when the revival with its mourning songs arrives in town at the same time as the carnival with its syncopated ragtime tunes. Sandy longs to go to the carnival with Harriett and his father, Jimboy, but is forced, because of his youth, to go to the revival with Aunt Hager and his mother, Annjee. He acts so badly at the religious gathering that Aunt Hager relents and lets him go to the show tents with Jimboy. They arrive in midafternoon when the performers are waiting around for the nighttime action. Leaving his father under a tree talking to carnival workers he seems to know from his travels, the boy goes off to see what's happening in the tents.

Attracted by a "piano tinkling" and "hands clapping as though someone was dancing," Sandy wriggles under the flap of the minstrel tent and sees "a slim black girl, with skirts held high and head thrown back, prancing in a mad circle of crazy steps" (CW 4:84). As in the backyard and at the dance hall, Sandy is once again a spectator of the dance rather than a participant, now lying on the ground and viewing from below. It takes only a moment for him to realize that the dancer is Harriett. While a large white man in a checkered vest sits and watches, she performs the kinds of moves she would be expected to do in the finale of the minstrel show and in a solo act, if she demonstrates she has enough material, skill, and presence to be a soloist.

From the skirt held high, head leaning back, prancing, circling, and

19. Stearns and Stearns, *Jazz Dance*, 73–74.

crazy steps, we know she's doing her own solo version of the cakewalk, following in the footsteps of Ada Walker. White female dancers of the period performed a similar dance, known as the skirt dance. It was "a mongrel style [which included] fast footwork, acrobatic stunts, manipulations of the skirt, twirls and curtsies. . . . Probably because it was not a set form . . . it gave the dancer a chance to display her own manner inside the dance."[20] A descendant of the solo mazurka, tarantella, and cancan of Europe, the American skirt dance was one of the earliest forms of the modern dance solo.

The cakewalk Harriett is dancing in the minstrel tent has a long history circling back from Broadway to the walk-around of the minstrel show to the ring shout of the plantation to the African circle dance. On the plantation, slaves received special privileges if they were good dancers. They were taken from one plantation to another and entered in contests with other slaves, while the owners wagered on the outcome. The prize was sometimes a cake, giving rise to the name *cakewalk*, or sometimes a dress for the woman and a suit for her partner. The Stearnses quote an informant who was a "strut gal" in the 1840s: "Us slaves watched white folks' parties, where the guests danced a minuet and then paraded in a grand march, with the ladies and gentlemen going different ways and then meeting again, arm in arm and marching down the center together. Then we'd do it, too, *but we used to mock 'em*, every step." This description links the cakewalk to European dances: the aristocratic manners mocked by the slaves came from the minuet of the seventeenth century, and the figures came from the grand march, which has origins in the medieval farandole. From the shuffling movement associated with the African circle dance, the cakewalk "evolved into a smooth walking step with the body held erect. The backward sway was added, and as the dance became more and more of a satire on the dance of the white plantation owners, the movement became a prancing strut."[21]

The cakewalk was a great exhibition dance with superb theatrical potential, realized on stage first in the walk-around of the minstrel show and

---

20. Kendall, *Where She Danced*, 36–37. The skirt dance was performed by famous dancers, including Loie Fuller, Isadora Duncan, Ruth St. Denis, and Maud Allan, but also by unknown dancers in the Midwest and other regions. All a young woman needed was a big skirt, some kind of audience, and the courage to dance whatever movements she knew. As jazz was developing to give voice to African Americans, modern dance was developing to give voice to American women.

21. Stearns and Stearns, *Jazz Dance*, 22; Lynne Fauley Emery, *Black Dance from 1619 to Today*, 208.

then on Broadway. In 1898, *Clorindy—The Origin of the Cakewalk,* written by composer Will Marion Cook with lyrics by Paul Laurence Dunbar, opened and was an instantaneous success. As Hughes commented in "The Negro and American Entertainment," "Performed by handsome couples, the women gorgeously gowned, and nobody in blackface, the dance was a joy" (*CW* 9:435).

Prior to its appearance on Broadway, the cakewalk was done as the walk-around at the end of the minstrel show to gather all the performers together and allow them to show off their craziest steps before strutting and prancing off the stage. In *Not without Laughter,* Hughes's remembrance of the minstrel finale in Swank's Shows has all the ingredients of the historic walk-around. As Sandy and Jimboy watch, "all the black actors came trooping back, clapping their hands . . . as each one in turn danced like fury, vigorously distorting agile limbs into the most amazing positions, while the scene ended with the fattest mammy and the oldest uncle shaking jazzily together" (*CW* 4:87).

Late that night with Aunt Hager out of the house taking care of a sick neighbor, Harriett packs her suitcase and tells Sandy she's going to join the carnival. Like many performers of the time, she starts out with high hopes but soon finds herself mistreated and cheated by the management. She quits the show, which moves on without her, and ends up stranded in a strange town with no money. Just before Christmas, she writes a letter to the family asking them to send her fare to come home, but all they can send is three dollars. As the snow is turning to slush at the end of a hard winter, she manages to return, thinner, grown-up, hard, and strange. When Annjee asks her if she found a job where she was stranded, she says satirically, sardonically, "Sure, I found a *job* all right." The step from cakewalking to streetwalking was a short one for black female dancers. The same was true for white skirt dancers. As historian Elizabeth Kendall notes, "A former dancing girl could not enter domestic service or work in a shop once she had been in the theater."[22] If she could not find another dance job, her options for earning a living were severely limited.

Harriett cannot move back to Aunt Hager's house. She goes to live with a friend and eventually moves to the Bottoms, the only part of town where ragtime music and dance flourish. Aunt Hager's worst fears for Harriett are realized when she's arrested and fined for streetwalking, and, sadly, the mother, who continues to cherish her daughter, does not live to see her climb out of the Bottoms, make her way to the stage in Kansas City, then

---

22. Kendall, *Where She Danced,* 6.

on to St. Louis, and from there to a successful run in Chicago, where a major national touring circuit has begun booking her act.

Hotel Lobby

The gaze has become a focus of recent dance scholarship—the gaze of domination and exploitation, in contrast to the "eyes of the tribe," noted by Frantz Fanon, that "protect and permit." One thinks of the ballet dancers pulling up their stockings and extending their legs in paintings by Edgar Degas and of the cancan dancers kicking up their stockinged legs in paintings by Henri Toulouse-Lautrec, as men in top hats sit or stand along the edges—watching, ogling, gazing, leering. Early in *Not without Laughter*, when Harriett dresses to go out with friends, she puts on "red silk stockings, bright and shimmering to her hips" (CW 4:45). Aunt Hager worries about her appearance attracting the wrong kind of attention, a fear Hughes addresses in the ironic poem "Red Silk Stockings":

> Put on yo' red silk stockings, gal,
> An' tomorrow's chile'll
> Be a high yaller.
>
> Go out an' let de white boys
> Look at yo' legs. (CW 1:105)

At the carnival, as Harriett auditions for the white boss, he keeps his eyes on her legs.

Sandy is growing up, working his first job in a barbershop, where he sweeps the floor and shines shoes. For the first time he's exposed to the talk of men, much of which revolves around sex, including insinuations about his Aunt Harriett. When a chorus girl, who is performing in *Smart Set* at the Opera House, comes into the barbershop looking for a copy of a newspaper, the men stop talking and stare. "'Whew! . . . Some legs!' the teamster cried as the door closed on a vision of silk stockings" (CW 4:138). An actor from *Smart Set*, wanting a shoeshine, also comes into the barbershop. He receives no exclamations about his legs but impresses Sandy with his brown button shoes and generous tip. The appearance of the chorus girl and the actor sets off a discussion about racism. One of the barbers says that for *Smart Set* the top gallery will be full of black people since "it's a jig show, but I ain't goin' anear there myself to be Jim-Crowed" (CW

4:137), using two expressions with origins in dance—*jig show* and *Jim Crow*—that came to be deeply associated with racism.

The jig, a folk dance of the British Isles, lent itself to syncretism with African dance on the basis of its fast rhythmic footwork and was danced by slaves on the plantations in the form of jig contests, where the challenge was to move the feet as fast as possible while performing a feat with the upper body, such as balancing a glass of water on top of the head without spilling a drop.[23] However, it was through blackface minstrelsy, the most popular form of American entertainment from the mid-1800s to the early 1900s, that the word *jig* changed from a general name for a dance with fast rhythmic footwork to a term for Negro dancing and dancers (as in "jig top," "jig show," and "jig dancer") to an epithet for Negro.[24] "A lot of minstrels—that's all niggers are!" says the higher-class black Mr. Siles in *Not without Laughter*. "Clowns, jazzers, just a band of dancers" (*CW* 4:202). He could have said just a band of jiggers. Summed up in the word *jig* as a pejorative term is the low status of those who danced the jig, the low status of the minstrel shows in which jigs were danced, and the low status of dance itself in the eyes of the dominant society.

The trope *Jim Crow* was also spread by blackface minstrelsy. Dance historians trace the origins of the term to a lame old black man, named Jim Crow, who did odd jobs in a livery stable behind a theater in Louisville, Kentucky. He would amuse the actors with a song and dance he improvised, which contained the following refrain:

> Wheel about, turn about
> Do just so,
> An, ebery time I wheel about,
> I jump Jim Crow![25]

White actor Thomas Dartmouth Rice, who became known professionally as Daddy "Jim Crow" Rice, saw the original song and dance in 1828, imitated it successfully on stage in blackface, and thereby laid the cornerstone of minstrelsy. As a commentator in the *Baltimore Afro-American* put it in 1934: "Rice's 'Jim Crow' gave to our stage a type and to our language a striking phrase that ever after was to stigmatize our physical and psychic segregation of the Negro."[26] No one has expressed the dehumaniz-

23. Emery, *Black Dance*, 90–91.
24. Stearns and Stearns, *Jazz Dance*, 36, 49.
25. Ibid., 40.
26. Emery, *Black Dance*, 185.

ing effect of the minstrel stereotype on the black dancer better than
Hughes did in the second verse of his poem "Minstrel Man":

> Because my mouth
> Is wide with laughter,
> You do not hear
> My inner cry?
> Because my feet
> Are gay with dancing,
> You do not know
> I die? (CW 1:171–72)

While one man in the barbershop scene of *Not without Laughter* refuses
to go to the shows at the opera house because of the Jim Crow seating, another man says that seeing the shows is more important than where he
sits. From a letter Hughes wrote to Carl Van Vechten in 1925, we know
that as a boy Hughes sided with the second man: "When Ruth St. Denis,
the first real artist I ever saw, came to town to dance I had been about a
month saving the fifty cents to go. But then I had a whole row to myself.
They had reserved the last row for colored folks and no other one but me
went!"[27]

Both the musical review *Smart Set* and the modern dance program of
Ruth St. Denis would have played at Lawrence's Bowersock Opera
House, built in 1912 as a venue for traveling shows.[28] In *Black Magic*,
Hughes and Meltzer included an advertisement for *Smart Set*, which
starred "Ma Rainey, the Great Blues' Singer," and boasted

27. Emily Bernard, ed., *Remember Me to Harlem: The Letters of Langston Hughes and
Carl Van Vechten, 1925–1964*, 32. Ruth St. Denis (1879–1968) was a pioneer of modern
dance whose performances bore enough resemblance to variety shows to allow her to
tour on the vaudeville circuit. She created dances that told stories of Japan, India, Cam-
bodia, Egypt, Java, and China, with no thought of being accurate to the dances of those
countries. When Hughes saw her in 1915, she had just married a young dancer in her
company, Ted Shawn, who came from Kansas City. Hughes probably saw their first
joint choreography, a duet called *The Garden of Kama*, a love idyll set in the garden of
a high-caste Indian family, with Ruth, as the daughter of the house, arranging herself
in decorative postures of yearning, strumming a lute, and singing, while Ted, as the
love god Kama, pursued her with lush arabesques echoing the love darts drawn in his
bow. Also on the program of the 1915 coast-to-coast tour was a new St. Denis solo, *The
Legend of the Peacock*, in which Ruth strutted and preened as a rajah's favorite dancing
girl, doomed by his jealous wife to inhabit the body of a peacock (Suzanne Shelton,
Divine Dancer: A Biography of Ruth St. Denis, 124–25).
28. Bowersock Opera House is still standing but is now called Liberty Hall.

50 Celebrated Theatrical Circus and Operatic Stars
America's Greatest Singing and Dancing Chorus With the Most
  Wonderful Costumes
The Biggest Bevy of Singing and Dancing Girls you've ever
  seen
Imperial Troupe of Tossing Turning Tumbling Clowns
Everything Clean, Moral and Refined[29]

There is no indication in *Not without Laughter* that Sandy went to the opera house, but, according to his biographer, Hughes "haunted the place" whenever he had the money to go.[30]

Sandy leaves the safe circle of the black barbershop for a higher paying job in a hotel for white guests only, where he experiences the gaze of racist domination turned on him. He shines the shoes of a burly white southerner, who has been drinking and telling dirty stories. When the boy stands up for his pay, he receives instead a command to dance. The word *dance* instantly changes from a call for the free and expressive motion of the human body into a threat to obey or be punished. The southerner gathers other white men, who are lounging in the hotel lobby, so that Sandy is standing in the middle of a "smoky circle of grinning white men." The protective and permissive circle of friends in the backyard and dance hall has turned into a constricted and hostile circle of enemies. The dancer has become the victim of the spectators like an animal surrounded by hunters or a slave surrounded by owners and buyers.

Using the racial epithets *coon, nigger,* and *boy* again and again, the big white man demands: "let's see you hit a step. . . . Come on, boy, snap it up! . . . I want to see you dance!" For the first time in the novel, Sandy cannot remain an observer but has been ordered to dance himself. "I can't . . . I don't know how to dance," he says with a frown and somehow manages to push his way out of the terrible circle, but the southerner grabs him. Then the boy's anger gives him the strength to yell, wriggle free, and head for the door. As he exits, he hurls his bootblack box at the group of white men and runs out into the falling snow (*CW* 4: 152–53). In contrast to the rough grasp of the white man and entrapment in a perilous ring comes the light touch of the white snowflakes and the motion of running, running to escape, running toward freedom.

The white southerner in his grandstanding for the circle of hotel

---

29. Hughes and Meltzer, *Black Magic*, 69.
30. Rampersad, *Life*, 1:20.

loungers makes clear reference to pre–Civil War and Reconstruction days when whites could command blacks to dance and receive immediate satisfaction. Dance on command has a long history, going back to Egypt, Greece, and Rome when dancers "were slaves, while the services of their bodies were always the properties of their masters."[31] Hughes and Meltzer discussed the open deck of a slave ship as the first dance stage for captive Africans. "There, on the way to the Americas, blacks in chains, when herded up on deck for exercise, were forced to sing and dance . . . for the amusement of the crew." If they went about it reluctantly or did not move with agility, they were flogged.[32] The pattern of dancing on command continued on the plantations, often through contests, such as the jig and cakewalk contests, which pitted slave against slave for the entertainment of wagering owners. While slaves could be ordered to dance on the plantations, they could also be ordered not to dance, depending on the religious views of the masters. Harriett, who dances, and Aunt Hager, who tries to stop her, reveal how African Americans might have picked up the opposing views of the white masters.

Aware of dance and slavery in the experience of African Americans, Hughes delved into the issue in a 1934 article he wrote for *Theater Arts Monthly*, based on his travels in Central Asia. The focus of the article is the Uzbek dancer Tamara Khanum, the first woman to dance in public performance in Central Asia, known as much for her "bravery in breaking the fetters hobbling women"as for her "Eastern genius in the dance" (*CW* 9:123).[33] When Uzbekistan became part of the Soviet Union in the 1920s, there was an effort to free women from the confines of the harem, though even after Sovietization it was dangerous to dance in public. From his Uzbek hosts, Hughes heard stories of women killed by irate relatives, who thought it bad enough to take off the veil, let alone to go on stage. Boy dancers were also treated like slaves. At certain times of the year, there were dancers' markets, where the best and most handsome of the youthful performers competed against each other, displaying their steps before a vast gathering of men seated around an enormous outdoor space. Prospective buyers came from miles around to bargain for the dancers, who were bought to entertain invited guests at private feasts.

Having written *Not without Laughter* before his travels in Central Asia,

31. Lincoln Kirstein, *Dance: A Short History of Classic Theatrical Dancing*, 332.
32. Hughes and Meltzer, *Black Magic*, 2.
33. The description of Tamara Khanum is from the caption to a photograph introducing Hughes's article in *Theater Arts Monthly* 18:11 (1934): 828.

with Harriett as a model of how African Americans developed their own performance styles by putting together elements learned from relatives, friends, fellow performers, and acts seen at carnivals and circuses, Hughes would have identified with Khanum's creation of her own dance patterns from the wedding dances she performed as a young girl, from steps of the boy-dancers, and from the rhythms and frenzied whirling of the dervishes. When he saw her dance on stage in a folk-opera, she entered with a dynamic stride, stamped out a swiftly postured rhythm, and whirled to the "deafening whir of drums and wail of flutes." He described her dancing as "strong like the wind . . . clean-cut and sharp as the sky-peaks . . . neither male nor female, but wind-like, torrent-like, sand-like" (CW 9: 122–23).

Hughes often links dance to nature as a means for freeing the human body from the traps of race, gender, religion, and class. One thinks of the dance hall scene, where Hughes builds his dance of ecstasy and liberation by virtually removing the walls, roof, and floor of the building, thus allowing the circle of dancing bodies to define the space and the dancers to join their movements to the movements of the universe. One also thinks of an early poem, which dances in words:

> To fling my arms wide
> In some place of the sun,
> To whirl and to dance
> Till the white day is done.
> Then rest at cool evening
> Beneath a tall tree
> While night comes on gently,
>   Dark like me,—
> That is my dream! (CW 1:33)

Interestingly, the image of flinging the arms wide and whirling comes from the religious Hager as well as the dancing Harriett. When Hager dies, and Sandy moves into the home owned by his Aunt Tempy and her husband, Mr. Siles, he misses her "whirling around in front of the altar at revival meetings . . . arms outstretched as though all the cares of the world had been cast away." And he also misses Harriett eagle-rocking in the backyard (CW 4:202). Mr. Siles is a mail clerk on the railroad, and he and Tempy are property owners who socialize only with "people of standing in the darker world—doctors, school-teachers, a dentist, a lawyer" (CW 4:168). In the Siles household there is no "Ballin' the Jack," "Goin' to

Kansas City," or even spirituals, all of which are associated with lower-class African American life. Here Sandy confronts a different kind of opposition to dance. Mr. Siles sees black people as "just a band of dancers—that's why they never have anything" (*CW* 4:202). In his view, the whites have the money, which buys everything including respect, and if Negroes want any, they better stop dancing and learn to get the dollar (*CW* 4:168).

Sandy refuses to accept Mr. Siles's division of the world into those who work and those who dance, a division characterizing Calvinistic America.[34] "A band of dancers. . . . Black dancers—captured in a white world. . . . Dancers of the spirit, too. Each black dreamer a captured dancer of the spirit" (*CW* 4:202). But as Hughes and Fanon contend, dance is also a way to move toward liberation, exorcism, and explanation.

Chicago Theater

The last chapter of *Not without Laughter* is titled "Princess of the Blues" and centers on Harriett's successful performance in a Chicago theater. Sandy is in the audience with his mother Annjee, having left the Siles household in Kansas for a job as an elevator boy in Chicago, a job he soon realizes he must leave if he is to go back to school and keep moving along the pathway of great men like Booker Washington and Frederick Douglass (*CW* 4:201). Hughes describes the response of the theater audience as typical of the Chicago Black Belt:

> laughing uproariously, stamping its feet to the music, kidding the actors, and joining in the performance. . . . Everybody having a grand time with the vaudeville, swift and amusing. A young tap-dancer rhymed his feet across the stage, grinning . . . stepping . . . ending with a series of intricate and amazing contortions. . . . Then a sister act came on [and sang ballads] with their hips moving gaily at every beat . . . their thighs shaking.
> "Aw, step it, sweet gals!" (*CW* 4:204)

---

34. Nathaniel Hawthorne dramatized the conflict between work and dance in "The Maypole of Merry Mount," a short story based on an 1628 incident in Plymouth Colony. Condemning dancing as a wanton, pagan activity, the hard-working churchgoers of a village overcome the dancers of a neighboring village, cut down their Maypole, stop the dancing that has brought Native Americans and Europeans together, and put the dancers to work.

The comments of the audience echo Jimboy's words encouraging Harriett to dance in the backyard circle as well as the exchanges that pushed the dancers to do more and more in the dance hall circle. Thus, in Hughes's portrayal, the urban Black Belt audience becomes an extension of the permissive circle.

Two minstrel dancers break into *Walking the Dog*. Although the song was published by composer Shelton Brooks in 1917, a source interviewed by the Stearnses claims the dance was much older. He saw it in Kansas City in 1909 and put it into his act, adding the Quiver for an ending.

> Get 'way back and snap your fingers
> Get over Sally one and all,
> Grab your gal and don't you linger
> Do that Slow Drag 'round the hall
> Do that step the Texas Tommy
> Drop, like you're sittin' on a log
> Rise slow, that will show
> The dance called Walkin' the Dog.[35]

The minstrel dancers in *Not without Laughter* do their own version of *Walking the Dog*, "flopping their long-toed shoes, twirling their middles like egg-beaters," and exiting to a roar of laughter.

The tap-dancer, the sister act, and the minstrel dancers are openers for Harriett, the star of the show, who enters in a dress of glowing orange and sways toward the footlights. As she croons a new song, she begins to snap her fingers, putting a slow, rocking pep into the chorus. For her second appearance, wearing an apron of blue calico and a bandanna around her head, she walks slowly as she sings the old familiar folk blues. Her final climactic number is a dance-song, which she performs in a sparkling dress of white sequins, ending "with a mad collection of steps and a swift sudden whirl across the whole stage" (CW 4:205–6).

From the backyard to the dance hall, the carnival to the Bottoms, to theaters in Kansas City, St. Louis, and Chicago—Hughes insists on widening the permissive circles and overcoming the constrictive ones as he chronicles the dances of his time. Harriett has kept on singing and dancing, and, true to Jimboy's prediction, she's following in the footsteps of Ada Walker. She's still performing in the Chicago Black Belt, but she has bookings on the Orpheum circuit, which can lead to Broadway. In keeping with

35. Stearns and Stearns, *Jazz Dance*, 108.

Hughes's belief in the possibility of reconciling workers and dancers, saints and sinners, heaven and hell, he concludes *Not without Laughter* with Harriett closer than Annjee or Tempy to Aunt Hager's ambitions and dreams for her progeny. It is Harriett who, at the conclusion of the novel, insists that Sandy leave the elevator job and go back to school, and she slips him money to help him *dance* far beyond the limitations imposed by poverty and racism (CW 4:202). Thus Hughes presents dance as moving people closer to the earth and stars; as bringing together the truth of the physical and the mental; as protecting and permitting the effort to exorcise, liberate, and explain; and, therefore, as fundamental to an ethos of wholeness.

The Essayistic Vision of Langston Hughes

Christopher C. De Santis

Among the most prolific of American writers, Langston Hughes gained international attention and acclaim in nearly every genre of writing, including poetry, the short story, drama, the novel, history, autobiography, journalistic prose, works for children and adolescents, the libretto, and song lyrics. While scholars and general readers have enjoyed relatively easy access to most of these writings, however, one genre in Hughes's vast oeuvre—the essay—has gone largely unnoticed. From his radical pieces supporting revolutionary socialist ideology in the 1930s to the more conservative "Black Writers in a Troubled World," which he wrote especially for a 1966 writers' colloquium at Dakar, Senegal, a year before his death, Hughes used the essay form as a vehicle through which to comment on the contemporary issues he found most pressing at various stages of his career. Although Hughes is best known as a poet, he generated some of his most powerful critiques of economic and racial exploitation and oppression through the genre of the essay. It was also the essay as a literary form that allowed Hughes to document the essential contributions of African Americans to U.S. literature, music, film, and theater and to chronicle the immense difficulties that black artists faced in gaining recognition, fair remuneration, and professional advancement for these contributions. Finally, it was in his essays that Hughes most fully represented the unique and endearing persona of the blues poet in exile. While never literally forced out of the United States, Hughes nevertheless sought temporary refuge from American class prejudice and racial discrimination in locales that, for various reasons, seemed more conducive to the spirit and ideals of democracy than did his own nation.

Hughes viewed himself early on as a poetic chronicler of the democratic ideal, but he also turned to the genre of the essay to help launch his long writing career. At the age of only eighteen, he had gained the attention of Jessie Redmon Fauset, the literary editor of the youth-oriented *Brownies' Book* and the prestigious *Crisis* magazine of the National Association for the Advancement of Colored People (NAACP), with several poems written for children that he submitted for publication in the fall of 1920. Fauset was impressed with the submissions, promised to publish one poem in an upcoming issue of *Brownies' Book,* and inquired whether Hughes had written any children's articles or stories about Mexico (he was living with his father in Toluca at this time). Hughes responded by sending a brief piece on Mexican games, an essay about daily life in Toluca, and a third article about a Mexican volcano, all of which Fauset accepted and published, respectively, in the January, April, and December 1921 issues of *Brownies' Book.*[1] Fauset published a fourth Hughes essay, "The Virgin of Guadalupe," in *The Crisis* that same year. Thus, at the very beginning of his writing career, Hughes demonstrated promise as an essayist and as a poet.

This initial promise was further substantiated with two additional essays Hughes contributed to *The Crisis* while still in his early twenties, both reflective of the wanderlust that would compel him to travel and live in numerous places throughout the United States and abroad over the course of his writing career. The first, "Ships, Sea and Africa" (1923), is an impressionistic series of brief, vivid images that Hughes recorded while a crew member aboard the *West Hesseltine,* a freighter bound for the west coast of Africa from New York, where he had taken up residence. Arriving at the port of Dakar in Senegal on July 3, 1923, Hughes would remain in Africa for nearly three months. There, poetic and essayistic inspiration coalesced, resulting in a lovely essay that reads at times like a prose poem: "Evening . . . The copper-gold of the Congo sunset . . . Blue-green twilight . . . The hot, heavy African night studded with stars" (*CW* 9:27). If Africa impressed Hughes with its abundance of new sights, sounds, and smells, equally provocative to the young writer were his experiences in the great cities of the United States, Mexico, and France, which he recollected in an essay that won second prize in a *Crisis*-sponsored literary con-

1. Arnold Rampersad, *The Life of Langston Hughes: Volume 1, 1902–1941, I, Too, Sing America,* 45–48.

test. "The Fascination of Cities" (1926), like the earlier "Ships, Sea and Africa," is impressionistic in technique, as when Hughes describes Chicago as a "vast, ugly, brutal, monotonous city, checker-boarded, hard," or Paris as "a sorceress-city making herself beautiful with jewels" (*CW* 9:27; 31). Hughes beautifully evokes the childlike wonder of discovery in this essay, softening the harsher aspects of city life behind a veil of grandeur: "New York is then truly the dream-city, city of the towers near to God, city of hopes and visions, of spires seeking in the windy air loveliness and perfection" (*CW* 9:30). Evident here as well, however, are the brutal instances of racial injustice that would become central to so much of Hughes's nonfiction. Marveling at Chicago's cultural diversity, the young writer is interrupted in his romantic reverie by a simple, blunt statement: "We don't 'low no niggers in this street" (*CW* 9:28).

"The Fascination of Cities" hinted both at the major themes Hughes would pursue and at his maturing talent in creative nonfiction. It was the publication of "The Negro Artist and the Racial Mountain" (1926) in the *Nation*, however, that signaled Hughes's transformation from a promising writer of nonfictional prose to one of America's most engaging essayists. At stake in the essay was no less than the very existence of a distinct African American aesthetic, an art originating in the confluence of African folk culture and the black experience of the Middle Passage, slavery, Reconstruction, and the long era of segregation. Hughes had touched on this subject implicitly in his most famous poem, "The Negro Speaks of Rivers" (1921), but it would take a controversial essay by another African American writing for the *Nation*, George S. Schuyler, to provoke a more explicit articulation of a distinct black art. Schuyler's "The Negro-Art Hokum" challenged the very premise that art produced in the United States is in any way influenced by race. In the midst of the intense excitement surrounding the publication of Alain Locke's anthology *The New Negro* (1925), which heralded an awakening in African American visual arts, literature, music, and scholarship, Schuyler registered strong and bitingly sarcastic skepticism that the movement commonly called the Harlem Renaissance was anything more than racial propaganda and the self-promotion of an elite few:

> Negro art "made in America" is as non-existent as the widely advertised profundity of Cal Coolidge, the "seven years of progress" of Mayor Hylan, or the reported sophistication of New Yorkers. Negro art there has been, is, and will be among the numerous black nations of Africa; but to suggest the possibility of any such development among the ten million

colored people in this republic is self-evident foolishness. Eager apostles from Greenwich Village, Harlem, and environs proclaim a great renaissance of Negro art just around the corner waiting to be ushered on the scene by those whose hobby is taking races, nations, peoples and movements under their wing. New art forms expressing the "peculiar" psychology of the Negro were about to flood the market. In short, the art of Homo Africanus was about to electrify the waiting world. Skeptics patiently waited. They still wait.

Central to Schuyler's argument is the idea that "race" is a cultural construct, a product of social class, caste, and physical environment rather than a biological determinant. Schuyler correctly points out that the concept of fundamental differences among the races was historically used in the United States to erect a white supremacist ideology that cast African Americans as inherently inferior to white Americans. Schuyler insisted that celebrations of a distinct African American art—which might be translated by whites as a "peculiar art"—could only serve to legitimize such an ideology.

Hughes understood the merits of Schuyler's argument concerning "fundamental differences" among races, but he was incensed by Schuyler's suggestion that "the Aframerican is merely a lampblacked Anglo-Saxon." In a letter to the editor of the *Nation* that appeared shortly after Schuyler's essay was published, Hughes made his own position clear: "For Mr. Schuyler to say that 'the Negro masses . . . are no different from the white masses' in America seems to me obviously absurd. Fundamentally, perhaps, all peoples are the same. But as long as the Negro remains a segregated group in this country he must reflect certain racial and environmental differences which are his own" (CW 9:552). Hughes had enumerated these differences two months prior to this letter in "The Negro Artist and the Racial Mountain," his finest essay and a virtual declaration of independence for the younger artists and writers of the Harlem Renaissance. Troubled by what he perceived to be a reliance on dominant white standards of art and culture among the African American middle classes and intelligentsia, Hughes challenged black artists and writers to embrace a racial aesthetic and a source of creativity generated from within the black communities in the United States rather than from without. In creating a truly racial art, the black artist could not be swayed by critiques of his or her subject matter or techniques, nor could fears of revealing aspects of black life that dominant standard-bearers of propriety frowned upon stand in the way of artistic inspiration. "An artist must be free to choose what he does," Hughes insisted, "but he must also never be afraid to do what he might choose" (*CW* 9:35). In this respect, Hughes believed that a vast storehouse of largely untapped artistic material resided within the culture of the African American working masses. Jazz, the spirituals, and the blues offered the artist a wealth of resources for the creation of a distinct black aesthetic, and the often conflicted relations between black and white people in the United States furnished "an inexhaustible supply of themes" for the writer and dramatist (*CW* 9:33). In utilizing these resources, the black artist could—indeed, *must*—begin to challenge and overturn dominant white standards of beauty that limited the representation of blackness to minstrel-show stereotypes. Hughes dismissed Schuyler's argument that environment and economics had transformed African Americans into darker Anglo-Saxons, issuing in its place a code of responsibility to the artists of his generation: "[I]t is the duty of the younger Negro artist, if he accepts any duties at all from outsiders, to change through the force of his art that old whispering 'I want to be white,' hidden in the aspirations of his people, to 'Why should I want to be white? I am a Negro—and beautiful!'" (*CW* 9:35).

"The Negro Artist and the Racial Mountain" anticipated the themes Hughes would pursue in his essays for the next decade, particularly in its strong critique of white racial prejudice but also in its condemnation of the black bourgeoisie's complicity in perpetuating racist attitudes. Uncompromising in his belief that the younger generation of African American artists and writers was being held back by timeworn attitudes, Hughes chastised "the best Negroes" in "These Bad New Negroes: A Critique on Critics," published in the *Pittsburgh Courier* in 1927, for rejecting the work of writers such as Jean Toomer and Rudolph Fisher on the basis of their representations of conflict and violence within African American communities. He also took a controversial stance in the essay on the issue of Carl Van Vechten's sensationalistic novel, *Nigger Heaven* (1926), which had caused a firestorm among the black literati and intelligentsia for its grossly stereotypical depictions of Harlem society and nightlife. A combination of his friendship with Van Vechten, a desire to shock the black bourgeoisie, and perhaps a sincere conviction that he was correct compelled Hughes to pronounce the novel "true to the life it pictures" (*CW* 9:39). Addressing charges by critics that his own work was mired in the lives of the lowest classes of African America, Hughes posed an honest question: "Is life among the better classes any cleaner or any more worthy of a poet's consideration?" (*CW* 9:40). He answered this question in the ironically titled "Our Wonderful Society: Washington" (1927), an essay that appeared in the National Urban League's *Opportunity* magazine. Eager to experience the "'wonderful society life' among Negroes in Washington" that he remembered hearing about even as a child, Hughes found only small-minded snobbery and intraracial prejudice among many of the black elite of the nation's capital to whom he was introduced: "Speaking of a fraternity dance, one in a group of five college men said proudly, 'There was nothing but pinks there,—looked just like 'fay women. Boy, you'd have thought it was an o'fay dance!'" (*CW* 9:41, 43).

Concerned as he was with issues affecting the black communities in the United States, Hughes was no provincial; his increasing engagement with the political Left was fueled as much by an active awareness of global class and racial oppression as it was by his commitment to represent the voices of the African American working masses. A trip to Haiti in 1931 confirmed for Hughes the extent to which U.S. imperialism had cast an ugly net of racism and economic exploitation over a once proud people—a people descended from Toussaint L'Ouverture, Jean-Jacques Dessalines, and Henri Christophe, heroic leaders who freed their land from slavery and established the first independent black republic. When Hughes arrived in the small country, signs of the American occupation were everywhere. U.S. military intervention, purportedly arranged on humanitarian grounds after a 1915 coup d'état resulted in the overthrow and death of the Haitian president and the execution of political prisoners, had stripped the Haitian government of all vestiges of independence; the Haitian military, finances, and legislative powers were firmly under U.S. control. Hughes discovered that the occupation affected far more than the daily workings of the country, however. In "A Letter from Haiti" (1931), sent to the radical *New Masses,* a magazine to which he contributed poems and essays frequently in the 1930s, Hughes reported, "Haiti is a hot, tropical little country, all mountains and sea; a lot of marines, mulatto politicians, and a world of black people without shoes—who catch hell." Searching in vain for signs of Haiti's heroic past—Christophe's great Citadel "stands in futile ruin now"—Hughes found only extreme poverty and illiteracy among the Haitian masses, corruption and greed among the ruling elite (*CW* 9:554). In "People without Shoes" (1931), an impassioned essay also published in *New Masses,* Hughes noted that the "barefooted ones care for the rice and cane fields under the hot sun. They climb high mountains picking coffee beans, and wade through surf to fishing boats in the blue sea. All of the work that keeps Haiti alive, pays for the American Occupation, and enriches foreign traders—that vast and basic work—is done there by Negroes without shoes" (*CW* 9:47). By contrast, Hughes discov-

ered that the cultural and political elite of Haiti—those fortunate enough
to have shoes—seemed largely unconcerned with the squalid huts and
shops near the waterfront, the ragged child beggars, or the lack of ade-
quate roads, factories, and schools in the country. Rather than working toward agricultural or commercial development, they contented themselves with luxury items acquired through government loans from abroad
while drawing sharp class lines between themselves and the poverty-
stricken masses.

Hughes's love of foreign travel was fed in part by a desire to temporarily escape the racial prejudice and discrimination of the United States.
Learning of the color line between the mulattoes and the blacks, and that
the Haitian ruling class segregated itself from the workers, was thus a
painful blow to the young writer, reminding him again of the ways in
which class lines and color lines often intersect. The discovery that soldiers of the American occupation enforced Jim Crow customs in Haiti,
however, did not surprise Hughes in the least. Signs of the white American presence—and its negative influence—abounded in Haiti. Having
strayed from its supposedly humanitarian purpose, Hughes pointed out
in "White Shadows in a Black Land" (1932), an essay published in *The Crisis*, the American occupation had determined nearly every aspect of life
in Haiti:

> Before you can go ashore, a white American Marine has been on board
> ship to examine your passport, and maybe you will see a U.S. gunboat
> at anchor in the harbor. Ashore, you are likely to soon run into groups
> of Marines in the little cafes, talking in "Cracker" accents, and drinking
> in the usual boisterous American manner. You will discover that the
> Banque d'Haiti, with its Negro cashiers and tellers, is really under the
> control of the National City Bank of New York. You will become in-
> formed that all the money collected by the Haitian customs passes
> through the hands of an American comptroller. . . . The dark-skinned lit-
> tle Republic, then, has its hair caught in the white fingers of unsympa-
> thetic foreigners, and the Haitian people live today under a sort of mil-
> itary dictatorship backed by American guns. They are not free. (*CW*
> 9:51–52)

Hughes returned from Haiti to an equally troubled United States. The
Great Depression had brought to an abrupt halt the sense of joy and hope
with which he had proclaimed in the 1920s a new and shining moment in
African American art. The gaiety of the Harlem Renaissance had given
way to the stark reality of economic crisis, and African Americans all over

the nation were facing record levels of unemployment. Having exposed in his essays of the mid-1920s the effects of white racial prejudice on African American artists—and the ways in which the valuation of whiteness among blacks contributed to an often impassable color line within African America—Hughes focused in the early 1930s on the broader racist and classist attitudes that seemed to be increasing as the nation moved deeper into economic depression. The 1931 Scottsboro trials especially reinforced in Hughes's mind the connections between race and class, further convincing the young writer that conservative thinking among blacks and whites alike was leading the nation—and particularly its millions of black citizens—toward disaster.

The Scottsboro case involved nine African American youths who had been arrested in Alabama in 1931 and charged with the rape of two young white women on an open railroad freight car. Eight of the youths were quickly convicted by all-white juries and sentenced to death, while the ninth of the "Scottsboro boys," as they were called in the media, received life imprisonment.[2] From the outset, reaction to the Scottsboro case took on sensational dimensions. To many white southerners, the alleged rapes represented crimes not merely against two women who happened to be in the wrong place at the wrong time but against white womanhood in general. In this racist context, the youths involved in the incident came to be seen as representatives of the moral dissipation among African Americans in the South that had resulted from the collapse of slavery. Indeed, one Alabama newspaper reporter referred to the Scottsboro boys as "beasts unfit to be called human," and mobs of white townspeople, intent on seeing the youths lynched for their alleged crimes, were held back only by the Scottsboro sheriff's foresight to ensure the security of the jail by calling in the National Guard.[3] Contributing to the sensationalism that tended to shift the nation's focus away from the young African Americans themselves was the legal atmosphere surrounding the incident. Immediately after the original death sentences were handed down by the juries,

2. In March 1932 the Alabama Supreme Court reversed the conviction of the youngest of the nine youths, and in November 1932 the U.S. Supreme Court overturned guilty verdicts against the other seven. The next four years brought a series of retrials, appeals—some of which reached the U.S. Supreme Court again—and more retrials, even though Ruby Bates, one of the alleged victims, recanted her charges of rape on the witness stand and admitted that she had fabricated the entire story. In the end, none of the youths was put to death for the alleged crime. See Dan T. Carter, *Scottsboro: A Tragedy of the American South*, and James Goodman, *Stories of Scottsboro*.

3. Quoted in Goodman, *Stories of Scottsboro*, 13.

the International Labor Defense (ILD)—a legal defense organization controlled by members of the Communist Party—offered to represent the nine youths, convinced that its participation in the case would not only help the defendants but also bring both recognition to its antilynching crusade and new members to the party. The ILD persuaded some of the teenagers' parents that it was in the best position to defend their sons effectively, quickly obtaining signed agreements granting the organization full control over the case. NAACP officials, by contrast, hesitant to act until details of the case were better known, had avoided public comments on the indictments of the Scottsboro boys. After the teenagers were convicted, however, the association rallied. According to Mark Naison, "the NAACP recoiled in horror at the thought of Communists handling their appeal." Failing to convince the youths' parents to repudiate the ILD's participation in the case, NAACP executives began to wage a drawn-out battle against the Communist Party that alienated many African Americans and abated only when the ILD agreed to allow the NAACP to raise funds in behalf of the defendants.[4]

For Hughes, the NAACP's hesitancy to act represented an alarming trend among conservative black leaders to place status and fears of white reprisal before the welfare of the race. The Scottsboro case thus further strengthened Hughes's embrace of the radical Left, a political commitment that had been building at least since high school, when he had immersed himself in Max Eastman's *Liberator*. As he journeyed through the South on a reading tour in the winter of 1931, the connections between the nine youths imprisoned at the Kilby State Penitentiary in Montgomery, Alabama, the fear of some black leaders to take a vocal stand against injustice, and the broader issues of southern racial intolerance and violence became brutally clear to him. Concerned that the Scottsboro boys would perish by actual or legal lynchings, Hughes published two powerful essays—"Southern Gentlemen, White Prostitutes, Mill-Owners, and Negroes" (1931) and "Brown America in Jail: Kilby" (1932)—that dramatized the vagaries of a racist southern justice system and implicitly critiqued black leaders who remained silent about the trials. The first essay, published in the progressive magazine *Contempo: A Review of Books and Personalities*, was particularly virulent, demonstrating in bold terms Hughes's disgust and anguish over Scottsboro:

> But back to the dark millions—black and half-black, brown and yellow, with a gang of white fore-parents—like me. If these 12 million Negro

4. Naison, *Communists in Harlem during the Depression*, 58, 83.

Americans don't raise such a howl that the doors of Kilby Prison shake until the 9 youngsters come out (and I don't mean a polite howl, either), then let Dixie justice (blind and syphilitic as it may be) take its course, and let Alabama's Southern gentlemen amuse themselves burning 9 young black boys till they're dead in the State's electric chair. (*CW* 10:209)

In the second essay, published in *Opportunity*, Hughes recognized the Communist Party and a number of revolutionary writers for their interest in challenging the racist treatment of the Scottsboro boys. Hughes had visited the eight youths in the death house at Kilby, however, and witnessed firsthand the immense harm the experience of the trials had done to their spirits. The tone of "Brown America in Jail: Kilby" is thus more somber and desperate than Hughes's first Scottsboro essay, suggesting the frustration of seeking justice in a social order that refuses to listen to the voices of the oppressed: "For eight brown boys in Alabama the stars have fallen. In the death house, I heard no song at all. Only a silence more ominous than song. All of Brown America locked up there. And no song" (*CW* 10:211).

While the Scottsboro case weighed heavily on Hughes as he traveled through the South in the winter of 1931–1932, reading his poems at schools and colleges and visiting with students, professors, and administrators, two additional incidents occurred that further reminded him that he was in a land of racial bigotry and violence. Juliette Derricotte, the dean of women at Fisk University and a renowned speaker on issues relating to black colleges and education, died from injuries sustained in a car accident after being refused admission to the nearest hospital, which treated whites only. That same weekend, a recent graduate of Hampton Institute, en route to watch the football team he coached play its first game of the season, was beaten to death by a white mob. Outraged by the incidents, students at Hampton, where Hughes was lecturing at the time, attempted to band together and protest the racial violence. Hughes agreed to speak at their meeting, but soon discovered that school administrators, both white and black, refused to allow the students to stage a protest. Hampton Institute, he and the students were told, was an educational institution, not a site for protests.

The refusal of Hampton's administrators to allow students an outlet for the anger and pain caused by southern white bigotry was one of several serious problems Hughes discovered in the black schools and colleges he visited on his tour through the South. While he himself was universally received with kindness and hospitality by students, faculty, and administrators alike, behind the genial facade were attitudes and practices that compromised both the educational mission and the struggle for civil rights and racial justice. Hughes found that Victorian codes of conduct prevailed on many campuses, with administrators doing their best to prevent students from smoking, playing cards, dancing, and engaging in sexual activities. Committed as he was to speaking out against racial intolerance, Hughes was shocked to find that many students and teachers at Tuskegee Institute knew nothing (or pretended to know nothing) about the Scottsboro trials, despite the fact that Tuskegee was only a short drive from Scottsboro. Additionally, he discovered colleges that expelled students for organizing protests against Jim Crow theaters, black campuses that maintained "whites only" guest houses, teachers afraid to discuss communism with their students, and administrators who consistently acquiesced to the wishes of white trustees and the customs of the color line.

Hughes revealed these findings in one of his most scathing essays, which he published in *The Crisis* two years after his reading tour. Addressed to the teachers and administrators he had met in the South, "Cowards from the Colleges" (1934) boldly accused many of them of insidious patterns of behavior that ultimately encouraged the social codes that served to keep African Americans on the margins of society: "To combine these charges very simply: Many of our institutions apparently are not trying to make men and women of their students at all—they are doing their best to produce spineless Uncle Toms, uninformed, and full of mental and moral evasions" (CW 10:216). Particularly distasteful to Hughes were the sources of funding on which many institutions depended, sources that "have such strings tied to them that those accepting them can do little else (if they wish to live easy) but bow down to the white powers that control this philanthropy. . . . To me it seems that the day must come when we will not be proud of our Jim Crow centers built on the money docile and lying beggars have kidded white people into contributing" (CW 10:220).

Hughes's personal experiences with white patronage during the Harlem Renaissance certainly contributed to the honest conviction with which he criticized such philanthropy in the 1930s. He had been well supported by a wealthy white woman, Charlotte Mason, while writing his first novel, thoroughly enjoying the opportunity to focus on his art without having to worry about where his next paycheck would come from. The moment Hughes's work took on a radical edge of social critique, however, Mason withdrew her patronage. This kind of hypocrisy, which seemed to fester behind philanthropic fronts, troubled Hughes long after the end of the Harlem Renaissance and the largesse of wealthy patrons who supported it. Addressing in absentia the first American Writers' Congress (1935)—organized by politically committed writers on the Left and out of which grew the radical League of American Writers—Hughes called on African American writers to reveal through their art "[t]he lovely grinning face of Philanthropy—which gives a million dollars to a Jim Crow school, but not one job to a graduate of that school; which builds a Negro hospital with second-rate equipment, then commands black patients and student-doctors to go there whether they will or no; or which, out of the kindness of its heart, erects yet another separate, segregated, shut-off, Jim Crow Y.M.C.A." (*CW* 9:132). In this radical statement, which was published in essay form under the title "To Negro Writers," Hughes championed the transformative powers of the written word and urged writers to use their art to effect social change. Black writers *must* use their talents, Hughes argued, to overturn minstrel stereotypes and establish racial unity "on the *solid* ground of the daily working-class struggle to wipe out . . . all the old inequalities of the past." They *must* reveal, he continued, "the sick-sweet smile of organized religion" and the false leaders within black communities who fear speaking out against injustice (*CW* 9:132).

Three years prior to the first American Writers' Congress, Hughes had made a trip to the Soviet Union that would substantially shape many of the ideas expressed in "To Negro Writers" and other radical essays that he wrote in the 1930s. Traveling with a group of twenty-two young African Americans to make *Black and White*, a film about American race relations commissioned by the Meschrabpom Film Corporation of the Worker's International Relief, Hughes arrived in Moscow on June 26, 1932. In "Moscow and Me" (1933), the first of many essayistic pieces to come out of this trip, Hughes wrote of the city with an exuberance matched only by that with which he had described his arrival in New York in "The Fascination of Cities" six years earlier: "Moscow and freedom! The Soviet Union! The dream of all the poor and oppressed—like us—come true" (*CW* 9:57). The contrast between the Soviet Union and the American South, where Hughes had just spent more than four months on his speaking tour, could not have been more pronounced. Warmly greeted, hugged, and kissed by the white Muscovites gathered at the train station to meet them, Hughes and the other African American travelers were whisked across Red Square in luxury sedans to the Grand Hotel, where they found courteous attendants and clean, comfortable rooms. "Everything that a hotel for white folks at home would have," Hughes remarked in "Moscow and Me," "except that, quite truthfully, there was no toilet paper. And no Jim Crow" (*CW* 9:58). In this essay and "Negroes in Moscow" (1933), both published in *International Literature,* Hughes emphasized the courtesy with which African Americans were treated in the city and elsewhere in the Soviet Union. Sympathetic with oppressed groups throughout the world, Russians were especially so with black Americans. Hughes discovered that the exploitation of black workers in the United States was a topic discussed frequently in Moscow newspapers, schools, and theaters, and always with a great deal of respect.

The relative lack of racial distinctions was one of many aspects of life in the Soviet Union that intrigued Hughes. Although the production of *Black and White* was called off due to artistic disagreements among the many people involved with the film, he chose to remain in the Soviet Union for a year and write about his experiences. Hughes discovered that in the Soviet Union, unlike the United States, he *could* make a living entirely from writing, and many of the cultural activities denied him at home because of his race were now open to him. This served him well when he accepted an assignment to write a series of articles about Soviet Central Asia for the newspaper *Izvestia,* several of which concerned transformations in theater and dance since the Bolshevik Revolution of 1917. Published as a small book, *A Negro Looks at Soviet Central Asia,* in 1934, the *Izvestia* pieces constituted at this point in his career Hughes's most sustained treatment of (and support for) revolutionary socialist ideology. While Hughes would maintain later in his career that he had never been a member of the Communist Party, he wrote about Soviet life after the Revolution with unabashed—and, as biographer Arnold Rampersad has pointed out, with *uncritical*—admiration.[5] As he headed south on a train in Russia, painful memories of verbal insults and inferior accommodations on Jim Crow modes of travel in the United States were juxtaposed with the pleasure he felt being surrounded by people of various shades of skin color, all sharing a camaraderie based on a fundamental respect for human beings and a recognition of the importance of the common worker. Life had certainly not always been this way, however. Soviet Central Asia, Hughes was told by a new friend, was "truly a land of Before and After." Before the Revolution, emirs, khans, mullahs, and beys had ruled. Now, power was in the hands of the workers. Rampant illiteracy had begun to be addressed, and education was no longer limited to the wealthy elite. Factories now existed in Asia itself, its raw materials no longer pillaged by cap-

5. See Rampersad, *Life,* 1:265.

italists. Hughes was told, moreover, that racial persecution and segregation had been banished—"Russian and native, Jew and gentile, white and
brown, live and work together" (*CW* 9:74). The Revolution had transformed nearly every aspect of life in Soviet Asia, but most remarkable to
Hughes were the changes it had brought about in the status of women. In
the *Izvestia* pieces and in two essays that he published in *Woman's Home
Companion* and *Travel*—"In an Emir's Harem" (1934) and "Farewell to Mahomet" (1935), respectively—Hughes wrote passionately of the women
who suffered persecution for daring to lift their veils and those who es-
caped the stultifying atmosphere of the harem to lead meaningful, politically committed lives after the Revolution. "Today the torch of liberated
womanhood burns throughout Soviet Asia," Hughes concluded in "Farewell to Mahomet," "and the whisper of its brightness sweeps across the
frontiers into Persia, India, even into China where strange and barbaric
customs still prevail" (*CW* 9:140).

Hughes wrote essays on an eclectic range of subjects upon returning
from the Soviet Union in 1933, including the International Longshore-
men's Association strike of 1934 (he himself came under fire from right-
wing reactionaries for supporting the strike through participation in the
radical John Reed Club), the photography of Henri Cartier-Bresson and
Manuel Alvarez Bravo, tourist attractions in Paris, and the Russian writer
Alexander Pushkin. His sheer productivity as an essayist during his stay
in the Soviet Union, however, would not be matched until 1937, when he
traveled to Madrid on assignment to cover the Spanish Civil War for the
Baltimore Afro-American. Anticipating the passion with which he would
write about the Loyalist struggle against Fascism in Spain, Hughes addressed the delegates to the Second International Writers' Congress in
Paris shortly before departing for Madrid. In his speech, published in *Volunteer for Liberty* under the title "Too Much of Race" (1937), Hughes again
demonstrated a strong awareness of the global dimensions of economic
and racial exploitation and oppression. Foregrounding his comments
with a reminder of the disfranchisement, segregation, and physical violence suffered on a daily basis by African Americans, Hughes spoke out
against such tyrants as Hitler, Mussolini, Batista, and, in Spain, Franco,
warning delegates about the Fascists' "lies of race": "Just as in America
they tell the whites that Negroes are dangerous brutes and rapists, so in
Germany they lie about the Jews, and in Italy they cast their verbal spit
upon the Ethiopians" (*CW* 10:222). Fascism, Hughes argued, represented
the most immediate and harmful threat to the friendship and peace that
the workers of the world desired to establish among all races.

Hughes continued these themes in the series of articles he wrote for the *Afro-American*. Touching on subjects ranging from his own experience in an air raid to the heroic acts of black soldiers who had left the United States to join the International Brigades, Hughes blended journalistic reportage with the conversational quality of memoir to give readers back home a sense of both the politics of the war and day-to-day life in a besieged city. Like his writings for *Izvestia*, the *Afro-American* pieces were anything but nonpartisan. As Arnold Rampersad notes, "the articles viewed the war from a perspective that merged the narrowly racial *Afro-American* view with Hughes's proletarianism and anti-fascism. The result was excellent propaganda for the left, aimed directly at the black American world."[6] Hughes's political passions were nowhere more apparent than when addressing the subject of Franco's Moorish troops, brought over from Morocco. "As usually happens with colored troops in the service of white imperialists," Hughes pointed out, "the Moors have been put in the front lines of the Franco offensive in Spain—and shot down like flies" (*CW* 9:164). As horrifying as the destruction and bloodshed of the war were to him, however, Hughes found among the people gathered at the headquarters of the Alianza de Intelectuales Antifascistas, where he stayed while in Madrid, a good deal of hope. The Alianza, an outgrowth of the first International Writers' Congress in Paris, was an organization composed of artists and intellectuals who used their various talents to disseminate pro-Loyalist information throughout Spain. In a radio speech on September 3, 1937 (published that same year in *Volunteer for Liberty* under the title "Madrid's House of Culture"), Hughes spoke lyrically of the work done by these people and the broader importance of the center that housed the Alianza: "It is a place where now, today, art becomes life and life is art, and there is no longer any need of a bridge between the artists and the people—for the thing created becomes immediately a part of those for whom, and from whom, it was created. The poem, the picture, the song is only water drawn from the well of the people and given back to them in a cup of beauty so that they may drink—and in drinking, understand themselves" (*CW* 9:152).

Themes of economic and racial oppression remained central to Hughes's essays in the years following his departure from Madrid in November 1937, as did his belief that artists must maintain politically committed perspectives if their creations are to have social significance. Addressing the Paris meeting of the International Writers Association for the Defense of

6. Ibid., 1:351.

Culture on July 25, 1938, he was adamant that to be a good writer, one could not afford to ignore global events. Because of the interrelatedness of international politics, Hughes argued, "a creative writer has no right to neglect to understand clearly the social and economic forces that control our world" (*CW* 9:199). The revolutionary zeal with which Hughes addressed these themes in his writings on the Soviet Union and the Spanish Civil War, however, was somewhat tempered in his later nonfiction. Hesitant to champion his radical socialism after the announcement of the Nazi-Soviet Nonaggression Pact of 1939, Hughes offered instead a measured essayistic voice that framed social critique in the rhetoric of American democratic idealism. Nowhere was this shift more evident than in a series of articles he wrote in the early 1940s about the status of blacks in American society. In "What the Negro Wants" (1941), an article published in the Common Council for American Unity's official magazine, *Common Ground*, Hughes argued that the desire for basic civil and social rights among African Americans—economic and educational opportunities, decent housing, full participation in government, justice before the law, public courtesy, and social equality—was a truly *American* desire. "We want nothing not compatible with democracy and the Constitution," Hughes maintained, "nothing not compatible with Christianity, nothing not compatible with sensible, civilized living" (*CW* 10:232). Hughes echoed these convictions in essays such as "What Shall We Do about the South?" (1943), "The Future of Black America" (1943), and "My America" (1944). Unafraid to voice his position on Jim Crow customs and other forms of racial prejudice, Hughes did so with a good deal of rhetorical savvy, almost always emphasizing during this period of his career that the status of African Americans was a barometer for the progress and future of America itself.

Hughes perhaps had good reason to create in his essays of the 1940s the persona of the dedicated American citizen committed to the ideals of democracy, for he was increasingly under attack by organizations and individuals on the Right that threatened to compromise his position as one of African America's most respected writers. Hoping to publicize the first volume of his autobiography, *The Big Sea*, at a 1940 "Book and Author" luncheon in California, Hughes instead was greeted by an angry crowd of protesters. Aimee Semple McPherson, the head of the fundamentalist Temple of the Four Square Gospel in Los Angeles, had arranged for a contingent of picketers to spread awareness of Hughes's impious poem "Goodbye Christ" (1932), in which he had sarcastically mentioned the evangelist. Shaken by the protest, Hughes was mortified to discover a month later that the *Saturday Evening Post*, which also came under fire in the poem, had reprinted "Goodbye Christ" without his permission.[7] Rather than revel in the spotlight on his radicalism, Hughes immediately sent a statement, "Concerning 'Goodbye, Christ'" (1941), to friends, publishers, and foundations. In this piece he reaffirmed his opposition to the systems of global oppression that had prompted his satirical words in the early 1930s. Nevertheless, he ultimately dismissed the poem as a product of the political fervor of his youth: "Now, in the year 1941, having left the terrain of 'the radical at twenty' to approach the 'conservative of forty,' I would not and could not write 'Goodbye, Christ,' desiring no longer to *épater le bourgeois*" (*CW* 9:209). Perhaps as a follow-up gesture to prove this statement, Hughes commemorated his twentieth anniversary as a contributor to *The Crisis* with an essay that was decidedly conservative. "The Need for Heroes" (1941) emphasized a moral responsibility among black writers to celebrate the strongest individuals and best achievements of the past and present rather than the faults and defeats of African America, a theme Hughes would revisit often in his essays of the 1940s, 1950s, and 1960s. Hughes took such novels as Richard Wright's *Native Son* and his own play, *Mulatto*, to task for emphasizing degradation and sorrow, imploring writers, "We have a need for books and plays that will encourage and inspire our youth, set for them examples and patterns of conduct, move and stir them to be forthright, strong, clear-thinking, and unafraid" (*CW* 10:225). The most obvious source of material for these books, Hughes maintained, was the heroic and ongoing history of the African American struggle against adversity.

The fact that this struggle was far from over was especially apparent to Hughes as he considered the many ironies inherent in the nation's fight against Fascism in World War II. African American soldiers, both overseas and in U.S. training camps, found themselves treated with the same humiliating disrespect as their fellow black civilians. Separate and less desirable living and eating quarters, little opportunity for advancement, and even segregated latrines, made life for the African American soldier quite unbearable. Moreover, the separation of "white" and "Negro" blood by the American Red Cross blood banks was an act that at once infuriated Hughes and caused him to chuckle at the lengths to which whites would go to maintain the illusion of racial supremacy. In "White Folks Do the Funniest Things" (1944), an article published in *Common Ground*, Hughes

7. See ibid., 1:390–392.

explored the tragicomic nature of the racial jokes popular during the war years. Humor was an integral tool for survival, Hughes believed, but he was all too aware that those who perpetuated racial prejudice and discrimination were utterly blind to the absurdities of their practices. "I suppose the greatest killers cannot afford to laugh," he mused. "Those most determined to Jim Crow me are grimly killing America" (CW 9:245). Despite the segregated troops, discrimination in the U.S. war industries, and the daily racial insults suffered by black civilians, Hughes believed in and supported the war effort as a necessary measure toward the realization of true democracy in his nation and the obliteration of Fascism worldwide. In one of his most inspired essays of this period, "Negro Writers and the War" (1942), Hughes revisited his position from the 1930s on the responsibility of writers to use their art for social change. Published three months prior to Hughes's inaugural column in one of African America's most influential newspapers, the *Chicago Defender*, this essay recognized members of the black press for their leadership in bringing the war effort—and its meaning to African Americans in particular—to the masses. African American writers in general needed to follow their lead, Hughes maintained, taking it upon themselves as a basic duty to demonstrate in their writing the international dimensions of American racism. Racial conflicts at home were, after all, "part of the great problem of world freedom everywhere." It was thus the duty of black writers

> to show how our local fascists are blood brothers of the Japanese fascists—though they speak with a Dixie drawl, to show how on the great battle front of the world we must join hands with the crushed common people of Europe, the Soviet Union, the Chinese, and unite our efforts—else we who are American Negroes will have not only the Klan on our necks in intensified fashion, but the Gestapo, as well. (And the Nazis, I am sure, could teach the Klan a few things, for the Germans do not bother with silly crosses and childish nightshirts. Death and the concentration camp are more effective.) (CW 9:217)

Hughes continued to write passionately about the war effort and its aftermath in his *Chicago Defender* columns, championing once again the Soviet Union and drawing connections between reactionary Cold War propaganda and the continued oppression of minority groups in the United States. His nonjournalistic essays of the late 1940s and early 1950s, however, evidenced less of the radical young troublemaker and more of the reflective, middle-aged writer beginning to take stock of his life and career. This was particularly apparent in the increasingly reminiscent and autobiographical nature of his essays. Recounting his brushes with censorship and his conflicts with the reactionary Right in "My Adventures as a Social Poet" (1947), an essay published in Atlanta University's *Phylon* magazine, Hughes charmingly compared himself to poets whose lyrics of love, roses, and moonlight enabled them to float above the earth with their heads in the clouds. "Unfortunately, having been born poor—and also colored—in Missouri," he quipped, "I was stuck in the mud from the beginning. Try as I might to float off into the clouds, poverty and Jim Crow would grab me by the heels, and right back on earth I would land" (*CW* 9:269–70). While Hughes made it clear in this essay that he was proud of his past work as a social poet, the reminiscent tone suggests a distance between the radicalism of his younger years and how he chose to define himself as an increasingly public figure in his middle age. This distance would become more pronounced a few years later, when he sat for an interview with the editors of *Phylon* to discuss the current state of African American literature. In "Some Practical Observations: A Colloquy" (1950), Hughes charted the many positive advances made by African American writers since the Harlem Renaissance, noting in particular a publishing industry and reading public more "willing to accept Negro problems and Negro art" than they had been in the past. There was a cost to this acceptance, of course. Taking a position that would contradict his earlier advice to black writers to expose systems of oppression through their art, Hughes argued that "the Negro writer has to work especially hard to avoid the appearance of propaganda" (*CW* 9:307, 309).

Despite his attempts to position himself as politically moderate, individuals and organizations on the Right refused to allow Hughes to forget his radicalism of the recent past. The FBI had targeted him as a subversive after the incident in 1940 with Aimee Semple McPherson, maintaining a file that listed him as a member of the Communist Party and a potential threat to the white race. He was also denounced by the House Un-American Activities Committee (HUAC)—established in 1938 to investigate subversive political groups and individuals in the United States—for his membership in radical organizations. Right-wing reaction to Hughes came to a head in 1953, when he was subpoenaed by a U.S. marshal to appear before Sen. Joseph McCarthy's Senate Permanent Sub-Committee on Investigations to explain and account for his "un-American," radical past. Understandably fearful of McCarthy's witch-hunts for communists, Hughes prepared a statement that effectively repudiated his radical writings and saved him from serious charges by the committee.[8] In "Langston Hughes Speaks" (1953), a version of this statement published in *The Crisis*, he charted his revolutionary socialist writings as "coinciding roughly with the beginning of the Scottsboro Case and the depression of the 1930's and running through to the Nazi-Soviet Pact" (*CW* 10:245). Balancing a rejection of Communism with a recitation of his family's historic role in the struggle for civil rights, the statement served an important purpose: it signaled an end to the kind of essays that some readers would consider Leftist propaganda while reaffirming his commitment to writing critically about issues affecting African America.

That commitment was especially apparent when Hughes addressed the National Assembly of Authors and Dramatists at a symposium in May 1957. Speaking on "The Writer's Position in America," Hughes explained that African American writers "have been on the blacklist all our lives." Facing constant censorship, denied publication and opportunities on the lecture circuit, and barred from jobs in Hollywood and the publishing industry, Hughes suggested, the black writer works against overwhelming obstacles in attempting to make a living. Coupled with these realities, recent violence against African Americans drove many of the best black writers to live and work in other countries: "Why? Because the stones thrown at Autherine Lucy at the University of Alabama are thrown at them, too. Because the shadow of Montgomery and the bombs under Rev. King's house, shadow them and shatter them, too. Because the body of little Emmett Till drowned in a Mississippi river and no one brought to justice, haunts them, too" (*CW* 9:358).

If the violence surrounding the civil rights movement was an extreme reminder of the difficulties African American writers faced on a daily basis, the victories won by Rosa Parks and Martin Luther King Jr., the Little Rock Nine, the Freedom Riders, and other individuals and groups at the forefront of the struggle for civil rights reinvigorated in Hughes a sense of the writer's importance in helping people make sense of their world. They also compelled him to reexamine his earlier beliefs about the duty of the black writer. In the "Negro Artist and the Racial Mountain" he had boldly stated that "[w]e younger Negro artists who create now intend to express our individual dark-skinned selves without fear or shame," at

---

8. For information on Hughes's troubles with HUAC and his involvement in the McCarthy hearings, see Rampersad, *The Life of Langston Hughes: Volume 2, 1941–1967, I Dream a World*, 90–98, 209–222.

whatever cost to one's "respectability" in the eyes of black or white America (*CW* 9:36). In the 1950s and 1960s, however, Hughes grew increasingly uncomfortable with some of the literature being produced by the younger generation of African America writers. "Pride, nobility, sacrifice, and decency," he argued in "The Task of the Negro Writer as Artist" (1965), a brief statement published in the *Negro Digest*, "are qualities strangely lacking in some of the most talented outpourings by or about Negroes these days." Surrounded by the heroism of men and women committed to making full equality a reality for African Americans, Hughes reminded black writers, "There is today no lack within the Negro people of beauty, strength and power—world shaking power. If I were a young writer, I would try to put some of these qualities on paper and on stage" (*CW* 9:425).

Thus, almost forty years after his stunning manifesto of the Harlem Renaissance, Hughes found himself in the very position occupied by those members of the black intelligentsia in 1926 who worried that the younger artists and writers were not doing justice to the positive qualities of African American culture. In concluding "The Task of the Negro Writer as Artist," however, Hughes would reaffirm a belief in the political potential of African American writers that remained consistent throughout his forty-six-year professional writing career: "Ours is a social as well as a literary responsibility" (*CW* 9:425). Such a belief resounds everywhere in Hughes's essayistic nonfiction, a remarkable body of work that represents the testament of a man committed to the possibilities of language to generate social awareness and, ultimately, to compel social change.

Langston Hughes and the Movies

The Case of *Way Down South*

Thomas Cripps

"We were no longer in vogue, anyway, we Negroes. Sophisticated New Yorkers turned to Noel Coward" (*CW* 13:249), wrote the poet Langston Hughes perhaps only days after a movie producer, Sol Lesser, had warned his staff that "Messrs. Hughes and [Clarence] Muse are to be given the utmost liberty in developing the Second Draft Screenplay [of *Way Down South*]."[1] For Hughes, the two events must have seemed only a typical moment in African American history when a small triumph rivaled a predictable reversal—not so much the march of progress as a struggle to stay even by "pluggin' away," as Paul Laurence Dunbar put it.

At his most sanguine, Hughes could write "I, too, sing America," but as often he despaired. Once, his friend Carl Van Vechten had hopefully predicted a New York theatrical season (1936), listing a half dozen black headliners on Broadway: "I think this is likely to be a NEGRO WINTER . . . a pretty good record, I call it."[2] But only a couple of years later, Hughes, addressing the Third American Writers' Congress in Carnegie

1. Lesser's comments on *Way Down South*, February 15, 1939; this draft was revised from a first draft by Michael Simmons, February 8, 1939, in Langston Hughes Papers, Beinecke Rare Book and Manuscript Library, Yale University, New Haven, Conn.
2. Van Vechten to James Weldon Johnson, September 27, 1935, Johnson Collection, Beinecke Library, Yale.

Hall, reported doors to the arts "as tightly closed to us in America as if we were pure non-Aryans in Berlin" (*CW* 9:204). It was not that he thought Van Vechten naive or wrongheaded, but rather that as the legal pillars of racism eroded there seemed to be endless advance and retreat rather than progress. One such sore memory occurred in 1932 when Hughes had gone to the Soviet Union to make *Black and White*, a film that exposed American racism while arguing for an interracial, working-class solution to it. Sadly, this visual hymn to workers' solidarity across racial lines evaporated at the hint that the incoming Roosevelt government might grant diplomatic recognition to the USSR. "Thou too, Comrade!" said a wry cartoon in the *Amsterdam News*.[3]

In yet another instance, America first celebrated Jesse Owens's four gold medals in the "Nazi Olympics" in Berlin in 1936, shamelessly attributing his triumph to the American way of life, only later to take from him the rest of his career for a minor infraction of rules governing conduct of amateur athletes. As though ratifying his exile from sporting life, the B-movie *Charlie Chan at the Olympics* (1937) all but obliterated the presence of African Americans at an international event that they had dominated. Who knows? Perhaps there was a matter of rights to footage shot in Berlin; but racial exclusion always seemed some small thing rather than an actual Jim Crow law.

Even when a persuaded racial liberal acted, it often brought an unforeseen result. Early on in preproduction, for example, David O. Selznick told the first of several writers on his outsized 1939 movie of Margaret Mitchell's bestseller, *Gone with the Wind*, "I, for one, have no desire to produce an anti-Negro film," especially "in these fascist ridden times." The result? A "structuring out," as critic James Snead, put it, of all the edgy, prickly black roles in favor of the more unctuous figures. There were such roles, even a black leader of a slave rebellion, in Stark Young's novel *So Red the Rose* and King Vidor's 1935 movie of it, but they were lost in the blare attending the epic *Gone with the Wind*.[4]

---

3. *Amsterdam News*, October 5, 1932; an image of the cartoon is in Thomas Cripps, *Slow Fade to Black: The Negro in American Film, 1900–1942*, 215; see also Ted Poston to Claude A. Barnett, Associated Negro Press, September 21, 1932, in Barnett Papers, microfilm, Chicago Historical Society, Chicago, Ill.; George S. Schuyler oral history, 434–41, Oral History Research Office, Columbia University, New York City, N.Y.; and Eugene Lyons, *Assignment in Utopia*, 508–9.

4. Selznick to Sidney Howard, January 6, 1937, in Rudy Behlmer, ed., *Memo from David O. Selznick*, 151; see James Snead's "Recoding Blackness: The Visual Rhetoric of Black Independent Film," 103.

Perhaps the most abrasive disappointment for black moviegoers was in the sense that African Americans, compared with their onscreen plight in early times, were standing in the wings, ready to go on but rarely called. The venerable black filmmaking pioneer William Foster wrote to James Weldon Johnson of the NAACP on the eve of the first cycle of musical films in 1929, pleading that "if a colored producing co dont [*sic*] make the Grade now it will be useless later on after all the Big Co.s . . . set about controlling the Equipment." Johnson, former U.S. consul, litterateur, social activist, and author of "Lift Every Voice," "the Negro national anthem," replied to Foster, hoping for a black future in "talkies": "I myself have noticed that their voices record much better than white voices."[5]

But such was not to be. Early on, in 1929, King Vidor's *Hallelujah!* and Alan Crosland's *Hearts in Dixie* and the two-reeler *St. Louis Blues* flashed across the nation's screens revealing, apart from the lingering reliance on hoary black stereotypes, what richly varied roles black voices and music could expect in the American cinema. *St. Louis Blues* in particular featured the husky voice of Bessie Smith, the music of W. C. Handy, and the lithe dancing of Jimmy Mordecai. With the doors ajar, a few other gems made it to the screen, among them two symphonic pieces by Duke Ellington, *The Black and Tan Fantasy* (1929) and *Symphony in Black* (1935). Then the door clicked shut. Marc Connelly had won a Pulitzer for *The Green Pastures* in 1929, a musical "fable" derived from Roark Bradford's *Ole Man Adam and His Chillun,* an anthology of Old Testament tales as told by a rural black preacher. Connelly's play tried to impart a folkish charm and dignity to southern black folk religion and its music, yet it took half a decade before it reached the screen, having fallen victim to Hollywood's voices of "cold feet" that dismissed all of the African American material that had gone before as a mere "cycle."

It was into this milieu of backing and filling, inching along and sliding back, that Hughes and his coauthor, Clarence Muse, were to slip as through a cracked door, surely believing that *this time* would be the charm, the break into open ground, free of the baggage of racial convention and stereotype.

Hughes drifted into Los Angeles in the autumn of 1938, unknowingly on the verge of making more urgently needed money in a short time than in any other period of his writing life. Perhaps the tempo, the clatter of the

---

5. William Foster to James Weldon Johnson. He was referring specifically to *Hallelujah!* and *Hearts in Dixie,* two Hollywood efforts at black southern authenticity. Johnson to Foster, August 15, 1929, apparently in reply, Johnson Collection.

industry, the story conferences inside the studio gates where no black man had ever trod, blurred the shaky scaffolding of the project; when Muse brought it to him the old urge to do a movie rose as though a trout to a fly. Perhaps out of the welter of Hollywood life—pitching ideas, developing treatments, tweaking scripts—somehow a good movie might avoid the graveyard of the smothered, stifled, thwarted projects of other African Americans.

The times seemed as ready in 1939 as they had been when Bill Foster wrote to James Weldon Johnson in 1929 when the door cracked. On the eve of World War II, racism was brought to the fore by the world's concern for the plight of Jews in Germany—Kristallnacht, the worst anti-Semitic pogrom in recent memory, had only just happened in November 1938. The then dying Federal Theatre had brought African American material to the stages of Broadway and the nation in such productions as J. A. Smith and Peter Morell's *Turpentine* and W. E. B. Du Bois's *Haiti*. In 1933, Eugene O'Neill's *The Emperor Jones*, starring the rising Paul Robeson, had come to the screen minus much of its linkage between Freudianism and savagery and strengthened by an African American backstory, written by, among others, James Weldon Johnson, thereby promising that black culture might be brought into a white medium if filtered through black sources.

Even Broadway seemed ready. Orson Welles and John Houseman's *Black Macbeth* struggled to be born. There were other crossovers from white to black idiom that had already reached the stage, among them Mike Todd and Bill Robinson's *The Black Mikado*, which played the New York World's Fair; *Swingin' the Dream* (a black *Midsummer Night's Dream*); a black *Beggar's Opera*; and a *Carmen Jones*.[6]

All of a piece, everything seemed ready for Hughes's entrance. At first with Arna Bontemps, then later on his own, he began the year lecturing on writing for the young, a gig funded by the Philippa Pollia Foundation.[7] Then, almost simultaneously, he took on two jobs of writing. First, *God Sends Sunday*, a novel by the Harlem worthy Countee Cullen, was to become a musical called, as though an echo of W. C. Handy's, *St. Louis Woman*. "I think it will make a swell show," Hughes told Van Vechten, "a kind of Negro Diamond Lil" (a racily erotic role made famous by Mae West). Bontemps and perhaps Clarence Muse, the actor who had taken

6. For a contemporary chronicle of African Americans in theater, see Edith J. R. Isaacs, ed., *The Negro in the American Theatre*, chap. 7.

7. On the lecture series, see Arnold Rampersad, *The Life of Langston Hughes: Volume 1, 1902–1941, I, Too, Sing America*, 366.

over the "Negro unit" of the Federal Theatre in Los Angeles, were to be collaborators. Sadly, the project stalled until MGM picked it up as a vehicle for recently signed Lena Horne, tried it out on Broadway, only then let it die after Walter White of the NAACP warned the principals, "We have a racial stake . . . which can be lost or tragically damaged if we make the wrong movies."[8]

Left standing was the project of which Hughes may have been most fond: *Way Down South.* At least, it drew him into the orbit of Hollywood few African Americans had ever reached—the ranks of screenwriters—and thus opened an opportunity to transform the image of black Americans in movies.

Sol Lesser, the producer, had seen Muse's production of Hall Johnson's *Run Little Chillun,* a twenty-one-week sellout at the Los Angeles Federal Theatre, and imagined Muse as the screenwriter of some sort of vehicle for Bobby Breen, a pudgy boy-tenor who was riding the crest of a brief vogue. The setting was to be in the South of the nineteenth century, but with local color and idiom, and the black place in it, as written by Hughes and Muse. In the beginning, the two black writers must have fairly sung with optimism. They even had the memorandum from Lesser in hand in which he seemed to offer no restraints, no nods to Hollywood racial convention: "Messrs. Hughes and Muse are to be given the utmost liberty in developing the Second Draft Screenplay, so that it will contain every element of their conception of the story."

Not only had Lesser's liberal stance been confirmed, but he would soon name as director Bernard Vorhaus, a known activist on behalf of the Republican cause in the Spanish Civil War who was eventually revealed as a Communist—not in themselves indicators of an openness to decent racial portrayals, but nonetheless markers of a sort. More to the point, a half century later, Vorhaus recalled his enthusiasm at the outset. "I persuaded Lesser to use as a screen-writer Langston Hughes, who was quite a distinguished poet," he told an interviewer. Besides, he thought of the writers, "as black people they would get some feeling into this story."[9]

---

8. Hughes to "Carlo" [on *Diamond Lil*], February 25, 1939, in Emily Bernard, *Remember Me to Harlem: The Letters of Langston Hughes and Carl Van Vechten, 1925–1964,* 144. See Walter White to Louis B. Mayer, September 19, 1945, and White to "Countee," n.d., NAACP Records, Library of Congress, Washington, D.C.

9. Vorhaus interviewed by John Baxter, in Patrick McGilligan and Paul Buhle, *Tender Comrades: A Backstory of the Hollywood Blacklist,* 657–70; Vorhaus turns up frequently in the literature on the Hollywood "blacklist." See for example, Bernard F. Dick, *Radical Innocence: A Critical Study of the Hollywood Ten,* 168–69.

What could go wrong? Nothing that they could actually see, but then there were the Hollywood intangibles. They were writers there, not "authors"—and their work was subject to "story conferences" and "rewrites"—not necessarily by people they might actually meet. And producers were, indeed, producers. Even a B-movie producer like Lesser might rewrite. Then there were the Hollywood conventions—the rules of thumb, the recipes—for making it at the box office. Thus they referred back to successes, not *forward* to the new. "The same, only different," as Sam Goldwyn was supposed to have said. "The colored man's point of view?" Of course, but we need "a little pickaninny of the Stymie Beard type," as Lesser would put it in his memorandum of February 15. Besides, if a scene violated the often silent code, censors both in the "Breen Office" of the Motion Picture Association of America and on various state and local censor boards—which were particularly strong and influential in the South—might ruin an offending movie by crude and discontinuous cutting. Such offense was often perceived as any scene that challenged or called into question the rigid racial arrangements of the South, an issue defined in many studios by a resident white southerner who advised on specific movies.[10]

In the beginning, Hughes had little formal knowledge of this system. And Muse was probably of scant help. He was widely admired for the intelligence and decency he brought to his usually stereotypical roles, but he was also regarded by the NAACP, for example, as an old veteran who got along in the system a little too well. "A keen operator," Vorhaus thought him, and "not a particularly talented actor or writer."[11] Thus Hughes probably faced the Hollywood institutional system alone.

So, even if he felt free to write from an untrammeled black angle, he could not have known that some agency in the system was always looking over Lesser's shoulder. The ideological weight of these silent forces hobbled Hollywood even as the country at large began to shed the grosser forms of southern racial baggage. Moreover, Lesser was not the figure that Hughes reckoned him to be: not an arm of RKO, but merely a B-movie man who turned out off-the-rack "programmers," as the trade papers called them. One year it might be a Saturday serial based on the comic strip *Dick Tracy*; another might bring forth *Tarzan's Revenge*, a "cheap

10. The literature on Hollywood vis-à-vis African Americans is ponderous. Begin with Evelyn Brooks Higginbotham et al., eds., *The Harvard Guide to African-American History*, chap. 12, "Film and Television." For a bibliography on censorship, see Gregory D. Black, *Hollywood Censored: Morality Codes, Catholics, and the Movies*.
11. McGilligan and Buhle, *Tender Comrades*, 670.

quickie" in Lesser's own view; and still another might see *Way Down South* into release. If any thread held them together it was some form of contest between modernism and tradition, much like the religious clash that caught Lesser's eye in *Run Little Chillun*.[12]

Against these odds, Hughes and Muse began their work. Hughes was earning more money than he had ever imagined and was so famous that he was writing his autobiography before the age of forty. Muse, in addition to directing *Run Little Chillun*, had only just done some of his best work: acted the slave rebel in *So Red the Rose*; directed and starred in *Broken Strings*, a well-crafted "race movie" about a black maestro of the violin; and claimed the honor of writing Louis Armstrong's theme music, "Sleepy Time Down South."

There is no telling how many previous drafts Lesser had received from other writers. But the two writers turned out a draft so remote from Lesser's wishes, Vorhaus's idea of a good Bobby Breen vehicle, and the Hollywood formula version of the fabled Southland that he called a meeting in mid-January. Hughes and Muse had set their story at the site of a new dam that would light and heat the houses of black and white alike—"even the tent of the Negro revivalist." It was the New South of Henry Grady's capitalism and the boosterism of the *Atlanta Constitution*. A sort of John Henry figure drawn from black folklore was the moral center of an integrated workforce. And though he died in a landslide, "he has taught Bobby his songs" and so his spirit lived on.

Lesser hastily reined in his writers with a dictated story "for Mr. Hughes" in which he set forth the obligatory images of the Hollywood South. Bobby Breen would be a poor white boy, singing for coins on the streets of New Orleans so he could save up to buy a showboat. Playing "Jim" to this little "Huck" of the streets was to be Gumbo, "a little pickaninny of the Stymie Beard type." Using this "light" opener they could "gradually" expose "the slave situation" (as though no one knew of it). Perhaps, Lesser thought, they could have Bobby attend a black church— just like the one in *Run Little Chillun*—where he might learn of the tragedy of black southern life. And in a dreamy revision of history, he imagined Lincoln encountering Stephen Foster and Dred Scott meeting John Brown in Missouri, which, he thought, "would give us an opportunity to use the song, 'John Brown's Body.'" Indeed, he thought Bobby might even run into John Wilkes Booth—anything to avoid the dreary truth of black life

12. See Allen Woll, *Black Musical Theatre: From Coontown to Dreamgirls*, 157–58; and Gabe Essoe, *Tarzan of the Movies*, 100.

under slavery. Or if "history" failed him, Lesser imagined a black preacher, lightly comic, perhaps like the Reverend Deshee in *The Green Pastures,* whose "quaint dignity, earnestness and sincerity," might open access to "the colored man's point of view." To further avoid offending the southern box office, why not include a coarse "Yankee," perhaps an agent for "London businessmen," who "knows nothing of the fine relations that existed between plantation owners and their slaves." And in a socko climax, Bobby Breen could save the slaves from auction, after which, Lesser wrote, "we will probably go into another spiritual situation." At every turn, he reshaped the material to fit the precast templates of Hollywood convention, even as he imagined they were striving "to avoid the typical hackneyed Hollywood story." But of course, each new suggestion not only buried them deeper in the mire of Hollywood practice but also carried the movie away from Hughes's and Muse's hopes.[13]

Thereafter, the only course for the two black screenwriters was to salvage as much authentic local color as they might. Probably by then, from January 22 through March 1939, the work had become Hughes's, if for no other reason than that he had spent a few days in the Los Angeles Public Library boning up on black history. His scene-setting prose offered a rich, aromatic, densely fetid Louisiana crammed with sugar mills; rice marshes; harvests of yams, goobers, persimmons, and pecans; a smokehouse; a black smithy; black cane cutters who are "magnificent women, strong men."

When the two kids, black and white, go to New Orleans, Bobby is all but marinated in the black streetscape, the night- and morning-song of the street "Arabs." Out in the canebrake's rice terraces, Hughes picked up the sounds as well as the scenes: the workers' grunts, the swish of the cane knives, the splash of bare feet setting out rice shoots, the wind in the pecan trees. Similar ambient textures colored the images themselves. There were cane dances that got "wilder and wilder"; cane choppers bending to their chores, each in turn picking up the line of a work chant; a slave who refuses to be whipped; men concealing voodoo drums in the dark; slaves hearing an ancient African tale.[14]

How much were white people to be privy to this black world, and what were they to make of it? There was the rub, never a flashpoint between

13. Anon. story for Bobby Breen, n.d., typescript; Breen southern story "dictated by Mr. Lesser" for "Mr. Hughes," carbon, January 13, 1939, Hughes Papers.

14. Version dated from January 22, 1939, to March 1939, including fragments labeled "scenes to be saved from Lesser's continuity," as though to suggest a running fight over what stayed and what was cut, Hughes Papers.

Lesser and Hughes, or at least never one that survived in the memorandums, but always an issue at stake on which the artistic, social, and commercial weight of the movie would hang. Bobby is always on the side of the angels. He might need to sing on a showboat to raise money to save the slaves and plantation from sale. On another page, Bobby and his black friend—his "Jim"—seek refuge in a black church from a pursuing sheriff, thereby replicating the lives of runaways. Or Hughes might give social heft to the dialogue, if only by avoiding a "mumbling" carriage driver and by cutting one "massa" too many.

Lesser's white people, on the other hand, seem not to observe slavery, except as its paternal masters. These outsiders were always the heavies, either Yankees or "sleek vultures" from the city. Finally, after distilling all he could from Hughes's (and Muse's) scripts and from their essay "A Résumé of Life in America, 1846," Lesser invoked rank in late March and set forth the thrust he wished for the release print. With an eye toward Hollywood conventions and formulas, as well as the southern censors and box offices, he reasserted the Hollywood "Southland." Only a few onionskin revisions from March reveal how heavy his hand would be. Evil could never be done by the hand of a southerner, only by a Yankee. Why? Because "being a Northerner he does not understand . . . the sentimental and emotional relationship that exists" between master and slave. How else preserve the mood of "the whole happy spirit of mellow and joyous Southland"? Granted this formulation, the dramatic conflict would be between Yankee heavy and southern hero (rather than between master and slave), thereby resulting in a proper Hollywood ending: "sympathetic Southern people have the proper viewpoint, thereby restoring happiness on the plantation." Curiously, until the end Lesser shared much of the politics of his writers and wrestled inwardly with them. The same sensibility that allowed him to accommodate to Hollywood's happy "Southland" also embraced a leftist, not to say Marxist, mentality. "In those days it was slave labor that created an economic issue," he wrote in one of his first memorandums to his writers, "whereas today it is the enslavement of labor."[15]

The movie, as released, revealed some of the tensions that brought it to life. Bobby Breen, the boy tenor, had aged some during the gestation pe-

15. "Discarded scenes" of Simmons's first-draft continuity [February 6, 1939]; *Dialogue & Music for Way Down South*, Hughes and Muse, n.d.; and, especially, Lesser's revisions, March 1939 and his notes of March 28, 1939; *Way Down South*, Lesser's revision of the Simmons script, February 15, 1939, Hughes Papers.

riod, and with maturity his cute kid aspect waned and his voice seemed no longer able to carry a sentimental scene. Hughes and Muse were then stuck with only two models: whatever of the southern mise-en-scène had been obliged by its Hollywood origins—the catering to a southern box office, the silent threat of southern censors, the softness of Hollywood's own censorship code toward the South, and the producer's own internalized formulas and conventions that had "worked" in the past—and, most sadly, the cadre of African Americans who earned their keep playing whatever Hollywood asked of them. The latter clung to their day jobs, fretted over losing a white friend on the inside, and feared losing credits and slipping into some chorus line as a "creole cutie" or into the ranks of uncredited spear-carriers. "What's an actor going to do," said the veteran Willie Best (who appeared in *Way Down South* as an uncredited chimney sweep). "Either you do it or you get out."[16] Even the dignified Muse and the fine Hall Johnson Choir gave their white bosses what they wanted.

From the main titles to the end, these forces were at work, silently nibbling away at the politics that Lesser and his writers had begun with. A prologue, shot as though on parchment, set the scene. The "system of slavery" was ruled by an "aristocratic" class driven to care for its "faithful retainers" by a sense of noblesse oblige. Unavoidably, it seemed to say, any breach in these harmonious old ways must come from some alien source. Indeed, the establishing shots reveal this in the person of a Yankee lawyer with an accountant's heart who wheedled a debt-ridden plantation from its kindly patriarch who knows that this new man can "never understand" southern ways. The plot is set afoot with the death of the old master and the decision of the lawyer (and executor) to sell off the slaves to cover debts.

Thereafter, the flow of the plot takes on a cadence, intercutting between the writers' use of southern idiom and local color to sketch in an African American slave culture as never before seen in a movie and Lesser's mediation between North and South, slave and free. The tensions between his black writers and Lesser may be seen most vividly in the slave quarters. Hughes and Muse have their way in the daily round of toil—baling cotton, chopping sugar cane, stoking the sugar mill—and in the ominous threat embedded in all slavery: being dealt off from a benign regime to a harsher one, "down the river." But Lesser has his happy slaves as they sing and chant at their work and celebrate its bounty when the crops are in. In this equation between writers and producer—indeed between real-

16. Clipping from *Silhouette*, in George P. Johnson Collection, Research Library, University of California at Los Angeles.

ity and legend—a softening accommodation always seems within reach. Hot, harsh work in the sugar mill? Two kids rub their bellies awaiting the "drippin's." Back-wrenching toil in the laundry house and in the fields? Let fly a work song or a chant. And at the end of the harvest with all of its lengthening days, let us have the slaves revel in the bounty of the harvest, as though indeed it were *their* bounty.

The relations between the lowly and their betters also serve to sentimentalize the system. Old Uncle Caton (Muse himself), the liveried butler, is allowed a bit of both latitude and attitude, as though both serving and guiding his master along the right paths. The child-hero, Tim (Breen), has a black playmate (Stymie Beard), and together they romp about, cadge rides in the family carriage, and josh with Uncle Caton. In contrast, for the Yankee lawyer such closeness is unseemly. Indeed, farm life itself seems distasteful. For him the value of the slaves is only in their price, with which he will keep his befrilled courtesan (Steffi Duna) in flashy baubles. Too close to stereotype for comfort, the slaves are allowed an emotional range while these white people are kept as stiff as lords in a restoration farce.

The death of Tim's father and the resulting threat of losing the plantation (and the slaves) to the greedy Yankee lawyer sets the plot on its tortured course. The slaves (and Tim) hold a wake, mourning their plight, singing "Oh, dem Golden Slippers," "My Lord Delivered Daniel," and Tim's solo, "Sometimes I Feel Like a Motherless Child." Then, in a lightning-streaked night, the two allies, white Tim and black Gumbo, rush to New Orleans, where they successfully plead for the restoration of Tim as executor of his father's estate, thereby saving the slaves from auction at the hands of the Yankees, a sequence that ends in the slave quarters with yet another ringing chorus of praise for God's gift of "good" white masters.

As though covertly placing their stamp on the movie, the two black writers slipped in two throwaway lines, no more than puns, actually, that whispered their dashed hopes: when the Yankee lawyer is appointed "executor," Uncle Caton primly refers to him as "executioner"; and later, at the wake, as the slaves pray for Tim's regaining *his* legal power over the estate, a slave woman sharply utters a *black* wish—"Yes, *power*," she says, emphatically.[17]

Had anything been achieved in this small struggle between two African

17. *Way Down South* (1939). The surviving print is about sixty minutes in length, suggesting that Lesser chose to cut Breen's "star turns" such as a showboat scene, thereby giving proportionally more screen time to the work of Hughes and Muse.

American writers and the Hollywood system? Yes, somewhat. The writers had achieved a "first," as far as we know: they had penetrated a lily-white preserve. They had not only gotten credit—*sole* credit—for a Hollywood screenplay and story but had also gotten credit for two songs. Moreover, although it was only a B-movie, Lesser managed to open it on Broadway at the RKO Palace (albeit on a double bill with *Each Dawn I Die*, a dernier cri of the 1930s cycle of gangster yarns). However, a week after the film opened, the Luftwaffe bombed Warsaw, thereby stunting whatever celebrity it might have earned as a groundbreaker.

Nonetheless, the shrewdest observers of movies, the critics who wrote for the trade papers, caught some of the often subtextual merits of the film. *Daily Variety* not only led with a claim of its "breaking away from sharper lines of formula" but credited the two writers by name for both their story and their songs, which, together with the music and pacing, held to "high standards." The *Hollywood Reporter* carried the black angle even further, attributing the film's reaching "above the standard set by the producer in his previous efforts" to its setting in "the colorful period" of antebellum New Orleans. Moreover, it singled out Muse and the Hall Johnson Choir for their "capably enacted" work, a reckoning shared by *Film Daily*. The *New York Times* agreed, citing the "humanitarian ideals" of the protagonists.[18]

Perhaps a release under more favorable circumstances might even have allowed *Way Down South* its moment in the movement of the NAACP to press Hollywood to generate wartime movies that expressed the sentiments of wartime slogans embodied in the catchwords *equality, brotherhood,* and *tolerance.* For Walter White of the NAACP, the coming war seemed a "rising wind" on the wings of which black fortunes might improve, a prospect, he imagined, in which Hollywood might have a significant hand.[19]

Certainly, in Muse's reckoning *Way Down South* held a special place. Forever afterward he not only listed the picture in his résumé but also flew

18. *Daily Variety,* July 23, 1939 (cited also in *Amsterdam News,* July 29, 1939); *Hollywood Reporter,* July 19, 1939; *Film Daily,* July 25, 1939; *Motion Picture Herald,* July 22, 1939; *New York Times,* August 18, 1939, courtesy Linda Harris Mehr, Margaret Herrick Library, Academy of Motion Picture Arts and Sciences, Beverly Hills, Calif. The *New York Herald Tribune,* August 17, 1939, added a liberal political note, praising the Breen role "on the right side of the audience . . . by taking up the cause of the slaves."
19. For an account of this wartime sea change in Hollywood racial imagery, see Thomas Cripps, *Making Movies Black: The Hollywood Message Movie from World War II to the Civil Rights Era,* chaps. 2–5.

it like a proud flag at the top of the masthead of his personal stationery. As for Hughes, he felt the sting of criticism not so much from the mainstream press as from his friends on the Left, notably Louise Thompson, who had been with him on his aborted moviemaking jaunt to the Soviet Union in 1932. She all but relished telling him her "unpleasant news" of "what they are saying about the picture" in New York. Yet the experience did little to dampen his enthusiasm for the future of movies as a black medium. Over the years his files thickened with ideas for an African American presence on the screen: among others, a "personable" black astronaut who had learned to love science and history at his grandmother's knee; a "western" about the Kansas Exodusters' migration of 1879; a film of his own "The Negro Speaks of Rivers," at the urging of Arna Bontemps; and, like Sergei Eisenstein before him, an idea for Paul Robeson as the poet Alexander Pushkin.[20]

Yet, as was true for so many accomplished writers, perhaps Hollywood was the wrong place for him. Perhaps as an American he had soaked up so much of the Hollywood idiom that he could not keep it at a distance. Not surprisingly, one of his own unrealized film ideas called for "a happy ending" in the Hollywood manner. Indeed, at one point his biographer, Arnold Rampersad, seemed impatient with Hughes's uncritical warmth toward Hollywood when, in an early draft of *Way Down South*, "he had already given Breen an old black mammy," a sign that, wrote Rampersad, "Langston appeared to have no difficulty in creating stereotypes."[21] In any case, Hughes is entitled to credit for having taken a small step, perhaps too early to matter, toward the wartime alliance among the NAACP, the leftists within the Office of War Information who monitored movies for conformity to war aims, and the left wing of Hollywood "moguls" who, together, set Hollywood on a course toward cycles of wartime "unity" and "brotherhood" movies, followed by a round of so-called message movies after the war and an eventual opening of the powerful Hollywood craft guilds to African Americans.

20. Thompson's remarks cited in Rampersad, *Life*, 1:371. A file of various proposals is in the Hughes Papers; Muse's letterhead, author's possession.

21. The proposed ending is for the "Exodusters" film. Rampersad quoted in *Life*, 1:367.

Bibliography

Aaron, Daniel. "Reds, Whites, and Blues: *The Life of Langston Hughes.*" 1988. In his *American Selected Notes: Essays.* Boston: Northeastern University Press, 1994.

Achebe, Chinua. "An Image of Africa." 1975. In *Chant of Saints: A Gathering of Afro-American Literature, Art, and Scholarship,* ed. Michael S. Harper and Robert B. Stepto. Urbana: University of Illinois Press, 1979.

Aldrich, Elizabeth. *From the Ballroom to Hell: Grace and Folly in Nineteenth-Century Dance.* Evanston: Northwestern University Press, 1991.

Allen, Samuel W. "Négritude and Its Relevance to the American Negro Writer." In *The American Negro Writer and His Roots,* ed. John O. Killens et al. New York: American Society of African Culture, 1960.

"Alumni Will Be Banned When Band Plays at First-ever Dance." *Lawrence (Kansas) Journal-World.* December 10, 1988.

Anderson, Sherwood. *Dark Laughter.* 1925. Reprint. New York: Liveright Publishing Corporation, 1970.

———. "Paying for Old Sins" Review of *The Ways of White Folks.* 1934. In *Langston Hughes: Critical Perspectives Past and Present,* ed. Henry Louis Gates Jr. and K. A. Appiah. New York: Amistad Press, 1993.

Anissimov, Julian. "Kinship." Trans. Langston Hughes. *International Literature* 4 (1933): 61.

Attwood, Lynne. "The New Soviet Man and Woman." In *Soviet Sisterhood,* ed. Barbara Holland. Bloomington: Indiana University Press, 1985.

Attwood, Lynne, and Catriona Kelly. "Programmes for Identity: The 'New Man' and 'New Woman.'" In *Constructing Russian Culture in the Age of Revolution, 1881–1940*, ed. Catriona Kelly and David Shepherd. Oxford: Oxford University Press, 1998.

Bakhtin, Mikhail. *The Dialogic Imagination.* Austin: University of Texas Press, 1981.

Baldwin, James. "Sermons and Blues." *New York Times Book Review,* March 29, 1959.

Baldwin, Kate. *Beyond the Color Line and the Iron Curtain: Reading Encounters between Black and Red, 1922–1963.* Durham: Duke University Press, 2002.

Baraka, Amiri. *The LeRoi Jones/Amiri Baraka Reader.* Ed. William J. Harris. New York: Thunder's Mouth Press, 1991.

———. "SOS" and "Black Art." 1966. In his *Black Magic: Collected Poetry, 1961–1967.* Indianapolis: Bobbs-Merrill Company, 1969.

Barksdale, Richard K. "Hughes: His Times and His Humanistic Techniques." In *Langston Hughes: Critical Perspectives Past and Present,* ed. Henry Louis Gates Jr. and K. A. Appiah. New York: Amistad, 1993.

Barrett, Lindon. "The Gaze of Langston Hughes: Subjectivity, Homoeroticism, and the Feminine in *The Big Sea.*" *Yale Journal of Criticism* 12.2 (1999): 383–97.

Batker, Carol. "'Love Me Like I Like to Be': The Sexual Politics of Hurston's *Their Eyes Were Watching God*, the Classic Blues, and the Black Women's Club Movement." *African American Review* 32.2 (1998): 199–213.

Behlmer, Rudy, ed. *Memo from David O. Selznick.* New York: Viking Press, 1972.

Bennett, Juda. "Multiple Passings and the Double Death of Langston Hughes." *Biography* 23 no. 4 (Fall 2000): 670–693.

Bennett, Tony. *Formalism and Marxism.* New York: Methuen, 1979.

Berlant, Lauren, and Michael Warner. "Sex in Public." *Critical Inquiry* 24:2 (Winter 1998): 547–66.

Bernard, Emily. *Remember Me to Harlem: The Letters of Langston Hughes and Carl Van Vechten, 1925–1964.* New York: Alfred A. Knopf, 2001.

Berry, Faith. *Langston Hughes: Before and beyond Harlem.* Westport, Conn.: Lawrence Hill and Co., 1983.

Bessie, Alvah, ed. *The Heart of Spain: Anthology of Fiction, Non-fiction, and Poetry.* New York: Veterans of the Abraham Lincoln Brigade, 1952.

Black, Gregory D. *Hollywood Censored: Morality Codes, Catholics, and the Movies.* Cambridge: Cambridge University Press, 1994.

Bloch, Ernest, et al. *Aesthetics and Politics.* London: NLB, 1977.

Bloom, Harold, ed. *Langston Hughes.* New York: Chelsea House, 1989.

Bontemps, Arna, ed. *Golden Slippers: An Anthology of Negro Poetry for Young Readers.* New York: Harper and Brothers, 1941.

Booker, Bobbi. "Langston Hughes's Centennial Celebration." *Philadelphia Tribune,* February 1, 2002.

Borden, Anne. "Heroic 'Hussies' and 'Brilliant Queers': Genderracial Resistance in the Works of Langston Hughes." *African American Review* 28 (1994): 333–45.

Bordwell, David. *The Cinema of Eisenstein.* Cambridge: Harvard University Press, 1993.

Boykin, Keith. *Beyond the Down Low: Sex, Lies, and Denial in Black America.* New York: Carroll and Graf Publishers, 2005.

Boym, Svetlana. *Common Places: Mythologies of Everyday Life in Russia.* Cambridge: Harvard University Press, 1994.

Brecht, Bertolt. "Against Georg Lukács." In *Aesthetics and Politics,* ed. Ernest Bloch et al. London: NLB, 1977.

———. *Brecht on Theater.* Trans. J. Willet. London: Eyre Methuen, 1978.

Briggs, Cyril V. "Alien Education." *The Crusader* 1 (September 1918): 5.

Brown, Henry Billings. "Majority Opinion in *Plessy v. Ferguson.*" In *Desegregation and the Supreme Court,* ed. Benjamin Munn Ziegler. Boston: Heath, 1958.

Brown, Sterling A. Review of *Not without Laughter,* by Langston Hughes. 1930. In *Langston Hughes: Critical Perspectives Past and Future,* ed. Henry Louis Gates Jr. and K. A. Appiah, New York: Amistad Press, 1993.

Burkhardt, Barbara. "The Blues in Langston Hughes's *Not without Laughter.*" *Midamerica: The Yearbook of the Society for the Study of Midwestern Literature* 23 (1996): 114–23.

Burleigh, Robert. *Langston's Train Ride.* New York: Orchard, 2004.

Butler, Judith. *Bodies That Matter: On the Discursive Limits of "Sex."* New York: Routledge, 1993.

———. *Gender Trouble: Feminism and the Subversion of Identity.* New York: Routledge, 1990.

Carbado, Devon W., et al., eds. *Black Like Us: A Century of Lesbian, Gay, and Bisexual African American Fiction.* San Francisco: Cleis Press, 2002.

Carby, Hazel. "'It Jus Be's Dat Way Sometime': The Sexual Politics of Women's Blues." In *Gender and Discourse: The Power of Talk,* ed. Alexandra Dundas Todd and Sue Fisher. Norwood, N.J.: Ablex, 1988.

———. "Policing the Black Woman's Body in an Urban Context." 1992. In

Identities, ed. Kwame Anthony Appiah and Henry Louis Gates Jr. Chicago: University of Chicago Press, 1995.

————. *Reconstructing Womanhood: The Emergence of the Afro-American Woman Novelist.* New York: Oxford University Press, 1987.

Carter, Dan T. *Scottsboro: A Tragedy of the American South.* 1969. Baton Rouge: Louisiana State University Press, 1990.

Chauncey, George. *Gay New York: Gender, Urban Culture, and the Making of the Gay Male World, 1890–1940.* New York: Harper Collins, 1994.

Chin, Timothy S. "'Bullers' and 'Battymen': Contesting Homophobia in Black Popular Culture and Contemporary Caribbean Literature." *Callaloo* 20.1 (1997): 127–41.

Chinitz, David. "Rejuvenation through Joy: Langston Hughes, Primitivism, and Jazz." *American Literary History* 9.1 (1997): 60–78.

Chisholm, Anne. *Nancy Cunard: A Biography.* New York: Knopf, 1979.

Cole, Lester. *Hollywood Red.* Palo Alto: Ramparts Press, 1981.

Conrad, Joseph. *Heart of Darkness.* 1902. Reprint. Boston: Bedford/St. Martin's, 1996.

Cook, Mercer. "Léon-Gontran Damas: The Last Four Decades." 1978. In *Léon Gontran Damas, 1912–1978: Founder of Negritude,* ed. Daniel L. Racine. Washington, D.C.: University Press of America, 1979.

Cripps, Thomas. *Making Movies Black: The Hollywood Message Movie from World War II to the Civil Rights Era.* New York: Oxford University Press, 1993.

————. *Slow Fade to Black: The Negro in American Film, 1900–1942.* New York: Oxford University Press, 1977.

Cullen, Countee. "Poet on Poet." 1926. In *The Opportunity Reader,* ed. Sondra Kathryn Wilson. New York: Modern Library, 1999.

Cunard, Nancy. "Three Negro Poets." *Left Review* 3 (October 1937): 529–36.

Damas, Léon. "Négritude in Retrospect." 1974. In *Léon Gontran Damas, 1912–1978: Founder of Negritude,* ed. Daniel L. Racine. Washington, D.C.: University Press of America, 1979.

Dawahare, Anthony. "Langston Hughes's Radical Poetry and the 'End of Race.'" *MELUS* 23.3 (1998): 21–41.

————. *Nationalism, Marxism, and African-American Literature between The Wars: A New Pandora's Box.* Jackson: University Press of Mississippi, 2003.

de Andrade, Mario. *La poésie Africaine d'expression Portugaise.* Trans. Jean Todrani and Andre Joucla-Ruau. Rouen: Pierre Jean Oswald, 1969.

Deutsch, Babette. "Waste Land of Harlem: A Review of *Montage of a Dream Deferred.*" *New York Times Book Review,* May 6, 1951, p. 12.

Dick, Bernard F. *Radical Innocence: A Critical Study of the Hollywood Ten.* Lexington: University of Kentucky Press, 1989.

Doyle, Laura. *Bordering on the Body.* New York: Oxford University Press, 1994.

Du Bois, W. E. B. "Russia and America: An Interpretation." Cat. 1–318, Microfilm 85, frames 395–527, W. E. B. Du Bois Papers. University of Massachusetts, Amherst.

———. *The Souls of Black Folk.* 1903. Reprint. New York: Signet, 1969.

duCille, Ann. *The Coupling Convention: Sex, Text, and Tradition in Black Women's Fiction.* New York: Oxford University Press, 1993.

Duggan, Lisa. "Theory in Practice: The Theory Wars, or Who's Afraid of Judith Butler?" *Journal of Women's History* 10.1 (1998): 9–19.

Edwards, Brent Hayes. "Three Ways to Translate the Harlem Renaissance." In *Temples for Tomorrow: Looking Back at the Harlem Renaissance,* ed. Geneviève Fabre and Michel Feith. Bloomington: Indiana University Press, 2001.

Eliot, T. S. "The Love Song of J. Alfred Prufrock." In his *Collected Poems, 1909–1962.* New York: Harcourt, Brace, and World, 1963.

Emery, Lynne Fauley. *Black Dance from 1619 to Today.* Princeton: Princeton Book Company, 1988.

Eng, Robert. *Racial Castration: Managing Masculinity in Asian America.* Durham: Duke University Press, 2001.

Essoe, Gabe. *Tarzan of the Movies.* Secaucus, N.J.: Citadel Press, 1973.

Fabre, Michel. *From Harlem to Paris: Black American Writers in France, 1840– 1980.* Urbana: University of Illinois Press, 1991.

———. "The Harlem Renaissance Abroad: French Critics and the New Negro Literary Movement (1924–1964)." In *Temples for Tomorrow: Looking Back at the Harlem Renaissance,* ed. Geneviève Fabre and Michel Feith. Bloomington: Indiana University Press, 2001.

Feelings, Tom. *Soul Looks Back in Wonder.* New York: Dial Books, 1993.

Fitzgerald, F. Scott. *This Side of Paradise.* New York: Charles Scribner's Sons, 1920.

Ford, Karen. "Do Right to Write Right: Langston Hughes's Aesthetic of Simplicity." *Twentieth-Century Literature* 38 (Winter 1992): 436–56.

———. "Making Poetry Pay: The Commodification of Langston Hughes." In *Marketing Modernisms: Self-Promotion, Canonization, Rereading,* ed. Kevin J. H. Dettmar and Stephen Watt. Ann Arbor: University of Michigan Press, 1996.

Freud, Sigmund. *Three Essays on the Theory of Sexuality.* Trans. James Strachey. 1905. Reprint. New York: Basic Books, 1975.

Fuss, Diana. "Fashion and the Homospectatorial Look." *Critical Inquiry* 18 (1992): 713–37.

Garber, Eric. "A Spectacle in Color: The Lesbian and Gay Subculture of Jazz Age Harlem." In *Hidden From History: Reclaiming the Gay and Lesbian Past*, ed. Martin Duberman et al. New York: New American Library, 1989.

García Lorca, Federico. *Obras Completas*. Vol. 1. Madrid: Aguilar, 1986.

Gates, Henry Louis, Jr. "The Black Man's Burden." In *Fear of a Queer Planet: Queer Politics and Social Theory*, ed. Michael Warner. Minneapolis: University of Minnesota Press, 1993.

———. "Introduction: Darkly as through a Veil." In *The Souls of Black Folk*, by W. E. B. Du Bois. New York: Bantam Books, 1989.

———. *The Signifying Monkey: A Theory of Afro-American Literary Criticism*. New York: Oxford University Press, 1988.

———. "A Tragedy of Negro Life." Intro. to *Mule Bone: A Comedy of Negro Life*. By Langston Hughes and Zora Neale Hurston. New York: Perennial, 1991.

Gates, Henry Louis, Jr., and K. A. Appiah, eds. *Langston Hughes: Critical Perspectives Past and Present*. New York: Amistad Press, 1993.

Gates, Henry Louis, Jr., and Nellie McKay, eds. *The Norton Anthology of African American Literature*. 2nd ed. New York: W. W. Norton, 2004.

Gilman, Sander L. "Black Bodies, White Bodies: Toward an Iconography of Female Sexuality in Late Nineteenth-Century Art, Medicine, and Literature." In *"Race," Writing, and Difference*, ed. Henry Louis Gates, Jr. Chicago: University of Chicago Press, 1985.

Gilroy, Paul. *The Black Atlantic: Modernity and Double Consciousness*. Cambridge: Harvard University Press, 1993.

———. "Exer(or)cising Power: Black Bodies in the Black Public Sphere." In *Dance in the City*, ed. Helen Thomas. New York: St. Martin's Press, 1997.

Ginsberg, Elaine K., ed. *Passing and the Fictions of Identity*. Durham: Duke University Press, 1996.

Goodman, James. *Stories of Scottsboro*. New York: Vintage, 1995.

Graham, Maryemma. "The Practice of a Social Art." In *Langston Hughes: Critical Perspectives Past and Present*, ed. Henry Louis Gates Jr. and K. A. Appiah. New York: Amistad Press, 1993.

Griffin, Farah Jasmine. *"Who set you flowin'?": The African-American Migration Narrative*. New York: Oxford University Press, 1995.

Hamalian, Leo. "D. H. Lawrence and Black Writers." *Journal of Modern Literature* 16 (1990): 579–96.

Hamilton, Russell G. *Voices from an Empire: A History of Afro-Portuguese Literature.* Minneapolis: University of Minnesota Press, 1975.

Handy, W. C., and Tim Brymn. "Aunt Hagar's Children's Blues." Alice Leslie Carter. Bell P103, 1921. Reissued on *Female Blues Singers, Vol. 4,* Document DOCD 5508, 1996. Compact disk.

Harper, Phillip Brian. *Are We Not Men? Masculine Anxiety and the Problem of African-American Identity.* New York: Oxford University Press, 1996.

Hawkeswood, William G. *One of the Children: Gay Black Men in Harlem.* Ed. Alex W. Costley. Berkeley: University of California Press, 1996.

Hemphill, Essex. "Looking for Langston: An Interview with Isaac Julien." In *Brother to Brother: New Writings by Black Gay Men,* ed. Essex Hemphill. Boston: Alyson Publications, 1991.

———. "Undressing Icons." In *Brother to Brother: New Writings by Black Gay Men,* ed. Essex Hemphill. Boston: Alyson Publications, 1991.

Higginbotham, Evelyn Brooks, et al., eds. *The Harvard Guide to African-American History.* Cambridge: Harvard University Press, 2001.

Hine, Darlene Clark, and Kathleen Thompson. *A Shining Thread of Hope: The History of Black Women in America.* New York: Broadway Books, 1998.

Hinton, Robert. "Black Dance in American History." In *The Black Tradition in American Modern Dance.* Project booklet. Durham, N.C.: American Dance Festival, 1988.

Hudson, Wade. *Pass It On: African-American Poetry for Children.* New York: Scholastic, 1993.

Hughes, Langston. *Carol of the Brown King: Nativity Poems by Langston Hughes.* New York: Atheneum Books for Young Readers, 1998.

———. "A Cuban Sculptor." *Opportunity* 8 (November 1930): 334.

———. *Good Morning Revolution: Uncollected Social Protest Writings.* Ed. Faith Berry. New York: Lawrence Hill and Company, 1973.

———. "Harlem Literati in the Twenties." *Saturday Review of Literature,* June 22, 1940, pp. 13–14.

———. "Letter to the Academy." *International Literature* 5 (1933): 112.

———. Papers. Yale Collection of American Literature, Beinecke Rare Book and Manuscript Library, Yale University, New Haven, Conn.

———. "Review of W. C. Handy's *Blues: An Anthology.*" *Opportunity* 4 (August 1926): 258.

Hughes, Langston, ed. *The Book of Negro Humor.* New York: Dodd, Mead, 1966.

Hughes, Langston, trans. "A Page of West Indian Poetry." [Poems by

Nicolás Guillén, Regino Pedroso, and Jacques Roumain] *The Crisis: A Record of the Darker Races* 40 (December 1931): 424.

———. "Gypsy Ballads." 1937. Unpublished draft translation of Lorca's *Romancero Gitano*. James Weldon Johnson Collection. Beinecke Rare Book and Manuscript Library, Yale University, New Haven, Conn.

———. "Gypsy Ballads." 1937. Unpublished draft translation of Lorca's *Romancero Gitano*. The Langston Hughes Collection, Box 6, Folder b65, Schomburg Center for Black Research and Culture, New York Public Library, New York, N.Y.

———. "Gypsy Ballads." *Beloit Poetry Journal* 2:1 (Fall 1951).

Hughes, Langston, and Milton Meltzer. *Black Magic: A Pictorial History of the Negro in American Entertainment*. Englewood Cliffs: Prentice-Hall, 1967.

Hunter, Jane Edna. *A Nickel and a Prayer*. Cleveland: Elli Kani Publishing Co., 1940.

Hurston, Zora Neale. *Their Eyes Were Watching God*. 1937. Reprint. New York: Harper and Row, 1990.

Isaacs, Edith J. R., ed. *The Negro in the American Theatre*. New York: Theatre Arts, 1947.

Jackson, Gabriel. *The Spanish Republic and the Civil War, 1931–1939*. Princeton: Princeton University Press, 1965.

Jefferson, Blind Lemon. "Broke and Hungry." Paramount 12443, 1926. Reissued on *Blind Lemon Jefferson: The Complete 94 Classic Sides*. JSP 7706, 2003. Compact disk.

Jefferson, Wilson. "Life Comes 'Not without Laughter' to Kansas Negroes." 1930. In *Langston Hughes: The Contemporary Reviews*, ed. Tish Dace. Cambridge: Cambridge University Press, 1997.

Jemie, Onwuchekwa. "Or Does It Explode?" In *Langston Hughes: Critical Perspectives Past and Present*, ed. Henry Louis Gates Jr. and K. A. Appiah. New York: Amistad. 1993.

Johnson, Pauline. *Marxist Aesthetics*. London: Routledge and Kegan Paul, 1984.

Jones, Howard Mumford. Introduction to *Dark Laughter* by Sherwood Anderson. New York: Liveright Publishing Corporation, 1970.

Kaplan, Caren. *Questions of Travel: Postmodern Discourses of Displacement*. Durham: Duke University Press, 1996.

Karenga, Maulana Ron. "Black Art: Mute Matter Given Force and Function." 1968. In *New Black Voices*, ed. Abraham Chapman. New York: New American Library, 1972.

Kelley, Robin D. G. "'This Ain't Ethiopia, But It'll Do.'" In *African-Americans in the Spanish Civil War*, ed. Danny Duncan Collum. New York: G. K. Hall, 1992.

Kellner, Bruce, ed. *The Letters of Carl Van Vechten.* New Haven: Yale University Press, 1987.

Kelly, Catriona, Hilary Pilkington, David Shepherd, and Vadim Volkvo. "Why Cultural Studies?" In *Russian Cultural Studies,* ed. Catriona Kelly and David Shepherd. Oxford: Oxford University Press, 1998.

Kendall, Elizabeth. *Where She Danced.* Berkeley: University of California Press, 1979.

Kennedy, Ellen Conroy, ed. *The Negritude Poets: An Anthology of Translations from the French.* New York: Viking Press, 1975.

King, J. L. *On the Down Low: A Journey into the Lives of "Straight" Black Men Who Sleep with Men.* New York: Broadway / Random House, 2004.

Kirstein, Lincoln. *Dance: A Short History of Classic Theatrical Dancing.* New York: Dance Horizons, 1969.

Kusmer, Kenneth L. *A Ghetto Takes Shape: Black Cleveland, 1870–1930.* Urbana: University of Illinois Press, 1976.

Lauter, Paul, ed. *The Heath Anthology of American Literature.* 5th ed. Vol. D. Boston: Houghton Mifflin, 2006.

Lawrence, D. H. *The Lovely Lady.* 1930. Reprint. London: Secker, 1932.

Lewis, David Levering. *When Harlem Was in Vogue.* New York: Knopf, 1981.

———. *W. E. B. Du Bois: The Fight for Equality and the American Century, 1919–1963.* New York: Henry Holt and Co., 2000.

Lipsitz, George. *The Possessive Investment in Whiteness: How White People Profit from Identity Politics.* Philadelphia: Temple University Press, 1998.

Locke, Alain. "Black Truth and Black Beauty: A Retrospective Review of the Literature of the Negro for 1932." *Opportunity* 11 (January 1933): 14–18.

———. "The Legacy of the Ancestral Arts." In *The New Negro,* ed. Alain Locke. New York: Atheneum, 1992.

———. "Negro Angle." Review of *The Ways of White Folks,* by Langston Hughes. *Survey Graphic* 23 (1934): 565.

———. "Spiritual Truancy." *New Challenge* 2.2 (1937): 81–85.

———. "Sterling Brown: The New Negro Folk-Poet." 1934. In *Negro: An Anthology,* abridged edition, ed. Hugh Ford. New York: F. Ungar Publishing Co., 1970.

Looking for Langston: A Meditation on the Harlem Renaissance. Dir. Isaac Julien. New York: Third World Newsreel, 1989.

Loughram, David, trans. and ed. *Gypsy Ballads and Songs.* By Federico García Lorca. Hanover: Ediciones del Norte, 1994.

Lukács, Georg. "Realism in the Balance." In *Aesthetics and Politics,* ed. Ernest Bloch et al. London: NLB, 1977.

Lyons, Eugene. *Assignment in Utopia.* New York: Harcourt, Brace and Co., 1937.

Malone, Jacqui. *Steppin' on the Blues.* Urbana: University of Illinois Press, 1996.

Marshall, Paule. Untitled conference luncheon speech. Let America Be America Again: An International Symposium on the Art, Life, and Legacy of Langston Hughes. University of Kansas, February 9, 2002.

Marx, Karl. *The Grundrisse.* 1941. In *The Marx-Engels Reader,* ed. Robert C. Tucker, 2d ed. New York: W. W. Norton and Co., 1978.

———. *A Contribution to the Critique of Political Economy.* 1859. In *The Marx-Engels Reader,* ed. Robert C. Tucker, 2d ed. New York: W. W. Norton and Co., 1978.

Matich, Olga. "Remaking the Bed: Utopia in Daily Life." In *Laboratory of Dreams: The Russian Avant-Garde and Cultural Experimentation,* ed. John E. Bowlt and Olga Matich. Stanford: Stanford University Press, 1996.

Maxwell, William J. *New Negro, Old Left: African-American Writing and Communism between the Wars.* New York: Columbia University Press, 1999.

McDowell, Deborah. "'That nameless . . . shameful impulse': Sexuality in Nella Larsen's *Quicksand* and *Passing.*" In her *"The Changing Same": Black Women's Literature, Criticism, and Theory.* Bloomington: Indiana University Press, 1995.

McGilligan, Patrick, and Paul Buhle. *Tender Comrades: A Backstory of the Hollywood Blacklist.* New York: St. Martin's Press, 1997.

McKay, Nellie. "Response to Arnold Rampersad." In *Afro-American Literary Study in the 1990s,* ed. Houston Baker and Patricia Redmond. Chicago: University of Chicago Press, 1989.

McPherson, James M. *Ordeal by Fire: The Civil War and Reconstruction.* 1982. Reprint. New York: McGraw-Hill, 1992.

Medina, Tony. *Love to Langston.* New York: Lee and Low Books, 2002.

Miller, Carol Poh, and Robert A. Wheeler. *Cleveland: A Concise History, 1796–1996.* 2d ed. Bloomington: Indiana University Press, 1997.

Miller, James E., Jr., ed. *The Heritage of American Literature*. Vol. 2. New York: Harcourt Brace Jovanovich, 1991.

Miller, R. Baxter. "'Done Made Us Leave Our Home': Langston Hughes's *Not without Laughter*—Unifying Image and Three Dimensions." *Phylon: The Atlanta University Review of Race and Culture* 37 (1976): 362–69.

———. *Langston Hughes and Gwendolyn Brooks: A Reference Guide*. Boston: G. K. Hall, 1978.

Morrison, Toni. *Playing in the Dark: Whiteness and the Literary Imagination*. Cambridge: Harvard University Press, 1992.

Mudimbe-Boyi, M. E. "Harlem Renaissance et l'Afrique: Une aventure ambiguë." *Présence Africaine*, no. 147 (1988): 18–28.

Mullen, Edward J., ed. *Critical Essays on Langston Hughes*. Boston: G. K. Hall & Co., 1986.

———. *Langston Hughes in the Hispanic World and Haiti*. Hamden, Conn.: Archon Books, 1977.

Naison, Mark. *Communists in Harlem during the Depression*. Urbana: University of Illinois Press, 1983.

Nash, Gary. "The Hidden History of Mestizo America." In *Sex, Love, Race: Crossing Boundaries in North American History*, ed. Martha Hodes. New York: New York University Press, 1999.

Navasky, Victor. *Naming Names*. Harmondsworth, U.K.: Penguin Books, 1981.

Nelson, Cary. *Repression and Recovery: Modern American Poetry and the Politics of Cultural Memory, 1910–1945*. Madison: University of Wisconsin Press, 1989.

———. *Revolutionary Memory: Recovering the Poetry of the American Left*. New York: Routledge, 2001.

Nelson, Cary, and Jefferson Hendricks. *Edwin Rolfe: A Biographical Essay and Guide to the Rolfe Archive at the University of Illinois at Urbana–Champaign*. Urbana: University of Illinois Library, 1990.

Nero, Charles I. "Re/Membering Langston: Homophobic Textuality and Arnold Rampersad's *Life of Langston Hughes*." In *Queer Representations: Reading Lives, Reading Cultures*, ed. Martin Duberman. New York: NYU Press, 1997.

Nichols, Charles H., ed. *Arna Bontemps–Langston Hughes Letters, 1925–1967*. New York: Paragon House, 1990.

Nowell-Smith, Geoffrey. "Eisenstein on Montage." In *S.M. Eisenstein, Selected Works Volume Two: Towards a Theory of Montage*, trans. Michael Glenny, ed. Michael Glenny and Richard Taylor. London: British Film Institute, 1991.

O'Daniel, Therman B. *Langston Hughes, Black Genius: A Critical Evaluation.* New York: William Morrow, 1971.

Ogren, Kathy. *The Jazz Revolution: Twenties America and the Meaning of Jazz.* New York: Oxford University Press, 1989.

Ovington, Mary White. "Praises Hughes an Unusual Colored Writer." 1930. In *Langston Hughes: The Contemporary Reviews,* ed. Tish Dace. Cambridge: Cambridge University Press, 1997.

Padgette, Paul, ed. *The Dance Writings of Carl Van Vechten.* New York: Dance Horizons, 1974.

Perdomo, Willie. *Visiting Langston.* New York: Henry Holt, 2002.

Pettinger, Alasdair, ed. *Always Elsewhere: Travels of the Black Atlantic.* New York: Cassell, 1998.

Povinelli, Elizabeth. "Notes on Gridlock: Genealogy, Intimacy, Sexuality." *Public Culture* 14 (2002): 215–38.

Preto-Rodas, Richard A. *Négritude as a Theme in the Poetry of the Portugese-Speaking World.* Gainesville: University of Florida Press, 1970.

Rabinowitz, Paula. *For the Love of Pleasure: Women, Movies, and Culture in Turn-of-the Century Chicago.* New Brunswick: Rutgers University Press, 1998.

Rampersad, Arnold. "Biography and Afro-American Culture." In *Afro-American Literary Study in the 1990s,* ed. Houston Baker and Patricia Redmond. Chicago: University of Chicago Press, 1989.

———. "Future Scholarly Projects on Langston Hughes." *Black American Literature Forum* 21.3 (Fall 1987): 305–16.

———. "Hughes's *Fine Clothes to the Jew.*" In *Langston Hughes: Critical Perspectives Past and Present,* ed. Henry Louis Gates Jr. and K. A. Appiah. New York: Amistad, 1993.

———. Introduction. In *The Big Sea* by Langston Hughes. New York: Hill and Wang, 1993.

———. "Langston Hughes and His Critics on the Left." *Langston Hughes Review* 5.2 (1986): 34–40.

———. *The Life of Langston Hughes: Volume 1, 1902–1941, I, Too, Sing America.* New York: Oxford University Press, 1986.

———. *The Life of Langston Hughes: Volume 2, 1941–1967, I Dream a World.* New York: Oxford University Press, 1988.

Reimonenq, Alden. "Hughes, Langston." *GLBTQ: An Encyclopedia of Gay, Lesbian, Bisexual, Transgender, and Queer Culture.* http://glbtq.com/literature/hughes_1.html.

Review of *Fine Clothes to the Jew,* by Langston Hughes. *Chicago Whip,* February 26, 1927.

Roberts, Kimberley. "The Clothes Make the Woman: The Symbolics of Prostitution in Nella Larsen's *Quicksand* and Claude McKay's *Home to Harlem.*" *Tulsa Studies in Women's Literature* 16.1 (1997): 107–30.

Rogers, J. A. Review of *Fine Clothes to the Jew* by Langston Hughes. 1927. In *Critical Essays on Langston Hughes*, ed. Edward J. Mullen. Boston: G. K. Hall and Co., 1986.

Rothenberg, Jerome, ed. *Revolution of the Word: A New Gathering of American Avant-Garde Poetry, 1914–1945.* 1974. Reprint. Boston: Exact Change, 1997.

Roumain, Jacques. *Ebony Wood / Bois d'Ebene.* 1944. Trans. Sidney Shapiro. New York: Interworld Press, 1972.

Rowell, Charles H. "Signing Yourself: An Afterword." In *Shade: An Anthology of Fiction by Gay Men of African Descent*, ed. Bruce Morrow and Charles H. Rowell. New York: Avon Books, 1996.

Russell, Michele. "Slave Codes and Liner Notes." In *All the Women are White, All the Blacks are Men, But Some of Us are Brave: Black Women's Studies*, ed. Gloria T. Hull, Patricia Bell Scott, and Barbara Smith. New York: Feminist Press 1982.

Schuyler, George S. "The Negro-Art Hokum." *Nation* 122 (June 16, 1926): 662–63.

Schwarz, A. B. Christa. *Gay Voices of the Harlem Renaissance.* Bloomington: Indiana University Press, 2003.

Sedgwick, Eve Kosofsky. *Between Men: English Literature and Male Homosocial Desire.* New York: Columbia University Press, 1985.

———. *Epistemology of the Closet.* Berkeley: University of California Press, 1990.

Senghor, Léopold Sédar. "Léon-Gontran Damas and the Origin of the Négritude Movement." In *Léon Gontran Damas, 1912–1978: Founder of Negritude*, ed. Daniel L. Racine. Washington, D.C.: University Press of America, 1979.

Shaw, Caroline. "São Tomé and Príncipe." In Patrick Chabal, *The Postcolonial Literature of Lusophone Africa.* Evanston: Northwestern University Press, 1996.

Shelton, Suzanne. *Divine Dancer: A Biography of Ruth St. Denis.* New York: Doubleday and Co., 1981.

Shields, John P. "'Never Cross the Divide': Reconstructing Langston Hughes's *Not without Laughter.*" *African American Review* 28 (1994): 601–13.

Shulman, Robert. *The Power of Political Art: The 1930s Literary Left Reconsidered.* Chapel Hill: University of North Carolina Press, 2000.

Silverman, Kaja. *Male Subjectivity at the Margins.* New York: Routledge, 1992.

Singer, Barry. *Black and Blue: The Life and Lyrics of Andy Razaf.* New York: Schirmer Books, 1992.

Sitkoff, Harvard. *A New Deal for Blacks: The Emergence of Civil Rights as a National Issue, Volume I: The Depression Decade.* New York: Oxford University Press, 1978.

Smethurst, James. *The New Red Negro: African American Writing and Communism.* New York: Oxford University Press, 1999.

Smith, Johanna M. "'Too Beautiful Altogether': Ideologies of Gender and Empire in *Heart of Darkness.*" In *Heart of Darkness: Complete, Authoritative Text with Biographical and Historical Contexts, Critical History, and Essays from Five Critical Perspectives,* ed. Ross C. Murfin. 2d ed. Boston: Bedford / St. Martin's, 1996.

Smith, Paul Julian. "Black Wedding: García Lorca, Langston Hughes, and the Translation of Introjection." *Papers in Spanish Theatre History* 4 (1996).

Smith, Rogers M. *Civic Ideals: Conflicting Visions of Citizenship in U.S. History.* New Haven: Yale University Press, 1997.

Snead, James. "Recoding Blackness: The Visual Rhetoric of Black Independent Film." *Whitney Museum of American Art: The New American Filmmakers Series* 23 (1985).

Somerville, Siobhan. *Queering the Color Line: Race and the Invention of Homosexuality in American Culture.* Durham: Duke University Press, 2000.

Soto, Isabel. "Crossing Over: Langston Hughes and Lorca." In *A Place That Is Not a Place,* ed. Isabel Soto. Madrid: Gateway Press, 2000, 115–32.

———. "Langston Hughes: The Poetics of Reciprocity." In *Tendencias actuales en los estudios filológicos Anglo-Norteamericanos,* ed. Elena Ortells Montón and José Ramón Prado Pérez. Castelló de la Plana: Pulicacions de la Universitat, 2003.

———. "The Poetry of Langston Hughes." In *Tendencias actuales en los estudios filológicos Anglo-Norteamericanos,* ed. Elena Ortells Montón and José Ramón Prado Pérez. Castelló de la Plana: Pulicacions de la Universitat, 2003.

Spillers, Hortense J. "All of the Things You Could Have Been by Now if Sigmund Freud's Wife Was Your Mother: Race and Psychoanalysis." *Boundary 2* 23.3 (Autumn 1996): 75–141.

———. "Interstices: A Small Drama of Words." 1984. In her *Black, White, and in Color: Essays on American Literature and Culture.* Chicago: University of Chicago Press, 2003.

Stearns, Marshall, and Jean Stearns. *Jazz Dance: The Story of American Vernacular Dance.* New York: Schirmer Books, 1968.

Steiner, Wendy. "The Diversity of American Fiction." In *Columbia Literary History of the United States,* ed. Emory Elliott. New York: Columbia University Press, 1988.

Stites, Richard. *The Women's Liberation Movement in Russia: Feminism, Nihilism, and Bolshevism, 1860–1930.* Princeton: Princeton University Press, 1978.

Tenreiro, Francisco-José. "Fragmento de Blues." 1943. In *A Horse of White Clouds: Poems from Lusophone Africa,* trans. Don Burness. Athens: Ohio University Center for International Studies, 1989.

Téten, Carol. *Dances of the Ragtime Era, 1910–1920.* Kentfield, Calif.: Dancetime Publications, n.d. Videotape.

Thomas, H. Nigel. "Patronage and the Writing of Langston Hughes's *Not without Laughter:* A Paradoxical Case." *CLA Journal* 42.1 (1998): 48–70.

Thomas, Lorenzo. *Extraordinary Measures: Afrocentric Modernism and Twentieth-Century American Poetry.* Tuscaloosa: University of Alabama Press, 2000.

Thurston, Michael. "'Bombed in Spain': Langston Hughes, the Black Press, and the Spanish Civil War." In *The Black Press: New Literary and Historical Essays,* ed. Todd Vogel. New Brunswick: Rutgers University Press, 2001.

———. *Making Something Happen: American Political Poetry between the World Wars.* Chapel Hill: University of North Carolina Press, 2001.

Tidwell, John Edgar. Introduction. In *Livin' the Blues: Memoirs of a Black Journalist and Poet* by Frank Marshall Davis. Madison: University of Wisconsin Press, 1992.

Tolson, Nancy D. "Introduction." *Obsidian III: Literature in the African Diaspora* 3.1 (Spring–Summer 2001): 9–11.

Tracy, Steven C., ed. *A Historical Guide to Langston Hughes.* New York: Oxford University Press, 2004.

———. *Langston Hughes and the Blues.* Chicago: University of Chicago Press, 1988.

Tucker, Robert C., ed. *The Marx-Engels Reader.* 2d ed. New York: W. W. Norton and Co., 1978.

Uebel, Michael. "Men In Color: Introducing Race and the Subject of Masculinities." In *Race and the Subject of Masculinities,* ed. Harry Stecopoulos and Michael Uebel. Durham: Duke University Press, 1997.

Untermeyer, Louis. *The New Era in American Poetry.* New York: Henry Holt, 1919.

Vaillant, Janet G. *Black, French, and African: The Life of Léopold Sédar Senghor.* Cambridge: Harvard University Press, 1990.

Vaughn, Robert. *Only Victims: A Study of Show Business Blacklisting.* New York: G. P. Putnam's Sons, 1972.

Venuti, Lawrence. *The Translator's Invisibility.* New York: Routledge, 1995.

Walker, Alice. *Langston Hughes: American Poet.* New York: HarperCollins / Amistad, 2002.

Wall, Cheryl. "'Whose Sweet Angel Child?' Blueswomen, Langston Hughes, and Writing during the Harlem Renaissance." In *Langston Hughes: The Man, His Art, and His Continuing Influence,* ed. C. James Trotman and Emery Wimbish Jr. New York: Garland Publishing, 1995.

Way Down South. 61 mins. RKO, 1939.

Webb, W. Prescott. "Notes on Folk-Lore of Texas." *Journal of American Folklore* 28 (1915): 291–96.

Whitman, Walt. *Walt Whitman: Complete Poetry and Prose.* Ed. Justin Kaplan. New York: Library of America, 1982.

Wiegman, Robyn. *American Anatomies: Theorizing Race and Gender.* Durham: Duke University Press, 1995.

Williams, John A. *Captain Blackman.* 1972. Reprint. New York: Thunder's Mouth Press, 1988.

Wirth, Thomas. "Introduction." In *Gay Rebel of the Harlem Renaissance* by Richard Bruce Nugent. Durham: Duke University Press, 2002.

Woll, Allen. *Black Musical Theatre: From Coontown to Dreamgirls.* Baton Rouge: Louisiana State University Press, 1989.

Woods, Gregory. "Gay Re-readings of the Harlem Renaissance." *Journal of Homosexuality* 26:2/3 (1993): 127–42.

———. *A History of Gay Literature: The Male Tradition.* New Haven: Yale University Press, 1998.

Žižek, Slavoj. "Introduction: The Spectre of Ideology." In *Mapping Ideology,* ed. Slavoj Zizek. London: Verso, 1994.

Notes on the Contributors

Giselle Liza Anatol is Associate Professor of English at the University of Kansas. Her research areas include contemporary Caribbean women's literature and representations of race and ethnicity in writing for children. She edited the volume *Reading Harry Potter: Critical Essays* (2003) and has published articles in *Callaloo, African American Review, Mosaic, Small Axe, MaComère,* and *Mango Season.* She regularly teaches courses on Caribbean literature, multicultural U.S. literature, Toni Morrison, and literature for young people. She was named a Conger-Gabel Teaching Professor from 2001 to 2004.

Kate A. Baldwin is Associate Professor in American Studies at Northwestern University, where she teaches comparative twentieth-century American and Russian literatures and specializes in transnational cultural studies. Her *Beyond the Color Line and the Iron Curtain: Reading Encounters between Black and Red, 1922–1963* (2002) addresses the involvement of African American intellectuals with Soviet communism and underscores the Russian intellectual heritage of black modernism. Her current project, "Authenticating Nations: Cultural Fictions of U.S. and Soviet Women during the Cold War," reads Russian and American texts and contexts dialogically, documenting how femininity was used by both superpowers as a site upon which to wage cold warfare.

Kimberly J. Banks is Assistant Professor of English at Arcadia University in Pennsylvania. Her specialty is African American literature, especially the Harlem Renaissance. Her "'Like a violin for the wind to play': Lyrical Representations of Lynching in Short Stories by Langston Hughes, W. E. B. Du Bois, and Jean Toomer" appeared in *African American Review*. She edited a forthcoming collection of Jessie Fauset's letters to appear in *Kindred Hands*. She is currently working on a manuscript, "Framing Diasporic Memory," that situates Caribbean immigrants to Harlem and their imaginations of the Caribbean against African American writers' travels to the Caribbean and their imaginations of the same space.

Juda Bennett is the author of *The Passing Figure: Racial Confusion in Modern American Literature* (1994), an exploration of shifting representations of racial passing. His essays, many of which also historicize the trope of passing, have appeared in *African American Review, Biography,* and other journals, and his fiction and poetry can be found in literary journals, such as *Quarterly West, Wisconsin Review,* and *Puerto del Sol.* He is an Associate Professor at the College of New Jersey.

Thomas Cripps, University Distinguished Professor Emeritus at Morgan State University, has written several books, including *Slow Fade to Black: The Negro in American Film, 1900–1942* (1977), and an impressive number of articles and television scripts, including his award-winning script *Black Shadows on a Silver Screen* (1976). He has held fellowships from the Rockefeller, Guggenheim, and Dedalus foundations and has been resident fellow in the National Humanities Center, the Woodrow Wilson International Center for Scholars, and the Rockefeller Center in Bellagio, Italy. His visiting professorships include positions at Stanford and Harvard.

Christopher C. De Santis is Associate Professor of American and African American Literature at Illinois State University. De Santis is the editor of *Langston Hughes and the "Chicago Defender": Essays on Race, Politics, and Culture, 1942–62* (1995) and two volumes in *The Collected Works of Langston Hughes: Essays on Art, Race, Politics, and World Affairs* (2002) and *"Fight for Freedom" and Other Writings on Civil Rights* (2001). His most recent book is *Langston Hughes: A Documentary Volume* (2005). De Santis has also published numerous articles and reviews in *African American Review, American Studies, American Book Review, CLA Journal, Contemporary Literary Criticism, Langston Hughes Review, The Oxford Companion to African American Literature, Southern Quarterly,* and other books and journals.

Sandra Y. Govan is Professor of English at the University of North Carolina–Charlotte, where she teaches American and African American literatures. A Langston Hughes and Gwendolyn Bennett scholar, Govan also writes about African American science fiction writers Steven Barnes, Octavia E. Butler, and Samuel R. Delany. Her essays have appeared in such journals as *Black American Literature Forum, MELUS,* and *Langston Hughes Review* and as chapters in *Erotique Noire, Sexual Politics, Langston Hughes: The Man His Art and His Continuing Influence* and *Recovered Writers/Recovered Texts.* Govan belongs to the Wintergreen Women Writers' Collective, a group of African American women who have met annually since 1987 to discuss their writing projects.

Trudier Harris is J. Carlyle Sitterson Professor of English at the University of North Carolina at Chapel Hill, where she teaches courses in African American literature and folklore. Author and editor of more than twenty volumes, she is currently at work on "The Scary Mason-Dixon Line: African American Writers and the South." Her memoir, *Summer Snow: Reflections from a Black Daughter of the South* (2003), was selected to inaugurate the One-Book, One-Community Reading Program in Orange County, North Carolina in 2003–2004. In 2005, she won the UNC System Board of Governors' Award for Excellence in Teaching.

Cheryl R. Ragar is Visiting Instructor in the Interdisciplinary Studies Center at Drury University in Springfield, Missouri. She is currently completing her dissertation at the University of Kansas on the life and work of Harlem Renaissance painter Aaron Douglas, entitled "Aspects of an Artist's Life: Reimagining the Significance of Aaron Douglas as Painter, Teacher, and Public Intellectual."

Elizabeth Schultz retired in 2001 from the University of Kansas, where she was the Chancellor's Club Teaching Professor in the English Department. The author of *Unpainted to the Last: Moby-Dick and Twentieth-Century American Art* (1995) and *Shoreline: Seasons at the Lake* (2001), she has published extensively in the fields of African American fiction and autobiography, nineteenth-century American fiction, American women's writing, and Japanese culture; she continues to publish poetry, short stories, and essays on nature. A founder of the Melville Society Cultural Project in New Bedford, Massachusetts, she has curated several exhibitions related to Melville and the arts and has coedited *Melville and Women* (2006), a collection of essays.

Jeffrey A. Schwarz graduated with a Ph.D. in English from Saint Louis University in May 2004. His fields of study include American literature and culture of the 1920s and 1930s and ethnic literature. His essay entitled "Who's the Foreigner Now? Rethinking 1920s American Prejudice in *A Farewell to Arms*" recently appeared in the collection *Hemingway's Italy: New Perspectives* (2006).

Isabel Soto teaches in Spain's Universidad Nacional de Educación a Distancia. She has been Visiting Scholar at Vassar College and Honorary Fellow of the Schomburg Institute for Research and Black Culture. In 2000 she cofounded the independent scholarly publisher Gateway Press, devoted to publishing work on liminality and text. Her interests lie in liminality theory and African American studies. She has published and lectured widely on Langston Hughes's relationship with Spain. Her article "Boundaries Transgressed: Modernism and Miscegenation in Langston Hughes's 'Red-headed Baby,'" appeared in the April 2006 issue of *Atlantic Studies*. She is currently Deputy Vice-Rector for International Relations of her university.

Joan Stone teaches dance history and choreography at the University of Kansas. A graduate of Sarah Lawrence and Yale, she has used her background in anthropology and urban studies to create an unusual repertory of historic, narrative, and environmental dances for solo dancers and groups, which have been performed in the United States, Europe, Tajikistan, and India. Her writings on dance and politics, the history of dance in the Midwest, and literature and art as preserves of dance history have appeared in various regional and national publications since the 1970s.

Lorenzo Thomas, late of the University of Houston–Downtown, had a long acquaintanceship with the blues. In the 1960s, he joined Umbra, a writing workshop whose experimentation with art gave rise to the Black Arts movement. During a varied career, his position as writer-in-residence at Texas Southern University in 1973 caused him to adopt the Southwest as his home. Throughout his life, he maintained ties to grass-roots communities as well as intellectual ones. His participation in the Texas Commission on the Arts and Humanities and the Cultural Arts Council of Houston enabled him to serve the community and preserve black aesthetic traditions.

Michael Thurston is Associate Professor of English at Smith College. He is the author of *Making Something Happen: American Political Poetry between the World Wars* (2001) and of essays on Muriel Rukeyser, Ernest Hemingway, Eavan Boland, and Gillian Clarke, as well as Langston Hughes. His current project is "Going to Hell: The Underworld in Twentieth-Century Poetry."

John Edgar Tidwell, Associate Professor of English at the University of Kansas, has edited Frank Marshall Davis's *Livin' the Blues: Memoirs of a Black Journalist and Poet* (1992), Davis's *Black Moods: Collected Poems* (2002), and *Writings of Frank Marshall Davis, a Voice of the Black Press* (2007). With Mark Sanders of Emory University, he has edited Sterling A. Brown's travelogue *A Negro Looks at the South* (2007). He is currently at work on "Oh, Didn't He Ramble: The Life of Sterling A. Brown."

Steven C. Tracy is Professor of Afro-American Studies at the University of Massachusetts, Amherst. He is the author of *Langston Hughes and the Blues* (1988), *Going to Cincinnati* (1998), *A Brush with the Blues* (1993), and the introduction to a 2006–2007 edition of Howard W. Odum's "Black Ulysses" trilogy of novels; editor of *Write Me a Few of Your Lines: A Blues Reader* (1999), *A Historical Guide to Langston Hughes* (2004), and *A Historical Guide to Ralph Ellison* (2004); and general coeditor of *The Collected Works of Langston Hughes*. A blues singer-harmonica player, he has toured and recorded with his own band and various blues singers.

Carmaletta M. Williams is Professor of English and African American Studies at Johnson County Community College (JCCC) in Overland Park, Kansas. She earned her doctorate in English at the University of Kansas. Her many awards include the Carnegie Foundation for the Advancement of Teaching's Kansas Professor of the Year, the League for Innovations Award for her videotape *Sankofa: My Journey Home* about her Fulbright-Hays experience in Ghana, and the first JCCC Diversity Award. Among her many publications are *Langston Hughes in the Classroom: Do Nothin' Till You Hear from Me* (2006), published by the National Council of Teachers of English.

Regennia N. Williams holds a Ph.D. from Case Western Reserve University and is a faculty member in the Department of History at Cleveland State University. Her publications include *Cleveland, Ohio*, in the Black America Series by Arcadia Publishing; "Race Women and Reform" in the proceedings of the 2002 Meeting of the Ohio Academy of History; a chapter in *Education and the Great Depression*; and "Griots and Grace: The Art of Oral History and the History of African American Religion" in *Black*

History Bulletin. Williams is cofounder of Cleveland's Langston Hughes Literary Society, and she served as Chair and Project Director for the award-winning 2002 Greater Cleveland Langston Hughes Centennial Celebration.

Robert Young is Associate Professor of English at the University of Alabama. He is currently at work on a book project that advances a materialist conception of African American cultural and literary theory.

Index

Permissions

We wish to gratefully acknowledge Kate Baldwin for granting us permission to reprint a revised version of her "The Russian Connection: Interracialism as Queer Alliance in Langston Hughes's *The Ways of White Folks*," which appeared initially in *Modern Fiction Studies* 48.4 (2002): 795–824. Elizabeth Schultz and the Johns Hopkins University Press were kind enough to allow us to publish here her revised "Natural and Unnatural Circumstances in Langston Hughes's *Not without Laughter*," which first appeared in *Callaloo* 25.4 (2002): 1177–87. For permission to cite Hughes and other archival material, we thank Harold Ober Associates, Inc.; the Langston Hughes Collection of the Manuscripts, Beinecke Rare Book and Manuscript Library, Yale University; the Archives and Rare Books Division of the Schomburg Center for Research in Black Culture; and the Astor, Lenox and Tilden Foundations.